The Politics of Immigration

THE POLITICS OF
IMMIGRATION
Questions and Answers

JANE GUSKIN
AND DAVID L. WILSON

MONTHLY REVIEW PRESS
New York

Library of Congress Cataloging-in-Publication Data:

Names: Guskin, Jane. | Wilson, David L. (David Leigh), 1946–
Title: The politics of immigration : questions and answers / Jane Guskin and
David L. Wilson.
Description: New York : Monthly Review Press, [2017] | Includes
bibliographical references and index.
Identifiers: LCCN 2017018183 (print) | LCCN 2017021029 (ebook) | ISBN
9781583676387 (trade) | ISBN 9781583676394 (insitutional) | ISBN
9781583676363 (pbk.) | ISBN 9781583676370 (hardcover)
Subjects: LCSH: United States—Emigration and immigration. | United
States—Emigration and immigration—Government policy. |
Immigrants—United States. | Immigrants—Government policy—United
States.
Classification: LCC JV6465 (ebook) | LCC JV6465 .G87 2017 (print) | DDC
325.73—dc23
LC record available at https://lccn.loc.gov/2017018183

Typeset in Minion Pro

MONTHLY REVIEW PRESS, NEW YORK
monthlyreview.org

5 4 3 2 1

Contents

This book is dedicated with respect and admiration to everyone who is resisting deportation, detention, discrimination, exploitation, and oppression.

Acknowledgments

WE THANK JOHN MAGE AND CAROL SKELSKEY SOTO at Monthly Review Press for suggesting the original idea for this book and trusting us to write it, and the whole team at Monthly Review for their support and patience.

Our sincere gratitude goes to all the people who took the time to review the manuscript and share their thoughts and suggestions. We are especially thankful to Sam and Phyllis Guskin, David B. Wilson, and Amy Gottlieb (of American Friends Service Committee), for helpful feedback on both editions. For the second edition we were fortunate to receive valuable input from Donald Anthonyson (Families for Freedom), Diana Eusebio (New York State Youth Leadership Council), Ishan Ashutosh, Oriana Sanchez, Ron Hayduk, Partha Banerjee, and Eleazar Castillo. For help with research questions we are grateful to Ronald Coleman at the United States Holocaust Memorial Museum, Tory Johnson at the American Immigration Council, Katy Long, sociologists Annette Bernhardt, Douglas Massey, and Rubén Rumbaut, and historians Richard Breitman, Peter Staudenmaier, and John Womack. For advice on technical matters related to the second edition, we thank Anthony Arnove, Ramsey Kanaan of PM Press, and Greg Ruggiero at City Lights.

We remain indebted to those who contributed feedback on the first edition: Amy Sugimori (La Fuente, a Tri-State Worker & Community Fund), Carter Wilson, Aarti Shahani (Families for Freedom), Ken Estey, Arnoldo García (National Network for Immigrant and Refugee Rights), David Bacon, Mark Dow, and Will Coley.

Special thanks go to the people who organized and hosted dialogues and speaking events with us: Martin Alvarado, Judy Ancel, Dahoud André, Ernest Banatte, Scott Borchert, Marta Caminero-Santangelo, Dick Eiden, Bill and Connie Flores, Jon Flanders and Nancy Wallace, Leo J. Garofalo, Ursula Levelt, Star Murray, Emily Noelle Sanchez Ignacio, Eric Schuster, and Moisés Villavicencio Barras (with apologies to those not mentioned here by name). We also recognize the contributions of everyone who, through their participation in these events, gave us ideas and helped to shape our thinking on the issues.

Naturally, we take full responsibility for any errors or shortcomings that may be found in the book.

Introduction

THE FIRST EDITION OF THIS BOOK was written in the wake of the massive demonstrations, strikes, and walkouts that immigrants and their supporters carried out in the spring of 2006, and as churches across the United States were banding together to forge a new "sanctuary" movement in support of immigrants and their families resisting deportation.

That resistance has continued, taking new forms. Thousands of immigrant youth who grew up in the United States—sometimes referred to as "dreamers"—have forced a major shift in public perception by "outing" themselves as "undocumented, unafraid and unapologetic" and adopting increasingly radical tactics of active nonviolence. When civil disobedience actions like blocking streets, occupying politicians' offices, or camping out in front of government buildings didn't win their demands, these young activists upped the ante: some deliberately turned themselves in to immigration enforcement authorities in order to reject fear and organize resistance within the detention centers where they were locked up, and some left the country and returned en masse to nonviolently confront border authorities and demand reentry to the country where they came of age.

This kind of grassroots organizing and mobilizing is often effective, but it can also provoke backlash. A major goal of this book is to diminish that backlash by addressing people's concerns about immigration.

Since the first edition of this book was published, we have facilitated numerous dialogues on immigration with students, activists, and others in communities throughout the United States. These dialogues have reinforced our impression that many people are open to a deeper understanding of immigration and the forces that drive it.

As we said in 2007: "Every day, more people are realizing that immigrants are here to stay. They are our friends, our parents, our partners, our neighbors, ourselves. Either we condemn them to live as a permanent underclass, or we look for ways to integrate them into a more just and inclusive society."

This is not an easy task. The problems with our immigration system grow out of the history and legacy of slavery and colonialism, and are closely linked to the systems of labor exploitation and imprisonment that remain in effect today.

Following the gains of the civil rights movement in the 1960s, overtly racist rhetoric grew less acceptable within our legal framework, so policymakers claimed to be "colorblind" as they developed new systems to maintain the old racist structures. Politicians and the media shifted from openly slurring specific ethnicities and nationalities to branding groups of people as "criminals," "welfare queens," "gangsters," "illegals," "invaders," and "terrorists." These and many other labels are used to keep people "in their places" as racial others: behind walls, in cages, and stripped of power on the job in fields, forests, homes, and restaurants.

This book challenges such labels. We start with a demographic overview in chapter 1: what does the data say about who comes to the United States, from where, and how many? In chapter 2, we explore *why* people come here: what are the circumstances that impel them to leave their countries? Chapter 3 takes a look at how our country has treated refugees, now and in the past. Chapters 4 and 5 address questions about "illegality": what does it mean, why do so many people end up without legal status, and what challenges do they face? We then discuss the impact of immigration on the economy (chapter 6), and on health, environment, and culture (chapter 7). Chapter 8 challenges the myths that paint immigrants as criminals or terrorists. In chapter 9 we consider various approaches to immigration enforcement, both at the border and in the country's interior: how do these systems work, what do they accomplish, and at what cost? Because harsher enforcement often comes packaged with "softer" measures like amnesty and guest worker programs, we move in chapter 10 to the impact of such programs. In chapter 11, we return to enforcement, focusing on detention and deportation practices. We finish the book by considering the meanings of "open borders" and imagining what a more open immigration policy might look like in practice.

We hope this book contributes to deep, critical dialogues about the ways in which racism, exclusion, and exploitation are embedded within the politics of immigration in the United States. We believe such dialogue can help to strengthen movements that resist oppression, build solidarity, and develop strategies toward a more just political system.

Authors' Notes

What's new in the second edition?

THIS SECOND EDITION IS MORE than a simple update of the 2007 version. Many illuminating articles, books, reports, and academic papers on the topic of immigration have appeared over the past ten years, and these have enabled us to expand and improve the content. We've also revised, edited, and reorganized the text in an effort to make it clearer; in doing this we've benefited greatly from our experience facilitating dialogues on immigration, and from suggestions, critiques, and other feedback from many people.

Several chapters, notably chapter 3 (on refugees) and chapter 11 (on detention and deportation), have been substantially expanded and almost completely rewritten. Entirely new sections have been added to chapter 2 ("Why are children coming here from Central America?"); chapter 9 (about "Operation Streamline" and the post-2008 slowdown in unauthorized immigration); and chapter 10 (about "Deferred Action").

We have added brief introductions to the start of each chapter, summarizing the main points that follow. There is a greater emphasis on how the social construction of race has shaped immigration policy. The immigration law chronology that was left out of the first edition (but was posted on the website for the book) has been included here, and expanded.

The entire book is more rigorously researched and cited. Sources are provided for virtually every piece of information in the book. There are more than twice as many endnotes in this edition as there were in the original book, and a number of the endnotes include additional details or data as well as sources.

Where did these questions come from?

People who complain about immigrants often rely on arguments that are mostly based on myths. These myths are powerful because they tap into fears about jobs, wages, and changing communities. Well-funded anti-immigrant organizations and politicians try to exploit such fears to gain political advantage.

Even if we reject the anti-immigrant myths, we sometimes lack the tools we need to respond effectively when they emerge from the mouths of co-workers, family members, neighbors, or friends.

The idea of this book is to address people's fears with facts and honest arguments, to encourage everyone to take a deeper and broader look at immigration and its root causes, and to suggest some possible courses of action. We hope this book will reach people with genuine concerns about immigration, and be a useful source for immigrants and their supporters seeking to foster public dialogue around the issue.

Who are we talking to?

We hope this book is read by all kinds of people: immigrants and U.S.-born citizens, people with and without legal immigration status. We have alternated between referring to these different groups of readers as "you," "we," or "they" at various times over the course of the book. This is not meant to offend or exclude anyone, or to distance ourselves from anyone, but rather to acknowledge the diversity of our readers and encourage them to occasionally step into someone else's shoes and see things from a different perspective.

Disclaimer

This book is not designed to explain to immigrants how they can legalize their status in the United States. That would require a whole book about immigration law, and it would undoubtedly be out of date before it reached the publisher. As readers will likely notice, at the date of publication there are very few avenues open to people trying to legalize their status. Anyone who wants to know if they qualify should consult a reliable lawyer or legal service agency for advice. Try to get referrals from trusted friends or community-based organizations; there are unfortunately a lot of people out there who will be happy to charge a fee and promise to get you legal documents. If you're not careful, you may lose your money and end up in deportation proceedings.

Terminology

We use several terms in this book to describe people who are living in the United States without permission from the federal government. "Out of status" is the most accurate term and reflects the transitory nature of immigration status, but it is sometimes awkward, especially when used repeatedly. "Unauthorized" is less clumsy but still accurate and neutral, and is often used by researchers and policy analysts. "Undocumented" is more popularly used in the United States by those who reject the term "illegal." "Without papers" is especially common in Europe. (Occasionally we use "illegal," in quotes, just to make sure everyone understands that what so many people call "illegal" is what we are referring to as out of status or undocumented.)

As of April 1, 1997, to conform with laws passed in 1996, the immigration agency began using the term "removal" instead of "deportation" to describe the process of sending immigrants back to their home countries. Removal is a more legally precise term, but deportation is more widely recognized and understood. In this book we use the terms interchangeably.

1. Who Are the Immigrants?

IMMIGRANTS CURRENTLY MAKE UP AROUND the same proportion of the U.S. population as they did during the "great wave" of migration between the 1880s and 1920: between 13 and 14 percent. As happened during the first wave, some people view the newcomers as "too different" to integrate into U.S. society. The earlier waves mostly came from Europe. Jews, Catholics, and others from Eastern and Southern Europe were not necessarily seen as fully white at the time, but eventually they were accepted as white Americans.

Since 1965, a majority of immigrants have come from Asia, Latin America, and the Caribbean. Restrictive immigration laws push millions of them into a situation of "illegality," and many face a hostile racial climate that views them as second-class citizens and perpetual outsiders. Will the changing demographics of the United States lead us to expand our ideas about who is American? Or will we continue to put up walls and to consolidate a caste system that limits rights and opportunities for large numbers of people?

How do we define immigrants?

Immigrants are people who move into one country from another in order to settle there. They are immigrants—incoming migrants—from the perspective of their new home. They are emigrants—outgoing migrants—in relation to the country they are leaving.

"Migrants" can also refer to people who move from one area to another within their own country. Over the decades following the Civil War, millions of African Americans fled oppressive conditions in the rural South to seek a better life in northern cities, or in the West.[1] Because the United States had been reunited, these migrants didn't have to cross a national border, so they weren't immigrants. If the war had ended differently, African Americans might have had to cross into another country in order to escape—just as some 20,000 to 30,000 of them did between 1820 and 1860, fleeing slavery in the South and dodging bounty hunters in the northern states to reach freedom in Canada through the Underground Railroad.[2]

The U.S. government uses the term "alien" to cover all the different types of people who come here from another country and are not U.S. citizens. Demographers—people who study populations and how they change—generally use the category "foreign born," which includes naturalized citizens.

Foreign-born people living here with a legal status recognized by the federal government may be referred to as "authorized migrants" or "authorized immigrants." The government includes in a category of "non-immigrants" those people who come here from other countries but don't plan to stay, such as tourists and other visitors, temporary foreign workers, and international students. In reality, some "non-immigrants" end up settling here, while some immigrants decide to return to their country of origin.

Terms such as "unauthorized," "out of status," or "undocumented" are used to describe immigrants who are living here without permission from the federal government, or who are violating the terms of their stay.

The government, some media outlets, and many ordinary people describe out-of-status immigrants as "illegal aliens," "illegal immigrants," or just "illegals." But these terms contribute to a political climate that dehumanizes immigrants. The word *illegal* only makes sense when describing actions, not people—and in any case, unlawful presence in the United States is not a crime.[3] At a meeting with immigration officers after the arrests of immigrant workers at a factory in Wisconsin in the summer of 2006, Sandra Jiménez, an authorized migrant from Mexico, asked an immigration officer to stop calling the detainees "illegal aliens." "The word makes me think of strange little creatures," Jiménez said. "I am not a Martian."[4]

How many immigrants are here?

As of 2013, about 44 million foreign-born people had settled in the United States. Nearly half of them—19.3 million—had become naturalized citizens. Another 13.5 million people were lawful permanent residents (known in legal jargon as LPRs, often referred to as green card holders because the residency document used to be green). Over 100,000 refugees and asylees—people who were granted protection here after fleeing their home countries because of persecution, but who had not yet gained permanent residency—were also living in the United States. Another million or more "temporary legal residents" were here on work visas, as students, or as diplomats.[5]

It's harder to figure out how many people are living here out of status. Most estimates now are based on a residual method, taking the number of foreign-born people counted in the surveys or by the U.S. Census Bureau, and then subtracting the number of authorized migrants reported by immigration authorities. Demographers know that some out-of-status immigrants evade census takers, so they add in a certain percentage to compensate for the undercount.

As of 2014 the Pew Research Center, a nonprofit research group in Washington, D.C., estimated the unauthorized population at 11.3 million, including people who had been granted temporary relief from deportation. This number had not changed much over the past five years.[6]

About 8.1 million undocumented immigrants were working or looking for work in 2012, making up about 5.1 percent of the total U.S. labor force, according to the Pew Research Center's estimates. These figures too had been basically stable since 2007, when unauthorized workers reached a peak of 5.4 percent of the labor force.[7]

Are immigrants different from everyone else?

Compared to the general population, a larger proportion of immigrants are young adults, since immigrants tend to come here when they are at peak working age—that is, between twenty and fifty-four years old.[8]

In terms of family income, immigrants lag a bit behind people who were born here. In 2013, the median annual income for a household headed by a U.S.-born citizen was $52,500, compared to $48,000 for a household headed by an immigrant (regardless of status). When you compare immigrants from different regions, a stark contrast emerges: households headed by immigrants from South or East Asia had median incomes of $70,600, while those headed by immigrants from Mexico took in only $36,000.[9]

There is one major area in which immigrants are strikingly different from the general population: race and ethnicity. As of 2014, an estimated 77.5 percent of the overall U.S. population identified as white, whereas just 48 percent of the foreign born reported their race as white. Only 17.4 percent of the overall population identified as "Latino" or "Hispanic"—terms for people of Latin American heritage or their descendants, who may identify as any race or combination of races. Some 46 percent of the foreign born reported having Hispanic or Latino origins.[10]

Who are the undocumented immigrants?

Out-of-status immigrants make up a little more than a quarter of the foreign-born population, but they are often the focus of political debate and media stories. People sometimes use "immigrants" as shorthand for undocumented immigrants—and also make generalizations about the undocumented that are incorrect or overly broad.

There's a common assumption that all out-of-status immigrants are Mexican, or at least Latino or "Hispanic." Mexicans in fact make up the majority: about 52 percent of the estimated 11.7 million out-of-status immigrants in 2012 came from Mexico, according to the Pew Research Center—six million people. This is a slight decline from 2010, when Pew estimated that some 58 percent came from Mexico, with about 23 percent coming from Central and South America and the Caribbean, 11 percent from Asia, 4 percent from Europe and Canada, and 3 percent from Africa.[11]

People sometimes assume all out-of-status immigrants "jumped the border." Probably about half to two thirds of them come here without permission ("enter without inspection," in immigration jargon): they slip across the Mexican or Canadian border in secret, take a boat from a Caribbean island, or use false papers to come through a port of entry. Some present themselves at a border post to request asylum. But many people enter with permission and then fail to leave when that permission expires—they become "overstays." The overstays are more likely to come from Europe or Asia, rather than from Latin America or the Caribbean.[12]

The undocumented are often stereotyped as agricultural laborers. Many did work on farms in the past, and as of 2012 they made up just over a quarter of the U.S. agricultural labor force. But farmworkers are a small minority of the unauthorized immigrant labor force—about 4 percent.[13] Some 18 percent of out-of-status workers were employed in leisure and hospitality (working in restaurants and hotels, for example), 16 percent in construction, 13 percent in manufacturing, and 22 percent in professional, business, or other services, a broad category that includes legal services, advertising, landscaping, nail salons, car washing, and more.[14]

Another stereotype is that the undocumented all work "off the books," that is, in the informal, or underground, economy. In 2005, the New York Times quoted a Social Security Administration (SSA) official as saying the agency assumed that about 75 percent of unauthorized immigrants were working in the formal economy, paying the same income, Social Security, and Medicare taxes as other workers. The proportion later shrank as the government cracked down on people who were using false documents to work on the books. In a 2013 report, the SSA estimated that as of 2010 about 44 percent of undocumented workers were employed on the books, while 56 percent were working in the informal economy.[15]

One common perception is true: many of the undocumented work at low-paying jobs. A 2009 Pew report found that while households headed by the native-born had a median yearly income of $50,000, median income for households headed by out-of-status immigrants was just $36,000, even though these households generally had more members who worked.[16]

There's also a common assumption that most unauthorized immigrants are recent arrivals. Yet as of 2015 the vast majority—probably about 85 percent—had been living here for more than a decade.[17]

Is there a "new wave" of immigration?

In 2013 the U.S. population was over 316 million, according to the U.S. Census Bureau, and about 44 million foreign-born people were living here that year. This means that a little more than one in eight people—13.9 percent or less of the total population—came from somewhere else. The 11.3 million undocumented immigrants were 25.7 percent of the immigrant population, or 3.6 percent of the entire U.S. population.[18]

In 1965, just 4.4 percent of the total population in the United States was foreign born. The proportion of immigrants rose gradually to 6.2 percent in 1980, then more rapidly to 7.9 percent in 1990 and to 11.1 percent in 2000.[19] The foreign-born population was 19.8 million in 1990; it had jumped to 31.1 million by 2000, a 57 percent increase.[20] The 1990–2000 growth rate was even faster for out-of-status immigrants. Their numbers rose at an annual rate of 500,000 a year, more than doubling from 3.5 million in 1990 to 8.5 million in 2000.[21]

The undocumented population continued to grow at the same rate until it reached 12.2 million in 2007. But with the onset of the "Great Recession" that year, the growth stopped—in fact, the estimated number of undocumented immigrants fell to about 11.2 million in 2010, and rose only slightly to about 11.3 million by 2013. In addition to the economic crisis in the United States, other factors slowing the flow of unauthorized immigrants include a significant reduction in birth rates in Mexico over the past half-century.[22]

Is the "new wave" really new?

At 13.9 percent, the proportion of immigrants in the U.S. population of 2013 was comparable to what it was during much of the sixty-year period between 1860 and 1920, when the foreign-born population never dropped below 13.2 percent.[23]

The number of new immigrants started to decline after 1924, when Congress approved a law severely restricting immigration from Southern and Eastern Europe. Immigration from Asia had already been curtailed by a number of laws barring Chinese and other Asians. Because most immigrants at the time came from Europe and Asia by sea, it was relatively easy to slow immigration by blocking entry at the major ports where ships docked. The lack of opportunities here during the Depression also cut back immigration from Europe and Asia in the 1930s, as did the virtual suspension of commercial sea travel during the two world wars in the first half of the century.[24]

The result was that for fifty years, from 1940 to 1990, the foreign born made up a much smaller proportion of the population, ranging from 4.7 to 8.8 percent.[25]

Some people look at these numbers and see two waves of immigration, the current wave since 1990 and the earlier one between 1860 and 1920. But it makes as much sense to see current levels of immigration as the norm, and the fifty-year period of lower immigration—largely the result of restrictionist policies designed to keep out certain ethnic or national groups—as the exception.

In contrast to the wave of immigration at the turn of the twentieth century that brought new arrivals mainly from Europe, a large proportion of immigrants now, both documented and undocumented, come from Latin America, Asia, or the Caribbean.[26]

Another distinction is in the places where immigrants settle. Since 2010, more than half of the foreign born live in the suburbs of the country's largest 100 urban areas; another third live inside these major cities, and the rest live in smaller towns or in rural areas. Immigrants are increasingly arriving directly into these suburbs and smaller cities, especially in southeastern and midwestern states, instead of settling first in traditional gateway cities like Los Angeles, Miami, and New York City.[27] Because of long-standing stereotypes around race, native-born whites are often apprehensive about demographic shifts that bring people of color—immigrant or otherwise—into areas where whites are accustomed to being the dominant group.

Are politicians stirring up a panic about immigration?

In November 1973, under President Richard Nixon, former marine officer Leonard F. Chapman took office as commissioner of the Immigration and Naturalization Service (INS). Chapman told congressional committees in 1976 that there were at least six to seven million out-of-status immigrants in the United States at that time, and maybe as many as ten to twelve million. On January 17, 1972, *US News & World Report* warned its readers: "Never have so many aliens swarmed illegally into [the United States]—millions, moving across the nation. For government, they are becoming a costly headache." According to a December 29, 1974, *New York Times* article on the "silent invasion," one million undocumented immigrants lived in the New York metropolitan area at that time. On June 23, 1976, a *New Orleans Times-Picayune* headline announced: "Illegal Aliens: They Invade U.S. 8.2 Million Strong." On August 26, 1982, the *Saginaw News* in Michigan reported: "As many as fifteen million are already here."

In fact, a study by Census Bureau demographers concluded in 1980 that the number of undocumented immigrants that year was "almost certainly below six million, and may be substantially less, possibly only 3.5 to five million."[28] The Census Bureau's estimate may have been too high, in fact: after Congress passed a broad amnesty for the undocumented in the 1986 Immigration Reform and Control Act (IRCA), only three million people applied to legalize their status.[29]

Public perceptions of immigration continue to be highly exaggerated, according to Transatlantic Trends, an annual survey conducted in fifteen nations by the German Marshall Fund of the United States, the Compagnia di San Paolo, and the Barrow Cadbury Trust. For the 2011 survey the researchers asked people in the United States and ten European nations to estimate the proportion of immigrants in their countries. Respondents in the eleven countries tended to overestimate the immigrant population. On average, U.S. respondents thought that the foreign born made up 37.8 percent of the U.S. population—nearly three times the actual number.[30]

2. Why Do People Immigrate?

PEOPLE HAVE MANY REASONS FOR migrating, but major waves of migration are generally triggered by "push factors" such as economic or political problems in migrants' home countries, and "pull factors" such as better opportunities in their new country. When we analyze the push factors, we often find that the countries where migrants arrive—the United States, for example—played a major role in creating the problems that caused people to leave their countries in the first place.

Our current immigration and trade policies do nothing to stem these push factors, and often make the situation worse. Why not focus on solving the problems that displace people from their homes, instead of making it harder for people to get here, and punishing them when they arrive?

What are the "root causes" of migration?

Some people are nomadic and don't settle down in one place for any length of time. But most people prefer to remain in a relatively stable community in a particular area. Sometimes people are uprooted from their homes by violence, or by economic, social, or political pressures.

This "forced displacement" can push people from rural areas into cities or refugee camps, from one region to another, or across borders into other countries.

The series of events in Ireland known as the "Great Famine" triggered the migration of some 1.7 million Irish people to the United States in the 1840s and 1850s. People fleeing China to escape the violence and economic turbulence that accompanied the Taiping Rebellion (1850–64) were a large part of the wave of immigration that brought more than 105,000 Asians here by 1880. Many of the two million Eastern European Jews who immigrated to the United States from 1881 to 1914 came because of sporadic anti-Semitic pogroms as well as discriminatory policies in Tsarist Russia that limited opportunities for a decent life.[1]

Millions of people continue to migrate because their communities are devastated by poverty and violence. For others, it may be possible to survive in their communities, but by migrating they can get jobs that pay more, allowing them to seek a better future for their families. Many migrants hope to return home as soon as economic and political conditions in their homeland improve. Often these hopes are dashed, as conditions only worsen, and family members left behind increasingly depend on their support for basic needs.

Any of us might make the decision to migrate if we faced similar conditions. "I'm a retired cop," said a Long Island man during a public meeting shown in the 2003 award-winning documentary *Farmingville*. "I was in the Marine Corps. I have a lot of respect for the laws of the United States. If I lived in Mexico and I knew I had some advantage here to help my family back in Mexico, I'd be wading across the Rio Grande myself. I'd be on a raft floating from Haiti, I'd be crossing the border from Yugoslavia into Germany. I'd be going into England. I'd do anything I can to help my family."[2]

Why do people come to the United States?

Many people consider the United States to be a land of freedom and opportunity, and believe that people from around the world are eager to come here. For most people who are driven to migrate, a combination of three main factors influences where they choose to go: economic opportunities in the destination country; the presence of family or friends there who can help them get a job and a place to live; and the distance, difficulty, and expense of the trip.

The United States has a large economy with a range of job opportunities, and material goods tend to be cheaper here relative to income levels than in other countries. Our history as an immigrant nation means many foreign citizens have family or friends—or even entire communities from their homeland—already living here, and can help the newcomers adjust.

Some immigrants are drawn to the United States because it promises certain freedoms, like freedom of speech and religion. And despite persistent economic and social inequalities and racial discrimination in the United States, immigrants sometimes feel they can leave behind the class and caste prejudices of their home countries and make a fresh start here.

The United States is not the only country with high rates of immigration. As of 2013 more than 230 million people were living outside the country where they were born, about 3.2 percent of the world's population. The approximately 44 million immigrants in the United States accounted for about one-fifth of these people.[3]

Immigrants generally settle in economically stronger, more stable countries that are comparatively easy to reach. Migrants from Mexico, Central and South America, the Caribbean, and parts of East Asia tend to settle in the United States; migrants from Africa and West Asia often prefer to go to Europe. Sometimes these patterns reflect historical relationships of colonialism that leave behind cultural, political, or linguistic links: for example, when North Africans go to France, or people from the Indian subcontinent move to Britain.[4]

Is it our fault other countries have so many problems?

In recent decades, immigrants to the United States have come largely from places where the U.S. government carried out major military, political, or economic interventions in the past. Of the top ten countries of origin for the million people who became permanent legal residents in 2012, seven experienced major U.S. interventions: Mexico, the Philippines, the Dominican Republic, Cuba, Vietnam, Haiti, and South Korea.[5]

Claiming a need to stop influence by the Soviet Union, in the 1980s the U.S. government funded and promoted wars against leftist revolutionary movements in Central America. Some 300,000 people, mostly civilians, were killed: 200,000 in Guatemala, 70,000 in El Salvador, and 30,000 in Nicaragua. This represented about one death for every hundred inhabitants in the region.[6] The United States has spent billions on a similar armed strategy in Colombia, where some 220,000 people have been killed and millions displaced over the last half-century as government forces tried to crush leftist insurgencies.[7] The U.S. government has also trained Latin American military officers who have been accused of abducting, torturing, and murdering civilians throughout the hemisphere.[8]

The United States likewise bears a large share of responsibility for most of the economic crises that have sparked mass migration since the 1980s. These crises have their roots in economic policies dictated either directly by the U.S. government through its regional trade agreements, or indirectly through its influence over international lending institutions like the World Bank and the International Monetary Fund (IMF).[9]

How do U.S. economic policies affect migration?

The IMF and the World Bank function by making loans to countries that are already heavily indebted, on the condition that their governments follow an economic model promoted by U.S. economists and the media as "open markets," "free trade," and "globalization." Analysts in Latin America and much of the rest of the world call this model "neoliberalism." (This comes from the old sense of "liberalism," which referred to the free trade policies of classical economists like Adam Smith and David Ricardo.)[10]

The neoliberal model and its "structural adjustments" involve reducing the supply of money; selling off state-owned industries and services to private companies; scaling back and privatizing health-care, education, and other social programs; and eliminating or sharply reducing tariffs that protect domestic industries and agriculture. Such measures generally reduce inflation and stabilize currency exchange rates, but at a cost. Privatization throws tens of thousands of public employees out of work and reduces government revenues. Service cutbacks leave people without a social safety net when they fall on hard times. "Free trade" forces local farmers and manufacturers to compete with huge multinational corporations that are often subsidized by the governments of the wealthy countries where the multinationals are based.

The most dramatic result of such policies was a series of economic crises that followed their implementation: in Mexico in 1994 and 1995, in several Southeast Asian countries in 1997 and 1998, in Russia in 1998, in Brazil in 1999, and in Argentina in 2001.[11] But even in areas without major crises, these neoliberal policies cause exactly the sort of economic hardships that lead people to migrate.

Why do so many Mexicans come here?

After its 1910 revolution, Mexico grew from a primarily agricultural country to what in 2013 was the fifteenth-largest economy in the world, right behind Spain and South Korea. Until the 1980s its economic growth rate was frequently as high as 6 percent a year. Poorer Mexicans often didn't share equally in the benefits of this growth, but life did improve for many people: the illiteracy rate was cut in half and mortality rates fell dramatically.[12]

In the early 1980s, Mexico suffered a financial crisis brought on by a worldwide recession and the government's overborrowing during the 1970s oil boom. To get out of the crisis, the government started implementing a neoliberal economic model. Proponents of the change claimed that unemployment and other dislocations caused by these policies would be more than made up for by foreign investment, expanded trade, and a rapid expansion of industrial jobs in the *maqui-ladoras*—the largely tax-exempt assembly plants producing goods for export, including hundreds of factories along Mexico's border with the United States.

Mexico forged ahead with the plan, signing a letter of intent to sell off 1,200 state-owned companies in 1984, and then amending the Mexican constitution in 1992 to allow the privatization of many *ejidos*, the campesino-controlled cooperative farms that were the heart of Mexico's agrarian reform in the 1930s.[13]

In the early 1990s, the government of Mexican president Carlos Salinas de Gortari negotiated a model neoliberal trade accord with the United States and Canada—the North American Free Trade Agreement, better known as NAFTA.

Mexico's economy had shown no sign of recovery by the time NAFTA went into effect on January 1, 1994, but the United States promoted the Mexican experience as an example for the rest of Latin America. In December 1994, U.S. president Bill Clinton hosted a "Summit of the Americas" in Miami, with thirty-four heads of state meeting to ratify a plan for a Free Trade Area of the Americas, which was supposed to extend NAFTA to the whole hemisphere by 2005. Two weeks later, the Mexican peso collapsed. On January 31, 1995, fearing a total breakdown of the Mexican economy that would affect a large number of U.S. investors, the Clinton administration patched together a $48.8 billion bailout package of loans and credit lines for Mexico from various countries and financial institutions. The U.S. share was $20 billion.[14]

Under NAFTA and other trade agreements that forced the reduc-tion or elimination of protective tariffs, more than 1.5 million Mexican farmers lost their sources of income and had to sell or abandon their farms; total agricultural employment fell from 8.1 million in the early 1990s to 5.8 million in the second quarter of 2008. Consumer prices were supposed to decline under NAFTA, yet while the prices paid to farmers for their products plummeted, consumer food prices rose in all three NAFTA countries. As of 2005, Mexican farmers earned 70 percent less for their corn than they did before NAFTA while Mexican consumers paid 50 percent more for tortillas, a corn-based staple of the Mexican diet. Without the protection of tariffs, Mexico became increasingly dependent on food imports: in 1995 the country's grain imports jumped to ten million tons a year, from five to seven million tons previously. The dependence on imports means that when the local currency loses value against the U.S. dollar, real prices for food can double or triple.[15]

It's true that the *maquiladoras* added some 660,000 manufacturing jobs after NAFTA took effect, but this wasn't nearly enough to offset the loss of 2.3 million jobs in agriculture—and the *maquiladora* sector itself started losing jobs in 2000-2001 because of competition from countries like China.[16] Meanwhile, the real purchasing power of the Mexican minimum wage fell by nearly three-fifths from 1980 to 1996.[17] It continued to fall after NAFTA went into effect in 1994—by 25 percent from 1994 to 2009.[18]

Rising unemployment and shrinking pay resulted in a growing gap between Mexican and U.S. wages. Up to the 1970s, Mexican workers were paid about one-fourth to one-third of what their U.S. counterparts got. (The cost of living in Mexico is generally much lower than it is in the United States, although items like electronics, cars, and name-brand clothes usually cost more.) After the decline of real wages in the 1980s, Mexican workers in manufacturing in the late 1990s were making about one-eighth what they would be making for the same job in the United States; in some occupations Mexican workers were being paid one-fifteenth what they would get north of the border.[19]

In 1981, a Mexican factory worker could have made three or four times as much money by crossing the border, not necessarily enough of a difference to make up for the risks and hardships of immigration. Just a few years later, the same factory worker's actual purchasing power in Mexico had dropped to about one-third of its previous level but now the worker could get paid eight to fifteen times more by going north. A 2009 study by the Carnegie Endowment for International Peace concluded that "one of the paradoxes of NAFTA, which leaders promised would help Mexico 'export goods, not people,' is that

Mexico now 'exports' more people than ever and more of them reside permanently in the United States without documents."[20]

Why don't people stay home and fix their own countries?

In the 2001 documentary *Uprooted: Refugees of the Global Economy*, "Maricel," an immigrant from the Philippines, tells how she ended up going overseas as a domestic worker. Seeing ads everywhere encouraging people to work abroad, and facing a lack of opportunities at home, Maricel made a tough decision. "I realized that it's just a waste of time for me to go to college," she said, "because those people who went to college, they wasted four years studying hard, and then they have to go abroad to work as domestics. And I said that I just don't want to waste any more time. I'm just going to go abroad."

At the time, the Philippines had a total foreign debt of more than $52 billion.[21] "On top of that the economy is not doing well, and you have this loan that [has] to be paid off, and people are talking about even like ten generations will pass and we won't be able to survive," explains Maricel. "So, realistically speaking, when is it going to be better? Is there a possibility that the economy gets better? You're paying the debt, and on top of it you have this big, big interest. It's not very realistic that you will come out of it, like the Philippines will come out of it in one piece." With no opportunities in her home country, Maricel ended up in New York City, and eventually became an organizer helping other domestic workers fight exploitation.[22]

When people have no hope that things will get better, they are more likely to uproot themselves and go elsewhere to survive. If they believe they can improve the situation in their countries, they are less inclined to leave. And if things do get better in their home countries, many people who left will return.

Starting in 1910, an estimated one to one and a half million Mexicans crossed the northern border to escape the violence of the Mexican revolution. Mexico's population was about fifteen million at the time, so this was a major migration—almost one out of every ten Mexicans. But many returned to Mexico once the violence let up and the revolution opened new opportunities back home, including social programs such as a sweeping agrarian reform.[23]

What happens when people do try to fix their countries?

In the Central American nation of Nicaragua, an earthquake struck on December 23, 1972, killing as many as 10,000 people and destroying or damaging about 80 percent of the buildings in the center of the capital city, Managua. The country's U.S.-backed dictator, Anastasio Somoza Debayle, funneled much of the international aid into his own family's pockets, leaving the population without help. Yet the disaster did not provoke a massive wave of migration. A movement to overthrow Somoza had been building for the past decade, and many Nicaraguans stayed home to push for change.[24]

Washington continued to support Somoza, despite the earthquake aid debacle and a series of worsening human rights abuses, but in the end it could no longer prop him up against widespread opposition. On July 19, 1979, an insurrection led by the leftist Sandinista National Liberation Front (FSLN) toppled Somoza and began to transform Nicaragua from a dictator's feudal estate into a real country, with political pluralism and a "mixed economy" based on the economic models of countries like France and Sweden, which combine public and private ownership of important economic sectors.[25]

Nicaragua's real Gross Domestic Product (GDP) grew by a total of 7.67 percent per capita from 1979 to 1983; this was at a time when the real GDP *fell* by 14.71 percent per capita for Central America as a whole.[26] But with fiercely anti-communist Ronald Reagan as president, the U.S. government chose not to tolerate the way Nicaraguans were fixing their country; it started funneling money, weapons, training, and other "assistance" to recruit local fighters, known as the contras, for a proxy war that targeted civilian supporters of the Sandinista government. The war halted economic progress. Eleven years and some 30,000 deaths later, the United States won its war of attrition when Nicaraguans, tired of fighting, voted the FSLN out of office in February 1990.

For all their struggles and sacrifice, Nicaraguans were cheated out of the chance to fix their country. The new U.S.-backed government quickly imposed IMF-sponsored "structural adjustment" programs that brought a sharp rise in unemployment and triggered a recession, plunging the already impoverished population into desperate misery. Many Nicaraguans fled to neighboring Costa Rica, whose 1984 census counted 45,918 Nicaraguans; by 2000 the country had 226,374 Nicaraguan residents, two-thirds of whom said they had arrived during the 1990s.[27]

In El Salvador and Guatemala, the U.S. government backed rightwing regimes as they tried to crush revolutionary leftist movements similar to Nicaragua's. These wars ended with peace accords—in 1992 in El Salvador and in 1996 in Guatemala—that allowed the leftist forces to regroup as political parties. But 70,000 Salvadorans and 200,000 Guatemalans had been killed, the vast majority of them by the U.S.-backed regimes, which remained in power and began imposing neoliberal economic programs. The wars left deep wounds in the countries' social and economic fabric. By 2005, El Salvador's homicide rate of fifty-four murders per 100,000 people was the highest in Latin America;[28] nearly half of the country's rural population lived below the poverty line, and 61 percent had no access to water piped into the home.[29]

The U.S. Census reported that 44,166 Nicaraguans were living in the United States in 1980, shortly after the overthrow of the Somoza regime; the number jumped to 168,659 over the next decade. The number of Salvadorans living in the United States rose from 94,447 in 1980 to 465,433 in 1990, and the number of Guatemalans went from 63,073 to 225,739 during the same period, when the wars in those countries were at their worst. The numbers rose almost as much again during the 1990s, as neoliberal economic programs were imposed: by 2000 there were 220,335 Nicaraguans, 817,336 Salvadorans, and 480,665 Guatemalans in the United States.[30]

Haitians suffered a similar fate. In December 1990, Haitians seized an opportunity for change, overwhelmingly electing popular priest Jean-Bertrand Aristide as president. Turnout was about 63 percent of eligible voters, according to official figures, with 67.5 percent voting for Aristide, compared to 14.2 percent for his closest competitor. Haitians hoped Aristide would carry out his promises to oppose IMF programs and raise the standard of living in the hemisphere's poorest country.

But less than a year later, in September 1991, Aristide was overthrown in a military coup. Army officers and right-wing paramilitaries unleashed massive repression against grassroots and leftist activists. According to reports judged credible by Human Rights Watch, the U.S. Central Intelligence Agency funded the main paramilitary leader, Emmanuel Constant. The military regime and its supporters killed an estimated 3,000 to 4,000 people before being forced to give up power in September 1994.[31] Their hopes for change crushed, Haitians fled. U.S. Coast Guard data showed a notable drop of migrants fleeing Haiti by boat after the December 1990 elections, followed by a dramatic upturn after the 1991 coup.[32]

Aristide was returned to office in October 1994 after then-president Bill Clinton ordered a U.S. military intervention—once Aristide had agreed to a U.S.-inspired neoliberal economic program, including a "drastic reduction" of the tariffs that protected Haitian food producers from foreign competition. Many Haitian farmers, especially rice producers, were forced out of business, and Haitians became largely dependent on imported rice. Clinton later apologized for the tariff reduction policy. "I have to live every day with the consequences of the lost capacity to produce a rice crop in Haiti to feed those people, because of what I did," he told the U.S. Senate in March 2010.[33]

Haitian migration to the United States swelled after the 1991 coup, and continued as the 1994 neoliberal program took effect. About 200,000 people born in Haiti lived in the United States in 1990. By 2009, that number had reached nearly half a million.[34]

Why are children coming here from Central America?

Although the total number of undocumented immigrants in the United States fell by nearly one million after 2008, in the middle of 2014 there was a sharp rise in unauthorized border crossing by children. Most came from Mexico and three Central American countries—El Salvador, Guatemala, and Honduras. The U.S. Customs and Border Protection (CBP) agency detained 57,525 unaccompanied children—those traveling without a parent or guardian—at the Mexico-U.S. border from October 2013 through June 2014, more than twice as many as for the same period the year before. The number of children apprehended with a parent or guardian also jumped dramatically: 22,069 accompanied children were detained from October 2013 to June 2014, almost three times the number for the year before. About 16 percent of the unaccompanied children were under the age of thirteen, as were a full 81 percent of the children who were accompanied by a parent or a legal guardian. The upsurge in child migration started tapering off in the second half of 2014.[35]

Poverty and fear of violence seemed to be the main reasons for this sudden increase in child migrants. In March 2014 the United Nations High Commissioner on Refugees (UNHCR), the UN refugee agency, reported the results of a survey it had made of underage immigrants from Mexico and the three Central American countries. The researchers found that "no less than 58 percent of the 404 children interviewed were forcibly displaced because they suffered or feared harms that indicated a potential or actual need for international protection." A survey of 322 underage migrants from El Salvador published by the Immigration Policy Center in June 2014 found that "59 percent of Salvadoran boys and 61 percent of Salvadoran girls list[ed] crime, gang threats, or violence as a reason for their emigration."

The UNHCR report noted that the increase in migration from the three Central American countries wasn't just affecting the United States. Asylum requests by people from these countries to Belize, Costa Rica, Mexico, Nicaragua, and Panama jumped by 435 percent from 2009 to 2012.[36]

Experts on Central American history noted that continuing effects of the wars of the 1980s and the neoliberal policies of the 1990s had contributed to high poverty and crime rates in Central America.[37] Political repression added to the new level of violence in the area, especially in Mexico and Honduras, and so did a militarized approach to fighting the trafficking of drugs through the region to the United States. More than 60,000 people died in drug-related violence in Mexico from 2007 to 2014, but instead of stopping the drug cartels, the fighting in Mexico just seemed to encourage the spread of narco-trafficking into El Salvador, Guatemala, and Honduras. The U.S. government had helped fund this militarized approach since 2007 through a $2.5 billion program, the Mérida Initiative.[38]

In Honduras another factor was government corruption following a 2009 military coup. Despite evidence of links between security forces and drug gangs, the Honduran military continues to get millions in U.S. aid. As of 2014, Honduras had the highest murder rate in the world. A Human Rights Watch report noted "rampant crime and impunity for human rights abuses," including violent attacks on journalists and peasant organizers.[39]

How can we address the root causes of immigration?

Many people around the world are trying, often at great personal risk, to build a better future for themselves, their families and their communities, and a more equitable society for everyone. Those of us who live in the United States can join them in these efforts, generally without risking our lives.

During the 1980s, many thousands of people in the United States spoke out against their government's intervention in Central America. Activists protested and lobbied Congress; many traveled to Central America to provide assistance and bring back information on conditions in the region, seriously undercutting the Reagan administration's public relations campaign to depict Central American leftists as a threat to the United States. This activism seems to have had an impact on public opinion: a *New York Times*/CBS poll in April 1986 showed some 62 percent of U.S. respondents opposed financial aid to the U.S.-backed contras in Nicaragua, while just 25 percent supported it.[40]

In the early 1990s, labor unions and activists led a campaign against NAFTA, and in late 1999, giant protests erupted in Seattle against the policies of the World Trade Organization (WTO), sparking a new "anti-globalization" movement in the United States. These protests took their lead from workers in Latin America and elsewhere, who had long been out in the streets fighting the same policies. Mexicans organized innumerable marches, rallies, strikes, sit-ins, and occupations of government buildings in the 1990s. Thousands of indigenous farmers rose up in southern Mexico on January 1, 1994, the day NAFTA went into effect. Naming their movement the Zapatistas—after Mexican revolutionary hero Emiliano Zapata—they denounced the trade pact as a "death sentence" for indigenous people.[41]

Starting in the mid-1990s, campus and labor activists in the United States built an anti-sweatshop movement that has made important gains in supporting successful local worker-organizing campaigns in Latin America and throughout the world.

For example, in 2002 and 2003 a group called United Students Against Sweatshops (USAS) exerted pressure through its Sweat-Free Campus Campaign to help workers at the BJ&B factory in Villa Altagracia in the Dominican Republic win the first union in a Caribbean "Free Trade Zone" in five years. The company closed the plant in 2007, despite international pressure to keep it open, but the factory reopened in 2010 under an agreement that South Carolina–based Knights Apparel signed with the Workers Rights Consortium, an independent U.S.-based monitoring organization, in collaboration with the former union leaders. Knights Apparel rehired some of the laid-off workers to produce college-logo apparel for a new "fair trade" brand, Alta Gracia. The workers are paid a living wage—three times higher than the country's minimum—and their union contract also guarantees health and safety standards and fair treatment.[42]

Such efforts are continuing. In November 2013 two major apparel manufacturers, Montreal-based Gildan Activewear Inc. and Kentucky-based Fruit of the Loom, announced that they would require their Haitian suppliers to stop violating the country's minimum wage laws. This followed a long-term campaign by Dominican, Haitian, Honduran, and Nicaraguan unions backed by Canadian and U.S. anti-sweatshop activists to end labor violations by Gildan and its suppliers.[43]

USAS and other groups have also been working to get U.S. brands to sign a legally binding agreement protecting worker safety in the Bangladeshi garment industry following the deaths of at least 1,129 people in the April 2013 collapse of a factory building at Rana Plaza in Dhaka. As of June 2014 the campaign had succeeded in convincing seventeen college clothing brands to sign the accord, while twenty-three universities had agreed to require their brands to sign it.[44] Worldwide, 200 companies have signed the accord.[45]

Major unions in the United States and Europe are also backing labor struggles in other countries, often by linking up with local unions. In October 2014, the Metal Workers Union of the Philippines (MWAP) won a new collective bargaining agreement for its members employed by Dutch multinational NXP Semiconductors, a supplier to Apple. The contract included reinstatement for twelve union officers and "decent severance" for another twelve who had been fired in a union-busting move. The union called the victory a "showcase of what international solidarity can do." It thanked the Geneva-based international union IndustriALL and online campaign organizations like SumOfUs, which mobilized 150,000 supporters to write to Apple, for putting pressure on NXP to respect workers' rights.[46]

In early 2015 a newly formed Panamanian dockworkers union, SINTRAPORSPA (Sindicato Industrial de Trabajadores/as Portuarios y Similares de Panamá), won a contract from a subsidiary of the Hong Kong–based Hutchinson Port Holdings Limited (HPH). The agreement would raise wages by 27 percent over the next four years. The Panamanian union is affiliated with a major U.S.-based dockworkers union, the International Longshore and Warehouse Union (ILWU), which had helped the Panamanian workers in their fight for union recognition.[47]

3. Does the United States Welcome Refugees?

U.S. REFUGEE POLICY DEVELOPED out of a Cold War focus on defeating communism. For many years, refugees were explicitly defined in U.S. law as people fleeing Communist rule. This priority resulted in unequal treatment for people attempting to reach safety—even after 1980, when the legal definition of a refugee was made politically neutral. People displaced by U.S.-sponsored wars, or fleeing U.S.-backed human rights violators, have historically been denied asylum, while those migrating from Communist countries have generally been given the benefit of the doubt. The asylum process has gradually evolved away from its Cold War origins, yet many forms of bias still affect who is granted protection.

What's a refugee?

In ordinary usage the word *refugee* refers to people forced to leave their country because of war, persecution, or natural disaster. The term has a narrower definition in international law.

The 1951 United Nations Convention Relating to the Status of Refugees and its 1967 Protocol define a refugee as "a person who is outside his or her country of nationality or habitual residence; has a well-founded fear of being persecuted because of his or her race, religion, nationality, membership of a particular social group or political opinion; and is unable or unwilling to avail him- or herself of the protection of that country, or to return there, for fear of persecution."[1] In other words, you must be part of a group specifically targeted for persecution. Wars or disasters that affect the whole population don't count. Under regional conventions in Africa and Latin America, the definition of a refugee has been expanded to cover migrants fleeing foreign aggression, occupation, internal conflicts, foreign domination, massive human rights violations, or events seriously disturbing public order. However, these broader criteria have not been adopted by the United Nations.[2]

Refugees are people whose claim to refugee status has been established; you are considered an asylum seeker if your claim hasn't been evaluated yet.[3] The office of the United Nations High Commissioner for Refugees (UNHCR) includes refugees and asylum seekers in a broader category of forcibly displaced people, along with internally displaced people (sometimes referred to as IDPs), who flee their homes due to violence or persecution but do not cross an international border.

At the end of 2015, the UNHCR counted 65.3 million people as forcibly displaced worldwide, the highest level since 1989, when the agency began tracking this data. Included were 40.8 million internally displaced people and 3.2 million asylum seekers; the other 21.3 million were refugees, or people in what the UNHCR calls "refugee-like situations." Some 16.1 million of these refugees were under the UNHCR's mandate, more than half of them from Syria, Afghanistan, and Somalia. Another 5.2 million were Palestinians under the mandate of the United Nations Relief and Works Agency for Palestine Refugees in the Near East (UNRWA). The proportion of forcibly displaced people among the world's population remained relatively stable at between 0.6 and 0.7 percent from 1996 until 2011, when Syria's civil war began, triggering what the UNHCR calls "one of the largest displacement crises in recent history." Since then, this figure has increased rapidly and steadily, reaching 0.9 percent in 2015.[4]

What's the difference between a refugee and an immigrant?

Refugees have special rights to protection under national and international law, compared to people who are seen as migrating for economic or other reasons. Some people use terms like "survival migrants," "forced migrants," "people in distress," or "vulnerable irregular migrants" to describe migrants who don't necessarily fit the strict definition of a refugee but who didn't voluntarily leave their countries.[5]

For most refugees and other migrants, there are complex political, economic, social, structural, and personal factors that determine why, when, and how they leave, and where they end up. Each time a humanitarian crisis erupts somewhere in the world, or a particular group is subjected to persecution, some people feel they have no choice but to flee—sometimes abandoning homes, land, livelihood, possessions, family, and community—while others make an equally difficult decision to remain, in the hopes of surviving and, in some cases, of taking action from within to effect social change. Many who seek safety as refugees also get involved in efforts to influence political and social conditions in their home countries. Some people stay behind not by choice, but because they lack the minimum resources or conditions needed to migrate.[6]

How do we decide who the "real" refugees are?

In the United States until 1980, a patchwork of laws and provisions allowed for the entry of individual refugees and groups of refugees based on ethnicity, nationality, and specific geographic or political circumstances. Several of these laws, starting with the Displaced Persons Act of 1948, provided quotas or access to a certain number of nonquota visas for refugees and other displaced persons. Refugees were generally still required to fulfill the standard immigration criteria of the time: they had to have job offers, a place to live, and proof that they would not become a "public charge."[7]

Throughout the Cold War period, the U.S. government's active opposition to communism guided refugee and asylum policy; U.S. law generally defined refugees as people fleeing a "Communist or Communist-dominated country." Accepting and even encouraging refugees and asylum seekers from such countries served to discredit their governments as oppressive regimes, recruit away their educated elites in what's referred to as "brain drain," and bolster exile-led opposition movements to attack them. Not until the Refugee Act of 1980 did the U.S. government finally adopt the politically neutral definition of a refugee established by the 1951 UN Convention and its 1967 Protocol, and lay out procedures for the processing of refugees and asylum seekers.[8]

But foreign policy still plays a role in asylum policy: "Immigration judges are required to consult and incorporate in their decisions the official country report published by the United States Department of State in any asylum case," Dana Leigh Marks, an immigration judge in California and the president of the National Association of Immigration Judges, told a reporter in 2011. "Obviously our foreign relations position with regard to a country from which the asylum seeker comes is an important factor in the judge's decision."[9]

FLEEING THE NAZIS

As people persecuted on the basis of their religion and their perceived ethnic characteristics, the Jews fleeing the German Nazi regime in Europe from the 1930s to 1945 clearly fit today's definition of refugees. Unfortunately, most were not able to reach safety, as worldwide anti-Jewish and anti-immigrant sentiment led many countries to close their doors.

In the 1930s, the United States was facing the widespread unemployment and poverty of the Great Depression. From the mid-1930s through the mid-1940s, polls showed the U.S. public firmly opposed to accepting more refugees from Europe or elsewhere; polls also reflected strong anti-Jewish sentiment in the United States during this period.[10]

The U.S. Immigration Act of 1924 had imposed strict nationality caps and economic requirements on people seeking to come here. There was no exception for people fleeing persecution. Many European Jews had family and friends in the United States who tried to help them escape, as well as the support of a large and active Jewish community here. Some U.S. citizens made extraordinary efforts to save the refugees by providing information—sometimes falsified—about family relationships, financial support and job offers for U.S. visa applications.[11] U.S. diplomatic officials rejected the vast majority of visa applicants, claiming they were "likely to become a public charge."[12]

In May 1939, the German ocean liner *St. Louis* sailed from Hamburg to Havana with 937 passengers, nearly all of them Jews seeking asylum from the Nazis. The Nazi government backed the voyage as part of its efforts to encourage Jews to leave Germany voluntarily.[13]

The Nazis also hoped the voyage would justify its anti-Semitic policies by highlighting the world's rejection of Jews. This rejection was already apparent in July 1938, when delegates from thirty-two countries, including the United States, met at the French spa town of Évian-les-Bains to discuss the European refugee crisis. Only one country at the Évian conference agreed to accept Jewish refugees: the Dominican Republic, whose brutal dictator Rafael Trujillo believed European immigration could "whiten" his country's largely African-descended population. The other countries declined to increase their limited quotas or to take any action to save Jews or others fleeing persecution.[14]

The majority of the *St. Louis* passengers hoped to wait in Cuba while the U.S. government processed their visa applications. But the Cuban government, then a close U.S. ally, allowed only twenty-eight passengers to disembark—four Spanish citizens, two Cubans, and twenty-two people who already had valid U.S. visas. After six days, the ship left Havana and sailed toward

Miami as passengers cabled President Franklin Roosevelt asking to be allowed to come ashore. The U.S. State Department answered that they had to "await their turns on the waiting list and then qualify for and obtain immigration visas before they may be admissible into the United States."

Unable to land anywhere in the region, the *St. Louis* turned back toward Europe on June 6, 1939. Because of the high profile of the voyage, Jewish organizations were able to negotiate entry visas to Britain for nearly a third of the passengers, and to the Netherlands, Belgium, or France for the rest. Of those who went to the European continent, more than 40 percent—254 people— died in the Holocaust.[15]

The *St. Louis* was one of many ships carrying desperate refugees from Europe, seeking to enter the United States. At the end of May 1939, 104 German, Austrian, and Czech Jewish refugees aboard the French ship *Flandre* were turned away from Havana and forced to return to France. Another two hundred refugees from Germany aboard the *Orinoco* were denied entry to the United States and were returned to Germany in June 1939. The fate of these rejected refugees remains unknown.[16]

At least half a million European Jews managed to flee to safer countries, and many later found their way to the United States to join friends and relatives already living here. Others were trapped by the war and unable to escape. Once the war started, the United States closed its doors to the refugees, seeing them as potential spies.[17]

When the war ended in 1945, an estimated six million Jews had been killed in the Holocaust.[18] Could more have been done to save those fleeing genocide? Some people broke laws and took personal risks to help the refugees, including individual diplomats from a number of nations who issued unauthorized travel documents and visas. But the United States played a minimal role in such rescue efforts.[19]

Most of the activity that helped European refugees to escape was illegal, violating not only the unjust laws of the Nazi regime but often the restrictive immigration laws of allied and neutral nations. In an April 1997 speech at the United States Holocaust Memorial Museum in Washington, then-UN High Commissioner for Refugees Sadako Ogata noted that those who managed to escape Nazi-occupied Europe "often did so by using fraudulent documents," an action for which asylum seekers are now criticized.

"In looking back, the refugee issues of the 1930s and 1940s seem simple," observed Ogata. "Yet at the time, the issues seemed to be as complex as similar issues appear today."[20]

Does the United States accept too many refugees?

The number of people who arrived in the United States as refugees averaged just over 80,000 a year between 1980 and 2013, ranging from a high of 207,000 in 1980 (a year that saw nearly 130,000 migrants arriving from Cuba) to a low of 26,800 in 2002, after the September 2001 terrorist attacks prompted a review of the refugee program, dramatically slowing admissions. In fiscal year 2013, just under 70,000 people entered the United States as refugees.[21]

Each year the U.S. president sets a cap on refugee admissions after consulting with Congress. Since 1980 the number of refugees admitted has reached this limit only once—in 1992. Actual admissions plummeted after 2001, even as the cap stayed at 70,000 to 80,000 a year. Between 2002 and 2012, actual admissions averaged less than 70 percent of the allotted number. Since 2013, each year's 70,000 limit has essentially been reached.[22]

The U.S. government granted asylum status in an additional 23,000 cases each year on average between 2000 and 2013.[23]

Can't refugees go somewhere else?

Most refugees *do* go somewhere else. The vast majority of the world's refugees—86 percent in 2015—are living in "developing" countries, generally near the country they fled, often in temporary shelter under precarious conditions.[24]

Many refugees spend years or even decades awaiting a resolution to their situation; by the end of 2013, the average time spent in a situation of displacement was seventeen years.[25] The UNHCR lays out three "durable solutions" for refugees: voluntary repatriation to their country of origin when it is safe to return there; integration in the country where they have sought refuge; and resettlement to a third country when voluntary repatriation is unsafe and integration in the country hosting them is not possible.[26]

Refugees may prefer a particular "durable solution," but they don't generally have much power to choose. The political situation that led them to flee their country often stretches on, while the country where they sought refuge denies them any permanent status or rights. Many hope for resettlement, but only a tiny fraction will be lucky enough to get it. Sometimes refugees return to their homeland even though it remains unsafe, because conditions end up being worse in the country where they sought asylum. While this may count as "voluntary" repatriation, it is hardly a free choice.[27]

A country that is temporarily hosting refugees and doesn't want to grant them any permanent status is likely to see their repatriation as a preferred solution. When arranging for repatriation, the UNHCR tries to ensure that conditions are adequate in the home country and that returnees won't face persecution.[28] Some refugees have been so traumatized that they don't want to return to their native country under any circumstances; in some cases, they have nothing left to return to. The 1951 Refugee Convention recognized that some refugees with "compelling reasons arising out of previous persecution" may never go back to their countries of origin.[29] (The Convention was drafted after the Second World War, when most Holocaust survivors had no homes or communities to return to, and could not imagine living among neighbors who had participated in their persecution.)

As migration scholar Katy Long notes, a real integration of returned refugees requires "a meaningful citizenship and full political membership of the community from which they were previously excluded." It's not enough for the returnees to be simply tolerated by society, and safe from persecution, in their home country. They must also be able to play an active role in influencing the political environment there, so that they and future generations can enjoy full rights and opportunities.[30]

For these reasons, resettlement—a permanent move to a diaspora community, generally in a more developed country—can seem preferable to returning to a devastated homeland.[31] But fewer than 1 percent of refugees are ever accepted for permanent resettlement. Refugees get priority for resettlement when they are living in especially perilous situations, or have specific needs that cannot be addressed in their country of first refuge.[32]

Most of the people who enter the United States as refugees come through the resettlement program. As a large and diverse country with many resources and extensive diaspora communities, the United States is a logical option for resettlement. Refugees can move to locations where they will receive support from extended family and community networks and can integrate quickly and become self-sufficient. Refugees and asylum seekers who are able to select a destination will often base their choice on similar criteria.

In 2015, at least twenty-three countries, mostly in the "developed" world, provided permanent status to 107,100 refugees through resettlement. The United States consistently resettles more refugees than all other countries combined—66,500 in 2015. The total U.S. population is also much larger than that of other countries offering resettlement. Canada, Norway, and Australia all resettled more refugees per capita than the United States did in 2015.[33]

How do refugees get here?

People whose refugee status is granted outside the United States, including refugees selected for resettlement, enter the country through the U.S. Refugee Admissions Program (USRAP), a collaboration between various U.S. government agencies and international and domestic humanitarian partner organizations.[34] Resettled refugees generally arrive on special flights arranged by the U.S. government; the nonprofit agency hosting them reimburses the government for their airfare, then collects payment from the refugees through a loan program.[35]

Asylum seekers come to the United States the same ways other migrants arrive: at a land or sea border, or through airports. If they don't have a valid visa, and immigration authorities try to stop them from entering the country, they may ask for asylum on the basis that they have been persecuted in their country of origin and are afraid to return there. Those who are able to enter the United States legally (or who manage to enter undetected) may apply for asylum through an "affirmative" process within a year after arriving.[36] People who are ordered deported from the United States can apply for asylum, "withholding of removal," or protection under the Convention Against Torture through a "defensive" process if they are afraid to return to their country of origin.[37]

People who succeed in winning asylum have the same rights and status as people who arrive in the United States as refugees.[38]

SPECIAL TREATMENT FOR CUBANS

Discriminating based on national origin would seem to violate basic principles of fairness. But in the case of Cubans, their privileged treatment is written into law.

Some 800,000 Cubans immigrated to the United States between 1960 and 1980. They left Cuba for many reasons: some were opposed to the leftist revolution of 1959 and feared persecution; wealthy and middle-class Cubans lost property or economic opportunities because of socialist policies; and poorer Cubans fled the island later as its economy stagnated, at least in part because of a U.S. embargo. But they were able to come here because the U.S. government actively encouraged Cubans to immigrate.

From 1959 to 1961, about 125,000 Cubans arrived in the United States. The U.S. Coast Guard did nothing to stop them from entering the country, and the administration of John F. Kennedy then used executive parole authority to admit them, and those who followed, without regard to the quota limits established by the 1952 Immigration and Nationality Act.[39]

In 1966 Congress passed the Cuban Adjustment Act, which allowed Cuban immigrants to apply for permanent resident status after two years in the United States; the 1980 Refugee Act reduced the wait time to one year. Most restrictions on other immigrants are waived for Cubans; they can apply for resident status even if they entered without permission.[40] The government even supplied assistance to Cuban immigrants as they arrived—$1.4 billion by 1980.

Welcoming Cuban immigrants fit in with U.S. efforts in the early 1960s to bring down President Fidel Castro. The policy provided a pool of people who could be recruited to fight the Cuban government; at the same time, it hurt the Cuban economy by luring away academics, scientists, professionals, and experienced managers. And the streams of refugees fleeing the island hurt the reputation of the Cuban revolution.[41]

Over a seven-month period from April 15 to October 31, 1980, starting just a few weeks after the passage of the Refugee Act, some 130,000 Cubans landed in Florida in a "freedom flotilla" from the Cuban port of Mariel. This time the migrants were primarily young working-class men, many of them black.[42] The Refugee Act now provided a process for determining whether individual migrants qualified for asylum, but the administration of then-president Jimmy Carter chose not to apply the Act's provisions to the new wave. Instead, Carter used executive authority to parole the *Marielitos,* as they became known, into the United States under a new category of "Cuban-Haitian entrants."[43]

The United States was happy to receive the first wave of Cuban immigrants, who were "disproportionately well-educated, white, and of upper-echelon occupations and income," according to New York University professor David M. Reimers. But as the later waves of Cubans turned out to be less well educated and less white, they "were not as welcome as earlier groups had been." A Gallup poll in 1980 indicated that 59 percent of the U.S. public felt immigration by the *Marielitos* wasn't good for the country, with only 19 percent feeling it would be good.[44]

The U.S. government changed its policy in 1994 and 1995 after a series of negotiations with the Cuban government. The two countries agreed to let 20,000 or more Cubans apply for U.S. immigrant visas each year from inside Cuba, and the U.S. government modified its treatment of Cubans who try to enter the United States without permission. Under what became known as the "wet-foot, dry-foot" policy, Cubans who make it to land are still accepted under the old Cuban Adjustment Act, while Cubans who are intercepted by the U.S. Coast Guard while at sea are returned to Cuba—although they may be treated as refugees and settled in a third country if they express a credible fear of persecution in Cuba.[45]

Why should we accept refugees?

So-called developed nations have more resources for hosting refugees than poorer nations do. These richer countries are often also partly responsible for the plight of refugees because they help to trigger or deepen the conflicts that cause people to flee "underdeveloped" or "third world" nations. Governments and their corporate allies in the United States, Canada, Australia, and Western Europe expand their power and profits by extracting resources, selling weapons, and engaging with corrupt and brutal leadership in less-developed countries.

For example, in eastern Congo, militia forces profit from the global demand for coltan, a mineral used in manufacturing computers and mobile phones. The militias are responsible for the violent persecution of local residents, provoking displacement.[46] Meanwhile, the West's four major arms exporting countries—the United States, Germany, France, and the United Kingdom—are engaged in exporting arms "to countries which serve supplying states' domestic economic and security interests" without consideration of human rights records or other ethical factors, according to researchers Richard Perkins and Eric Neumayer. In fact, the researchers found that countries known to abuse human rights received a greater than average share of U.S. weapons transfers.[47]

Do asylum seekers have it easy?

If you're fleeing for your life, you may have a hard time obtaining valid travel documents before you leave, let alone gathering proof of the harm you suffered. And if you arrive without valid documents, or are caught trying to enter the United States without permission, you will be subjected to a process called "expedited removal."[48]

This means the border agency can send you back to your country without giving you a chance to plead your case to an immigration judge. If you tell border agents that you are afraid to return to your country, they are supposed to grant you a "credible fear interview," where you can try to convince an asylum officer that your fear of persecution is real, and that there is a "significant possibility" that you will win your asylum case.[49]

Under UNHCR guidelines, anyone fleeing persecution is supposed to be granted a meaningful opportunity to seek asylum. But in practice, this doesn't always happen: the advocacy group Human Rights First reported in 2012 that a number of asylum seekers who had expressed a fear of return were not referred by U.S. officials for credible fear interviews. In particular, migrants from Haiti who arrive by sea and are intercepted by the U.S. Coast Guard are generally not informed that they may be entitled to a credible fear hearing.[50]

For those who do get a chance, the wait time for a credible fear interview is generally about two weeks.[51] In the meantime, you'll be locked up under jail-like conditions in crowded immigration detention facilities or holding cells. As an "arriving alien," your detention is mandatory under the restrictive provisions of the 1996 Illegal Immigration Reform and Immigrant Responsibility Act (IIRIRA). You have no right to free legal representation. Even if you can afford a lawyer, it's hard to find one when you're in detention. Many detention facilities actively try to block effective legal representation.[52]

If your credible fear claim is rejected, you can ask that an immigration judge review the decision. But if the reviewing judge rejects your claim, you'll be summarily returned to your country of origin.[53]

If you pass the "credible fear" test you *might* be paroled or bonded out of detention to await an immigration court hearing on your asylum case. But it's up to the discretion of the immigration agent in charge of your case, and if you don't have a lawyer to help you win parole, or you can't afford to pay a bond, you will likely remain locked up.[54] If you've suffered torture or abuse, you may be re-traumatized by the conditions you experience in detention, where you will generally be treated as a criminal, whether or not you have violated any laws.[55]

Asylum seekers and migrants detained at the border are routinely subjected to extremely cold temperatures in the short-term holding cells of U.S. Customs and Border Protection (CBP). Border agents refer to the cells as "*hieleras*," Spanish for iceboxes or coolers. Exposing people to cold temperatures appears to be part of a strategy to deter them from pursuing options to stay in the United States. Some detainees remain in the *hieleras* for more than a week.[56] Ironically, U.S. federal courts have recognized forced exposure to extreme cold as a form of torture that can serve as a basis for granting asylum.[57]

If you pass your credible fear interview but are denied asylum, you can appeal the decision. The appeals process may take years; in the meantime, even if you are able to avoid detention, you may have trouble supporting yourself. Asylum seekers have to wait at least six months before they qualify for permission to work. Immigration judges and asylum officers have discretion to extend the waiting period, and it often stretches out for additional months or years. (This policy is another legacy of the 1996 IIRIRA.) Asylum seekers are also barred from receiving any government benefits. While many countries pose restrictions on asylum seekers, the United States is alone among the wealthier nations in denying them both work authorization and government benefits.[58]

Is the U.S. asylum system fair?

The asylum process may look impartial on paper, but studies suggest that in practice it is plagued with disparities. For example, the criteria for granting asylum aren't supposed to be applied differently to people who enter the United States with a valid visa, compared to people who cross the border "without inspection," enter with false documents, or request asylum on arrival. Yet researchers from the Georgetown University and Temple University law schools found that applicants who entered with a visa were 45 percent more likely to be granted asylum by the Department of Homeland Security (DHS) than those who did not. Applicants from Latin America, the Caribbean, and China were more than twice as likely to be granted asylum if they entered with a visa. "This factor probably favored wealthier and more educated applicants, as they were more likely to have been granted tourist, business, student, or other visas by U.S. consular officers and had no need to evade border inspection," the researchers concluded.

Legal representation also generally improved the chances of winning asylum—especially for applicants who entered without inspection, for those without dependent children in the United States, and for single men, who make up "the least sympathetic category" of asylum applicants, according to an unnamed senior asylum official interviewed by researchers.[59] In 2010, immigration courts granted asylum to 11 percent of unrepresented applicants, compared to 54 percent of those who were represented, according to Transactional Records Access Clearinghouse (TRAC), a nonpartisan research organization associated with Syracuse University.[60] A 2009 report from the U.S. Commission on International and Religious Freedom found that among asylum seekers detained in the "credible fear" process, those with legal representation were granted asylum at a rate twelve times greater than those who were unrepresented.[61]

Asylum grant rates for applicants of the same nationality were dramatically different between the eight regional DHS offices. Within each office, grant rates also varied depending on the characteristics of the asylum officers who handled them: whether they had law degrees; whether they were married, single or divorced; how much experience they had on the job; and where they were born.[62]

Similar disparities emerge among immigration judges, who review the cases that DHS asylum officers reject. Immigration judges also decide "defensive" asylum cases, removal proceedings, and other kinds of immigration cases. At thirteen of the nineteen busiest immigration courts, with all other factors being equal, if you were assigned the judge who granted asylum most often, your chances of winning asylum were at least four times greater than if your case was heard by the judge in the same court who rejected the most cases.[63]

The imposition as part of the 1996 IIRIRA of a one-year filing deadline for asylum claims has deprived a number of genuine refugees of a fair hearing on their asylum cases, and has delayed thousands of cases by shifting them into the backlogged immigration court system. An independent academic analysis found that between 1998 and 2009, more than 21,000 refugees would likely have won asylum through an administrative process, without the need for further litigation in the immigration courts, if not for the filing deadline.[64]

A September 2008 review by the United States Government Accountability Office (GAO) cited nine factors affecting the asylum decisions of immigration judges, including nationality of the applicants, whether the applicants were represented or detained, whether they applied within the one-year time limit, and whether they applied affirmatively or defensively. Other factors included the length of time the asylum decision took, and the gender and length of experience of the immigration judge. After statistically controlling for these factors, the GAO found major disparities among different immigration courts: affirmative applicants in San Francisco were twelve times more likely to be granted asylum than those in Atlanta.[65] These findings confirmed what TRAC had reported in 2007. "The unusual persistence of these disparities—no matter how the asylum cases are examined—indicates that the identity of the judge who handles a particular matter often is more important than the underlying facts," noted TRAC.[66]

In a separate study, researchers concluded that strong diaspora communities and the presence of refugee support organizations in a particular area increased the local asylum grant rate. Local economic and employment factors also had an impact; for the average immigration judge, high unemployment in the surrounding community decreased the likelihood of granting asylum.[67]

Since there is no systematic follow-up with asylum seekers who lose their cases and are deported from the United States, there is no way to determine how many legitimate refugees may be rejected. The consequences can be dire. Researchers who have tracked asylum seekers returned by the United Kingdom, Australia, and other nations have exposed cases of imprisonment, torture, murder, and forced disappearance. Returnees may be persecuted for the same reasons they sought refuge. They may face persecution as deportees, or because they are seen as influenced by foreign cultures or governments. They may be subjected to harsh treatment based on their connections to politically active exile groups, or simply because they brought unwanted attention to their country's human rights record by seeking asylum.[68]

HAITIANS FACE "FLOATING BERLIN WALL"

The nonprofit Human Rights Watch estimates that some 20,000 to 30,000 civilians were murdered by Haitian authorities during one of the most brutal regimes in the history of the hemisphere: the twenty-nine-year dictatorship of Haitian "presidents for life" François Duvalier ("Papa Doc," 1957–1971) and his son Jean-Claude Duvalier ("Baby Doc," 1971–1986).[69]

Thousands of Haitians began fleeing to the United States by boat in the 1970s. U.S. immigration authorities declared almost all of them "economic migrants" and sent them back to Haiti. Nearly 5,000 Haitians charged the U.S. government with discrimination in a lawsuit, *Haitian Refugee Center v. Civiletti*. The U.S. District Court for the Southern District of Florida ruled for the Haitians in July 1980. The court's detailed and scathing decision said the plaintiffs had "proven their claim" that the U.S. immigration agency engaged in "impermissible discrimination on the basis of national origin" when it used a special expedited processing program to reject their asylum claims summarily without review.

A similar program had been created for Cubans, except that it was used to swiftly approve, not reject, their cases. The court suggested "a possible underlying reason why these plaintiffs have been subjected to intentional 'national origin' discrimination. The plaintiffs are part of the first substantial flight of *black* refugees from a repressive regime to this country. All of the plaintiffs are black. In contrast, for example, only a relatively small percent of the Cuban refugees who have fled to this country are black." The court noted that nearly all the Cubans were granted asylum, while none of the Haitians were accepted. "No greater disparity can be imagined," the court declared.[70]

This decision came in the midst of the 1980 Mariel boatlift of migrants from Cuba, which coincided with a dramatic increase in the number of Haitian "boat people." About 25,000 Haitians arrived by boat to South Florida that year. The administration of U.S. president Jimmy Carter responded by including the Haitians with Cubans in a special category, "Cuban-Haitian entrants," and releasing them in the United States with parole status. Most of the Haitians who arrived in that period eventually became permanent residents through the 1986 amnesty.[71]

The administration of Ronald Reagan, inaugurated in January 1981, came up with a new policy. In September 1981 it made an agreement with the Duvalier regime allowing the U.S. Coast Guard to stop Haitians in international waters and summarily return them to Haiti. In exchange, the Haitian authorities gave "assurances" that they wouldn't prosecute the returnees unless they were charged as smugglers. Migrants captured under this "interdiction program" were not generally offered a chance at asylum. From 1981 through 1990, during the final years of the Duvalier dictatorship and the turbulent interim regime that followed, the U.S. government stopped 22,940 Haitians at sea; only eleven of them were allowed to apply for asylum.[72]

In 1990 many Haitians put their hopes in the presidential campaign of the popular priest Jean-Bertrand Aristide, who won by a landslide but was deposed by a right-wing coup in late September 1991.[73] The number of Haitians fleeing fell dramatically during the 1990 campaign, and rose again just as dramatically in the repression that followed the coup, with

37,618 Haitians intercepted at sea in 1992 alone. Between November 1991 and April 1992, a U.S. military joint task force helped the Coast Guard seize Haitian migrants and take them to the U.S. naval base at Guantánamo Bay, Cuba. (After 2001, that same base became known worldwide as a prison where the U.S. government holds Muslim men alleged to be "enemy combatants" as part of its "war on terror.")

Fewer than a third of the more than 34,000 Haitians who passed through the Guantánamo camp during that period were eventually found to have a credible fear of persecution and were paroled into the United States. The rest were sent back to Haiti. In May 1992, once the base was at capacity with more than 12,000 Haitians, President George H. W. Bush ordered the Coast Guard to intercept all Haitians and immediately return them to Haiti without trying to determine whether they were at risk of persecution.[74]

Although Bill Clinton denounced the interdictions as "cruel and unjust" during his campaign, and pledged to close the Guantánamo camp, he maintained the policy after becoming president in January 1993. At that point the Coast Guard had a fleet of at least twenty-two ships and patrol boats encircling Haiti's coastline, along with a dozen aircraft. Aristide spokesperson Reverend Antoine Adrien called the blockade a "floating Berlin Wall, around those seeking freedom."[75]

A combination of litigation, public pressure, and a hunger strike by the detainees finally led to the closure of the Guantánamo camp in June 1993. At that point the camp held about a hundred and fifty Haitians deemed to be HIV-positive or suffering from AIDS; all were flown to the United States.[76] President Aristide terminated the interdiction agreement after returning to power in 1994, but the United States has continued to stop Haitians at sea, at a rate of more than a thousand a year since 1998.[77]

How are refugees treated?

Like asylum seekers, refugees who arrive in the United States through the resettlement program have survived persecution, torture, war, and other trauma prior to arriving in the United States. Unlike asylum seekers, they are not detained upon arrival. Resettled refugees arrive with legal status and permission to work, can apply for certain family members to join them, and are eligible for permanent residency after one year. They even get some limited temporary cash assistance to help them get on their feet, and can apply for certain other needed benefits.

But that doesn't mean resettled refugees have it easy. They have often spent years or even decades languishing in refugee camps with no opportunities for employment or higher education. Many arrive speaking little or no English, and some have limited literacy or education in their native language. Others are highly educated but unable to make use of their qualifications in the United States. Despite these impediments, resettled refugees are required to find employment quickly after arriving; most benefits run out after ninety days. Like many other migrants, they are forced to accept physically challenging jobs with low pay, low status, no benefits, and long hours.

Refugees who are resettled in the United States are assigned to specific communities where they are "hosted" by nonprofit organizations working under contract with the federal government. Many of these communities are smaller cities, often with high rates of unemployment, where arriving refugees may face discrimination and resentment. After arriving, refugees are free to relocate on their own to anywhere within the United States, but when they do so, they may lose access to resettlement services and benefits. Still, many do move, especially to follow jobs. The meatpacking industry actively recruits recently arrived refugees.[78]

Are refugees sent home when their countries become safer?

In the United States, refugee and asylum status are supposed to offer permanent protection. A year after entering the United States, refugees must apply for permanent resident status; people who win asylum status may also seek permanent residency after a year but are not required to do so. After five years of residency, refugees and people who have been granted asylum can apply for U.S. citizenship.[79]

If they don't become citizens, and are convicted of certain criminal offenses, even longtime permanent residents who came here as refugees can be sent back to their countries. This has happened, for example, to hundreds of Cambodian refugees—most of whom came to the United States as young children.[80]

In 1990, the U.S. government created Temporary Protected Status (TPS) as a reprieve from deportation for migrants whose homelands have suffered a severe environmental disaster, armed conflict, epidemic or other "extraordinary and temporary" conditions. TPS is not for refugees who flee these conditions, but rather for migrants who are already living in the United States when the traumatic event happens, to protect them from being sent back to a country in crisis. Anyone convicted of a felony or two misdemeanors is not eligible for TPS. As of July 2014, some 340,000 people were beneficiaries of TPS, more than 60 percent of them Salvadorans (212,000).

TPS temporarily protects beneficiaries from detention and deportation, and allows them to work legally here, but it doesn't provide a path to lawful permanent residence or citizenship. The special status can be renewed—and has been, repeatedly, for nationals of several countries. But if the U.S. government doesn't renew the status, its protections expire, and its beneficiaries can again be returned to their countries, no matter how long they have been in the United States. Even while the status remains available, those who qualify are required to re-register for it and renew their work authorization every year or so, a process that costs hundreds of dollars.[81]

CENTRAL AMERICANS: ASYLUM DENIED

From 1984 to 1990, while war raged in Central America, the United States granted asylum to 25 percent of the 48,000 applicants from Nicaragua, whose leftist government the U.S. administration violently opposed. Over the same period, only 2.6 percent of the 45,000 applicants from El Salvador and 1.8

percent of the 9,500 Guatemalan applicants won asylum—the rest were dismissed as "economic migrants." At the time, both El Salvador and Guatemala had brutal right-wing governments closely allied with the United States and widely known to be responsible for serious human rights violations.[82]

U.S. religious and activist groups pressed the government to loosen its restrictions. More than 150 religious congregations openly defied immigration laws by offering sanctuary in places of worship for out-of-status refugees from Central America. The American Baptist Churches brought a class action suit against the U.S. government on behalf of the asylum seekers, which the government finally settled in 1991 by agreeing to reopen the cases of Salvadorans and Guatemalans who had applied for and been denied asylum in the 1980s.[83]

But by then the conflicts were ending. IIRIRA, the Illegal Immigration Reform and Immigrant Responsibility Act, which Congress passed in 1996, allows the government to deny asylum by claiming that there has been "a fundamental change in circumstances" in the applicant's country.[84]

A year later, in 1997, Congress passed the Nicaraguan Adjustment and Central American Relief Act. Even as it addressed the disparate treatment of Central Americans, NACARA continued to privilege Nicaraguans, allowing those who had failed to win asylum to gain permanent legal residency, while granting some Guatemalans and Salvadorans a chance to seek "suspension of deportation" under pre-1996 terms. Under heavy pressure from the Haitian immigrant community, in 1998 Congress passed the Haitian Refugee Immigration Fairness Act (HRIFA), allowing nearly 50,000 Haitians to finally seek permanent residence under a process similar to that extended to Nicaraguans under NACARA.[85]

4. Why Can't They Just "Get Legal"?

SOME PEOPLE THINK WE'VE ALWAYS had two distinct types of immigrants in the United States: "legal" and "illegal." The "legal" ones are people who "follow the rules" and "wait their turn in line," whereas the "illegal" immigrants are seen as criminals who for some reason decided to "flout our laws" and "cut ahead in line."

Such views suggest a sort of permanent caste system into which immigrants have always been sorted. In truth, immigrants have continued to come to the United States over the years in much the same ways they did in the past. What changed was not the immigrants but the laws. Illegality was constructed, imposed on people, and maintained through increasingly restrictive immigration laws.[1] That means we can deconstruct it—and counteract its negative effects—by changing those laws.

What's the difference between "legal" and "illegal"?

The distinction between "legal" and "illegal" isn't as clear as many people imagine. Being without status is not a permanent condition.

Immigrants who arrive legally may fall out of status. Some who were once undocumented have become U.S. citizens. Asylum seekers who are ordered deported can win their cases in the appeals courts and eventually gain permanent residency. And immigrants who have had permanent resident status for many years have been "de-legalized," as the New York–based group Families for Freedom puts it, because of past criminal convictions, even minor ones.[2] In short, the difference between an immigrant who is "legal" and one who is not is simply that one has been granted an opportunity to gain and keep legal status, and the other is being denied that opportunity.

News reports sometimes claim that "illegal" immigration is an affront to immigrants who do things the "right way."[3]

But most authorized immigrants have family members and friends who are still trying to gain legal status, and they understand how difficult it is, so it's not surprising that a majority feel sympathy for the undocumented. In a telephone survey of 800 authorized immigrants taken by Bendixen & Associates in early 2006 for *New America Media*, 68 percent supported granting out-of-status immigrants a temporary work permit and a way to gain legal residency.[4]

A November 2014 poll by the Latino Decisions firm showed 89 percent of Hispanic voters backing a plan by President Barack Obama for giving temporary legal status to as many as five million undocumented immigrants. The poll didn't distinguish between native-born and naturalized voters, but after analyzing the poll, *TalkingPointsMemo.com* editor Josh Marshall concluded it was "pretty clear that legal immigrants do not feel victimized by leniency or legalization for undocumented immigrants."[5]

How did immigration become "illegal"?

Immigration opponents regularly claim that their ancestors came here legally; they even buy T-shirts and bumper stickers saying that. In fact, their ancestors may well have arrived long before people coming from other countries needed legal permission to enter the United States.

Far from restricting immigration, the thirteen British colonies actively sought people to settle here as a way of providing cheap labor and displacing the Native American population. Many people came against their will—including more than 388,000 Africans who were brought here as slaves between the mid-seventeenth century and 1860.[6] Most white colonists arrived voluntarily, but not all. Of the about 500,000 Europeans who had migrated to the colonies by 1775, some 55,000 were convicts deported from the British Isles and forced to work as indentured servants for periods of up to seven years. About 200,000 other whites also came as indentured servants; a small number of these were brought by force, according to historian Richard Hofstadter, and "a much larger portion came in response to deceit and misrepresentation" by recruiters.[7]

After the U.S. Congress banned the slave trade starting in 1808,[8] the country continued to encourage voluntary immigration. Another sixty-seven years passed before the federal government finally enacted its first law regulating immigration—the Immigration Act of 1875, often referred to as the Page Act or the Asian Exclusion Act.[9]

This law limited immigration by male Chinese laborers and Chinese women. It was followed in 1882 by the Chinese Exclusion Act, and then by other openly racist laws aimed at keeping out most people from Eastern Asia. Europeans continued to be admitted with few restrictions until Congress passed laws in 1921 and 1924 establishing quota systems. The Immigration Act of 1924 limited total immigration to about 165,000 people a year. Africans and Asians were almost completely excluded, and the quotas for Southern and Eastern European countries were set in a way that virtually shut out people from those areas. The European quotas reflected widespread prejudice among citizens of Northern European ancestry against the Italians and Eastern European Jews who had started arriving in larger numbers in the 1880s.[10]

Has Mexican immigration always been "illegal"?

Although the 1924 law was an effort to end most immigration from

Africa, Asia, and much of Europe, it didn't set quotas for most people from the Western Hemisphere.[11] These immigrants only needed to meet a few requirements when applying for visas, such as paying fees and taxes, and demonstrating good health, the ability to read, and the absence of a criminal record. In practice, some of these requirements were used to block Mexican laborers seeking to enter the United States; those allowed in were forced to strip naked and submit to a humiliating "delousing" bath and medical inspection at the border. Europeans and first-class passengers on ships or trains were not subjected to this treatment.

After 1924, the U.S. government actually encouraged a certain level of migration from Latin America. But Mexicans were wanted only as temporary manual laborers. "A settled resident workforce would have encouraged both labor organization and more stable communities, and all that they imply—higher wages, education, political participation, growth of a middle class," observes historian Mae Ngai. Restrictions introduced in 1924, including the creation of the Border Patrol and the expanded use of deportation, "ultimately served the interests of agribusiness by creating a vulnerable 'alien' workforce," Ngai notes.[12]

With the 1924 laws came talk from politicians and the media about the need to expel the newly "illegal" immigrants.[13] Deportations expanded, particularly of Mexicans, yet so did labor recruitment, for example through the 1942–64 *bracero* program.

The Immigration and Nationality Act of 1965 (also known as the Hart-Celler Act) set up new barriers for Latin American migrants. It removed the discriminatory quotas of the 1924 law, but it extended quotas to the Western Hemisphere for the first time, setting the limit at 120,000 a year.[14]

The 1965 law caused the number of unauthorized immigrants to swell further in the 1970s, and politicians and the media stepped up their scare-mongering about "illegal" immigrants "invading" and "swarming" over the southwestern border. "Illegality" quickly became the charge raised most often by people who opposed immigration. In the past immigration opponents openly expressed prejudices against the Chinese, for example, or Eastern European Jews. Civil rights gains in the 1960s made it less acceptable for public figures to voice prejudiced views, so the idea of illegality gave people holding such beliefs a cover. They could say they weren't against immigrants (or against Mexicans), they were just against "illegals."[15]

How "illegal" is immigration, anyway?

Law is not a neutral force. Throughout history, people at the top have made laws to uphold their power against threats from below. Even acts like robbery and murder, which seem to violate clear and strongly held social norms, have always been treated differently depending on who carries them out against whom and in what context.

Just because something is illegal doesn't make it harmful. It was illegal for people to flee slavery, and to help others escape; it was illegal for black people to sit at the front of the bus. Yet those were acts of courage that made history and inspired millions.

Laws can change when enough pressure is exerted. What was illegal yesterday may be perfectly legal tomorrow, or vice versa.

In any case, lacking immigration status isn't necessarily a crime even under our present laws. As of 2015, entering the United States without government permission (by "jumping the border," for example) is a criminal offense—a minor misdemeanor, with a maximum sentence of six months. Living or working here without permission, regardless of how you entered, is just a civil infraction, not a crime. While some local officials try to claim such "unlawful presence" is like trespassing, it's more comparable under the law to a ticket for jaywalking.[16]

Many out-of-status immigrants use false identification documents, usually in order to get legitimate jobs instead of working off the books. Federal law treats this as a crime, with a maximum sentence of five years.[17] Working for a living doesn't harm society, and most people consider it to be a good thing. But immigrants face more public condemnation, and harsher legal consequences, for using fake IDs to seek employment than U.S.-born teenagers do when they use fake IDs, for example, to buy alcohol. Immigration opponents charge that immigrants are committing a serious crime—identity theft—if they unknowingly use a real person's Social Security number to get a job, but the Supreme Court ruled in May 2009 that this use of false documents doesn't meet the legal definition for identity theft.[18]

Why don't immigrants "follow the rules"?

It's easy for U.S. citizens to go to most other countries. To enter Mexico as a tourist, for instance, you only need to show your passport, go through customs, and (if traveling beyond the border area) pay a small fee for a tourist card. Gaining permanent residency in Mexico takes more time and requires applicants to prove they can support themselves, but almost all U.S. citizens who apply to settle in Mexico are able to do so.[19]

Many people in the United States assume that undocumented immigrants could all have come here legally if they'd been willing to "stand in line." But as the American Immigration Council (AIC) points out, "There is no line available for them, and the 'regular channels' do not include them."[20] Otherwise why would so many risk their lives trudging across the desert for days without water, stuffed into sealed train cars or truck beds, stowed away in shipping containers, crawling through sewage tunnels, or floating on inner tubes across polluted rivers or shark-infested oceans?

About one million people manage to become "lawful permanent residents" in the United States each year. This is a large number, but nearly all of these people gain legal residence either because they have close relatives living here (66 percent), meet requirements for a special work visa (16 percent), win a "diversity visa" (5 percent), or qualify as refugees or asylees (12 percent).[21]

Immigration laws don't limit the number of refugees, asylees, and members of U.S. citizens' immediate families (spouses, parents, and minor unmarried children) who can get a green card, but there's a limit of 675,000 a year on the total granted residency under all the other categories. Because of complicated rules, the annual number of new permanent residents never comes close to this maximum; in fiscal year 2013 it was 430,907, and this was normal. Less than half the people who get permanent status are entering the United States from outside; the majority are already living here. The result is that the number of slots open for people coming from abroad is about 250,000 each year for everyone except refugees, asylees, and members of U.S. citizens' immediate families.

Within this number there are still more limits. For example, no country gets more than 7 percent of the immigrant visas available in a given year. In 2012, there were 1,316,118 Mexicans on waiting lists for the visas, while the highest number of Mexicans that could be accepted under the 7 percent rule was 47,250.[22]

Can't immigrants bring their extended families here?

If you're a U.S. citizen, you can generally apply to bring your "immediate relatives"—spouses, parents or unmarried children under twenty-one—here as permanent residents, although there are plenty of hoops to jump through, and it's not always quick or easy. For other types of "family preferences," an even more complex set of rules lays out "priority" categories and annual caps based on the family relationship and country of origin. Waiting times of ten to twenty years are not uncommon. In February 2015 the government was still processing family visa applications from as far back as August 1991. While they wait, applicants are disqualified from visiting the United States because they have shown "immigrant intent" by applying for immigrant visas.[23]

Some conservatives now object to the "family preference" system, but it was actually introduced into the 1965 Immigration Act as a concession to conservative politicians who wanted to keep Asians and Africans out of the United States. Family preferences would mean "there will not be, comparatively, many Asians or Africans entering the country," Representative Emmanuel Celler, a liberal New York Democrat who cosponsored the 1965 law, said in Congress during the final debate on the bill, "Since the people of Africa and Asia have very few relatives here, comparatively few could immigrate from those countries because they have no family ties to the U.S."[24]

What about the work visa and the "visa lottery"?

The government can also issue up to 140,000 immigrant visas a year for five categories of workers, and each of these has its own numerical limitations. The categories include professionals, people with special skills, and cultural or sports figures. There are openings for religious workers, former U.S. government employees, and investors, but only 5,000 visas can be issued to unskilled workers.[25]

In 1986, Congress created a temporary category of "diversity" visas to bolster immigration from Europe, which had slowed thanks to a growing European economy.[26] The Immigration Act of 1990 made the program permanent starting in 1995. The Diversity Immigrant Visa Program, often called the "visa lottery," allocates 50,000 immigrant visas to different parts of the world under a formula favoring regions that have sent relatively few immigrants in the previous five years. Natives of countries that have sent more than 50,000 immigrants to the United States during the past five years are disqualified from participating in the lottery.[27]

"YACHT PEOPLE"

The Immigration Reform Act, signed by President George H. W. Bush on November 29, 1990, created a new category of visa for millionaire investors. Up to 10,000 immigrant visas a year were made available under the EB-5 category to anyone investing $1 million into a U.S. business and creating at least ten jobs for U.S. citizens. The investment can be smaller—$500,000—if made in rural or "high unemployment areas."[28]

"We've done a great job on boat people," Harold Ezell, former Immigration and Naturalization Service (INS) western regional commissioner, said in 1991. "I see no problem with a few yacht people." After leaving his INS post in 1989, Ezell began

marketing investor visas to wealthy foreigners.[29] Ezell was one of a number of government officials who pushed for the investor visa program, then left for the private sector to reap profits from it, as revealed in a February 2000 *Baltimore Sun* exposé.[30]

Those profits were boosted when INS deputy general counsel Paul Virtue issued legal opinions in 1993 and 1995 loosening the rules for the investor visas. The controversial rules were reversed in late 1997, and the scandal led the U.S. Justice Department's inspector general to launch an investigation in 1998 into the "appearance of impropriety" in the behavior of high-level government employees. The investigation concluded that Virtue had arranged special access to key agency officials for a private company, American Immigration Services (AIS). The Inspector General's office closed the case without taking further action in October 1999, and its report was kept secret.[31]

The program started off slowly but grew each year, from 179 visas issued in 2005 to over 3,000 in 2012. In 2014 the number of visas issued reached the 10,000 maximum for the first time, with 9,128 of them going to Chinese nationals. One favorite "high unemployment area" has been Manhattan's West Side, where some 1,200 Chinese millionaires have invested in the $20 billion Hudson Yards project. *The Atlantic* noted in 2015 that the project actually "is on the edge of one of the richest neighborhoods in the country."[32]

Is it easy for people to come here as tourists?

As of December 2015, citizens of thirty-eight countries were eligible for the Visa Waiver Program (VWP), meaning they didn't need to apply for a visa to visit the United States for ninety days or less. This waiver covers most of Europe, New Zealand, Australia, and several of the wealthier Asian nations: Brunei, Japan, Singapore, South Korea, and Taiwan. Chile, added to the list in 2014, is the only Western Hemisphere country that qualifies. Citizens of Bermuda and Canada can visit without visas through a separate program.[33]

In the rest of the world, the average citizen has a difficult time qual-
ifying for a U.S. visitor visa (B visa). To apply, you may have to wait
in long lines, pay hefty application fees, and travel to another city for
an in-person visa interview. To get a visa, you must convince a consular officer that you don't plan to stay in the United States, generally
by demonstrating that you have a stable job or a profitable business,
close family ties in your country, several thousand dollars in the bank,
and a home or other property. Many people who would like to visit
don't bother applying, since they expect to be rejected.[34]

Consular officers have "sole authority to approve or deny" visa
applications; there is no appeal process for those who are denied.[35]
In the early 1990s, the U.S. consulate in São Paulo, Brazil, routinely
denied visas to applicants who "looked poor"—which generally meant
they had darker skin—regardless of other criteria. Officers would
mark applications with abbreviations such as "LP" (looks poor), "TP"
(talks poor), or "LR" (looks rough), according to a lawsuit brought by
a fired consular officer who objected to the discrimination. In January
1998, a U.S. federal judge ruled that the screening policies used at the
consulate in São Paulo from 1992 to 1994 were "clearly illegal."[36]

For those whose applications are approved, "a visa does not guarantee entry into the United States," as the U.S. State Department website
warned in 2015. The final decision on whether to let someone into
the country is in fact made by a U.S. immigration officer at the port of
entry. You can have a valid visa in hand and still be turned away at the
airport and put on the next flight home, with no explanation, because
of an arbitrary decision by an immigration officer.[37]

Aren't there lots of other ways to come here with visas?

There is a whole alphabet soup of temporary visa categories, each
with its own set of confusing and restrictive rules. Most of the people
who have been displaced by economic and political crises around the
world don't fit any of these categories.

To get a student visa, you have to show you have strong ties in your
home country and enough money to support yourself and pay your

full-time tuition without working outside school. A massive database known as SEVIS (Student and Exchange Visitor Information System), mandated under the 1996 Illegal Immigration Reform and Immigrant Responsibility Act (IIRIRA), links school records with government records, so the immigration service automatically revokes the visas of students who drop out, flunk out, or stop taking a full course load.[38]

There are also visa categories for exchange visitors, athletes, artists, entertainers, religious workers, "intracompany transferees," and others.[39]

Once immigrants have been here a while, can't they "get legal"?

Millions of immigrants have lived in the United States for many years without status and are eager to gain legal permanent residency. According to a survey by Bendixen & Associates in October 2005, 98 percent of the undocumented would try to get legal status if it was available to them.[40] Those who have a valid option for legalizing their status generally pursue it, even though the process can be expensive and can take years. In 2013, a total of 530,802 people—including documented and undocumented immigrants—managed to adjust their status to permanent resident, according to the Department of Homeland Security (DHS).[41]

But there are only a few ways to "get legal," and most out-of-status immigrants don't qualify. The process is difficult for people who entered the United States with visas (or under the visa waiver program) but stayed longer than allowed. It's close to impossible for people who came here without permission—"entered without inspection" (EWI) in immigration law jargon.

Even marrying a U.S. citizen doesn't usually help immigrants who entered without inspection. Instead of applying to adjust their status here, they must leave and apply for a visa from outside the United States. Once out of the country, they are trapped by the punitive provisions of Section 301 in the 1996 Illegal Immigration Reform and Immigrant Responsibility Act. Under those provisions, anyone who has been "unlawfully present" in the United States for more than 180 days is deemed "inadmissible" and barred from returning for three years; anyone with more than twelve months of "unlawful presence" is barred for ten years. If you can prove that your absence will cause your U.S. citizen spouse to suffer "extreme hardship," you can apply for a "provisional unlawful presence waiver" that may allow you to return to the United States sooner. Starting in 2013 people married to U.S. citizens could apply for this waiver while remaining in the United States.[42]

Is it ever easy to get a green card?

If you entered the United States with a valid temporary visa but overstayed it, you might be able to get permanent residency through family ties or employer sponsorship. If you overstayed more than 180 days, you'd technically be subject to the three-year or ten-year bars, but if you're married to a U.S. citizen you can generally avoid the bars by adjusting your status in the United States.[43]

Still, getting a green card is rarely easy, even for immigrants who haven't overstayed their temporary visas. Any encounter with the immigration bureaucracy is likely to be plagued with obstacles and frustrations.

Many people believe that getting a green card through marriage is just a matter of filling out a few forms and answering a few questions— as long as the relationship is legitimate. But the way the government looks at it, the burden is on you—the applicant—to prove your marriage isn't fraudulent. You and your spouse are expected to get a joint checking account, pay taxes jointly, and have bills and leases in both your names, among other steps (even though not all married couples routinely do these things).[44] The whole process from marriage to green card generally takes at least ten months if you're married to a U.S. citizen, but it can take longer. The process is much longer if the spouse sponsoring you is a permanent resident rather than a citizen.[45]

Before July 1, 2013, there was no way for a U.S. citizen to sponsor a same-sex spouse. After the Supreme Court struck down Section 3 of the Defense of Marriage Act (DOMA) in June 2013, the administration of President Barack Obama changed its policy and instructed federal employees "to review immigration visa petitions filed on behalf of a same-sex spouse in the same manner as those filed on behalf of an opposite-sex spouse."[46]

Getting an employer to sponsor you for permanent residency is especially complicated, and can often take more than five years. Employers are frequently reluctant to go along with the tax and salary requirements involved and prefer not to admit they've been hiring out-of-status workers. Before your file even gets to the immigration agency, the Department of Labor must certify that your employer tried unsuccessfully to find U.S. citizens or permanent residents who could do your job.[47] Although discrimination on the basis of national origin is illegal in the United States, a 2014 study of approval rates for labor certification petitions found significant disparities based on the nationality of the prospective employee, even when other factors like skills and experience were the same.[48]

What about the "anchor babies"?

Children born in the United States are U.S. citizens, even if their parents are out-of-status immigrants. Opponents of immigration like to call such children "anchor babies," implying that immigrant parents use their U.S.-born children as a way to establish themselves here. In July 2010 Senator Lindsey Graham (R-SC) claimed on Fox News that unauthorized women come to the United States simply to "drop and leave" their babies.[49]

Most citizen children of undocumented immigrants are actually born some time after their parents have settled in the United States, according to a study of babies born to immigrants from March 2009 to March 2010. Just 9 percent of the out-of-status parents had arrived in 2008 or later; most had been in the United States for a number of years when the babies were born—30 percent had arrived between 2004 and 2007, and 61 percent arrived before 2004. For its October 2006 survey, Bendixen & Associates asked undocumented immigrants to give their reasons for migrating to the United States. The respondents overwhelmingly cited work opportunities; having "anchor babies" didn't even rate a mention.[50]

In any case, having a U.S. citizen child doesn't help undocumented immigrants gain legal status, or even protect them from deportation. U.S. citizens have to be at least twenty-one years old to sponsor their parents for legal residency. Each year, thousands of people who have U.S.-born children are deported, leaving families shattered. A 2012 study by the New York University School of Law's Immigrant Rights Clinic found that 87 percent of New York City immigration cases involving parents of U.S. citizen children between 2005 and 2010 ended in deportation.[51]

Before 1996, out-of-status immigrants could sometimes win "suspension of deportation" by proving that they had lived in the United States for seven years and had good moral character, and that their removal would cause "extreme" hardship to themselves or to a family member with legal status. But IIRIRA, the 1996 immigration law, changed the rules. To be granted what is now called "cancellation of removal," applicants must prove they have lived here for ten years with good moral character, and their deportation would cause "exceptional and extremely unusual" hardship to a U.S. citizen or permanent resident parent, spouse, or child. It's very difficult to meet the hardship criteria: a child who is separated from a parent clearly suffers hardship, but the situation is not necessarily exceptional or extremely unusual. When such cancellation is granted, it usually goes to an immigrant parent who is the primary caregiver for a U.S. citizen child suffering from a severe, life-threatening medical condition.[52]

The 1996 law also set a limit of 4,000 on the number of people who can be granted this particular type of cancellation in any given year—not counting permanent residents seeking to reverse deportation orders, who are counted separately and are not subject to the cap. Complicated rules designed to prevent judges from granting more than 4,000 cancellations in any given year have resulted in a backlog of decisions.[53]

BIRTHRIGHT CITIZENSHIP

Some countries base citizenship on family heritage, but the British colonies followed English common law in automatically making people citizens of the place where they were born. The newly formed United States continued to recognize birthright citizenship; the Supreme Court assumed it as the basis for an 1804 decision.

However, women didn't have full citizenship until they won the right to vote in 1920, and many states originally denied voting rights to citizens without property. Slaves were denied citizenship altogether, and until 1870 only white immigrants were eligible to naturalize as citizens. The situation was more complicated for free native-born people of color: in most states they had limited citizenship, without the right to vote; at the time of the Civil War free men of African descent could vote in only six of the thirty-four existing states. Some Native Americans, but not all, were recognized as citizens in treaties with the federal government. In 1848 the Treaty of Guadalupe Hidalgo mandated U.S. citizenship for all Mexicans living in the southwestern territories taken from Mexico in the Mexican-American War.[54]

With the 1857 Dred Scott decision the Supreme Court ruled that birthright citizenship only applied to white people. The Fourteenth Amendment, ratified in 1868, specifically redressed this injustice by restoring birthright citizenship without reference to race or ethnicity. The Supreme Court upheld the principle in 1898 in the case of the Chinese-American citizen Wong Kim Ark.[55]

Conservative legislators like Sen. Graham and former Arizona state senator Russell Pearce have proposed amending the Constitution or finding some way to circumvent the Fourteenth Amendment so that children born in the United States to out-of-status immigrants would not be U.S. citizens.[56]

Revoking birthright citizenship might leave many children born here stateless, since their parents' countries may not automatically grant citizenship to children of their citizens.

This could violate international standards. The Dominican Republic's government, for example, eliminated birthright citizenship in 2010, a move motivated by racial animosity toward Dominicans of Haitian descent. The United Nations High Commissioner for Refugees (UNHCR) charged in December 2013 that this effort had created a "human rights problem," and the Inter-American Commission on Human Rights (IACHR) suggested that it had caused "grave violations of the right to nationality, to identity, and to equal protection without discrimination."[57]

If we ended birthright citizenship, what status would the U.S.-born children of undocumented immigrants have? Would they also be undocumented? In that case, ending birthright citizenship would *increase* the number of undocumented people in the country; the undocumented population would be at least 44 percent larger by 2050, according to a projection by the nonprofit Migration Policy Institute project.[58] In other words, revoking the country's long tradition of granting citizenship to everyone born here would expand and make permanent an underclass of vulnerable, easily exploited people without full rights—very much like the U.S. South under Jim Crow laws or South Africa under apartheid.

Can't immigrants apply to become U.S. citizens?

A total of 7,259,530 immigrants were naturalized as U.S. citizens from 2005 through 2014, an average of nearly three-quarters of a million each year.[59] But like most processes for immigrants, this one is far from simple. People who want citizenship must first become permanent residents, then wait five years before they can apply to be naturalized. (If you are married to a U.S. citizen, you can apply for citizenship three years after getting your green card; U.S. soldiers on active duty can take advantage of a more accelerated schedule.)

Some permanent residents hesitate to go through the naturalization process because it is expensive (at the end of 2016 the filing fee was $640) or too much of a bureaucratic hassle.[60] Others don't apply because their home country doesn't allow dual citizenship, and they may lose certain rights there by becoming U.S. citizens. Some permanent legal residents are barred from gaining citizenship because of prior criminal convictions.

For those who do seek citizenship, the process is not always straightforward. If your residency status was based on marriage to a U.S. citizen, immigration agents may raise questions about your marriage. If you travel outside the United States for more than a few months each year, your application can be denied (and the government may even try to take your green card away). Any past arrests will resurface through fingerprint record checks, and may get you deported.

Even if your record is clean, you may be confused with someone with a similar name and prior arrests. In one such case, a longtime permanent resident from Peru who had never received so much as a parking ticket was denied citizenship based on crimes committed by someone with the same first and last name and the same birth date, even though the person who committed the crimes was a foot taller, had a different middle name, and was a U.S.-born citizen with no reason to apply for naturalization. While such confusions would be easy to clear up quickly through fingerprint comparisons, immigration officials refused to fix the mistake and grant citizenship until they were sued in federal court.[61]

Citizenship applicants also face unexplained delays. California resident Mustafa Aziz, a military veteran who was only a year old when he and his family escaped war-torn Afghanistan and moved to the United States, applied for citizenship while on military duty in 2003. The government left Aziz waiting while it allegedly carried out a type of background check known as a "name check." "Despite serving in the U.S. Air Force, I have been waiting for my citizenship for more than two years," Aziz charged in August 2006. With the name check still dragging on and no end in sight, Aziz and nine others in similar situations sued the government with help from the American Civil Liberties Union (ACLU) of Southern California, the ACLU Immigrants' Rights Project, and the Council on American-Islamic Relations (CAIR); the goal was to get the immigration service to start following set deadlines on its name checks. In October 2006, two months after the suit was filed, the government announced it would finally grant citizenship to Aziz and six of the other plaintiffs.[62]

The problems continued, however. In 2013, the ACLU of Southern California reported that a covert U.S. Citizenship and Immigration Services (USCIS) program had since 2008 indefinitely delayed or rejected without cause the citizenship or residency applications of numerous Muslim, Middle Eastern, and South Asian immigrants. Those affected received no explanations for why their applications were singled out for delay or denial.[63]

5. Is It Easy to Be "Illegal"?

LIVING IN THE UNITED STATES WITHOUT valid immigration status was never easy, but it has become extremely difficult over the past two decades as politicians have enacted a multitude of anti-immigrant laws at the federal, state, and local level. Fear of being apprehended and deported limits opportunities and causes stress and anxiety that can have a negative impact on the physical and mental health of undocumented immigrants and their children.[1] Such fear, which intensifies anytime raids take place, also makes undocumented immigrants more vulnerable to labor exploitation and more likely to be victims of crime, and poses serious challenges to integration. Still, out-of-status immigrants can and do push back against this climate of fear by organizing to defend their rights and demand change.

What's it like to live here "illegally"?

Immigrants who lack documents may have trouble finding a place to live, opening a bank account, applying for jobs, registering for school, or getting medical treatment. In most states, laws block "out-of-status" immigrants from seeking driver's licenses. People without legal status often try to avoid traveling, since buses, trains, and even private cars may be stopped by officers checking immigration documents.

Such restrictions force many out-of-status immigrants into situations that are sometimes risky (such as keeping their savings in cash, and avoiding hospitals) or illegal (driving without a license). As they become more vulnerable, out-of-status immigrants are more likely to be exploited by unscrupulous employers, landlords, immigration law "consultants," and others who try to take advantage of them, knowing they will be hesitant to report abuses.

Even some immigrants with "permanent" legal residence are now at risk because a past arrest or conviction makes them eligible for deportation under retroactive laws passed in 1996. They too may be trapped, unable to travel, and living with the daily fear of being detained and deported.[2]

Undocumented immigrants are often separated from family members for years, even decades. Tightened border enforcement means they can no longer visit relatives or friends back home without risking everything they have built here—and sometimes their lives. Even those immigrants who have family members here have generally been forced to leave other loved ones behind. Many immigrants come from close extended families, making the separation especially painful.[3]

It's often the love they feel for their families that leads people to migrate. "Our situation doesn't give us the luxury to live together and live well; it can't be done," Mexican immigrant Ramón Castillo explained to filmmaker Heather Courtney in the 2001 documentary *Los Trabajadores* (The Workers). Unable to make ends meet in Mexico, Castillo left his wife and two daughters behind to find work in Austin, Texas. He sent most of the money he earned back home to pay for his daughters' schooling, in the hopes that they could become professionals and have a better future. "You either live well, or you live together. If you live together, you don't live well, because there isn't enough to live on. If you live well, you need to leave your family to make good money, so they can live well."[4]

How can you tell who's undocumented?

The United States has no national ID card for its citizens, because so many people see national ID cards as an infringement of privacy rights and civil liberties. This means there is no easy way for the authorities, or anyone else, to figure out who's an immigrant and who's not.

We can't distinguish a native-born U.S. citizen from an immigrant by their physical appearance or accent, since native-born citizens have diverse ethnic and linguistic backgrounds, just as immigrants do. The "equal protection" clause of the Fourteenth Amendment makes it unconstitutional to question people just because of the way they look or talk.[5]

In reality, law enforcement officers make judgments about whether someone is an immigrant based on their own prejudices, but it can be difficult to prove that they've engaged in racial profiling. The Supreme Court made it still more difficult in 1996 by ruling that to challenge an arrest, you need "to show that the government declined to prosecute similarly situated suspects of other races."[6] Still, the profiling of immigrants has at times been challenged successfully. In July 2005, an immigration judge in Arizona halted the deportation of four high school students arrested during a school trip to Niagara Falls, ruling that Border Patrol agents had illegally singled them out for questioning on the basis of their appearance. The four students were from Mexico, but had lived in the United States since they were children.[7] In May 2013 a federal judge found that the Sheriff's Office in Arizona's Maricopa County had used racial profiling in making traffic stops of Latinos. The judge ordered notoriously anti-immigrant Sheriff Joe Arpaio and his officers to undergo training to prevent further unlawful detentions, and required the county to compensate people who were detained in violation of the court order.[8]

If questioned by government officials, immigrants, even those who have become U.S. citizens, have the burden of proving they are in the United States legally. Native-born citizens, by contrast, cannot be required to show identification proving their status. It's a federal crime to lie to an agent, but if you decline to tell agents that you were born outside the United States, then unless they have evidence, the burden of proof remains on them to demonstrate that you lack legal status.[9] However, it can be extremely difficult to stay silent during questioning and to resist coercion; most of the time agents are experienced at getting people to admit that they are not native-born citizens. Even if you don't reveal your place of birth, they can detain you based on suspicion for several weeks.

Do undocumented people live in fear?

Out-of-status immigrants don't necessarily live in a state of permanent, intense fear, because it's too stressful to live that way, but many do experience ongoing, heightened levels of anxiety. Spouses or other relatives left caring for the home may worry daily about whether family breadwinners will fail to come home that evening because they have been detained at work. Children may be anxious and unable to concentrate at school because they are afraid their parents will be arrested and deported.

When immigration raids occur, they often set off a wave of terror within the affected communities and beyond. People become afraid to venture into the streets, even to shop for food or take their children to school. The kids who do make it to class spend the day worrying about losing their parents. In April 2006 immigration agents arrested 1,200 workers across the country in a single day as part of an investigation into the pallet company IFCO Systems; at the same time there were separate raids in Florida towns for immigrants who had been ordered deported. The sweeps sparked what Florida Immigrant Advocacy Center director Cheryl Little called "the worst climate of fear . . . in more than two decades."

"People are scared to even go in the streets now, fearing they are going to be picked up, questioned," said Dennis D. Grant, the Jamaican-American senior pastor of Restoration Ministries in Margate and Miramar, Florida. "They are in a state of panic right now."[10]

The same thing happened in early January 2016, when the federal government began rounding up Central American refugee women and children whose petitions for asylum had been denied. Rumors about the operation spread quickly, creating alarm even in communities where no raids had yet taken place. Nancy Hiemstra, a professor of migration studies at Stony Brook University, described how such raids set back immigrants' efforts to integrate into society. Noting the impact on one undocumented resident, the mother of a friend of her own children, Hiemstra wrote: "All fall she had been walking to a nearby church three times a week for English lessons, and proudly testing out her new language skills on neighbors. But now, she's too scared to continue." The woman told Hiemstra: "My husband says I shouldn't even go to the kids' school, not even for the concert coming up; we can't risk it."[11]

Are undocumented immigrants victims of crime?

Some people believe out-of-status immigrants are especially likely to commit crimes. That's a myth that multiple studies have proven false.[12] In reality, undocumented immigrants are disproportionately likely to be victims.

A 2009 survey the Southern Poverty Law Center (SPLC) carried out among 500 low-income Latinos in five areas of the South (including U.S. citizens and both documented and undocumented immigrants) found that the undocumented had "become prime targets for robbery and other crimes." Criminals know the victims "are unlikely to go to the police," the SPLC researchers wrote, and they know that "because most undocumented immigrants can't open bank accounts . . . they are more likely than others to be carrying large sums of cash." Muggers see immigrants as "walking ATMs," according to an immigrant rights advocate working in New Orleans.[13]

Immigrant victims of domestic violence also have a low rate of seeking help from authorities. A survey conducted by the Washington, D.C.-based nonprofit immigrant service agency Ayuda in 1993 noted that 83 percent of the battered immigrants interviewed did not contact law enforcement agencies about their abuse. One-fifth of the women surveyed reported that abusive partners had threatened them with deportation or refusal to file immigration papers.[14] A 2009 study by the Family Violence Prevention Fund had similar findings. Though intimate partner violence "is *not* more prevalent, and, in fact, is probably less prevalent, among immigrant and refugee population groups," the study said, factors like fear of deportation and discrimination "make it especially difficult for victims in these populations to seek or obtain help."[15]

Immigrants are also targeted in hate crimes. For example, in Farmingville, Long Island (New York), in 2000 two white men carried out a premeditated racist attack against two undocumented Mexican day laborers, beating them nearly to death. Because of the violence of the assault, and the publicity that accompanied it, the attackers were sentenced to twenty-five years in prison for attempted murder. In November 2008 Ecuadorian immigrant Marcelo Lucero was stabbed to death just a few miles away in Patchogue, Long Island, during an attack by a group of seven teens who had been regularly assaulting immigrants—a practice they called "beaner hopping." The teens received prison sentences ranging from six to twenty-five years.[16]

Attacks on immigrants seem to have jumped dramatically from 2004 to 2012, at a time of stepped-up anti-immigrant rhetoric from politicians and the media. The government's Bureau of Justice Statistics (BJS) estimated that although the overall number of hate crimes remained about the same over this period, the percentage of hate crimes that were based on ethnicity, including attacks on "foreigners," rose from 22 percent to 51 percent of the total. People living in households with an income under $25,000 were especially likely to be victims in the estimated 293,800 non-fatal hate crimes that took place in 2012, and Latinos had the highest rate of victimization in relation to their population share. Immigrants who are perceived as Muslim, Middle Eastern, or South Asian have also been targeted, especially after September 11, 2001. The BJS estimated that the percentage of hate crimes motivated by religious bias reached 28 percent in 2012, nearly three times what it was in 2004.[17]

Can immigrants get driver's licenses?

One major obstacle for many undocumented immigrants is the lack of official identification. Without government-issued IDs, they are frequently barred from opening bank accounts, signing contracts and leases, reporting crimes to police, or entering public buildings. Sometimes they can't even go to their children's schools for parent-teacher conferences.

Most states refuse to issue driver's licenses for people without legal status. Supporters of this policy claim that having a license allows immigrants to get benefits they aren't entitled to—and even helps terrorists. "One of the reasons the 9/11 terrorists were so successful was because they had access to official identification," Ira Mehlman, media director of the anti-immigration Federation for American Immigration Reform (FAIR), said in 2014. But the September 11 attacks had nothing to do with undocumented immigrants. The hijackers all came to the United States legally, with visas, and most of them still had valid status when they carried out the attacks. Eight of them had obtained non-driver IDs from the Department of Motor Vehicles in Virginia, a state that barred out-of-status immigrants from getting driver's licenses or non-driver IDs.[18]

Issuing licenses actually helps fight terrorism by getting accurate information into government databases, according to national security experts. There are also traffic safety issues: research suggests that expanding opportunities for drivers to get tested, licensed, and insured would reduce the frequency and cost of vehicle collisions.[19]

The situation seems to be changing. Eleven states had laws as of 2013 giving access to driver's licenses or other identification regardless of immigration status. In 2013 alone, eight states enacted laws expanding immigrants' access to licenses. Meanwhile, cities with large immigrant populations have begun making municipal ID cards available to all residents. New Haven, Connecticut, started the trend in 2007, and as of 2015 eleven other cities had issued their own cards, including Los Angeles, New York, San Francisco, and Washington, D.C. The New Haven program has "helped residents feel like New

Haven is home and they're a part of the community," the city's communications director, Laurence Grotheer, said in 2014. "For immigrants,
it begins the process of assimilation and puts them on the road to full
community participation."[20]

Do immigrants have the right to an education?

All immigrant children, regardless of their status, have the right to
public education through the high school level. The Supreme Court
upheld this principle in the June 1982 *Plyler v. Doe* decision, overturning a Texas state law that sought to deny school funding for
undocumented students.[21]

The situation is more complicated when it comes to higher education institutions such as universities and technical schools. Though
many countries consider higher education to be a universal right, the
United States generally treats it as a privilege. Still, many community
colleges and public universities in the United States provide accessible degree programs to city or state residents. Before 1996, it didn't
matter if those students were immigrants living here without permission from the federal government.

Section 505 of the 1996 Illegal Immigrant Reform and Immigrant
Responsibility Act (IIRIRA) barred states from granting reduced
tuition to undocumented state residents unless non-resident U.S.
citizens in the same circumstances get the same privilege. As of April
2006, only about 5 to 10 percent of undocumented young people who
graduated from high school went on to college, compared with about
75 percent of their classmates.[22] The result was that many thousands
of immigrants who came here as young children, had been educated
in U.S. public schools, spoke English just like people born here, and
felt as "American" as anyone else, now found themselves without a
future. Denied in-state tuition, unable to qualify for financial aid
under federal rules, and unable to work legally, they got stuck in low-
paying jobs and shut out of more promising opportunities.

Angela Perez, a Colombian immigrant, didn't even apply to college despite ranking fourth in her 2004 graduating class with a 3.8

grade-point average. "It feels awful," she wrote in an essay during her sophomore year. "I feel frustrated. I try hard until I accomplish something and I do not want all my accomplishments to be a waste of time. I want them to be valuable. I want to be able to pay my parents back after all their support and the difficulties they have lived in order to bring me here."[23]

Out-of-status students who did manage to get through college were still unable to pursue a career without legal status—like Kathy, another young immigrant, who graduated from Nyack College in New York with a degree in social work, but could only get a job as a nanny. "Graduation was the most depressing day of my life," she said.[24]

Since 2004, undocumented youth and students have organized to win substantial changes. By June 2014, at least seventeen states, the states where the majority of the country's undocumented immigrants live, had passed laws allowing undocumented students to qualify for in-state college tuition if they attended high school in the state for a certain number of years and graduated. (The state laws comply with the 1996 Act by allowing U.S. citizens who meet the same state high school attendance and graduation requirements to get the same tuition rate, even if they no longer live in the state.)[25]

Sustained organizing by undocumented young people led the Obama administration to launch the Deferred Action for Childhood Arrivals (DACA) program in June 2012, allowing many undocumented immigrants who came here as children to apply for two-year work permits and a temporary reprieve from deportation. By the end of fiscal year 2015, nearly 700,000 people had been granted DACA.[26]

What's it like to work here "illegally"?

Lack of legal status forces many undocumented workers into jobs where they earn less money and face more dangerous conditions than other workers. Not wanting to draw attention to their situation, and afraid of losing the jobs they have, undocumented workers are often reluctant to fight for better wages or working conditions. Many are scared to join unions, and until recently few unions made an effort to organize them. Those out-of-status immigrants who do try to defend their workplace rights face an uneven playing field. Employers may suddenly decide to fire workers who lack documents, or use the threat of raids and deportation to squelch organizing efforts.[27]

Several studies show that undocumented workers get paid less on average than authorized immigrants with similar skills and experience.[28] A lot of undocumented immigrants are paid poorly because they have less than a high school education, but they're still paid less than other workers without a diploma. Out-of-status men who worked off the books in Los Angeles County's huge underground economy made an average of $16,553 a year in 2004, according to a study by the Economic Roundtable, a nonprofit research organization; out-of-status women averaged just $7,630. Although they worked in major industries like apparel and textile manufacturing, these workers were paid far below industry standards, and much less than other workers who didn't finish high school; in 2004 the median earnings for male high-school dropouts nationally were $23,192 a year, and $17,368 for women.[29]

A 2012 study on working conditions in Durham, North Carolina, had similar results. Researchers interviewed 339 Spanish-speaking male immigrants in 2006 and early 2007. On average, the undocumented workers made about $17,268 a year; they were likely to be working off the books, and most didn't receive sick leave, paid overtime, or paid vacations. The survey ended just before the collapse of a housing boom. About 70 percent of the men surveyed worked in construction, so the "serious vulnerability of immigrant Hispanic men, already evident even under peak economic conditions, undoubtedly worsened further still with the [2007–2009] recession," wrote the study's author, University of Pennsylvania sociologist Chenoa Flippen.[30]

A higher proportion of people of color, women, and the foreign-born are paid less than the minimum wage, compared to whites, men, and the native-born. Undocumented workers in low-paid jobs get singled out for the worst treatment of all. A survey of more than

4,000 low-wage workers in Chicago, Los Angeles, and New York City in the first half of 2008 found that just 5.6 percent of native-born whites reported being paid less than minimum wage; the number was 16.6 percent for Latinos (including both immigrants and people born here). Black workers, both U.S.-born and foreign-born, were even more likely to report minimum wage violations than foreign-born Latino workers. Some 25.7 percent of the authorized immigrants who were surveyed experienced minimum wage violations, compared to 36.7 percent for unauthorized workers.

The workers who suffered the most were undocumented women: 47.4 percent said they had been paid less than the minimum wage. (Undocumented women are also most likely to serve as childcare or home care workers, and these occupations were most likely to be associated with wage violations among those surveyed.)[31]

Do immigrants work more dangerous jobs?

Undocumented workers appear to have a far higher rate of fatal injuries on the job than other workers. Fatal workplace accidents jumped 72 percent for Latinos between 1992 and 2005, while the rate for other workers dropped by 16 percent; by 2005 the fatality rate for Latinos was the highest for any group of employees, at 4.9 per 100,000 workers. Although most Latinos are not immigrants, a special report in the *Chicago Tribune* concluded that the victims were largely undocumented immigrants.

A 2009 article in the journal *Demography* reached similar conclusions. Although foreign-born workers accounted for about 11 percent of workplace fatalities in 1992, they made up 18 percent by 2005, with about 960 deaths each year. The authors noted that the immigrants' increased share in fatalities "coincide[d] with a surge of immigrant inflows, particularly of undocumented immigrants, in the wake of economic crises in Latin America."[32]

Workplace fatalities continued to decline slightly for most workers after 2005, but the rate for immigrants was still at 18 percent in 2011. The great majority of the 843 immigrant workers who died that year were Latino, and it's likely that most were undocumented. "As recession has taken hold, employers have tightened their belt," Migration Policy Institute director Muzaffar Chishti told WBEZ radio in Chicago. "And many of the labor standards, especially related to safety, go out the window." Chishti noted that undocumented workers are the most vulnerable, since they are less willing to speak up for their rights.[33]

An in-depth 2001 report in the Long Island daily *Newsday* suggested that the deaths of immigrant workers are also less likely to be investigated, especially if the workers are undocumented. The report charged that the government's Occupational Safety and Health Administration (OSHA) failed to investigate 874 of the estimated 4,200 job-related deaths of immigrant workers between 1994 and 1999. A report by OSHA's Office of the Inspector General disputed the charge but found that the agency needed to develop "a comprehensive strategy for reaching all non-English-speaking employees, including undocumented immigrants." A 2013 study of construction workplace deaths in New York City, where 74 percent of fatal falls in construction involved "Latino and/or immigrant" workers, found that OSHA was "ineffective" and "understaffed because of inadequate funding."[34]

Doctors and others who work with injured migrants say non-fatal workplace accidents are underreported, since out-of-status workers are afraid of losing their jobs or being deported. Dr. Eileen Couture, head of clinical care at Oak Forest Hospital in Cook County, Illinois, told the *Chicago Tribune*: "You say this [accident] has to be reported and they say, 'You don't understand, I need my job. You don't understand, I have to feed my family.'"[35]

Even when they do report an injury, out-of-status workers can't count on getting help. Francisco Ruiz, an undocumented Mexican, was injured in 1997 in Charlotte, North Carolina, when a crane hoisting him collapsed; the injury left him partially paralyzed and unable to work. His employer's insurance company, Companion Property & Casualty, refused to pay any compensation beyond his initial medical bills and fought him in court for nearly six years on the grounds that he was "illegal." His case drew attention because he was one of the few undocumented workers who have managed to fight back and win; the insurance company ended up having to pay him $438,000.[36]

Are immigrants protected by labor laws?

Under existing federal and state laws, as the courts have generally interpreted them, all workers, including immigrants, have certain rights, whether or not they have the federal government's permission to work here. Many workers don't know their rights, however, or are scared to exercise them because of their vulnerable immigration status. Despite these obstacles, undocumented workers have successfully defended their rights through the courts, or through grassroots public pressure campaigns, with the help of workplace justice advocates.[37]

All workers have a right to be free from discrimination in the workplace, including discrimination on the basis of race, religion, national origin, language, or accent.[38] All workers have the right to join a union, or to organize themselves in defense of their common interests. Most workers have the right to be paid minimum wage for the hours they have worked, plus overtime if they work more than forty hours a week. (There are a number of exceptions to federal minimum wage and overtime rights for some types of jobs. These exceptions aren't based on immigration status, although some of the affected labor sectors like agriculture and domestic work tend to have a high proportion of unauthorized workers.)[39]

All workers have a right to a healthy and safe workplace. As of April 2013, twenty-eight states provided compensation to all workers injured on the job, regardless of immigration status; a few excluded the undocumented, and other states hadn't confronted the issue. However, a 2008 survey of 1,432 workers in low-wage industries in New York City found that only 11 percent of those seriously injured on the job filed claims for the compensation to which they were entitled.[40]

Federal and state courts have generally upheld workplace rights for undocumented workers. For example, the courts agree that all workers should get compensation in cases of discrimination, and that employers who have violated wage or overtime requirements must compensate workers for the unpaid wages they earned.[41]

A number of judges have noted that it is unfair and harmful to all workers to allow employers to exploit undocumented workers and then escape their responsibilities in court by arguing that the workers' lack of immigration status means they have no right to compensation. In June 2002, U.S. district judge Whitman Knapp of the Southern District of New York ruled that clothing manufacturer Donna Karan International Inc. was not entitled to learn the immigration status of a group of workers who were charging the company with maintaining sweatshop conditions. Knapp said the possibility that the information would be used to intimidate plaintiffs outweighed its relevance to the case.[42] In a September 2002 case in Illinois, *Rodriguez v. The Texan*, a federal judge noted: "It surely comes with ill grace for an employer to hire alien workers and then, if the employer itself proceeds to violate the Fair Labor Standards Act . . . for it to try to squirm out of its own liability on such grounds."[43]

But in a March 2002 ruling (*Hoffman Plastic Compounds, Inc. v. NLRB*) the Supreme Court seriously undercut one important labor right guaranteed in the 1935 National Labor Relations Act (NLRA)—the right of workers to organize.

The employer in the case illegally fired an undocumented employee named José Castro in retaliation for his efforts to organize a union. Previously the company would have been forced to reinstate Castro and pay him the wages he would have earned if he hadn't been fired, but the Supreme Court ruled that since the worker was unauthorized, the company couldn't reinstate him and didn't need to pay him for the work he'd missed. "Back pay is the only out-of-pocket cost that an employer incurs by illegally firing a worker," four labor law experts noted in April 2003. "After *Hoffman*, an employer who violates the [NLRA] does so without suffering any economic loss" if the workers are undocumented. This "means that one of the most effective deterrents to further violations is no longer available."[44]

Still, the *Hoffman* decision doesn't affect most other labor rights.

The U.S. Equal Employment Opportunity Commission (EEOC) confirmed in June 2002 that it wouldn't inquire into the immigration status of workers claiming discrimination, and wouldn't consider such status when investigating cases. "Make no mistake, it is still illegal for employers to discriminate against undocumented workers," EEOC Commissioner Leslie E. Silverman insisted in a press release.[45] The U.S. Labor Department's Wage and Hour Division (WHD) confirmed in 2008 that it would enforce the minimum wage and overtime laws "without regard to whether an employee is documented or undocumented." However, because of *Hoffman*, undocumented workers who file discrimination claims usually won't be able to win reinstatement in their jobs.[46]

Do immigrants have constitutional rights?

The Bill of Rights (the first ten amendments to the Constitution, ratified in 1791) refers to the rights of "people," not citizens. The First Amendment specifically guarantees freedom of speech and of religion, and "the right of the people peaceably to assemble, and to petition the Government for a redress of grievances." Under the Bill of Rights, freedom from "unreasonable searches and seizures," from deprivation "of life, liberty, or property, without due process of law," from "excessive bail," "excessive fines," and "cruel and unusual punishments" are rights guaranteed to all persons—not only to the citizens of the United States. The Sixth Amendment guarantees any defendant in a criminal case, citizen or not, the right to a speedy public trial by jury with the assistance of a lawyer. Article One, Section 9, of the U.S. Constitution indicates that anyone can use the writ of habeas corpus to go before a judge to challenge his or her imprisonment.[47]

But all these and other rights were systematically and openly denied to most people of African descent from the beginning. Slavery remained legal and continued to exist for another seventy-four years after the Bill of Rights was ratified. The Supreme Court declared in the Dred Scott case of March 1857 that people of African descent, whether slave or free, did not have an inherent right to

U.S. citizenship.[48] Because it defended this injustice so blatantly, the Dred Scott ruling actually fueled the movement against slavery. In December 1865, after the Civil War, the Thirteenth Amendment was ratified, banning slavery, "except as a punishment for crime." In July 1868, the Fourteenth Amendment was ratified, stating:

> All persons born or naturalized in the United States, and subject to the jurisdiction thereof, are citizens of the United States and of the State wherein they reside. No State shall make or enforce any law which shall abridge the privileges or immunities of citizens of the United States; nor shall any State deprive any person of life, liberty, or property, without due process of law; nor deny to any person within its jurisdiction the equal protection of the laws.

Even here, where citizenship rights are defined, the last two clauses very clearly refer not to citizens but to "any person" and "any person within [a state's] jurisdiction." This language clearly extends due process rights and equal protection to immigrants, regardless of their legal status.

Do immigrants have the right to protest?

The First Amendment guarantees that everyone has the right to take part in public protests, including immigrants as well as U.S.-born citizens. Some people feel angry or resentful when they see immigrants exercising these rights, as when thousands marched and rallied across the United States between February and May of 2006 to defend immigrant rights. There seems to be an unspoken but widely held belief that out-of-status immigrants should stay "in their place" as silent cogs in the labor machine—hardworking, quiet, fearful, and out of sight.[49]

During the civil rights movement of the 1960s, African Americans who rose up against segregation and oppression saw similar reactions from whites, even among those who supported their civil rights in theory, but thought they should wait patiently for them rather than march.[50]

What rights don't immigrants have?

Today, equality under the law exists on paper for African Americans and other citizens of color, although in practice they suffer from pervasive discrimination and their rights are often violated with impunity. Non-citizens do not have true equality even on paper.

The way the courts have interpreted the laws and the Constitution, immigrants don't have the right to be here in the first place; even if you're a legal permanent resident, your presence here is considered a privilege.[51] Through this twist of logic, the government claims it can deport any non-citizen for virtually any reason, or for no reason at all, including longtime residents with green cards. So in practice, non-citizens can be denied a number of rights that should be guaranteed to "all persons," such as free speech, freedom from unjustified imprisonment, and freedom from cruel and unusual punishment. If you are a non-citizen, you can be deported for exercising your freedom of expression, imprisoned without being charged with a crime, or exiled for life from the country you consider your home.

The *Dred Scott* case is a reminder that even when the Supreme Court upholds discriminatory policies as the "law of the land," we can fight back and eventually win policy changes that reflect the values of freedom, justice, and equal rights. Court decisions don't happen in a vacuum; when the people move, the courts eventually follow. As Riva Enteen, program director of the National Lawyers Guild's San Francisco chapter, put it in a 2002 interview: "It takes a political movement to create a political context in which the courts respond and, frankly, do the right thing. So, if there wasn't a civil rights movement, the Supreme Court would not have [made its 1954 ruling in the] *Brown v. Board [of Education* case] to integrate the schools."[52]

"Power concedes nothing without a demand. It never did and it never will," noted prominent African-American writer, orator, and anti-slavery activist Frederick Douglass in a speech in August 1857, a few months after the Dred Scott decision.[53]

6. Are Immigrants Hurting Our Economy?

CONTRARY TO POPULAR BELIEF, a majority of unauthorized immigrants pay taxes. Young families with children in school, whether immigrants or not, tend to use more in services than they pay in taxes until the kids grow up. Immigrants "take" jobs by entering the labor market, but they also buy goods and services, creating jobs. Unauthorized status makes it harder for workers to assert their rights, and that does push wages down, but we could fix that by allowing everyone to work legally. Many immigrants send some of their earnings abroad, but so do we all, every time we buy a product made in China or Honduras.

Studies on immigration's economic impact generally don't address important questions like who benefits from economic growth, why so many large corporations don't pay their fair share, or whether the government spends our tax money in our best interests. People who support immigrant rights often say that immigrants are "good for the economy." That sounds nice, but what does it mean? Are people supposed to be good for the economy, or should the economy be structured so that it's good for people? And if so, what would that look like, and who gets to decide?

How much do immigrants cost us?

There have been dozens of efforts to determine the exact cost or benefit of immigration to the U.S. economy.[1] These studies generally focus
on how much immigrants increase or reduce economic growth, or
else compare how much immigrants pay in taxes to how much they
receive in services.

The results have been contradictory, showing how hard it is to
measure something so complex, and how much the results depend
on what assumptions we start with.

- Research by the generally pro-immigration Fiscal Policy Institute
  in 2009 found evidence that immigrants had helped the economy grow in twenty-five metropolitan areas. "Immigration and
  economic growth of metro areas go hand in hand," the study
  concluded.

- The Center for Immigration Studies (CIS), which calls for restricting immigration, claimed that families headed by undocumented
  immigrants were costing the federal government $10.4 billion a
  year in 2002, the difference between the taxes they paid and what
  the government spent on them (although the CIS study inflated
  the government's expenses by including some of the cost of
  enforcing laws that target immigrants).

- A 1997 study by the National Academy of Sciences calculated that
  immigration boosted economic growth by some $1 billion to $10
  billion a year, but that households headed by immigrants were
  costing households headed by native-born citizens about $166
  to $226 annually. However, the study found that the immigrant
  households made up for the costs later as the children started
  working and paying taxes.

The one thing that the studies usually agree on is that the overall
cost or benefit is relatively small, a few billion dollars either way each
year in a country with an annual gross domestic product (GDP) that
was about $16.8 trillion in 2014.[2]

To put those numbers in context, by October 2012 the U.S. government had lent $417 billion to financial firms under the Troubled Asset Relief Program (TARP), the "bailout" for the 2008 financial crisis. Even after all the loans are paid back, the government projects that U.S. taxpayers will have lost between $24 billion and $63 billion. The U.S. invasion of Iraq in 2004 has already cost us more than $2 trillion, according to the Costs of War Project sponsored by the Watson Institute for International Studies at Brown University, and that total will go up as we pay interest on the loans used to finance the war.[3] The estimated costs or benefits of immigration are also smaller than the annual cost of the main U.S. immigration enforcement programs, which totaled more than $17.9 billion in 2013.[4]

Do immigrants pay taxes?

As of 2013 some 74.4 percent of the country's 44 million immigrants were naturalized citizens or legal residents and were paying the same taxes as U.S.-born citizens. The other 25.6 percent of immigrants, those who lack legal status, were mostly paying the same taxes, too.[5] Everyone pays local sales taxes and contributes to property taxes when buying or renting a place to live (landlords include property taxes in the rents they charge). Unauthorized immigrant families paid some $10.6 billion in state and local taxes in 2010, according to estimates by the Institute for Taxation and Economic Policy (ITEP). This comes to about 6.4 percent of their annual income, a rate close to that of other taxpayers with similar incomes, according to the ITEP.[6]

The Social Security Administration estimated in 2013 that about 44 percent of this country's 8.1 million out-of-status workers were employed in the formal economy, working "on the books," generally using false Social Security numbers (SSN) or an individual tax identification number (ITIN).[7] These workers paid federal, state, and local taxes the same way citizens and immigrants with legal status did, and Social Security and Medicare payments were deducted from their paychecks.

The other 56 percent of undocumented workers—about 4.5 million—worked off the books in the informal, or "underground," economy. Their employers didn't report their income or pay for unemployment insurance, and their taxes weren't deducted from their paychecks. But these workers are still expected to pay income tax, and a number of them do, filing with an ITIN instead of a Social Security number.[8] Why would someone file a tax return if they work off the books? Many unauthorized immigrants hope to resolve their status as soon as the rules allow it, so they want to show that they have been following the law.

How much revenue are the U.S. and state governments losing because of the unauthorized immigrants who aren't paying income taxes? Workers in the underground economy are mostly paid very low wages; they tend to work irregular hours, if they even have steady work, and their employers often ignore minimum wage laws. Suppose these workers were all working full time in 2013 and were being paid the federal minimum wage; each of them would be making $15,080 a year. Based on the 1040 federal tax form for 2013 and assuming they had no dependents, they would each owe $508 in federal income tax. Even if all 4.5 million undocumented workers in the informal economy were failing to pay their federal income tax, the total loss each year would be about $2.3 billion.[9]

This may seem like a lot, but it's a small part of the country's annual tax losses. There were estimates in 2002 that as many as 25 million people, mostly citizens, were earning a large part of their income from the underground economy; the Internal Revenue Service estimated that the federal government was losing $195 billion a year in revenue from the informal sector. After the 2008 economic crisis, the situation got worse: formal employment crashed, and a growing number of people seem to have shifted into the informal economy—for example, renting out their homes to travelers or selling items on the internet. In 2013 economists estimated that the federal government was losing $450 billion to $500 billion in tax income this way each year, with another $50 billion lost by the states.[10]

As New York *Daily News* columnist Albor Ruiz has pointed out, "corporate giants" often pay less in taxes than the undocumented. Thanks to various loopholes, General Electric reportedly paid almost no U.S. federal taxes on the $14 billion it made in 2010. General Electric, Verizon, and Boeing were among twenty-six companies that made profits of at least $500 million between 2008 and 2012, yet paid zero in taxes on that income. By some estimates, U.S. corporations avoid paying some $100 billion in taxes each year through the use of foreign tax shelters. Wealthy individuals have also been able to use these shelters, depriving the U.S. Treasury of as much as $70 billion a year.[11]

Do immigrants collect welfare?

Immigrants who have become citizens get the same federal welfare and social services as native-born citizens. Undocumented immigrants and people here on temporary visas do not. Other immigrants, such as legal permanent residents and refugees, fall into a gray area.

"The United States welfare system is rapidly becoming a deluxe retirement home for the elderly of other countries," Robert Rector of the conservative Heritage Foundation complained to a congressional subcommittee in 1996.[12] In fact, the United States doesn't have a generous welfare state compared to other industrial countries, and immigrants are largely excluded from it. For example, the main programs benefiting seniors here are Social Security and Medicare. Immigrants are generally entitled to Social Security only if they are legal permanent residents and if they or a spouse worked legally in the United States. In any case, Social Security payments are relatively small. They came to 4.2 percent of our gross domestic product (GDP) in 2007, whereas in France, Germany, Greece, and Italy public pension payments totaled 10 percent or more of their GDPs that year.[13]

In 1996 Congress passed and President Bill Clinton signed the Personal Responsibility and Work Opportunity Reconciliation Act (PRWORA, known as the "welfare reform" bill), which drastically reduced public assistance for lawful permanent residents, especially for those who entered the United States after August 1996. The law cut permanent residents off from food stamps (now called the Supplemental Nutrition Assistance Program, or SNAP) and Supplemental Security Income (SSI), which provides assistance to the aged, blind, and disabled. The law also barred legal immigrants from access to Medicaid and Temporary Assistance for Needy Families (TANF, which replaced Aid for Families with Dependent Children) until they had lived in the country for five years, although states had some flexibility in applying this rule.

The 1996 law had a drastic impact: from 1994 to 1999, legal permanent residents' use of TANF benefits fell by 60 percent, food stamps by 48 percent, SSI by 32 percent, and Medicaid by 15 percent.

Lawmakers later softened some of the measures. For example, in 2002 Congress restored food stamps for children with legal status, and about half the states have stepped in to supplement some of the programs. But these changes have added to the complexity of the 1996 law, which was already difficult to understand. "Confusion about eligibility rules pervades benefit agencies and immigrant communities," the National Immigration Law Center (NILC) wrote in 2011. "Consequently, many eligible immigrants have assumed that they should not seek services, and eligibility workers mistakenly have turned away eligible immigrants."[14]

A 2013 study by the conservative Cato Institute found that "low-income non-citizen immigrants, including adults and children, are generally less likely to receive public benefits than those who are native-born. Moreover, when non-citizen immigrants receive benefits, the value of benefits they receive is usually lower than the value of benefits received by those born in the United States."[15]

How much do undocumented immigrants get in government services?

Even when they pay their full taxes, out-of-status adults generally can't get federal benefits or social services except in emergencies, although the government does sometimes pay for treatment in a hospital emergency room or for disaster relief. The 1996 "welfare reform" law specifically barred states from giving any federal welfare benefits to immigrants who lack status, although some state and local governments do provide certain services for the undocumented.[16]

The situation is more complicated for children. The approximately one million children who lack legal immigration status are entitled to free public education in the United States; in fact, education is mandatory—all school-age children must attend classes. As of 2011 the annual cost of public school education for all undocumented minors was at most some $12.6 billion. These costs are largely covered by local sales and property taxes, which everyone pays; in the 2004–2005 school year, 45.6 percent of financing for primary and secondary schooling came from state funds and 37.1 percent from local governments. Out-of-status children are also required to get vaccinations, in programs mostly funded by the federal government. Public education and health programs benefit all of us: our society needs educated people, and it needs to be able to prevent the spread of contagious diseases.[17]

Some out-of-status immigrants do seek benefits for their U.S.-born children, who are entitled to the same services as other U.S. citizens. For example, undocumented immigrants who file their federal income taxes are eligible, under the same rules as other taxpayers, for credits for their dependent children who are U.S. citizens or legal residents. These child tax credits are capped at $1,000 per child, and if the total amount of the credits is greater than what the taxpayer owes, the government may refund the difference.[18]

This is a benefit for the children, not the immigrant parent, and it's lower than benefits in many European child allowance programs, which often pay more than $100 a month per child.[19] Some politicians attacked the program after a 2011 Treasury Department investigation found that $4.2 billion had been paid out to accounts of unauthorized immigrants, but tax experts noted that the only real problem was with some fraud by a small number of taxpayers and tax preparers, not with the credit itself.[20]

Some low-income undocumented immigrants—children, as well as pregnant, elderly, and disabled individuals—can get medical care for certain emergency conditions through the joint federal-state Medicaid program. Emergency Medicaid costs about $2 billion each year, and almost all of the expense is for out-of-status immigrants. Childbirths and pregnancy complications account for the overwhelming majority of the costs; a four-year study in North Carolina found that 82 percent of the spending there was for these cases. Since the children will be U.S. citizens when they are born, the benefits are going to citizens as well as to their immigrant mothers.

The federal government could save money by funding prenatal care for undocumented women, since prenatal care reduces the chances of complications during childbirth, premature births, low birth-weight infants, and preventable birth defects, all of which require expensive emergency care. A 1989 study in New Hampshire showed that each additional dollar spent on prenatal care saved $2.57 in medical costs associated with low birth weight. As the advocacy organization Nebraska Appleseed noted in a fact sheet, "The immediate costs of premature and complicated births do not even capture the long-term costs to our health care and educational systems for babies who will struggle with physical, cognitive, and developmental challenges throughout their lives."[21]

Undocumented taxpayers pay into one system that they get *exactly nothing* back from: Social Security and Medicare. The Internal Revenue Service (IRS) estimated that out-of-status workers and their employers paid about $11.2 billion into Social Security in 2007 and $2.6 billion into Medicare; in 2013 the IRS increased the estimate for Social Security to $13 billion. This accounts for about 10 percent of Social Security's annual surplus. But undocumented workers are barred from receiving Social Security and Medicare. (They're eligible for the benefits if they get legal status or citizenship later, but most of them probably won't receive credit for the years they worked without authorization, especially if they paid into the system using false or expired Social Security numbers.)[22]

Are unauthorized immigrants a burden on our healthcare system?

Opponents of immigration often charge that undocumented immigrants strain health services by overusing hospital emergency rooms, where federal law requires that everyone must be treated. The claim is based on an assumption that the undocumented won't have health insurance to pay for regular medical care, since they often work off the books and at low-paying jobs that don't supply insurance. A study based on data from Los Angeles residents in 2000 supports that assumption: researchers estimated that slightly fewer than 22 percent of undocumented immigrants had health insurance. More would probably have gotten insurance recently through the Affordable Care Act of 2010 (ACA, or "Obamacare"), but Congress chose to exclude the undocumented from coverage.[23]

However, undocumented immigrants are generally much less likely than citizens to use health services. People who immigrate to look for work tend to be young and healthy, and fear of detection often keeps them from using hospitals, even in emergencies.[24]

A study of emergency room use nationwide in 2007 found that the uninsured didn't make significantly more trips to the emergency room than people with insurance. Although the national study didn't track immigration status, it showed that people of Latin American origin used emergency care less than either European Americans or African Americans. A study of healthcare use in California the same year found that undocumented immigrants of Latin American origin used emergency health services significantly less than either U.S.-born whites or U.S.-born Latinos.[25]

Politicians in border states sometimes blame problems in health services on the high number of immigrants in those states. But a survey of 46,000 people in sixty communities in the early 2000s found that the highest emergency room usage was in Cleveland and Boston, cities with relatively low percentages of uninsured patients and immigrants from Latin America. Administrators at hospitals in two Texas cities, Dallas and Fort Worth, told the *New York Times* in 2006 that most of their immigrant patients had jobs, paid taxes, and had a better record of paying their bills than low-income U.S. citizens do.[26]

THE 9/11 VICTIMS

The vast majority of unauthorized immigrants are too wary of detection to file for any government benefits, even when they are clearly entitled to them.

At least forty undocumented workers are known to have been killed in the September 11, 2001, attack on New York's World Trade Center, and the number is likely higher.[27] Five years later, only eleven survivors of these workers were receiving benefits from the federal government under the September 11th Victim Compensation Fund. The fund's rules specified that undocumented immigrants were eligible for the compensation and that immigration authorities wouldn't use the information to track them down. But the survivors were still reluctant to apply, and at least one widow had to be convinced by a lawyer that it would be safe—even though the benefits ranged from $875,000 to $4.1 million.

Fear of detection isn't the only thing that keeps survivors from applying. One, a widower, refused to apply because he didn't want "charity"; he finally decided to apply when his lawyer told him the money would help his preschool-age daughter. "It's all for her," he told a reporter. "That she becomes a doctor, a lawyer. That she's not the same as me."[28]

Do remittances drain the economy?

Many immigrants in the United States send a portion of the money they earn to relatives back home. In 2012, foreign-born U.S. residents sent some $51.1 billion in these remittances, which is about 64 percent more than the $31.2 billion in non-military foreign aid the U.S. government sent to other countries that year.

Based on statistics from earlier years, we can estimate that about two-thirds of the remittances went to countries in the Western Hemisphere, one-quarter to Asia and the Pacific, and the rest to Europe and Africa. Mexico received an estimated $19.9 billion in 2010; the Dominican Republic, El Salvador, and Colombia each got between about $3 billion and $4 billion. These payments are a huge part of the economies of many migrant-sending countries. For example, remittances made up 21.2 percent of Haiti's gross domestic product (GDP) in 2009.[29]

The total amount of remittances may seem large, but it doesn't have a significant impact on the total U.S. economy. By comparison, at the end of 2014, U.S. corporations were avoiding U.S. taxes by holding $2.1 trillion overseas, $200 billion more than the $1.9 trillion they were keeping in the United States.[30]

In any case, economic globalization means that money spent in one country is likely to end up in another one, frequently in the accounts of a giant multinational. The largest private employer in Mexico is Walmart, which is based in Arkansas. A full 35.6 percent of the clothes and shoes U.S. consumers purchased in 2010 were made in China; overall, about a third of the durable goods we buy in the United States, such as cars and electronics, are manufactured in other countries.[31]

U.S. corporations generally don't complain about the remittances. In 2002, immigrants paid about $4 billion in fees for sending remittances to Latin America and the Caribbean; most of this went to U.S. banks or to U.S. corporations like Western Union.[32]

U.S. politicians and elected officials sometimes use remittances to attempt to influence politics overseas. One example of this is El Salvador. Nearly one in four Salvadoran families count on remittances from the 1.1 million Salvadorans living in the United States. In 2014 some 212,000 Salvadorans resided here legally with Temporary Protective Status (TPS), a special immigration status that the U.S. government can withdraw. During El Salvador's 2004 presidential elections, then-U.S. Congress member Tom Tancredo (R-CO) and other politicians suggested that TPS for Salvadorans might end if the leftist Farabundo Martí Front for National Liberation (FMLN) carried the vote. Tancredo was quoted in campaign ads run by FMLN opponents. The FMLN's candidate lost that year. In 2009, however, the U.S. government explicitly ruled out the use of similar threats, and the FMLN-backed candidate won.[33]

Do immigrants take our jobs?

This is one of the few immigration questions that most economists can agree on. In 1994 the conservative Alexis de Tocqueville Institution concluded that the "evidence suggests that immigrants create at least as many jobs as they take, and that their presence should not be feared by U.S. workers."[34] Twelve years later, the liberal Pew Hispanic Center came to a similar conclusion based on a study of employment trends in the 1990s and the early 2000s.[35]

Immigrants work, but they also buy goods and services, creating more jobs. In fact, immigrants probably generate more jobs than many older residents: immigrants are younger and more likely to have children at home, so they spend much more of their income on goods like clothes and food, which involve labor-intensive production. Older and richer people are much more likely to put their money into luxuries and speculative investments, which generate relatively few jobs.[36]

Do immigrants just take jobs we don't want?

Although immigrants create as many jobs as they take, they can still compete with native-born workers for specific jobs, and employers can still replace native-born workers with immigrants who accept lower wages.

Employers—and some immigrant rights advocates—argue that immigrants generally get the jobs the native born won't do. James S. Holt, an economist for a labor management law firm, took that position in testimony to Congress in 1995. Agricultural jobs "entail physical labor under adverse environmental conditions of heat, cold, sun, rain, etc.," he said. "It is work that many Americans would be physically incapable of doing on a sustained basis, and that most of the rest would prefer not to do if there are better alternatives available."[37]

It's true that unauthorized workers made up about 48 percent of the hired crop labor force as of 2009, according to the Department of Labor. Still, 33 percent of hired crop workers were U.S. citizens, while 19 percent were born elsewhere but authorized to work in the United States.[38] And agriculture makes up a small part of the labor market. Most immigrants, including those who lack legal status, do jobs that native-born workers have traditionally done and continue to do. The native born remain a majority in these occupations, which include maintenance, construction, food preparation and service, and production. Workers without papers made up 10 to19 percent of the workforce in these areas in 2009. A survey in 2005 found that unauthorized workers were 36 percent of all insulation workers and 29 percent of all roofers and drywall installers. About 21 percent of private household workers were undocumented.[39]

According to the conservative Harvard economist George Borjas, himself an immigrant to the United States from Cuba, the reason that employers prefer immigrants for these jobs is probably just that immigrants will work for less money. There is no evidence, he says, "that natives would refuse to work in these jobs if the immigrants had never arrived and employers were forced to raise wages to fill the positions." Immigrants "take jobs that natives do not want *at the going wage*."[40]

Do immigrants bring down wages?

Economists disagree about immigrants' effect on wages. Some, like Borjas, say immigrants create a strong downward pressure, while others, such as Giovanni Peri from the University of California at Davis, think that by stimulating the economy immigrants actually raise wages. But Columbia University economist Moshe Adler notes that when he presents the economists' studies to students who are union construction workers, "they laugh them off. They have no use for complex mathematical models." They're familiar with construction sites that use undocumented labor at low wages, "and they know first-hand that this puts direct downward pressure on their own wages."[41]

The effect isn't huge. According to a 1997 study by the National Academy of Sciences, the increase in low-wage immigrant workers in the 1980s may have cut pay by 1 to 2 percent for "all competing native-born workers"—that is, people looking for the jobs that immigrants take, those that generally don't require a strong command of English or a high level of formal education. The effect was strongest on the 10 percent of U.S. workers who had dropped out of high school: competition from immigrant workers may have lowered their wages by about 5 percent between 1980 and 1994.[42]

These numbers are fairly small in terms of the U.S. workforce, but they are a serious matter for working people trying to survive on a low income. Five percent of the $25,376 median annual earnings for high school dropouts in 2014 comes to $1,269, a real hardship for a family struggling to get by.[43] About 20 percent of the low-wage workers likely to be affected are African Americans or U.S.-born Latinos.[44]

There is some evidence that the downward pressure on wages doesn't just affect the lowest-paid workers. In California's San Diego County—with one of the nation's largest pool of undocumented workers, plus commuters from nearby Tijuana, Mexico—production workers averaged $28,930 a year as of May 2005, 3.2 percent below the national average of $29,890. Transportation workers made $27,070, 6 percent below the national average of $28,820.[45]

Why do they work for less?

To the extent that immigrants bring down other workers' wages, it is largely because they themselves get paid less. and this forces native-born workers in the same occupations to accept lower wages in order to compete.

Some immigrants earn less because their English is weak, or because they lack the formal education or work experience required for better-paying jobs. Part of the wage gap can probably be attributed to supply and demand: as the pool of available low-wage work-ers grows, the price of their labor goes down. And immigrants may accept lower wages when they first come to the United States because they are used to receiving still lower wages in their home countries, although this effect tends to diminish as people stay and adjust to the cost of living here.[46]

Racial and ethnic discrimination also affects wages. A 2016 study found that only 58.3 percent of the wage gap between third-generation U.S.-born Mexican American and U.S.-born white workers is explained by known factors like education and skill level. Discrimination pre-sumably accounts for a significant portion of the rest. The situation is even worse for black workers: known factors account for only 48.3 percent of the difference between their wages and those of white workers.[47]

One important factor is often overlooked: legal status. A third of immigrant workers in the United States—about 8.1 million as of 2012—are undocumented, according to the Pew Research Center.[48] With no access to a social safety net when they're out of work, undoc-umented immigrants can't be too selective about the jobs they take. If they complain about low wages or unacceptable working condi-tions, or if they try to organize a union, employers may threaten to turn them in to immigration authorities. Fear of deportation keeps these workers from reporting safety violations to government agen-cies, even when they are injured on the job. Their lack of status makes them a vulnerable underclass of workers that employers can exploit with near impunity.[49]

Several studies have tried to determine how much difference legal status makes for undocumented immigrants' wages, either by compar-ing the pay of documented and undocumented workers with similar levels of skill, experience, and English proficiency, or by comparing how much more undocumented immigrants made after they got legal status through the 1986 amnesty. Because of the many variables, it's hard to determine the exact "wage penalty" for being undocumented, but there is no question that it's significant. The estimates in these studies range from about 6 percent to more than 20 percent.[50]

Who benefits from low wages for immigrants?

The post-1965 wave of immigration coincided with a stagnation of real wages for most U.S. workers. After rising 81 percent from 1947 to 1973, real wages fell 3 percent from 1973 to 1980 and had barely moved upward by 2006. This was despite dramatic increases in worker productivity—16.6 percent from 2000 to 2005, for example. At the same time, the country's richest 1 percent were benefiting from equally dramatic increases in their real income—by 135 percent between 1980 and 2004.[51]

There are a number of factors behind the wage stagnation, including government policies that reduce the ability of unions to organize and Congress's failure to raise the minimum wage between 1996 and 2007. (Even after an increase in 2007, the hourly minimum wage remained almost $2 lower than in 1968 when adjusted to current dollars.)[52] Certainly a large part of the explanation is a major change in the U.S. economy that has resulted in many jobs being shifted to low-paid, vulnerable workers: to the 8.1 million undocumented immigrants who work here; to some 8.5 million people, mostly single mothers, thrown out of the welfare system by the 1996 "welfare reform" law; and to the millions of workers employed in assembly plants in Asia, Latin America, and the Caribbean producing goods for U.S. firms to sell in the United States.[53]

The result is that workers are forced into what labor organizers call "the race to the bottom"; they must accept wretched wages and working conditions or they will lose their jobs to other workers who are willing to accept even less. And as wages stagnate or decline, the wealthiest individuals and corporations profit.

Corporate executives understand this. Many accept the idea of an immigration reform with the legalization of undocumented workers, but only if it includes an expanded "guest worker" program to bring in a new workforce of vulnerable, low-wage immigrants as an easily exploited substitute for the workers that get legal status. Randel Johnson, U.S. Chamber of Commerce vice president for labor, put it bluntly in April 2009: "As part of the trade-off for legalization, we need to expand the temporary worker program."[54]

What can we do about the "race to the bottom"?

When U.S. citizens and authorized immigrants feel their economic security is being threatened by undocumented workers, their first reaction is often to call for more enforcement of immigration laws. But a more logical step is to improve pay for unauthorized workers so their low wages no longer exert downward pressure on wages in general.

For one thing, this means supporting a full legalization for the 11.3 million out-of-status immigrants already in the country to ensure that they can exercise their full labor rights.

Anti-immigrant forces denounce legalization policies like the 1986 amnesty, which allowed some 2.7 million immigrants to adjust their status.[55] But all U.S. workers would benefit from the increase in real wages that would likely accompany an amnesty. According to the U.S. Department of Labor, within five years of the 1986 amnesty, real wages of the newly legal workers rose an average of 15 percent. If this happened now, with 8.1 million undocumented workers, there would be a strong upward pressure on wages for other workers in the same occupations. Wages would be likely to rise for all workers in the jobs with high concentrations of undocumented immigrants, according to a University of California-Los Angeles (UCLA) study from 2001: by about 5 percent in agriculture, 2.75 percent in services, and 2.5 percent in manufacturing.

At the same time, more of the newly authorized immigrants would work on the books and pay income taxes. Since they would earn higher wages, they would pay more in taxes and would buy more products and services, creating jobs for citizens and for other immigrants. Gaining permanent status would also make it easier for immigrants to plan for the future—for example, by purchasing a home and investing in education.

In a study published in 2009, UCLA professor Raúl Hinojosa-Ojeda, who headed the group that produced the 2001 UCLA report, called for legalization as a way to fight the "Great Recession" that followed the 2008 financial meltdown. He projected that a new amnesty "would result in a net income rise of $30-36 billion, support 750,000–900,000 new jobs, and generate $4.5 to 5.4 billion in net tax revenue."[56]

Legalization would also mean that immigrant workers would have a better chance of winning when they fight for improved wages and job conditions, and for better services for their communities. Even now, under adverse conditions, out-of-status workers have already led a number of successful organizing drives, often with the support of consumer boycotts and other community activism. The AFL-CIO grasped the importance of these efforts and in 1999 reversed its former support for stricter enforcement against undocumented immigration. The labor federation and most of its affiliates now officially back some form of legalization and encourage out-of-status immigrants to organize themselves and join unions.[57]

Retired University of California-Berkeley professor Carlos Muñoz argued in the early 2000s that immigrant workers would revitalize labor organizing in the United States as they "get forced into activity because of their situation. Many immigrants already have a heritage of participation in movements of workers in the countries they come from," he said. "Immigrants will change us more than we'll change them."[58]

Workers at the Republic Windows and Doors plant in Chicago provided an example of this kind of organizing. The company closed down suddenly in December 2008 without giving notice or severance pay. The workers, mostly African Americans and immigrants from Mexico and Central America, occupied the plant until they won a $1.75 million settlement from the company, becoming "symbols for hundreds of thousands of U.S. workers facing layoffs" in the 2008 economic crisis, according to Chicago Public Radio reporter Chip Mitchell.

There had been racial tensions at the plant, and some of the African Americans "felt that they were being discriminated against because they were black," Republic worker Melvin Maclin explained. "And at one point they were considering calling immigration, because they were saying things like, 'This person that is working here still isn't even a legal citizen.'" But the workers pulled together to fight the layoffs.

Maclin told Chicago Public Radio that "to see a lot of people standing up, willing to occupy the plant," despite fears of being detained and deported, "just raised my respect for them. . . . It's to the ceiling."[59]

7. Is Immigration Hurting Our Health, Environment, or Culture?

IDEAS ABOUT IMMIGRANTS AS A THREAT to health, environment, or culture generally revolve around concerns about a failure to assimilate, the idea that today's immigrants are not adapting to American society. In fact, research suggests that new immigrants assimilate at least as quickly as immigrants did a century ago. Unfortunately, as immigrants adapt to U.S. society over time, and the second and third generations become more "American," they generally experience a decline in health and in educational and economic success.

A positive model of integration would need to address obstacles such as racism, legal barriers to obtaining permanent residency, and insufficient investment in healthcare and education. "Integration involves a reciprocal relationship between immigrants and society," notes a comprehensive 2015 report by the National Academy of Sciences.[1] A study of official policies promoting multiculturalism in Canada and Australia suggests that recognizing a plurality of ethnicities and cultures, and encouraging people to retain heritage languages and cultures, enhances integration.[2] True integration also includes full and equal political rights—"Nothing about us without us," as the saying goes. Immigrants bring a wealth of knowledge, perspectives, and values that can enrich our nation, if we take down the barriers that block their participation.

Do immigrants endanger public health?

"There is a long, sad, and shameful tradition in the United States in using fear of disease, contagion, and contamination to stigmatize immigrants and foreigners," noted Arthur Caplan, director of the Division of Medical Ethics at New York University's Langone Medical Center, in a 2014 interview with NBC News.[3]

This tradition is embedded in the history of U.S. immigration law. The Immigration Act of 1891 mandated medical inspections of arriving immigrants and barred anyone "suffering from a loathsome or a dangerous contagious disease."[4] From the beginning, this policy was less about science and more about economics and morality: people with physical or mental illness or disability were deemed inadmissible because they would not be able to do manual labor and were "likely to become a public charge," and people with venereal diseases were seen as socially undesirable. Ethnicity and class also influenced how health inspectors treated the new arrivals: working-class Mexicans were forcibly sprayed with disinfectant at border crossings and forced to undergo physical exams, and Europeans at the same crossings were not. Lower-class Asian immigrants were also singled out for more medical scrutiny than Europeans.[5]

In the early 1980s, many news reports suggested that the HIV virus may have come to the United States from Africa via Haiti.[6] Simply being Haitian was considered a risk factor, and that led to discrimination against Haitian immigrants. From 1991 to 1993, U.S. officials subjected Haitian refugees seeking to enter the United States to routine HIV testing at the U.S. naval base in Guantánamo, Cuba; several hundred people who tested positive were kept segregated under squalid conditions in a special camp at the base until public pressure from human rights activists won their release.[7]

For more than twenty years, starting in 1987, the United States officially barred foreign nationals infected with HIV from entering the country, even to visit, and from gaining status as legal immigrants. After years of public campaigning by activist and advocacy groups, the HIV ban was finally lifted in 2010.[8]

Current immigration law still deems "inadmissible" anyone suffering from a "communicable disease of public health significance" as designated by the Centers for Disease Control and Prevention (CDC). As of 2016 these diseases include tuberculosis (TB), leprosy (also known as Hansen's Disease),[9] and five curable sexually transmitted infections.[10]

The only disease on the list that could potentially cause a public health crisis is tuberculosis, a respiratory illness spread by airborne bacteria. TB is common in Latin America, the Caribbean, Africa, Asia, Eastern Europe, and Russia. A majority of U.S. cases do occur among the foreign born, but the number of cases, the case rate, and the death rate from TB have all declined significantly since 1992, even as the foreign-born share of the U.S. population has increased. Cases of multi-drug-resistant TB, which is harder to treat, have also decreased: only ninety-one cases were reported nationwide in 2014, down from 484 in 1993.[11]

Medical exams, including TB testing, are required for refugees before they enter the United States, and for immigrants seeking resident status. Applicants must also be vaccinated against a number of "vaccine-preventable" ailments, and those who undergo their medical inspections outside the United States must be declared free of several other communicable diseases.[12]

These measures contrast with a lack of any routine health screening upon arrival for millions of visitors and U.S. citizens returning from trips abroad.[13] Asylum seekers are likewise not screened for illness when they arrive in the United States.[14] Arriving asylum seekers are often detained for days or weeks in crowded, unsanitary facilities, so if even one person were sick with an airborne illness like TB many others could quickly become infected.[15]

The main challenges to public health in the United States are non-contagious conditions like heart disease, cancer, injuries, and diabetes, none of which are transmitted through immigration, global travel, or trade.[16] "Americans die sooner and experience higher rates of disease and injury than people in other high-income countries," the National Research Council and Institute of Medicine reported in 2013.[17] Interestingly, foreign-born people in the United States are generally healthier and live longer on average compared both to native-born members of their ethnic groups and to the overall U.S.-born population. Immigrants are less likely than the native born to die from cardiovascular disease or cancer, and they have lower rates of obesity, depression, and alcohol abuse. However, this immigrant health advantage diminishes with time and over subsequent generations.[18]

Millions of U.S. citizens have no health insurance—they earn too much to qualify for Medicaid and their employers don't pay healthcare costs.[19] Most undocumented immigrants don't have health insurance, and they can't even buy it through the Affordable Care Act.[20] A lack of insurance discourages people from seeking timely medical attention; this increases the cost of care because later treatment is more expensive, riskier, and less effective. From a public health perspective, it makes more sense to ensure that everyone, regardless of ability to pay or immigration status, has access to quality preventive care and prompt medical treatment.[21]

Globally, public health is threatened by economic "austerity" measures, promoted by institutions like the World Bank and the International Monetary Fund (IMF). These measures force many impoverished countries to slash their social spending, slowing efforts to provide clean water and contain the spread of disease, while at the same time increasing the poverty that forces many people to migrate.[22]

Is immigration bad for the environment?

The environment is global; it doesn't stop at national boundaries. Immigration has little or no impact on any of the major environmental threats facing us, such as climate change, deforestation, radioactive and chemical waste, and air and water pollution. These threats to global ecology do, however, impact immigration: experts predict they will provoke massive displacement over the coming decades, causing a new wave of what some are calling "climate refugees."[23]

It's true that clandestine border crossings by large numbers of migrants in remote areas have hurt the local environment, especially in the Arizona desert. Trash left by border walkers includes empty water bottles, discarded clothing, garbage, and even old cars. Some of this trash causes long-term damage, although probably less damage than the patrolling and fencing that is meant to prevent border crossing. We could avoid such problems altogether by allowing people to come here legally, through airports and established border posts.[24]

Immigration opponents have argued that when people move here from countries with lower levels of consumption, they damage the global environment by using more energy than they would at home. The United States, with less than 5 percent of the global population, uses about a quarter of the world's fossil fuel resources.[25]

A 2008 study from the Center for Immigration Studies (CIS), a conservative nonprofit, claimed that immigration to the United States adds significantly to the greenhouse gases that cause global warming. Since the United States "leads the world's largest economies in per capita emissions" of carbon, the researchers wrote, immigrants produce about 482 million more tons of carbon each year than they would produce if they had stayed in their home countries. "The impact of immigration to the United States on global emissions is equal to approximately five percent of the increase in annual worldwide CO2 emissions since 1980," the CIS researchers concluded.[26]

But the amount of carbon emissions from a country depends on many things other than the number of people in it. For example, the biggest energy user in the United States is the military, which accounts for about one percent of all U.S. energy consumption. The majority of this is in fossil fuels, the largest source of greenhouse gases; if the Defense Department were a country, it would rank thirty-fourth in the world in average daily oil use, according to the 2005 *CIA Fact Book*.[27] There's no reason to think the military would burn less fuel if there were fewer immigrants in the United States. Immigrants are not responsible for the business practices and national policies that promote energy waste. Long before the current wave of immigration, the United States was investing in highways rather than mass transit; in trucking rather than shipment by rail; and in fossil fuels and biofuels rather than in solar power and other clean energy sources.[28] If we had energy policies here that seriously reduced carbon emissions, most immigrants wouldn't produce much more carbon than they did in their home countries.[29]

Are immigrants overpopulating our country?

The world has finite resources, and although overpopulation may be a real concern, it's a global one. The movement of people from one country to another doesn't change the size of the world's population.

Overpopulation also doesn't necessarily cause environmental problems in an individual country. As noted above, population size is only one of the factors affecting a country's environment. "In many countries, population growth rates have declined yet environmental conditions continue to deteriorate," the Committee on Women, Population, and the Environment (CWPE) pointed out in 1992. For example, Russia had a major drop in population during the 1990s, but its environmental problems didn't go away.[30]

When people express fear that the U.S. population is spiraling out of control, they often mean they feel uncomfortable seeing increasing numbers of people they perceive as different from themselves. Such fears have been exploited by white supremacists like David Duke, who proclaimed on his website: "I will fight to limit overpopulation and protect our environment by stopping illegal immigration and almost all legal immigration into America."[31]

Many people are also influenced by the stereotype that "foreigners" have far more children than U.S. citizens do. A 2005 study from the Center for Immigration Studies (CIS), which advocates restricting immigration, claimed the birth rate as of 2002 was 2.6 children per woman for authorized immigrants and 3.5 per woman for unauthorized immigrants. This was much higher than the rate for native-born women—two per woman—and actually higher than birth rates in the countries the immigrants came from. CIS warned that if the undocumented "are allowed to remain in the country… births alone will add some four million people to the U.S. population over the next decade."[32]

This population explosion failed to materialize: an estimated 340,000 babies were born to unauthorized mothers in 2008, well below the CIS forecast of 400,000 a year. From 2007 to 2010, birth rates for all foreign-born women fell by 14 percent, and for Mexican immigrant women by 23 percent. This helped bring the overall U.S. birth rate down by 8 percent, to "the lowest ever recorded," according to the Pew Research Center.[33]

"Demographic data from around the globe affirm that improvements in women's social, economic, and health status and in general living standards are often keys to declines in population growth rates," the Committee on Women, Population, and the Environment explained in 1992.[34]

Mexico is a good example. Its population grew dramatically during the twentieth century, from 15 million in 1910 to 105.3 million by the middle of 2004. This happened because better healthcare and sanitation meant that older people lived longer and more children lived to become adults; the annual death rate fell by two-thirds between 1910 and 1970. Since then, access to family planning and improved opportunities for women have brought the birth rate down. In 1976 the average Mexican woman was having about 5.7 children in her lifetime; by 2005 the birth rate had fallen to 2.1 children for the average woman, just a little more than enough to keep the population constant.[35]

Most activists concerned about global population recognize that blaming "foreigners" isn't a solution. "Instead of focusing on 'broken borders' rhetoric, we need to address the root causes of migration in our foreign policy and work with our neighbors to help improve educational and economic opportunities for people," wrote Brian Dixon, government affairs director of the nonprofit group Population Connection, in November 2006.[36]

Immigrants are sometimes accused of causing the overcrowding of certain urban or suburban areas, but overcrowding is impacted more by internal migration and economic changes than by immigration from abroad. Corporations turn once-industrial cities into ghost towns by moving their factories overseas to profit from cheaper labor. Seniors resettle in retirement communities. Rural people move to the cities; urban residents move to the suburbs. Real estate developers transform rural landscapes into urban sprawl. Schools, public transportation, hospitals, and other services are often slow to accommodate such changes. When community members are consulted in urban planning processes, they can organize to ensure that their needs are met.[37]

Do immigrants care about the environment?

Environmental degradation disproportionately affects low-income African-American, Native-American, Latino, and immigrant communities. Farm laborers and their families are exposed to pesticides in the fields, and in nearby homes and schools. Disenfranchised urban communities and isolated rural ones are poisoned by toxic waste. The same factories that pollute the air, land, and water are exposing low-wage workers, many of them immigrants, to dangerous chemicals.[38]

In a July 2015 survey of Latino voters, more than three-quarters of respondents thought it was important or very important to reduce smog and air pollution and to protect U.S. wildlife, public lands, and endangered species. Similar numbers supported mandates for clean energy sources like solar and wind power to prevent climate change. Some 66 percent believed global warming is caused by human activities, about 14 percentage points more than the general U.S. population. Although just under half of adult Latinos are immigrants, and just over half of all immigrants are from Latin America, the poll may reflect how Latino immigrants feel about the environment. "Latinos are aware of environmental degradation and climate impact in their countries of origin," the researchers noted, "and consider this when developing their views."[39]

A study based on survey data from 1993 found that immigrants who came to the United States at age sixteen or older were more likely to express concern about pollution and other environmental issues, and to engage in ecologically friendly behaviors such as recycling, than either non-immigrants or immigrants who came at a younger age. A 1996 survey found foreign-born New Yorkers more inclined toward pro-environment attitudes and behaviors compared to native-born New Yorkers. However, both of these studies found foreign-born respondents less likely to engage in political action around environmental causes—such as signing a petition—than the native born.[40]

This failure to take political action may be partly due to language constraints and a lack of outreach by environmental organizations, but it likely also reflects immigrants' fears that fighting publicly for better environmental conditions will expose them to consequences like detention and deportation. Philip Radford, executive director of the environmental group Greenpeace, wrote in 2013 that "current immigration policy forces vulnerable communities to keep silent about corporate pollution for fear of having their lives and families torn apart."[41]

Still, some immigrant communities overcome these barriers and lead efforts to clean up the environment. For example, in 1990 grassroots organizations representing immigrant and non-immigrant people of color in the southwestern United States formed the Southwest Network for Environmental and Economic Justice to join together in fighting toxins in their communities. In 1992 mostly Latino residents of Kettleman City, California, won a six-year battle against the Chemical Waste Management (ChemWaste) corporation's plans to put a hazardous waste incinerator in their town. The campaign included a lawsuit, filed in 1991 by a coalition of farmworkers and other community members, challenging the practice of having the meetings and notifications in the permit process for the incinerator held only in English.[42]

More recently, a coalition of environmentalists, unions, teachers, and the children of migrant farm workers in the largely Latino city of Watsonville, California, organized against the use of methyl iodide as a pesticide in nearby fields. The chemical is listed as a carcinogen and is known to cause birth defects. The campaign resulted in the manufacturer, Arysta Life Science, announcing in March 2012 that it was no longer selling the pesticide in the United States.[43]

Do immigrants learn English?

In 1751 Benjamin Franklin warned that German immigration would destroy the English language in Pennsylvania. "In a few years," he wrote, Pennsylvania would "become a German colony; instead of their learning our language, we must learn theirs, or live as in a foreign country."[44] If that sounds familiar, it may be because people who are uncomfortable with immigration today express similar concerns, often seeing a failure to speak English well as a sign that immigrants are uninterested in becoming full members of U.S. society.[45]

Immigrants from countries like India, Philippines, Nigeria, Kenya, Jamaica, Trinidad, Guyana, Ireland, the United Kingdom, and Canada, to name a few, come here already speaking English as a native language, even if their accents sound foreign to many U.S.-born citizens. But most immigrants from Latin America and China, who together accounted for 78 percent of the foreign born in 2013,[46] are unlikely to arrive in the United States already speaking English.

As the number of immigrants from those areas has grown, so has the number of the foreign born with limited abilities in English—reaching 25.3 million in 2011, up 81 percent from 1990. Speakers of Spanish and Chinese made up 72 percent of immigrants with limited English proficiency in 2010.[47]

It's not that the new immigrants don't want to speak English. Most are eager to learn English, so they can improve their job options, income, and other opportunities. But learning a new language can take time, especially for busy working adults and older people, and the available resources are limited. Nonprofit organizations that provide free or low-cost English classes are generally swamped with students, according to a September 2006 study by the National Association of Latino Elected and Appointed Officials (NALEO) Educational Fund.[48]

In 2014, the *New York Times* reported that free English classes offered by New York City's public library system "have become so popular in some neighborhoods that people stand in line for hours to sign up and many have to be turned away because there are not enough spots."[49]

The popular idea that today's immigrants are slower to learn English than previous generations is contradicted by at least two academic studies. Based on U.S. Census data, sociologists Claude S. Fischer and Michael Hout found that more than 75 percent of the people who immigrated between 1980 and 2000 spoke English on some level within their first five years in the country, whereas this was true of less than 50 percent of the immigrants who arrived between 1900 and 1920.[50] In 1910, thirty years after most immigration from Germany had ended, many immigrants and their descendants living in Wisconsin remained monolingual German speakers, according to a study by linguists Miranda E. Wilkerson and Joseph Salmons.[51] Then as now, immigrants who held on to their language and culture were sometimes viewed as a problem.

Perceptions that today's immigrants don't want to speak English may be partly based on the fact that newcomers with limited English are becoming increasingly visible in areas with historically low immigration rates. Traditionally, new immigrants settled in urban areas like New York, Chicago, Los Angeles, and Miami, joining large ethnic communities already established there. Although a majority still settle in such locations, the ten states with the greatest growth in people with limited English from 1990 to 2010 were generally less urban: Nevada, North Carolina, Georgia, Arkansas, Tennessee, Nebraska, South Carolina, Utah, Washington, and Alabama.[52]

Children growing up in a home where a language other than English is spoken generally become fluent very quickly in English, but they often lose fluency in the language spoken by their parents, which puts them at a disadvantage in an increasingly multilingual, globalized society. Researchers and policymakers see "heritage languages" as an important resource for the nation as well as for individuals, families, and communities. Research suggests that being bilingual improves cognitive development and academic success, helps build deeper cross-generational family bonds, and strengthens cultural identity.[53]

Are the new immigrants integrating into U.S. society?

People sometimes claim that new immigrants aren't assimilating—adapting into mainstream society—the way that earlier waves of immigrants did. Harvard political scientist Samuel P. Huntington argued in a 2004 book that because of Cuban and Mexican immigrants the United States "could change . . . into a culturally bifurcated Anglo-Hispanic society with two national languages."[54]

This kind of claim is generally based on two misconceptions: that immigrants from the 1880s through the 1920s did assimilate quickly and successfully; and that today's immigrants are either too different to fit in or are actively resisting integration.

James Smith of the California-based Rand Corporation, a conservative think tank that often produces analyses for the U.S. government, studied three generations of Mexican immigrants and Mexican-Americans. Smith wrote in 2003 that their rate of educational progress, a good measure of cultural assimilation, was the same as or greater than that of Europeans who immigrated in the late nineteenth and early twentieth century. In 2008 another study, by the conservative Manhattan Institute, found that recent immigrants "assimilated more rapidly than their counterparts of a century ago."[55]

When people suggest that these earlier immigrants, mostly from Europe, adapted well to mainstream U.S. society, what they often mean is that European immigrants didn't stand out in *white* mainstream society, so they were easily accepted into it. The earlier wave was not always seen that way, however. People from Europe were once considered "so distinct as to be referred to as 'races,'" according to a 1997 report on immigration by the National Academy of Sciences. Southern and Eastern European immigrants (especially Jews and Italians) were seen as genetically inferior at a time when eugenics—the idea of breeding a "superior" race based on a Nordic ideal—was popular in the United States. From 1907 to 1910, a joint Senate-House group known as the "Dillingham Commission" studied the issue and decided that immigration from Southern and Eastern Europe posed a serious threat to U.S. society and culture. Yet today the "children, grandchildren and great-grandchildren [of these immigrants] have intermarried to such an extent as to virtually erase differences in education, income, occupation, and residence," the National Academy of Sciences pointed out in 1997.[56]

The great wave of European immigrants to the United States "integrated" into a white identity by positioning themselves, consciously or otherwise, on the side of whites against black Americans within the country's existing race divide.[57] Meanwhile, black immigrants who came mainly from the English- and Spanish-speaking Caribbean integrated quickly into black America. In the memoir *Black Cuban, Black American*, Evelio Grillo recounts his youth growing up in the 1920s and 1930s in Tampa, Florida, and attending segregated black schools, where he learned African-American history and was transformed from a Cuban immigrant into a "black American."[58]

Black and white immigrants are generally perceived as "American" once they no longer have a foreign accent, and any differential treatment is based on their perceived race rather than their status as immigrants. People who have an appearance commonly associated with Asian or Latin American heritage have the opposite experience: they are seen as "perpetual foreigners," even if their families have been here for generations.[59]

The intermarriage among European immigrants and their native-born descendants that blurred ethnic differences into an American category of whiteness in earlier decades is not likely to erase racial or ethnic boundaries in the same way between today's more racially diverse immigrants, the National Academies of Sciences suggested in 2015.[60] This country's race divides are deep and complex. Asians may be perpetual foreigners, but they are now also widely seen as educational success stories. Latinos, regardless of skill or education, are stereotyped as manual laborers, domestic workers, or gang members. Black Americans—despite being recognized as "belonging" within this country, in contrast to the "perpetual foreigners"—are still largely relegated to the margins of society, their opportunities for socioeconomic advancement limited by pervasive discrimination. How we address this kind of discrimination and stereotyping will determine pathways to future integration.

How can we encourage immigrants to integrate?

Throughout U.S. history immigrants, especially those from outside Europe, have faced exclusion, discrimination, and outright violence. Instead of integrating Chinese immigrants into U.S. society, immigration opponents denied them the right to become naturalized citizens in the 1870 Naturalization Act, barred them from bringing their families to the United States, organized violent attacks on them, and segregated them into "Chinatowns." Other Asian immigrants were also barred from becoming citizens, and California banned Japanese immigrants from owning land in 1913. During the Second World War, the federal government confined 120,000 Japanese Americans, the majority of them native-born U.S. citizens, in internment camps.[61]

The denial of legal status to some immigrants is another form of exclusion that slows integration. The Manhattan Institute's 2008 study on the subject found that Mexicans had somewhat faster rates of cultural assimilation than immigrants from India and China but slower rates of economic and civic assimilation. One reason for this, according to the study's author, Duke University professor Jacob L. Vigdor, may be that so many Mexican immigrants lack legal status. "If you're in the country illegally, a lot of the avenues of assimilation are cut off to you," he told the *Washington Post*. "There are [a] lot of jobs you can't get, and you can't become a citizen."[62]

What does it mean to be an "American"?

If there is such a thing as a "real American," those who have the most right to that claim are the descendants of the millions of people who had been living in North America for thousands or even tens of thousands of years when the Europeans first arrived. Like these Native North Americans, a majority of the Latin Americans who immigrate here trace at least part of their ancestry to the hemisphere's indigenous peoples.

The English were latecomers to what is now the United States. The first European settlers came from Spain; this country's oldest continuously occupied European settlement is Saint Augustine, founded in 1565 and acquired by the United States when it purchased Florida from Spain in 1819. Texas and California and the southwestern states were part of Mexico, making up about 51 percent of Mexican territory at the time. The United States annexed Texas in 1845 and took control of the rest as its spoils from the U.S.-Mexican War of 1846–48. Some 200,000 Native Americans inhabited these territories at the time; so did 100,000 Mexican nationals, most of them Spanish-speaking and many of them mestizos, people of mixed Spanish and indigenous ancestry.[63]

U.S. place names reflect some of the diversity of origins that make up "real America." Throughout the country, hundreds of place names come from indigenous languages, including the names of at least twenty-one of our fifty states. Several other states get their names from Spanish. Most of California's best-known cities have Spanish names, including San Francisco, Los Angeles, and Sacramento. Like place names, U.S. culture has many different sources. The Europeans who settled here adopted a great deal from the Native Americans, including canoes, log cabins, moccasins, the idea for sign language, and major food crops like corn and squash.[64] People brought here by force from Africa also shaped U.S. culture with stories, words, music, and foods that reflect African traditions as well as their struggles to survive and escape slavery in the "New World."[65]

The U.S. media give a great deal of coverage to anti-immigrant sentiments, but a survey of U.S. residents in 2004 suggests broad acceptance of immigrants' cultural and ethnic diversity. Asked what should be "very or somewhat important in making someone a true American," only 17.4 percent of respondents cited "having European ancestors." Some 72.7 percent considered "carrying on the cultural traditions of one's ancestors, such as the language and food" to be an important part of being a "true American." "Respecting other people's cultural differences" was important for a full 96.7 percent of the respondents, and 92.7 percent cited "seeing people of all backgrounds as American."[66]

8. Are Immigrants a Threat?

RESEARCH SHOWS THAT IMMIGRANTS are less likely to commit crimes than native-born citizens, and that cracking down on immigrants doesn't make us safer. Yet many people accept the idea that immigrants who commit crimes should be deported. Fewer than a third of non-citizens deported for having criminal records were convicted of serious or violent offenses, and many longtime residents are deported for convictions that happened long in the past.[1] Regardless of what kind of offense was committed, should people suffer extra punishment just because of their citizenship status? Doesn't it make more sense for the severity of the penalty to be based on the seriousness of the crime?

The U.S. government has used public fears of crime and terrorism as a pretext to crack down on immigrants based on their religion, nationality, or political beliefs. If someone really posed a threat, why would we want to see the person deported over minor immigration violations instead of having to face justice in a criminal court?

Do immigrants commit more crimes than non-immigrants?

"Few stereotypes of immigrants are as enduring, or have been proven so categorically false over literally decades of research, as the notion that immigrants are disproportionately likely to engage in criminal activity," stated a 1997 paper jointly sponsored by two Washington-based nonpartisan research organizations, the Carnegie Endowment for International Peace and the Urban Institute. The results of these decades of research "are surprisingly unambiguous: immigrants are disproportionately unlikely to be criminal."[2]

A 1998 study analyzed Federal Bureau of Investigation Uniform Crime Reports and Census Bureau data from several dozen U.S. metropolitan areas and confirmed that recent immigrants had no significant effect either on crime rates or the change in rates over time. The authors also analyzed data from the National Longitudinal Survey of Youth and found that young people born abroad were significantly less likely than native-born youths to be criminally active.[3] Later studies have confirmed this trend. In fact, they show the last few decades' increase in immigration, including unauthorized immigration, actually coinciding with a *decrease* in crime. The undocumented population in the United States more than tripled between 1990 and 2013, but the violent crime rate declined 48 percent over the same period; the property crime rate was down by 41 percent.

Incarceration rates tell the same story: in 2010 the incarceration rate was around 1.6 percent for foreign-born men aged 18 to 39, about half the rate for native-born men in that age range. Researchers found that in a "paradox of assimilation," incarceration rates grow with the number of years immigrants have spent residing in the United States. Still, even those living here for sixteen years or longer had much lower incarceration rates than native-born citizens.[4]

If it's not true, why do we still associate immigrants with crime?

Distorted media coverage of crime and criminals probably contributes to perceptions that immigrants are linked to crime. A study published in 2002 in the *Journal of Research in Crime and Delinquency* reviewed television newscasts over a three-week period in Orlando, Florida, and reported that 28 percent of Hispanics appearing on the news did so in the role of criminal suspect—more than twice the rate for African Americans and 5.6 times the rate for whites. Both African Americans and Latinos (Hispanics) were presented as criminal suspects four times more often than they were presented as crime victims.[5]

Based on a sample of news broadcasts in Los Angeles between 2008 and 2012, including Spanish-language broadcasts, an April 2015 study found that Latinos were underrepresented in more sympathetic roles as officers and victims. The study also found that while whites made up just 13 percent of homicide victims listed in crime reports, they were 35 percent of the homicide victims portrayed on local television news.[6]

Most Latinos are not immigrants, and a slim majority of U.S. immigrants are from Latin America, but there is a general tendency in the United States for people to associate Latinos with undocumented immigrant status. A 2012 survey found that increased exposure to news or entertainment media portraying Latinos or immigrants in an unfavorable light made non-Latino respondents more likely to express negative or hostile perceptions about both groups.[7]

Because Latino ethnicity is conflated with immigration status, it's also likely that stark racial and ethnic disparities within the U.S. criminal justice system contribute to misconceptions about immigrants and crime.

"And Justice for Some," a comprehensive national report by the National Council on Crime and Delinquency, found that young people of color are treated more severely than white youths at every stage of the justice system—from arrest to incarceration—even when charged with the same offenses.[8] For youths charged with drug offenses, the incarceration rate for Latino youths was thirteen times the rate for white youths.[9]

The police often claim they don't disproportionately target people based on race, but their own statistics contradict this. According to

data from the U.S. Department of Justice, police nationwide chose
to search 6 percent of the African American drivers and 7 percent of
the Hispanic drivers they stopped in 2011, compared to 2 percent of
white drivers they stopped. White drivers were also less likely to be
ticketed.[10]

Shouldn't we deport immigrants who commit crimes?

Immigrant non-citizens who are arrested for crimes pose no more of
a threat to society than do U.S. citizens accused of the same crimes.
Yet many non-citizens, even if they are longtime permanent legal
residents, face a much harsher consequence for those crimes; after
completing their sentences, they are held in immigration jails for
weeks, months, or even years, and are then often deported.

The offenses that can lead to deportation are sometimes minor, and
are often the result of a plea bargain the immigrant made to avoid a trial.
Two exceptionally harsh 1996 laws—the Illegal Immigration Reform
and Immigrant Responsibility Act (IIRIRA) and the Antiterrorism
and Effective Death Penalty Act (AEDPA)—added a total of twenty-
one offenses to the list of crimes that trigger deportation.[11]

Often the distinction between a citizen and a non-citizen seems
arbitrary. Take Sacha Sealey, who enlisted in the U.S. Army at age
seventeen in 1983 and took part in the U.S. invasion of Grenada
in October of that year. After two years of service, Sealey suffered
from post-traumatic stress disorder, and like many combat veterans,
he struggled with addiction. But Sealey was born in Canada, and
although he had been living legally in the United States since he was a
toddler, he never got around to seeking citizenship. "I figured my card
said 'permanent residence,' that's permanent, not temporary. I didn't
think there was that much of a difference," Sealey later told a reporter
for the Long Island paper *Newsday*. Sealey pleaded guilty to a few
minor drug arrests, without realizing they would result in deportation. He had spent ten months in a rehab center and was fighting to
get his life back together when he went to the immigration office to
renew his green card on June 30, 2003. There Sealey was handcuffed

and thrown into immigration detention. For eight months he endured harsh conditions in New Jersey county jails. While he was detained, his sister died, leaving his widowed mother alone in Queens, New York. In March 2004, Sealey was deported to Montreal, barred from ever returning legally to the United States.[12]

For immigrants who have established their lives in the United States, deportation is exile, a cruel punishment that is not imposed on U.S. citizens. Many, like Sacha Sealey, came here as children; if they get involved in drugs or commit crimes, it's something they learned here, in the United States, not in the country where they were born. Deportees' families are generally punished as well, both emotionally and economically: the deportee is often the family breadwinner.[13]

Does deportation make us safer?

If deporting immigrants with criminal records made U.S. communities safer, we'd expect crime rates to go down in communities where the government had stepped up the rate of deportations. The government's 2008–14 "Secure Communities" program was specifically intended to identify and remove non-citizens with criminal convictions; it was implemented in 3,000 counties and led to about a quarter of a million people being deported. Two law professors published a study of the program's results in November 2014. They concluded that the program "led to no meaningful reductions in the FBI index crime rate. Nor has it reduced rates of violent crime—homicides, rape, robbery, or aggravated assault." The authors said their study "calls into question the long-standing assumption that deporting non-citizens who commit crimes is an effective crime-control strategy."[14]

Deporting someone for a violent crime may actually make us less safe. Deportation creates a climate of fear among immigrants that discourages people from reporting crimes or speaking out as witnesses.[15] In some cases, a person who has been victimized may *feel* safer if the perpetrator gets deported. Yet if the offender is truly a danger to others, deportation makes no sense. It simply takes offenders out of the parole system, and their criminal record may not follow them across the border. Whether they remain in their country of birth, go elsewhere, or return to the United States without permission, no one is monitoring them to ensure they don't put someone else at risk.[16] Don't all victims of violent crime deserve the same measures of justice and protection, regardless of the citizenship status of the person who harmed them?

Thousands of Central Americans were deported as "criminal aliens" after IIRIRA and AEDPA were enacted. Among them were youths who belonged to Mara Salvatrucha (known as MS-13), a Los Angeles-based street gang. Crime experts say the deportations made it possible for the U.S. gang to take root in Central America, especially in El Salvador, fueling criminal violence there. As a result of its connections in both Central America and the United States, MS-13 grew into a real force in the smuggling and distribution of drugs. In October 2012 the U.S. Treasury declared MS-13 a significant "transnational criminal organization" because of its "serious transnational criminal activities, including drug trafficking, kidnapping, human smuggling, sex trafficking, murder, assassinations, racketeering, blackmail, extortion, and immigration offenses." MS-13 members now reportedly see deportations from the United States as a way to get "free rides" to other countries in order to expand the gang's operations.[17]

Is there a link between immigration and terrorism?

Most terrorist violence in the United States comes from native-born U.S. citizens, the majority of them non-Muslim, but since September 11, 2001, when coordinated terror attacks left some 3,000 people dead in the northeastern United States, the image of terrorists as Muslim foreigners has held a persistent grip on this country's national consciousness.

The nineteen men who carried out the 9/11 attacks came here from other countries and were Muslim. (There were also more than five hundred foreign-born people, and more than two-dozen Muslims, among the victims.)[18] But the second-most deadly terrorist attack of all time on U.S. soil was carried out by a white, U.S.-born citizen and Gulf War veteran, Timothy McVeigh. That bombing killed 168 people, including nineteen children, at the federal building in Oklahoma City on April 19, 1995.[19]

No one suggests that white Gulf War veterans are inclined to be terrorists, or that they should be singled out for special scrutiny or arrested as suspicious when they approach federal buildings. So why should foreigners, especially those who are Muslims, or of Arab or South Asian descent, be treated as terrorists?

In a study published in June 2015, nearly three-quarters of 382 police and sheriff's departments surveyed in the United States cited anti-government violence as one of the three biggest threats from violent extremism in their jurisdictions, while only 39 percent included "Al Qaeda-inspired" violence on the list. That shouldn't come as a surprise, since between October 2001 and July 2016, white supremacists and other non-Muslim right-wing extremists carried out twice as many fatal U.S. terror attacks as did people identifying with Islam, according to New America, a Washington, D.C., research center. If we don't count the single largest attack during this period— Omar Mateen's June 2016 murder of 49 people at a gay nightclub in Orlando—then non-Muslim terrorists killed more people, too. Among those killers who did claim affiliations to Islam, all were U.S. citizens or legal residents.[20]

How did the September 11 hijackers get here?

All nineteen of the 9/11 hijackers came to the United States legally on valid visas, and once here, only two violated the terms of their visas. Fifteen were from Saudi Arabia, and two were from the United Arab Emirates; both countries are wealthy oil nations with close ties to the U.S. government. The other two suspects were Egyptian and Lebanese, but got their visas at the U.S. embassy in Berlin. As a 2003 report from the Migration Policy Institute points out, the hijackers had been "carefully chosen to avoid detection: all but two were educated young men from middle-class families with no criminal records and no known connection to terrorism."[21]

The hijackers did not face much scrutiny. U.S. diplomatic posts in Saudi Arabia had a policy of calling in fewer than 2 percent of visa applicants for interviews, and granting visas to nearly everyone who applied (only 3 percent of applicants were turned down in fiscal years 2000 and 2001, according to State Department figures). A similar policy was in place for the United Arab Emirates.[22]

When the General Accounting Office (GAO), the nonpartisan investigative arm of Congress, reviewed the visa applications submitted by fifteen of the hijackers in Saudi Arabia and the United Arab Emirates, it found that not one of them had filled in the documents properly, and only two had been interviewed. The applications for the other four were destroyed before investigators could review them.[23]

Did the government's post-9/11 crackdown help stop terrorism?

As of 2005 the administration of President George W. Bush was claiming that it had convicted more than 200 people in terrorism cases since September 11, 2001. A special Justice Department website, lifeandliberty.gov, now disabled,[24] claimed the government had prosecuted 401 people in "terrorism-related investigations," winning convictions or guilty pleas in more than 212 cases. In June 2005, the *Washington Post* examined those 212 convictions and found that only thirty-nine cases involved charges related to terrorism. Of those thirty-nine cases, most involved "broad-based charges of association with, or support of, a terrorist group, without any connection to actual terrorist actions," according to Georgetown University law professor David Cole.[25]

After reviewing prosecutions in "terror-related" cases, New York University's Center on Law and Security concluded that "the legal war on terror has yielded few visible results. There have been ... almost no convictions on charges reflecting dangerous crimes."[26]

The Justice Department also claimed on its website to have deported more than 515 foreign nationals linked to the investigation of the September 11 attacks. In fact, most of the deportations were carried out under a policy that barred deportation unless a person was first cleared by the FBI of any connection to terrorism.[27] In a February 2003 letter, FBI agent Coleen Rowley complained to her boss, FBI director Robert Mueller, that following the September 11 attacks the agency's headquarters "encouraged more and more detentions" of out-of-status immigrants "for what seemed to be essentially PR purposes," in order to create the appearance of "progress in fighting terrorism."[28]

Through a "special registration" program, started in September 2002, the immigration service fingerprinted, photographed, and questioned 80,000 male immigrants from twenty-four predominantly Muslim countries and North Korea. Another 8,000 people—mainly Arab and Muslim men—were interviewed by the FBI. In addition, 5,000 immigrants were detained, nearly all of them on minor immigration violations, in alleged connection to anti-terrorism investigations. None of the people swept up in these programs was ever convicted of a terrorist crime. "In what has surely been the most aggressive national campaign of ethnic profiling since World War II," notes Professor Cole, "the government's record is 0 for 93,000."[29]

Is the United States tough on terrorists?

In the 1980s, the United States made special visa arrangements to train terrorists to fight the Soviet Union's occupation of Afghanistan, according to Michael Springman, who headed the U.S. visa bureau in the Saudi Arabian city of Jeddah from 1987 to 1989. Springman said he was "repeatedly ordered by high-level State Department officials to issue visas to unqualified applicants," many of whom were not Saudi citizens and couldn't explain why they wanted to visit the United States.[30] In one case, Springman said, a refugee from Sudan who was unemployed in Saudi Arabia got a visa "for National Security purposes, after it was taken out of my hands by the chief of the consular section."[31] Springman said he eventually learned that the visas were being facilitated as part of a Central Intelligence Agency program "to bring recruits, rounded up by [Saudi terrorist leader] Osama Bin Laden, to the United States for terrorist training by the CIA. They would then be returned to Afghanistan to fight against the then-Soviets."[32]

"One country's terrorist can often be another country's freedom-fighter," noted Judge John Noonan in a June 2004 decision for the Ninth Circuit Court of Appeals, adopting a popular phrase to point out that the U.S. government had backed the right-wing "contras" who carried out terrorist attacks against civilians in Nicaragua. Judge Noonan ordered U.S. immigration officials to release Harpal Singh Cheema, a Sikh independence activist from India they had held on secret evidence since November 1997. "It is by no means self-evident that a person engaged in extra-territorial or resistance activities—even militant activities—is necessarily a threat to the security of the United States," wrote Noonan.[33]

The U.S. government kept Singh Cheema jailed in California for more than eight years, much of that time in solitary confinement. Eventually, Singh Cheema gave up his fight against deportation and agreed to return to India, where he had been tortured in the past. He was deported in April 2006, and six months later he was reportedly being held in prison in India's northwestern Punjab region.[34] Singh Cheema was eventually released; as of June 2015 he was in Punjab State serving as chair of the organization Sikhs for Human Rights.[35]

U.S. immigration officials detained the Mirmehdi brothers, four Iranians living in Southern California, for nearly four years, claiming they were members of a terrorist group, the Mujahedin-e Khalq (MEK). Two of the brothers had attended a June 1997 demonstration in Denver organized by the National Council of Resistance of Iran (NCR), a coalition linked to the MEK. It wasn't until four months later, in October 1997, that the State Department added the MEK to its list of terrorist organizations.[36]

The NCR continued to enjoy the support of at least two hundred members of the U.S. Congress, even after the State Department added the coalition to the terrorist list in 1999, claiming it was another name for the MEK. When the NCR held a rally in front of the United Nations in New York in September 2000, Missouri's two Republican senators sent a written statement of solidarity that was read aloud to the crowd. One of the two senators was John Ashcroft, who became attorney general in 2002 and fought to block the Mirmehdi brothers' release on bond. A Justice Department spokesperson later claimed Ashcroft's statement of solidarity did not "intend to endorse any organization."[37]

The Mirmehdi brothers were finally released in March 2005, a month after Ashcroft left office and as their case began to draw wider media attention. "This shouldn't happen in the United States," Mostafa Mirmehdi said of his family's ordeal. "If it took place in Iran, I would expect it, but I came here for freedom."[38]

TERRORIST OR FREEDOM FIGHTER?

As of 2015, the U.S. government was allowing at least one unauthorized immigrant associated with terrorism to live openly in Florida. Cuban-born Luis Posada Carriles, a longtime CIA asset, is believed to have orchestrated the 1976 bombing of a Cuban passenger jet that killed seventy-three people, and has been linked to several other terror attacks. "If Luis Posada Carriles does not meet the definition of a terrorist, it is hard to think of who would," observed Peter Kornbluh, director of the Cuba Documentation Project at the independent National Security Archive (NSA).

The U.S. government refused to charge Posada with terrorism and persistently ignored requests from Venezuela for his extradition in connection with the 1976 bombing case. Posada's Texas lawyer pointed out the U.S. government's dilemma: "How can you call someone a terrorist who allegedly committed acts on your behalf?"[39] Eventually the U.S. government did list Posada as a terrorist, and prosecutors charged him with immigration fraud; a federal jury in El Paso, Texas, acquitted him in April 2011, and he was allowed to remain in the United States.[40]

Does the crackdown on immigrants make us safer?

In 2002, six immigration experts, including former Immigration and Naturalization Service (INS) commissioner Doris Meissner, conducted an eighteen-month review of post–September 11 immigration measures for the Migration Policy Institute. Their June 2003 report found that the crackdown on immigrants put national security at greater risk by diverting resources away from in-depth, responsible intelligence work, and by alienating and intimidating communities that could have helped with terrorism investigations.

Among other measures, the report criticized the Justice Department's "efforts to enlist state and local law enforcement agencies into enforcing federal immigration law" as counterproductive to community safety and the fight against terrorism. "Such action undercuts the trust that local law enforcement agencies have built with immigrant communities, making immigrants less likely to report crimes, come forward as witnesses, or provide intelligence information, out of fear that they or their families risk detention or deportation."

The report also condemned the government's unchecked use of immigration detention in anti-terrorism cases. "Arresting a large number of non-citizens on grounds not related to domestic security only gives the nation a false sense of security," the report notes.[41]

The April 15, 2013, bombing at the Boston Marathon, in which three people died and an estimated 264 were injured, highlights the need for careful intelligence work rather than mass roundups of immigrants. The attack was carried out by Dzhokhar and Tamerlan Tsarnaev, two brothers of mixed Chechen ancestry who immigrated here from Russia in 2002.

A Russian intelligence agency sent the U.S. government two warnings about Tamerlan Tsarnaev in 2011, and an FBI agent interviewed him. Officials decided the case didn't warrant surveillance, but the CIA asked for Tsarnaev to be put on a watch list so he could be detained and questioned whenever he left or returned to the United States. Despite this, he reentered the country without any problems in July 2012 after spending six months in the Russian republic of Dagestan, where U.S. officials say he received terrorist training. The reason Tsarnaev wasn't detained and questioned at the airport was that his name had been misspelled as "Tsarnayev" in the watch list's database.[42]

Does the crackdown on immigrants violate the Constitution?

The Migration Policy Institute's June 2003 report argued that the government violated the First Amendment's protection of the public's right to be informed about government actions by deliberately hiding the identity, number, and whereabouts of immigrant detainees following the 9/11 attacks. "This right is at the heart of our democracy, and is crucial to maintaining government accountability to the public," the report said.

By targeting specific ethnic groups with its post-9/11 operations, the government also violated the Fifth Amendment's guarantee of equal protection. After reviewing the cases of 406 post-9/11 immigrant detainees and interviewing community leaders, lawyers, and advocates, the Migration Policy Institute concluded that many detainees were picked up "because of profiling by ordinary citizens, who called government agencies about neighbors, coworkers and strangers based on their ethnicity or appearance." The report notes that "law enforcement agencies selectively followed up on such tips for persons of Arab or Muslim extraction."[43]

The case of Tashnuba Hayder shows how the government is able to use immigration procedures to sidestep constitutional protections.

Hayder came to the United States from Bangladesh with her family at the age of five. She started following strict Islamic traditions as a teenager. U.S. intelligence became interested in Tashnuba in early 2005, possibly because she had listened to sermons by a radical Islamic cleric in an internet chat room. In March an FBI agent posing as a youth counselor questioned the girl, then sixteen, at her home in Queens, New York. Three weeks later a dozen federal agents raided the family home at dawn, seizing Hayder and removing her to a maximum security juvenile detention center in Pennsylvania, some 140 miles from New York, supposedly because her mother's immigration papers had expired.

Hayder and another New York teen, Adama Bah, an immigrant from Guinea, were questioned at the detention center for two weeks without the presence of their parents or a lawyer. Apparently the government had decided the girls were potential suicide bombers, and detained them on the pretext of immigration violations.

Officials allowed Bah to return to her East Harlem home in May—after the case began getting publicity—on the condition that she wear an electronic ankle bracelet and not discuss the case. But they refused to release Hayder until she accepted "voluntary departure" to Bangladesh, where she barely understood the language and would probably be unable to afford more schooling. The U.S. government refused to discuss the case with reporters, but presumably they determined that the teen wasn't a terrorist. As *New York Times* reporter Nina Bernstein noted, the "voluntary departure" option that let Hayder leave "requires a finding that the person is not deportable for endangering national security."[44]

Were there crackdowns like this before 9/11?

"The government's post-September 11 actions follow a repeating pattern in [U.S.] history of rounding up immigrant groups during national security crises," warned the Migration Policy Institute's 2003 report. "Like the internment of Japanese Americans during World War II, the deportation of Eastern European immigrants during the Red Scare of 1919–20, and the harassment and internment of German Americans during World War I, these actions will come to be seen as a stain on America's heritage as a nation of immigrants and a land where individual rights are valued and protected."[45]

In 1952, anti-Communist members of Congress pushed through the Immigration and Nationality Act (INA), also known as the "McCarran-Walter Act." The INA became the new body of immigration law, incorporating or replacing all previous laws with new provisions making it easier to detain immigrants, deny them release on bail, and deport them for alleged "subversion." The Act allowed immigrants to be excluded or deported based on purely ideological grounds, and barred "aliens afflicted with psychopathic personality, epilepsy, or mental defect"—a category expressly created by Congress to exclude people it referred to as "homosexuals and sex perverts." Most of the ideological provisions were formally repealed by Congress in 1990, as was the ban on homosexuals, although a number of them were reincorporated in the USA PATRIOT Act of 2001.[46]

In January 1987, under the administration of Ronald Reagan, the federal government arrested a group of eight leftist activists who were organizing for Palestinian rights in Los Angeles and tried to deport them under the INA's anti-communism provisions, using secret evidence. The "Los Angeles Eight" fought back through the courts. Twenty years later, in January 2007, an immigration judge threw out the last of the government's cases. The judge, Bruce J. Einhorn, called the government's actions in its unsuccessful pursuit of the activists "an embarrassment to the rule of law."[47]

Secret evidence is not allowed in criminal cases, but under the 1952 law the government is permitted to use it to block non-citizens from gaining political asylum, permanent resident status, naturalization, or release on bond. The Supreme Court extended this power with a February 1999 decision in the Los Angeles Eight case: the justices ruled that the government can target a group of foreigners for political reasons and can keep the reasons secret. New York Times columnist and legal expert Anthony Lewis labeled the court's action "a depressing performance."[48]

In 1997, under the administration of Bill Clinton, U.S. Attorney General Janet Reno used provisions of the INA to justify the detention of at least twenty immigrants—nearly all of them Arabs—on secret evidence. (Secret evidence was also used in at least two immigration cases involving members of the Irish Republican Army, but Reno suspended these cases in September 1997 after the State Department suggested that pursuing them could disrupt the peace process in Northern Ireland.)[49]

Several of the Clinton-era secret evidence cases, including that of Sikh activist Harpal Singh Cheema, lingered into the post-9/11 scenario. Palestinian scholar Mazen Al-Najjar was detained on secret evidence for three and a half years by the Clinton administration; he was released in December 2000 after a judge ruled the evidence against him was insufficient and his detention was unconstitutional. He was rearrested by the Bush administration in November 2001, and held in solitary confinement for nine months before being deported in August 2002.[50]

The Bush administration's post-9/11 secret detentions surpassed the Clinton-era ones in numbers: at least 1,200 people were swept up. As Georgetown University law professor David Cole observed, "Never in our history has the government engaged in such a blanket practice of secret incarceration."[51]

Are immigrant workers a national security risk?

Many people have prejudiced ideas about Muslim, Arab, and South Asian immigrants, which politicians and government officials seem to encourage and exploit to build support for "anti-terrorism" efforts. But people don't generally associate Mexican laborers or Haitian refugees with terrorism.

That didn't stop officials from trying to justify a broader crackdown on immigrant workers in the name of the "war on terror." In press releases describing the arrest of workers at "critical infrastructure" sites like airports and military bases, the U.S. Immigration and Customs Enforcement (ICE) agency acknowledged that the workers aren't terrorists, but claimed they pose a security risk because their undocumented status and use of false documents makes them vulnerable to blackmail by terrorists.[52]

In April 2003, then-attorney general John Ashcroft tried to extend the national security argument to refugees fleeing Haiti by issuing a legal opinion defending the continued detention without bond of eighteen-year-old Haitian asylum-seeker David Joseph. Ashcroft claimed that releasing Haitians like Joseph could trigger a wave of immigration by sea, threatening national security by overtaxing the Coast Guard, Border Patrol, and other agencies focused on preventing terror attacks. Ashcroft also claimed the government had noticed an increase in Pakistanis and Palestinians "using Haiti as a staging point for attempted migration to the United States."

That claim baffled the State Department's Consular Service. "We all are scratching our heads," said spokesperson Stuart Patt. "We are asking each other, 'Where did they get that?'"[53]

9. Enforcement: Is It a Solution?

IT'S NOT CLEAR THAT IMMIGRATION—even unauthorized immigration—is really a problem. The current scale of global migration is a symptom of serious problems like poverty, war, and human rights abuses, none of which can be solved by restricting immigration. But even if you believe in limiting immigration, enforcement is an expensive approach, and there's no evidence that it reduces the number of unauthorized immigrants who are here.

When people call for more policing of the border, or arresting undocumented people at their homes or workplaces, they often seem to forget about the costs in tax dollars and human suffering.

If enforcement doesn't reduce immigration, what does it do? It creates a vulnerable underclass that can be more easily exploited, pushing down working conditions and pay for society as a whole. Like other kinds of policing, immigration enforcement relies heavily on racial profiling to identify its targets, reinforcing a caste system based on physical appearance.[1] As geography professor Nancy Hiemstra explains, the government deploys enforcement "as a strategic spectacle . . . useful

for reassuring the anxious public that something is being done
to address their racialized security concerns."[2]

What if we deport all the "illegal" immigrants?

Politicians and others sometimes act as though we could simply
deport the estimated 11.3 million out-of-status immigrants living
in the United States. "There are eight million jobs in America now
held by illegal aliens, that's eight million job opportunities taken from
American citizens," claimed Representative Mo Brooks, a Republican
from Alabama, in an August 2014 television interview. Asked if he
wanted eight million people deported, Brooks replied, "Yeah, if that's
what's necessary to protect American jobs. Absolutely."[3]

Opinion polls suggest that the U.S. public wouldn't support a
mass deportation of millions of immigrants. A February 2014 survey
showed the population evenly split on the practice then in effect of
deporting about 400,000 immigrants a year; 45 percent backed the
policy and 45 percent were opposed. A full 73 percent said people
now living in the United States illegally should have a way to legalize
their status if they met certain requirements; only 24 percent were
against this.[4]

Many U.S.-born citizens would join immigrants in opposing, and
actively resisting, mass roundups of immigrant families and communities. It's one thing to have a discussion about the pros and cons
of immigration, but political views aside, most people don't want to
see their friends or neighbors led off in shackles just because of their
immigration status. (Not to mention their family members—more
than 36 percent of unauthorized immigrants live in mixed-status
families.[5])

On September 1, 2006, federal agents began rounding up out-of-
status immigrants in Stillmore, Georgia. The community of 1,000
people lost some 120 residents in the raids—more than 10 percent of its
population—and hundreds more fled, turning Stillmore into a ghost
town. David Robinson, who operated a trailer park there, watched
helplessly as the agents handcuffed residents and hauled them away.

To protest, he bought a U.S. flag and posted it upside down in front of the trailer park. "These people might not have American rights, but they've damn sure got human rights," Robinson said. "There ain't no reason to treat them like animals."[6]

Even without resistance, the cost of deporting all unauthorized immigrants would be prohibitive. In 1986, when Congress decided to extend amnesty, or limited legalization, to undocumented immigrants, one of the main reasons legislators gave was the difficulty of deporting the unauthorized population, then estimated at 3.5 million to five million. Representative Peter Rodino, a New Jersey Democrat, said he supported amnesty because, "In my judgment, we cannot deport these people. We would not, I am sure, provide the money to conduct the raids. It would mean billions of dollars in order to try to deport them."[7]

It would be much more expensive now. In 2010, the Center for American Progress estimated the cost of identifying, apprehending, detaining, processing through the legal system, and removing each unauthorized "alien" at $23,482. At that rate, deporting the current undocumented population of 11.3 million people would cost around $265 billion.[8]

Are we doing enough to secure the border?

The U.S. government has been stepping up its efforts to stop unauthorized entry at the border with Mexico since the early 1990s—at the same time it was negotiating the NAFTA trade pact with Mexico. In 1990, the U.S. Border Patrol started construction of a ten-foot-high welded steel fence along fourteen miles of the southwest border near San Diego, California, one of the main entry points for immigrants who come to the United States without permission.[9]

By the end of 1994, under the administration of President Bill Clinton, the Border Patrol had started three major enforcement operations at the Mexican border, using fences, barriers, high-tech surveillance methods, and an expanded force of border agents: Operation Blockade (later renamed Hold the Line) in El Paso, Texas;

Operation Gatekeeper in San Diego; and Operation Safeguard around Nogales, Arizona. In 1997, the Border Patrol initiated Operation Rio Grande in Brownsville, Texas. During this period, from 1993 to 1998, the number of Border Patrol agents in the Southwest more than doubled, from 3,389 to 7,357, and the annual cost to taxpayers rose from about $400 million in 1993 to $800 million in 1997.[10]

The increases have continued. By 2014 the Border Patrol's annual budget had jumped to $3.6 billion, more than thirteen times the $263 million budget in 1990.[11] The Border Patrol is only one part of Customs and Border Protection (CBP), the DHS agency that handles border enforcement. CBP's proposed budget for fiscal year 2015 was $13.1 billion, nearly twice what it was in 2005.[12]

Has border enforcement cut the flow of migrants?

The U.S. government uses the number of apprehensions of unauthorized border crossers to measure the flow of undocumented immigrants.[13] Even by this questionable measure, the various enforcement operations of the 1990s did not appear to have a significant impact on unauthorized entry: the number of migrant apprehensions on the Southwest border rose between 1994 and 2000, although afterward it declined to a low point in 2015.[14] Meanwhile, the number of unauthorized immigrants in the United States grew by some five million from 1990 to 2000, a significantly faster rate than in previous decades, and continued to rise until 2007, when it started leveling off as a major economic recession hit the United States.[15]

The stepped-up border enforcement operations of the 1990s likely discouraged some people from trying to immigrate, and they definitely cut unauthorized crossings near urban areas like San Diego and El Paso. But the main effect was just "squeezing the balloon"—forcing immigrants to change their routes and methods.[16] In January 2001, Georgetown University law professor Alex Aleinikoff, a former general counsel for the Immigration and Naturalization Service, warned that programs like Operation Gatekeeper weren't working. "Operation Gatekeeper has become our Vietnam," he said. Immigration service officials were "mistakenly thinking that if we added just a little more [to the buildup], then a little more, that we would get results."[17]

One result of "squeezing the balloon" is to push migrants into crossing through more remote and often dangerous terrain, where they are more likely to die en route. According to a 2009 report by the San Diego ACLU and Mexico's National Commission of Human Rights, at least 5,607 people died between 1994 and 2008 while attempting to cross the border, mostly along these riskier routes.[18] Alan Bersin, the Clinton administration official in charge of Southwest border policy from 1995 to 1998 and CBP head from 2010 to 2011, described the policy as "forc[ing] migrants into much more inhospitable and rugged places," adding that "the difficulty of passage is evidenced in the increased number of accidents and fatalities involving illegal entrants."[19]

Some researchers think stepped-up border enforcement has actually *increased* the number of out-of-status immigrants living in the United States. Because of the greater danger and expense of crossing the border, the undocumented are now far less likely than in the past to work here a few months and then return home for a period. Instead, they stay longer, and many settle down and send for their spouses and children to join them. According to Princeton sociology professor Douglas S. Massey, in the 1980s about half of all undocumented Mexicans returned home within twelve months of entry, but by 2000 the rate of return migration stood at just 25 percent. "If that is what is going on," Wayne Cornelius, a professor of political science at the University of California, San Diego, wrote in 2004, "it means that the U.S. border-centered immigration control strategy has been effective in bottling up illegal migrants within the United States, not necessarily in deterring them from coming in the first place."[20]

Can't we seal off the border?

In November 2005 DHS launched the Secure Border Initiative (SBI), claiming it would "secure America's borders and reduce illegal migration" by extending the existing fences to a total of 661 miles, about one-third of the southwestern border's 1,951 miles. The work was basically completed in February 2012.

The 651 miles of new fencing cost an average of $3.7 million a mile to build, suggesting that the expense of erecting similar fencing along the entire border would be about $7.4 billion. But this leaves out the money required for maintenance. An outside contractor estimated that the total cost of building and maintaining the current 651 miles of fence would be $6.5 billion over twenty years,— so the bill to tax-payers for a fence along the entire border for twenty years would be $19.5 billion.

Even this may be too low. The costs are expected to be much higher in rugged terrain or in areas where the government needs to buy more of the land; much of the current fencing is on land the government already owns. Moreover, the current fence isn't the sort of expensive double-wall barrier many politicians call for. Back in 1999 the U.S. Army Corps of Engineers estimated that maintaining a double-wall fence would cost from $16.4 million to $70 million per mile over a 25-year period, with $32.8 billion to $140 billion in maintenance alone for this type of fence along the entire border.[21]

That doesn't count the environmental costs. The current 651 miles of fencing puts at least fifty-six species of wildlife at risk, including at least four species already listed as threatened. Border Patrol vehicles tear up the desert, night lighting disturbs wildlife habitats, and every new wall or fence blocks animal migration while pushing human migrants farther into the most remote areas with the most fragile eco-systems. Another result is increased flooding in some border regions. One 5.2-mile stretch of fence in Arizona caused flooding in 2008 and 2011 that affected a restaurant, a post office, a shuttle company, and a duty-free store; a forty-foot section of the fence itself was knocked over in the 2011 flood.[22]

It would be even more expensive to attempt to close off the entire border by increasing the number of Border Patrol agents or using the military. In August 2011 then-CBP head Alan Bersin put the number of Border Patrol agents it would take to close off the border at 400,000 to 500,000. The U.S. public wouldn't accept the cost, he said. In fact, this would mean hiring at least twenty times the current number of agents, costing up to $16 billion or more per year.[23] Militarizing the border would presumably involve roughly the same number of soldiers. That would come to about one-third of the country's current active-duty forces, and more than twice the highest number of U.S. troops ever stationed in Iraq. The government estimates that it spends about $112,000 a year for each soldier, so deploying 400,000 of them to close the border would cost some $44.8 billion a year.[24]

In addition to pushing migrants onto more dangerous crossing routes, the militarization of the border can contribute to an us-versus-them combat mentality on the part of agents or soldiers, who see their role as protecting their country from an outside enemy. On-duty CBP agents killed at least forty-six people, including at least fifteen U.S. citizens, from 2004 to September 2014. Some of the victims were teenagers shot in the back while fleeing; some were shot while they were on the Mexican side of the border. CBP acting internal affairs chief Mark Alan Morgan told reporters in September 2014 that he didn't know of any agent who had been disciplined or terminated for any of these killings.[25]

The CBP commissioned the Police Executive Research Forum to conduct an independent review of sixty-seven shooting incidents that led to nineteen deaths between January 2010 and October 2012. In its February 2013 report, the Forum concluded that it was not clear whether the agency was "consistently and thoroughly" investigating such incidents. In an internal response, the CBP rejected the report's two main recommendations: that agents stop shooting at rock throwers when they can instead move out of range; and that they stop placing themselves in front of moving vehicles in order to justify the use of deadly force as self-defense.[26]

In a 2014 report, the American Immigration Council analyzed 809 formal complaints dating from January 2009 to January 2012, accusing Border Patrol agents of various abuses. Forty percent of the complaints were still "pending investigation." For the rest, the decisions took an average of 122 days—over four months—to reach, and in 97 percent of the cases, the result was "No Action Taken."[27]

Any deployment of military troops on the border would likely lead to more abuses, especially with such accountability issues unresolved. "When policing is done by soldiers, our communities become the enemy," said Pedro Rios of the American Friends Service Committee's San Diego office, citing the May 1997 killing of eighteen-year-old high school student Esequiel Hernandez, Jr.[28] Hernandez was tending his family's goats in Redford, Texas, when he was shot and killed by one of four U.S. Marines on a Joint Task Force 6 anti-drug mission. The Marines, who were wearing heavy camouflage and armed with M-16s, claimed self-defense. But Hernandez probably didn't even see them and certainly didn't realize they were soldiers when he fired in their general direction with an eighty-year-old, 22-caliber rifle, which he used for target practice. His death sparked an outcry, leading the Defense Department to suspend military missions on the border.[29]

Can we stop migrant smugglers?

The business of charging money to migrants to get them across borders without detection exists as a result of restrictive immigration and visa policies and harsh enforcement practices. When people have the option of entering a country through lawful means, they have no use for paid guides or smugglers. As border policies and practices become more restrictive, the process of crossing without permission gets riskier and more expensive for the migrant, and more lucrative for the smuggler. Enforcement measures that directly target smuggling operations and attempt to interrupt them, or target smugglers for arrest and prosecution, are not especially effective. The business is so profitable that when one smuggler is caught, another steps in, and when authorities manage to crack down on one method of getting people across the border, the smugglers find new methods.[30]

This can be seen clearly on the U.S.-Mexico border, where tightened enforcement appears to have increased the amount that migrants have to pay guides or smugglers to help them enter the United States. A number of studies have tracked this data; all show a marked increase in these costs from 1996 to 2005, after adjusting for inflation.[31] The average price for being smuggled through the San Diego area jumped from $300 to $2,500 between 1994 and 2005. Surveys of border crossers nationally indicate that average prices rose by 6.2 to 8.5 percent from 1993 to 2000. As of 2006, some 80 to 93 percent of border crossers used smugglers, at prices averaging between $1,400 and $2,100. The prices rose still higher even as Mexican migration slumped during the 2007–2009 recession, according to a report in the Los Angeles daily *La Opinión*. By the end of 2014, prices ranged from $3,000 to $20,000, depending on the mode of entry.[32]

Research concludes that the higher prices do discourage some migrants from trying to cross the border, even if the effect is minor. However, the higher cost may lead more undocumented immigrants to stay in the United States instead of crossing back and forth across the border, as many migrants used to do to stay connected with family. The higher prices may also attract larger and more ruthless criminal organizations to the smuggling business, squeezing out the smaller and more familiar operators who are based in the migrants' hometowns.[33] The report in *La Opinión* suggests that some of the smugglers whose income was reduced by the slowing of migration shifted their focus to other business practices, especially the kidnapping and ransoming of border crossers.[34]

The Organization for Economic Co-operation and Development (OECD) explains this phenomenon clearly: "If policy changes affect the profitability of the smuggling business, smugglers have three basic choices: (1) exit the market and refocus on other more profitable illicit activities, (2) increase prices, or (3) increase the number of people smuggled to maintain the same amount of profit. They may also shift routes and methods to maintain their profits."[35]

The rising cost of border crossing has another effect, which intersects with the shift in methods. "A spike in corruption incidents would be expected with a combination of new recruits and higher smuggling fees and so on," according to Brown University professor Peter Andreas, co-author of *Policing the Globe*, a 2006 book on international crime. "Smugglers have more resources to use for corruption, and they have a greater incentive to devote money for corruption."[36]

A 2012 study by the U.S. Government Accountability Office (GAO) found that "144 current or former CBP employees were arrested or indicted for corruption-related activities, such as the smuggling of aliens and drugs," from fiscal year 2005 through fiscal 2012, mostly along the border with Mexico. But this may understate the level of corruption: the GAO questioned whether the CBP had an adequate system to screen for corrupt officers and noted some "significant cultural resistance" to investigations.[37]

In 2006 James "Chip" Burrus, assistant director of the Criminal Investigative Division of the FBI, called the known corruption cases "the tip of the iceberg." "Nobody is seriously addressing corruption," complained Michael Maxwell, who resigned that year as head of internal affairs for the U.S. Citizenship and Immigration Services bureau of the Department of Homeland Security. "The corruption is pervasive," Maxwell said; 3,000 allegations of misconduct, including 100 reports of bribery, still hadn't been investigated when he left the agency.[38]

Can't we increase the penalties for border crossers?

While being in the United States without authorization is only a civil violation, crossing the border without authorization is a misdemeanor punishable by up to six months in prison. Reentering after deportation can result in a two-year sentence, or more if the migrant has committed other offenses.[39] But until 2005, the U.S. government rarely imposed criminal penalties on border crossers. Instead it used civil court procedures to deport them or, if they were Mexican, sometimes simply returned them to the Mexican side without a formal deportation process.

With politicians and others demanding stricter enforcement at the border, in 2005 George W. Bush's administration launched Operation Streamline. Under this program federal prosecutors bring criminal charges against a large number of border crossers each day. Most plead guilty in exchange for a reduced sentence; the average is thirty days for people who haven't been deported previously. Operation

Streamline started in Del Rio, Texas; by 2012 it had spread to six of the nine Border Patrol sectors on the border with Mexico. The number of convictions for unauthorized entry and reentry jumped from 27,694 in 2005 to 71,656 in 2011, and a total of 208,939 people had been processed by the end of September 2012.[40]

Operation Streamline is just one strategy in what the federal government calls its "Consequence Delivery System," a series of measures designed to impose enhanced penalties on migrants entering the United States without permission. It is not clear to what extent any of these policies are effective. Streamline's supporters claim it discourages migrants from trying to cross. According to the Border Patrol's data, only 10.3 percent of people convicted under the program in 2012 were caught crossing the border again in the same fiscal year, compared to 27.1 percent for those who were "voluntarily" repatriated after signing away their rights to a formal removal hearing. However, it is not clear whether those who were not caught again had given up on their migration plans, or had returned to the United States without detection that same year, or attempted return in the next fiscal year. A Congressional Research Service report suggests that the data used to measure repeat crossings is not conclusive, in part because it depends mainly on apprehensions to determine who is attempting entry.[41]

Surveys of migrants suggest that none of these efforts are likely to be very successful in preventing people from crossing. In a 2010 sampling, thirty-five deportees at a shelter in Nogales, Mexico, said they'd been convicted of border crossing; thirty of them said they would make another attempt, and only one gave fear of a longer jail sentence as the reason for not trying. A study by the University of California, San Diego, Center for Comparative Immigration Studies (CCIS) found that immigrants were much more concerned about "extreme climate," "border patrol," "gangs," and "not find(ing) work" than they were about "being incarcerated."[42]

"If [the prospect of] dying in the desert is not a deterrent, it's hard to imagine why spending no or little time in federal prison and being returned to your home country is a deterrent," University of Arizona law professor Marc Miller told National Public Radio in 2010; Miller specializes in criminal procedure and sentencing. Even some federal judges agree. James Stiven, a retired U.S. magistrate judge in California, said in 2010 that Operation Streamline had "no particular deterrent effect." Norbert Garney, a U.S. magistrate judge in El Paso, Texas, noted: "Ten to fourteen days [in jail] is a small price to pay for the opportunity to double, triple or even quadruple your income and start a better life for your family."[43]

Not all migrants arrested at the border are newcomers. Those with long-standing ties and family in the United States are especially unlikely to be deterred by harsher consequences for crossing illegally. According to the Migration Policy Institute, such consequences contribute "to an escalating criminalization of the unauthorized immigrant population, generating a growing class which may be ineligible for future immigration relief (because of multiple removals or criminal convictions) despite strong connections to the United States."[44]

Among a representative sample of nearly 2,000 migrants convicted of illegal reentry in 2013, the U.S. Sentencing Commission found that almost half had children in the United States, and more than two-thirds had other family members here. The study also found that 53 percent of those convicted of reentry had first entered the United States before the age of eighteen (the average age of entry was seventeen), and that nearly three-quarters had worked in the United States for more than a year at some time prior to being charged for reentry.[45]

What are the costs of Operation Streamline?

The government doesn't provide information about the costs of Operation Streamline, which are spread out over the Justice Department, the court system, and the federal prisons. These costs are certainly substantial.

The Justice Department had to hire more assistant U.S. attorneys because of the increased caseload for prosecutors, and federal courts must pay for defense lawyers for the migrants, usually at $125 an hour, since defendants in criminal cases are entitled to attorneys. The costs for defense attorneys in the Tucson, Arizona, court alone amounted to an estimated $2.4 million in fiscal 2011. The growing number of convictions also leads to increased expenses for the federal prison system. Grassroots Leadership, a nonprofit research and policy organization based in Charlotte, North Carolina, estimated that in 2011 the federal government spent over $1 billion a year to jail immigrants convicted of unauthorized entry or reentry, nearly double the $594 million spent in 2005.

"The expenses of prosecuting illegal entry and reentry cases (rather than deportation) on aliens without any significant criminal record [are] simply mind-boggling," Sam Sparks, a U.S. district judge wrote in a 2010 decision. "The policy presents a cost to the American taxpayer that is neither meritorious nor reasonable."[46] In 2011 immigration cases made up 36 percent of all federal criminal prosecutions, more than drug and fraud prosecutions combined. This was largely because of Streamline. Even with extra funding, the increase in immigration cases has strained courts and prosecutors' offices in the sectors near the border. Prosecutors and court workers describe the situation as "demoralizing" and say burnout is common.

All this takes resources away from prosecutions for serious crimes. In the border areas where Streamline is in effect, convictions for non-immigration felonies fell by an average 9.5 percent from the program's first year to 2009. Prosecutions for white-collar crime, weapons violations, organized crime, public corruption, and drug offenses have all declined in these areas. The rate of weapons prosecutions went down by 15 percent along the border from 2005 to 2009, and this was while drug-related violence in northern Mexico was leading to tens of thousands of killings there, often carried out using guns smuggled from the United States. "Are there public safety effects to making [immigration cases] the priorities over bank robbery?" Arizona law professor Miller asked in 2010. "Over white collar [crime], over fraud? Absolutely."[47]

What does Operation Streamline mean for our legal system?

Legal experts feel that programs like Streamline may violate constitutional rights. Migrants are brought before a magistrate judge in groups, usually shackled and in the same clothes they wore crossing the border and while held in detention. Most have only a few minutes to talk with a lawyer, and even with the aid of translators they are unlikely to understand their rights, the complexity of the U.S. legal system, or the possible consequences of a plea bargain. Delays in bringing the migrants to court may violate Fourth Amendment "probable cause" protections, and the brief meetings with defense attorneys may not meet the Sixth Amendment requirement for "assistance of counsel."

The courts have what are in effect daily quotas: the Del Rio court usually processes eighty migrants a day, for instance, while Tucson handles seventy among a much greater number of total apprehensions. This quota system results in arbitrary prosecutions. If you're caught crossing in the Del Rio sector, you're sure to go to court, but your odds of being prosecuted are less than 10 percent if you're caught in the much busier Tucson sector.

What sort of precedent is being set by these rushed mass trials, which even some of the judges describe as "assembly-line justice"? Fifth Circuit Court of Appeals judge Carolyn King has questioned whether we can "have a rule of law for the Southwest border that is different from the rule of law that obtains elsewhere in the country."[48]

Can't we cut off the "job magnet"?

Since unauthorized migrants come to the United States mainly to get work, many people argue that the best way to stop these migrants is to eliminate the "job magnet" that draws them here.

The "employer sanctions" included in the 1986 Immigration Reform and Control Act (IRCA) were supposed to make it harder for employers to hire unauthorized immigrants. The law set up a procedure under which employers must require each new person they hire to show documents demonstrating eligibility to work legally in the United States. As of 2008, employers who knowingly hire immigrants not authorized to work may face civil fines of $375 to $16,000 per employee. A pattern of knowingly employing undocumented workers can result in a criminal fine of $3,000 and up to six months in jail.[49]

But the sanctions policy came with a loophole: employers are required to check the documents of new hires, but they don't have to verify that those documents are valid or legitimate. So a major result of the policy has been a dramatic increase in the production and trade of false documents. When workers are found to have used false documents to get their jobs, it's the workers, not the employers, who are punished. In addition, enforcement of employer sanctions has been erratic. In 2000 a total of 312 employers were told to pay fines, adding up to $3.3 million, but by 2006 the number of fines had fallen to zero. The government then gradually went back to issuing fines; 495 employers were fined a total of $12.5 million in 2012.[50]

With undocumented immigration rising significantly since the 1986 law was passed, the government itself had to acknowledge that employer sanctions have been a failure. "The widespread availability of false documents made it easy for unauthorized aliens to obtain jobs in the United States," the GAO's Richard M. Stana told Congress in June 2006. "In addition . . . some employers knowingly hire unauthorized workers, often to exploit the workers' low-cost labor."[51]

How are employer sanctions enforced?

Immigration authorities have primarily enforced employer sanctions through workplace raids. These involve a scenario in which federal agents arrive at a job site and detain any workers who "look foreign" and who can't immediately prove they are authorized to be in the United States. These detentions are typically "administrative arrests"—that is, they don't involve criminal charges—but in recent years the government has increasingly prosecuted unauthorized workers in criminal court, especially if they are found to have used false documents to gain employment.

ICE administrative arrests in worksite operations jumped more than tenfold from 445 in 2003 to 5,184 in 2008, and criminal arrests went up from seventy-two to 1,103.[52] At the same time, the Bush administration stepped up a practice of sending "no match" letters to employers, notifying them that some employees' documents as listed on their I-9 (employment eligibility verification) forms didn't match Social Security or immigration records. This practice led to a kind of backdoor "silent raid" in which companies fired the workers rather than risk fines. In some cases, workers quit to avoid risking arrest by immigration agents.[53]

What both types of enforcement have in common is that the employers rarely face any serious consequences, while the workers are deported or, at best, are out of work. While the "silent raids" usually don't lead to deportation, they affect more workers and are harder to organize against. "It would be easier to fight if it was a big raid," Pramila Jayapal, executive director of the Seattle-based group OneAmerica, told the *New York Times*. "But this is happening everywhere and often."[54]

Another component of the "silent raids" is the use of E-Verify, a mostly voluntary option allowing employers to check a worker's documentation online by matching it against the Social Security Administration (SSA) and Department of Homeland Security databases via the internet. The government started E-Verify in 1997 as the "Basic Pilot Program"; the current name dates from 2007. President George W. Bush issued an executive order in 2008 requiring all federal contractors and subcontractors to use the program. More than 353,822 employers were enrolled in the program by January 2013.

Advocates of stricter enforcement want to make all of the country's 7.6 million employers enroll in E-Verify, which they claim can significantly reduce the number of undocumented immigrants. But the program has major flaws. In the early stages it regularly reported that foreign-born workers lacked work authorization when in fact their documents were in order. Improvements to the program reduced these errors, but some 20 percent of the rejections from the system are still mistakes; they affect about 1 percent of all the workers who are checked. And E-Verify isn't really very effective at catching immigrants without papers. An independent review by the Westat

Corporation found that E-Verify approved about 54 percent of the unauthorized workers being screened from April to June 2008.[55]

A Brief History of Immigration Raids

The U.S. government has carried out workplace raids off and on for decades, but the employer sanctions imposed in 1986 established a new basis for raids, making it illegal to hire immigrants who lacked work authorization from the federal government. The raids grew common in the mid- to late 1990s under the Clinton administration. In October 1998, grassroots immigrant rights groups carried out a nationwide campaign against the raids, drawing attention to their impact on families and the ways in which they violated civil and labor rights. A few months later, in March 1999, the immigration agency announced it would scale back the raids and focus on investigating "criminal aliens" and smugglers, and on discouraging employers from hiring unauthorized workers.[56]

In the wake of the September 11 attacks, the administration of George W. Bush revived the raids with a new premise: national security. The federal government started targeting airport workers in December 2001, then expanded the raids to other "critical infrastructure" facilities. At the same time, the agency was focused on deporting Muslim immigrants under the guise of fighting terrorism. Detention beds were filled with the targets of such crackdowns, and non-security-related enforcement took a back seat. In the post-9/11 climate of fear, the "critical infrastructure" raids mostly went unopposed. Activists in Chicago protested the arrests of workers at O'Hare Airport, but elsewhere in the country, there was little outcry. Many activists were busy responding to the crackdown on Muslim immigrants; others, especially in the labor movement, were trying to revive efforts, slowed by the terror attacks, to win legalization for unauthorized workers.[57]

In April 2006, as millions of immigrants were asserting their rights in a wave of unprecedented mobilizations, Immigration and Customs Enforcement (ICE) launched a new strategy: large, high-visibility worksite raids that culminated months-long investigations into hiring practices and brought mass arrests of workers. In the first of these raids, on April 19, 2006, ICE agents hit the pallet company IFCO Systems, arresting over 1,187 workers and seven managers in simultaneous operations at forty plants and related sites in twenty-seven states.

The scale of the operation, and the government's announcement that more such raids were being planned, set off a wave of fear in immigrant communities. At a news conference about the IFCO raid, Homeland Security Secretary Michael Chertoff announced: "Employers and workers alike should be on notice that the status quo has changed."[58]

On December 12, 2006, a thousand ICE agents arrested 1,282 immigrant workers in simultaneous raids at six meat processing plants in the Midwest owned by Swift & Co. Five of the six plants were unionized. More high-profile operations followed: 2007 and 2008 were particularly heavy years, with large raids at factories and especially at meat and poultry processing plants, and dozens of smaller raids targeting unauthorized immigrants at job sites, homes, on public transportation, and even at shopping malls.

As the raids grew more frequent and more visible, activists and community members responded with stepped-up protests, and advocates and lawyers worked to get legal and humanitarian assistance to those affected. These protests, and the visibility of the raids themselves, helped draw media attention to their human impact. Word spread about workers shackled on factory floors, breast-feeding mothers separated from their infants, and children returning from school to empty homes.[59]

One of the most dramatic raids—at the time, the largest at a single worksite—took place at the Agriprocessors kosher meatpacking plant in Postville, Iowa, on May 12, 2008. Hundreds of government agents surrounded the plant and arrested 389 workers, including eighteen children. Most of the arrested workers were from Guatemala. They were detained at a cattle association fairground converted into a temporary prison and courthouse, more than an hour's drive from the factory. Most were charged with crimes involving the use of false identity papers. In a process that resembled Operation Streamline, the shackled workers were moved in groups of ten along a line of judges, prosecutors, court-appointed defense lawyers, and interpreters, and pressed to accept plea bargains. A majority were deported after serving five months in prison.[60] The tactics used in the Postville raid caused outrage among labor and civil rights advocates, prompting a protest march in Postville in July that drew people from across the Midwest, and a congressional hearing in Washington that same month to determine if the workers' due process rights had been violated.[61] In a rare move, Agriprocessors plant manager Sholom Rubashkin was sentenced to twenty-seven years in prison, but on charges of financial fraud, not on immigration charges, which would have carried lesser penalties.[62]

An even larger raid took place in August 2008 at an electric transformer manufacturing facility in Laurel, Mississippi, where 595 workers were arrested.[63]

In November 2008, U.S. voters elected a new president, Barack Obama, whose campaign had generally promoted immigrant rights.[64] On April 30, 2009, Obama's 100th day in office, and the eve of the traditional May 1 mobilizations by and for immigrant workers, his administration announced "a revised worksite enforcement strategy," focusing on criminal prosecutions of egregious employers, and deemphasizing raids against workers.[65]

In practice, the new strategy relied largely on the "no-match" strategy of "silent raids." By the middle of 2010, the ICE agency had audited 2,900 companies in these operations and had imposed $3 million in fines. Administrative arrests fell to 1,224 that year, but thousands of workers lost their jobs.[66]

Has workplace enforcement worked?

If workplace enforcement is meant to keep undocumented immigrants from getting jobs, it's clearly a failure. There were over eight million undocumented immigrants working here in 2012, about eight out of every ten out-of-status adults; the rate had stayed about the same since 2000, despite the increase in worksite enforcement over that time.[67]

Workplace enforcement doesn't keep out-of-status immigrants from getting jobs, but it does succeed in pushing them into the underground economy, where they're less likely to be caught by E-Verify or "silent raids."

The government assumes that workplace enforcement has this effect. In 2008 the Congressional Budget Office (CBO) projected that expanding E-Verify would "decrease federal revenues by $17.3 billion over the 2009–2018 period" because of the loss of withholding tax income as large numbers of undocumented immigrants shifted to working off the books.[68] This may also explain why estimates of the number of the undocumented working on the books fell from 75 percent in 2005 to 44 percent in 2013, during a period when the government expanded E-Verify.[69]

Many businesses have avoided penalties by hiring their workers through subcontractors, so that the subcontractor rather than the employer is legally responsible if the workers are out of status. If one labor contractor gets shut down, another steps in and takes over the jobs—and the workers. "Employers in immigrant-heavy industries have shifted en masse to subcontracting in the wake of [the 1986 law]," Fordham Law School professor Jennifer Gordon testified before Congress in 2005. This practice is "now predominant in such industries as agriculture, janitorial, landscaping, and construction."[70]

One example is Walmart, the world's largest retailer. In 2003 federal agents raided sixty Walmart stores in twenty-one states and arrested 245 undocumented immigrants employed by cleaning contractors. U.S. law enforcement officials charged that top Walmart executives had known about the workers' immigration status, and the company ended up paying the U.S. government $11 million in fines in March 2005. But usually the larger companies get away with claiming ignorance; Walmart itself continues to use labor contractors for many of its jobs.[71]

Subcontracting "exerts downward pressure on wages in two ways," Professor Gordon testified. "Contracts are put out to bid, encouraging contractors to offer the lowest possible price, which translates directly into falling wages. In addition, subcontracting introduces a middleman who takes a cut of the contract, further lowering the wages that workers receive. And of course, once subcontracting becomes the standard arrangement in any industry, its impact on wages affects all workers, documented or not, in that industry."

"Far from protecting U.S. workers, then," Gordon concluded, "employer sanctions lower their wages and undercut their efforts to obtain jobs and improve working conditions."[72]

This effect was predicted: in November 1986, right after Congress passed employer sanctions, Mexican economist Rogelio Ramírez de la O warned that the United States would go on employing undocumented immigrants. "So the cost of this legislation is that for the illegal workers the salaries and working conditions will go down as the risk the employer takes becomes higher." It wasn't just economists who saw this. Gabriel Rocha García, a Mexican citizen waiting to cross into the United States, told the *New York Times*: "We will be hunted. The employers who are willing to hire us will take advantage of us. They will threaten to turn us in. They will want to pay us less because they will say they are taking a risk to give us jobs."[73]

Does workplace enforcement affect organizing?

Although there's no evidence that workplace enforcement stops people from coming here, there's plenty of reason to think that it intimidates immigrant workers and makes it harder for them to organize successfully for better pay and working conditions. Workers frequently report that employers threaten to turn them over to immigration authorities if they try to stand up for their rights. "Immigration law is a tool of the employers," Cristina Vasquez, a former garment worker who became a regional manager for the garment workers' union, UNITE, said in 1999. "They're able to use it as a weapon to keep workers unorganized, and the [immigration agency] has helped them."[74]

In December 2004 the Co-Op coal mine in Emery County, Utah, fired at least twenty-five workers allegedly because the SSA and U.S. Citizenship and Immigration Services (USCIS) had ordered an investigation of their Social Security numbers. The firings came a week before a scheduled union election; all of the suspended workers were supporters of the United Mine Workers of America (UMWA), according to UMWA organizer Bob Butero. "This company has accepted their Social Security numbers for years," Butero said. "Is it by coincidence that now that these workers want to exercise their rights in a union election, they suddenly want to confirm [the numbers]?"[75]

ICE's dramatic 2008 raid on the meatpacking plant in Postville came as the United Food and Commercial Workers (UFCW) was trying to organize workers there. The union's vice president, Mark Lauritsen, had written immigration authorities to warn that a raid on the plant could have a "chilling effect" on the workforce.[76]

The "silent raids" that the government has carried out since 2009 have thrown thousands of union members out of work, including janitors in the Service Employees International Union (SEIU) in Minneapolis, Seattle, and San Francisco. ICE "is going after employers that are union," Olga Miranda, the president of SEIU Local 87 in San Francisco, said in 2010. "They're going after employers that give benefits and are paying above the average."[77]

If we make life hard enough for immigrants, will they leave?

Some opponents of immigration argue for reducing the undocumented population through a strategy of attrition, by deporting as many out-of-status immigrants as possible while making life so difficult for the rest that they will be compelled to leave. A 2006 report from the Center for Immigration Studies (CIS) advocated a program to reduce unauthorized immigration through increased raids and removals, mandatory use of E-Verify, the tracking of people entering and exiting the United States on temporary visas, expanded use of state and local law officers to enforce immigration laws, and more state and local laws targeting immigrants.[78]

Various state and local governments had already begun applying this strategy. In 2002, the federal government began implementing a program known as "287(g)" that allows the Department of Homeland Security to deputize selected state and local law enforcement officers to perform the functions of federal immigration agents. Through agreements signed with the immigration agency, deputized local agents have access to federal immigration databases, may interrogate and arrest non-citizens believed to have violated federal immigration laws, and may lodge immigration "detainers" against alleged non-citizens held in state or local custody. Participation in this program grew explosively from the beginning of 2007, when only eight localities were signed up for it, to sixty-one at the end of 2008.[79]

Amid protests that the program encouraged racial profiling and violated civil liberties, the Obama administration started placing limits on the 287(g) program soon after taking office in 2009. At the same time, the administration began pushing instead for expansion of Secure Communities, a separate program introduced as a pilot in 2008 by the outgoing Bush administration. Under Secure Communities, local law enforcement officers were not allowed to make immigration arrests directly, but could cooperate with federal authorities to identify unauthorized immigrants in their custody for criminal offenses, and could then hold the suspects for immigration agents to detain.[80]

Meanwhile, state legislators wrote laws that, in the words of Alabama state representative Mickey Hammon, would "attack . . . every aspect of an illegal alien's life" and "make it difficult for them to live here so they will deport themselves." In April 2010 Arizona passed a law, SB 1070, that, among other provisions, required law enforcement officers to check the immigration status of anyone they encountered during lawful stops or arrests. Alabama, Georgia, Indiana, South Carolina, and Utah passed similar laws in 2011. The harshest was Alabama's HB 56, which made contracts invalid if one party was undocumented, and even required public schools to verify the immigration status of children registering to attend.[81] Spurred on by national anti-immigrant organizations, a number of towns and cities also passed local anti-immigrant ordinances, designed to make life harder for residents without legal status.[82]

These policies stirred up considerable opposition, from citizens as well as immigrants. Local police departments objected to enforcing immigration laws, partly because the extra duties strained their resources in a time of tight budgets, but also because they didn't want to discourage immigrants from reporting crimes or serving as witnesses.[83] Legal challenges to the new laws were costly for states and municipalities, and in the end federal courts threw out many of the clauses for violating anti-discrimination legislation or infringing on the federal government's control of immigration policy.[84]

Many native-born residents were upset to find their communities disrupted as friends and neighbors went underground or fled to other states. "I used to have a lot of Mexican clients who left, and I miss them," a barber told a researcher in Birmingham, Alabama, in October 2011. "I miss their money, and they're good people. As an African American, it broke my heart to see them have to go through what we had to go through."[85]

By 2012, the tide appeared to turn, with states and municipalities moving away from punitive anti-immigrant measures, and toward pro-immigrant measures such as opening up driver's licenses and in-state college tuition to undocumented immigrants.[86]

There's no evidence to suggest that the strategy of attrition would accomplish its stated goals. Some immigrants may return to their native countries if conditions there improve, as many young Irish immigrants did in the early 2000s when Ireland's economy suddenly boomed.[87] For many immigrants, no matter how bad things get here, the situation in their country of birth is still worse. Some who do go back find that the economic crisis has deepened in their absence, and the money they saved working here isn't enough, so they return to the United States and try again. Others will stay put even if the situation improves in their native country. They have made the United States their home for years, have friends and family here, and are integrated into local communities. In 2009 an estimated 85 percent of undocumented immigrants had been in the United States five years or more; 53 percent had been living here for at least ten years.[88]

What caused the drop in unauthorized immigration?

After growing for years, the number of undocumented immigrants in the United States began to decline sharply in 2007, falling from about 12.2 million to some 11.2 million in 2010.[89] Advocates of more enforcement were quick to credit their own policies for the reversal. Researchers from the Center for Immigration Studies wrote in 2008 that the decline "suggests it has been possible to cut the illegal population by inducing a large number to leave the country." At this rate the undocumented population could be "cut . . . in half within just five years," they claimed.[90]

There is no evidence to suggest that heightened enforcement was responsible for the drop in the undocumented population. After all, the government steadily intensified enforcement of immigration laws starting in the early 1990s, but the number of unauthorized immigrants kept on increasing right up to 2007.[91]

A more important factor was undoubtedly the change in job prospects. Apprehensions of border crossers began to decline significantly in 2007 just as the U.S. housing bubble started to burst and home construction, a major source of jobs for many undocumented immigrants, was falling dramatically. Unauthorized immigration continued to shrink with the official start of a recession in December 2007 and with a global financial crisis in September 2008. A graph from the organization Grassroots Leadership shows that since at least 1994, border apprehensions have tended to rise as the employment rate improved in the United States and fall as jobs become scarcer, as happened in the recessions of 2001 and 2007–2009.[92]

The huge enforcement buildup over the past twenty-five years seems not to have had much effect on how foreigners think about immigrating here. According to studies that the University of California San

Diego's Center for Comparative Immigration Studies (CCIS) has done in southern Mexico, people there are aware of the harsher enforcement measures at the border, but this apparently isn't an important influence on whether they decide to leave for the North.[93] And stricter enforcement inside the United States, even when combined with a major recession, doesn't seem to make immigrants "self-deport" after they've settled here: two studies, one by the Pew Hispanic Center and one by the RAND Corporation, indicate that Mexicans were slightly less likely to return to Mexico in the 2007–2009 period than they were before 2006.[94]

How much does enforcement cost us?

In 2013 the nonprofit Migration Policy Institute reported that the Homeland Security Department's main immigration enforcement programs were costing more than $17.9 billion a year. This was almost fifteen times what the government spent on immigration enforcement in 1986, and 24 percent more than the $14.1 billion cost of all other federal law enforcement programs combined—the Federal Bureau of Investigation (FBI), the Drug Enforcement Administration (DEA), the Secret Service, and the Bureau of Alcohol, Tobacco, Firearms, and Explosives (ATF). The total cost of immigration enforcement since 1986 came to an estimated $219.1 billion,[95] and this doesn't include state and local costs, such as the extra budget that police departments might need for the 287(g) program or the enforcement of state immigration laws.

The costs haven't stopped growing. For fiscal year 2015 the government requested $13.1 billion for CBP and $5.4 billion for ICE, a total of $18.5 billion for the two agencies.[96]

By comparison, the Department of Labor's 2015 budget request was $266 million for the Wage and Hour Division (WHD), which is supposed to enforce federal labor laws for some 135 million workers; it employs a total of 1,035 investigators. The Occupational Safety and Health Administration (OSHA) requested $565 million for about 2,200 inspectors to monitor workplace safety for some 114 million workers.[97] The government's Bureau of Labor Statistics reports that 4,405 people died in work-related injuries in 2013 and more than three million people were injured or sickened at work—and yet we spend thirty-three times as much on immigration enforcement as we do on workplace safety.[98]

Who profits from enforcement?

Employers profit indirectly from enforcement because it helps them to exploit workers and keep them from organizing. But immigration enforcement has also been a huge cash cow for many corporations.

In 2003 L-3 Communications took over a contract worth $429 million to set up a border surveillance system. In May 2004, the Accenture company and its partners won a $10 billion contract to set up "US VISIT," an entry-exit tracking system for people visiting the United States.[99] In September 2006, the aerospace and military company Boeing won a contract worth an estimated $2.5 billion to set up the "Secure Border Initiative Network" (SBInet), a web of new surveillance technology and sensors with real-time communications systems for the CBP.[100] After spending $1 billion on this "virtual fence," the government scrapped the project in January 2011, saying it "does not meet current standards for viability and cost effectiveness."[101] Private corporations make huge profits detaining immigrants for the federal government. Such profitable contracts give large, powerful companies a strong financial incentive to lobby Congress for expanded enforcement.[102]

10. What About Amnesty and "Guest Worker" Programs?

IF IMMIGRATION ENFORCEMENT IS HARMFUL to all workers, as discussed in chapter 9, then what is the solution? Providing amnesty—a path to citizenship for undocumented immigrants—would probably boost the economy and raise wages for everyone, at least temporarily, but unless we make ongoing changes to the immigration system, we would soon end up with a new underclass of exploited workers without papers.

Employers benefit from keeping wages down, so most aren't interested in seeing immigrants win rights. Some employers favor the status quo: just enough enforcement to keep workers from organizing, but not so much as to hurt business. Others prefer a legal alternative: "guest worker" programs, which bring people here from other countries for specific temporary or seasonal jobs, and require them to return home when the job is done. Critics argue that these guest worker programs are "inherently abusive and unfair" and "close to slavery," in the words of the Southern Poverty Law Center.[1]

Such conditions are tolerable only when compared to the dangers of crossing the border and working without permission. Forced to choose between guest worker status and the threat of enforcement, and denied any option for legalization, migrants are often exploited. Despite their vulnerability, many organize and fight back against abuse.

What do we mean by "amnesty"?

An immigration amnesty generally refers to a process allowing unauthorized immigrants—people who entered the United States without permission or overstayed their visas—to apply for legal status. Some rights advocates prefer other terms, such as "legalization" or "regularization," for programs granting legal immigration status. "Amnesty," from the classical Greek for "forgetting," often means a pardon granted to someone who has committed some kind of infraction. This could imply that out-of-status immigrants have done something wrong.

The word *legalization* has also been questioned by advocates who feel it suggests that the immigrants themselves are somehow "illegal." In any case, amnesty—*amnistía* in Spanish—has been a rallying cry for immigrant communities for about two decades, along with a common chant at immigrant marches: "*Aquí estamos, y no nos vamos, y si nos echan, nos regresamos*" (We are here, and we're not leaving, and if they throw us out, we'll come back).[2]

Haven't we already had an amnesty?

The United States first started granting amnesties in 1929 with a legal provision known as "registry." This offered a way to get legal permanent residence for immigrants who had lived continuously in the country since before the middle of 1921 but hadn't yet acquired legal status. People who had committed serious crimes were excluded. Registry was initially a response to 1921 and 1924 laws that drastically restricted legal immigration from Eastern and Southern Europe, leaving a number of immigrants from Europe without status.

Congress moved up the "registry date" several times over the years. The most recent change, included in the 1986 immigration reform known as IRCA, brought the date to January 1, 1972. Tens of thousands of people gained status though registry over the years; for example, about 60,000 benefited from registry between 1985 and 2001. The reason for continuing to advance the registry date, according to a 1938 report from the administration of President Franklin Roosevelt, was that "it is not in the best interests of the United States that there should be a considerable number of aliens here who have resided in this country for many years and who are otherwise eligible for naturalization and anxious to become citizens, but who are prevented from doing so" because they lack legal status.[3]

In addition to moving up the registry cutoff date, IRCA included two important new amnesty provisions:

- A legalization process for immigrants who could prove they had been continuously present in the United States since at least 1982.
- A Special Agricultural Worker program legalizing migrants who had done at least ninety days of farm labor between May 1985 and May 1986.

These provisions were different from registry: they covered recent arrivals, and all but the agricultural workers and elderly applicants had to establish some knowledge of the English language and U.S. history to qualify.[4] But the main difference from registry was the sheer number of people: about 1.7 million immigrants were able to gain permanent residency because they'd been present since 1982, and about 1.2 million others legalized their status through the "Special Agricultural Worker" program.[5]

Another major difference was the immigrants' countries of origin. Most of the applicants came from Latin America and the Caribbean, not Europe. This was partly because of an increase in immigration from the Americas, but it was also because of new restrictions on settling here. Before 1965 any number of people could immigrate legally from most Western Hemisphere countries, but a major immigration reform that year set an annual limit—initially 120,000—for the entire hemisphere.[6]

Unlike registry, the 1986 amnesty was politically controversial. In one of the usual legislative trade-offs, amnesty was packaged with stepped-up enforcement measures, including the "employer sanctions" that required workers to provide proof of legal status to get a job. President Ronald Reagan presented the 1986 law as a measure *against* unauthorized immigration, saying it "takes a major step toward meeting this challenge to our sovereignty."[7]

Before 1986, registry dates were moved up an average of every fourteen years, providing a way for out-of-status immigrants to gain legal residence for much of the twentieth century. Thirty years after the 1986 amnesty, many immigrants have lived and worked in the United States for more than a generation without any options at all to legalize their status. This includes thousands of people who arrived here as children, and know no other country than the United States.

Do other countries give amnesties?

Immigrant amnesties aren't limited to the United States. In February 2005, Spain granted amnesty to immigrants who had been in the country at least six months, were employed, and had a clean record.[8] Some 550,000 people were legalized through the program in 2005.[9] Even before the amnesty, immigrants in Spain had options to gain legal status through family ties, employer sponsorship, or proof they had lived there for at least five years; in 2003 nearly 236,000 immigrants legalized their status this way.[10] Italy has had several amnesties for immigrants, although the number of people applying has always exceeded the number of residency permits available. In March 2006, more than 500,000 people lined up for just 180,000 permits.[11] Overall, between 1996 and 2011, more than five million migrants gained some form of regularized status through a range of programs in different European countries. However, as in the United States, regularization has slowed in Europe as it has grown politically unpopular over recent years.[12]

Brazil enacted an amnesty in July 2009, granting temporary legal status and a pathway to permanent residence within two years to people who had entered the country illegally or overstayed their visas before February 1 of that year. An estimated 43,000 people took advantage of the measure. Brazil also had amnesties in 1988 and 1998; some 60,000 people benefited from the 1998 program.[13]

What impact would amnesty have in the United States now?

An amnesty would obviously bring many benefits to out-of-status immigrants, allowing them to travel abroad to visit family and friends, avoid exploitation on the job, and get driver's licenses more easily. No longer trapped in a cash economy, they would be less vulnerable to muggings and feel safer reporting to police when they were victimized. Permanent legal residency opens up options for immigrants to achieve greater economic integration and mobility, including buying homes and investing in their families and communities.[14]

An amnesty would likely also benefit the entire U.S. population. There are millions of citizens who have friends, co-workers, and relatives among the undocumented. In 2011 researchers at Pew Hispanic estimated that 16.6 million people were living in families with at least one unauthorized immigrant.[15]

Employers would have less excuse to pay workers "under the table" and cheat on taxes. Unions and workers' organizations would have greater success with campaigns that raise wages and improve labor conditions for everyone. The trade in false documents would drop off. Law enforcement agencies could stop wasting resources on the targeting of out-of-status immigrants. The travel industry would get a boost, since thousands of people who have been stuck here for years without status would finally be able to travel freely, within the United States and abroad.[16]

Won't amnesty cause more problems later on?

Opponents of amnesty regularly say the 1986 amnesty caused the increase in immigration during the 1990s and early 2000s. "Demographers trace the doubling of the number of Mexican immigrants since 1990 in part to the amnesty of the 1980s," the *New York Times* wrote in 2000. "Amnesties signal foreign workers that American citizenship can be had by sneaking across the border, or staying beyond the term of one's visa, and hiding out until Congress passes the next amnesty."

The editorial didn't cite any sources. Actual demographic studies indicate that the legalization's only effect was a short-term rise in unlawful entries into the United States in the late 1980s followed by a similar short-term drop in the early 1990s. In any case, the rise in immigration actually started well *before* the 1986 amnesty, as internal conflicts were heating up in Central America and economic conditions were deteriorating in Mexico. Census data indicates that the number of out-of-status immigrants in the United States almost doubled from about 1.1 million in 1974 to 2.1 million in 1983.[17]

But legalization is not a complete solution. Since an amnesty is generally a one-time reprieve for immigrants already here, its impact is short-lived; within a few years, more immigrants have arrived and a new underclass of out-of-status people is created. This happened with the IRCA amnesty in 1986. And when an amnesty comes packaged with stricter enforcement measures—as IRCA was, and as we see in most proposals for what policymakers and advocates call "comprehensive immigration reform"—the potential positive impact of legalization is especially likely to be outweighed by new problems.

Is "Deferred Action" an amnesty program?

In June 2012 President Barack Obama issued an executive order granting "Deferred Action for Childhood Arrivals" (DACA) to undocumented young people who arrived in the United States before their sixteenth birthdays. The move came after a decade of unsuccessful campaigning for the DREAM Act (Development, Relief, and Education for Alien Minors), which would have provided undocumented youth with a path to citizenship. DACA provides no such path, but allows beneficiaries to avoid deportation and obtain a work permit for a renewable two-year period. The applicant must have been under the age of thirty-one on June 15, 2012; have lived here continuously since at least June 15, 2007; and be in school, have graduated high school, or have served in the military.[18]

In November 2014 President Obama announced a broad expansion of DACA to include people over thirty-one and those who had lived in the United States since January 1, 2010, and a similar reprieve for undocumented parents of U.S. citizens or lawful permanent resident children, called Deferred Action for Parental Accountability, or DAPA. These expanded policies remained blocked by court challenges as of December 2016.

According to various estimates, some 1.2 million people were eligible for the original DACA program, although as of March 31, 2015, only 665,000 people had their petitions approved. Another 300,000 would be eligible for the expanded DACA, and 3.7 million would benefit from DAPA. This would add up to 5.2 million, a little less than half the estimated 11.7 million undocumented immigrants in the United States in 2012.

These executive orders would benefit millions of people, but they wouldn't be amnesties. An actual amnesty would be permanent and would have to be authorized by Congress. Deferred action is simply a directive from the president for immigration officials to exercise "prosecutorial discretion" by not deporting certain people. This is a long-established practice in both criminal and immigration law where the government chooses not to proceed with a case, often because of attenuating circumstances. The president can decide to extend the policies after the three-year limit, but can also simply end them, putting the beneficiaries back in an "illegal" state, where they are subject to arrest, detention, and deportation.[19]

In any case, a growing number of people are left out of amnesty and deferred action programs, including those who have returned after being deported or have been convicted of immigration offenses or other kinds of crimes.

Can migrants come here legally as guest workers?

There are some limited opportunities for people from other countries to come to the United States for temporary jobs. As of 2016, there are four main programs bringing these "guest workers" into the United States, usually referred to by the type of visa the government issues:

H-1B "specialty occupation" visas are for certain skilled workers with college degrees, mostly computer specialists. The visas are good for three years and can be renewed once. Unlike other temporary workers, H-1B visa holders can be sponsored for permanent residence (a "green card"). There is an annual cap on how many new H-1B visas can be granted: in 2015 the cap was 65,000, plus 20,000 more for people with advanced degrees from U.S. institutions. The demand is such that the limit is reached months in advance. There's also an H-4 visa that lets the members of an H-1B worker's immediate family stay in the United States without working themselves; these visas don't have a cap. (A visa for registered nurses, H-1C, was discontinued in 2009.)

H-2A visas are for seasonal agricultural workers. The visas are generally for one year or less and can be renewed three times. There is no annual cap.

H-2B visas are for other "lower-skilled" seasonal workers. They are valid for one year or less and can be renewed three times. The annual cap was 66,000 in 2015. As of 2012 the top three occupations for H-2B visa holders were landscape laborer, forest worker, and amusement park worker.

The J-1 visa was originally meant to promote cultural exchange with people from other countries. Administered by the State Department, these visas permit temporary work for fourteen categories of visitors, including professors, college students, camp counselors, and au pairs. Two categories that bring college students from abroad to the United States to work "have been particularly susceptible to exploitation," according to the Southern Poverty Law Center: the J-1 Summer Work Travel Program (SWT) and the J-1 Trainee and Intern Program. There is no annual cap on the two programs, but the State Department froze participation at the 2011 level—about 130,000—following news reports about abuses.

Employers petition the government to bring in temporary workers through the H-1 and H-2 programs. The employers are supposed to certify that they can't find enough U.S. residents to do the work, that they'll pay the prevailing wage for their areas, and that they don't have any ongoing labor disputes involving strikes or lockouts—in other words, that they aren't importing strikebreakers. None of these regulations apply to the J-1 program.

More than 300,000 temporary workers and family members are in the United States at any given time. For example, in 2012 H-1B visas were issued for 135,991 specialty workers, H-2A visas for 65,345 agricultural workers, H-2B visas for 50,009 other "lower-skilled" workers, and H-4 visas for 80,015 family members. Even though there's no cap on agricultural workers, only an estimated 10 percent of hired farm workers came in through the program that year; unauthorized immigrants made up about 55 percent of the hired agricultural workforce. The J-1 programs together bring some 130,000 people into the country each year, more than the two H-2 visa programs combined.[20]

How did we end up with these programs?

The Immigration Act passed in February of 1917 continued an existing bar on immigrants from Asia, but allowed in anyone from the Western Hemisphere who could pay a per-person "head tax" and pass a literacy test. The law also sought to ban the recruitment of foreign workers by denying admission to "persons . . . who have been induced . . . to migrate to this country by offers or promises of employment." In May 1917, one month after the United States officially entered the First World War, industry complaints about a farm labor shortage led the U.S. Department of Labor to set up a temporary worker program for Mexicans that suspended the head tax, the literacy test, and the bar on contract labor, allowing them to enter the United States "for the purpose of accepting employment in agricultural pursuits." The program was later expanded to allow some non-agricultural work. Between 1917 and 1921, as many as 81,000 Mexican workers were admitted to the United States under this program.[21]

Temporary worker programs resumed when the Second World War prompted new complaints about a labor shortage. In July 1942, the Mexican and U.S. governments signed an agreement to recruit temporary field workers from Mexico to work in the United States. These workers became known as *braceros*—manual laborers, from the Spanish word for arms, *brazos*. The Mexican Labor Program, better known as the "*bracero* program," grew quickly, from 4,203 workers in 1942 to 201,380 in 1953.[22] Most of the *braceros* worked in agriculture or on the railroads.

Under pressure from the agricultural lobby, this arrangement with Mexico was extended several times until 1964. Under a similar deal starting in 1943, sugar companies in Florida brought in workers from the Caribbean colonies then known as the British West Indies. That agreement ended in 1947, but the Caribbean workers kept coming under international contracts allowed by the provisions of the 1917 Immigration Act.[23]

In 1952, the Immigration and Nationality Act established the H-1 and H-2 visa categories, setting new rules for the continuing admission of temporary laborers. The H-2 category was largely a continuation of the British West Indies program; in 1986, the Immigration Reform and Control Act (IRCA) expanded it, creating the H-2A subcategory specifically for agricultural workers and the H-2B subcategory for workers in other lower-skilled industries. The law was amended in 1990 to split H-1 up into subcategories, principally H-1B. The J-1 program was authorized by the Fulbright–Hays Act of 1961, and amended later.[24]

SLAVERY IN THE CANE FIELDS

In Florida's sugarcane fields, guest worker programs got their start in the early 1940s after African American cane-cutters fought back against slavery conditions on the sugar plantations. In the 1990 documentary *H-2 Worker*, filmmaker Stephanie Black interviewed one of these workers, an African-American man named Samuel who started cutting cane in 1941, working

out of the Bare Beach labor camp in Clewiston, Florida. Samuel described brutal conditions at the camp: "They'd wake us up around two or three o'clock. They had a shack-rouser . . . [and] if you didn't get up when the shack-rouser roused you . . . he'd come 'round with a cane knife and a blackjack, beating you out [of] bed, and as you run out the door there was one with a rifle making you get back in line. And you were guarded. I found that it was almost the same as a prison."

The workers were not allowed to leave, but Samuel decided to try. "On Christmas Day in 1941, I took a walk from the camp," he remembered. "I walked past them with the rifles, and hit the railroad tracks." Samuel walked more than sixteen miles to South Bay, where he reported the abuses at the labor camp. "And I finally got them to come in at night, and they caught these five camps with human beings locked up to the beds at night, and they found some of them were bruised and beat up."

In 1942, the U.S. Sugar Corporation was indicted for conspiracy to enslave African-American workers. The next year, the sugar companies started using guest worker programs to bring in cane cutters from the British West Indies.[25]

What happened to the Mexican braceros?

Temporary workers from Mexico were actively recruited to work in the United States between 1917 and 1923, but after the Great Depression hit in 1929, Mexican workers suddenly made a convenient scapegoat. Arguing that the Mexicans were taking scarce jobs away from desperate U.S. workers, state and local authorities and the federal government launched a campaign against people of Mexican descent. Laws were passed barring the hiring of "aliens," and employers were urged not to hire anyone suspected of being Mexican. Businesses, local authorities, and even voluntary agencies sometimes bought train tickets to Mexico for entire families, and instructed them to leave. As many as one to two million people of Mexican descent were deported or forced out of the United States between 1929 and

1944. Sixty percent of them were U.S. citizens, including many U.S.-born children of Mexican immigrants.[26]

In July 2003, the Mexican American Legal Defense and Education Fund (MALDEF) filed a lawsuit on behalf of Emilia Castañeda, who was born in Los Angeles in 1926 and forced to leave with her family when she was nine years old. The lawsuit sought class action status to include other survivors of the sweeps. The state of California, the county of Los Angeles, the city of Los Angeles, and the Los Angeles Chamber of Commerce were named in the suit "because those entities were involved in a concerted effort to deport large numbers of Mexicans and also to create an atmosphere of fear," explained MALDEF lawyer Steve Reyes. The lawsuit was ultimately unable to proceed because the California state legislature failed to extend the statute of limitations in the case, but the legislature did approve a formal apology in 2005 for the state's role in the unconstitutional forced removals. In 2012, a plaque was installed at the Plaza de Cultura y Artes in Los Angeles to honor those displaced.[27]

In 1954, twelve years into the *bracero* program, the U.S. government again began targeting Mexicans, launching a massive deportation program officially named Operation Wetback. Starting in Texas in mid-July 1954, the crackdown targeted not only unauthorized Mexican workers but people of Mexican descent in general, including many U.S. citizens. Agents swarmed through Mexican-American neighborhoods, stopping anyone on the street who "looked Mexican" and asking them for identification.

The operation trailed off after a few months as funding began to run out, and public outrage over civil rights violations sparked opposition in Mexico and the United States. No one really knows how many people were deported, though the immigration agency claimed as many as 1.3 million people were either deported or returned "voluntarily" to Mexico because they feared being picked up in the sweeps.[28]

The *bracero* program continued to grow throughout the crackdown, under pressure from the agricultural industry in the southwestern U.S. states. The number of workers logged as going through the program rose from more than 300,000 in 1954 to over 400,000 each year from 1956 to 1959. The numbers started to drop in 1960, as Mexican-American civil rights activists and farm labor organizers including César Chávez pressured Congress to cancel the program, which was hurting efforts to organize for better conditions in the fields. The program officially ended in 1964.[29]

From 1942 to 1949, 10 percent of *braceros*' wages were held in trust, allegedly to be deposited in savings accounts and reclaimed, with interest, when the workers returned to Mexico. The funds, totaling an estimated $60 million, were to be transferred by Wells Fargo Bank to banks in Mexico, but somewhere along the way the money vanished, and the workers never got their pay. Sixty years later and after repeated protests, *braceros* or their survivors finally obtained an agreement from the Mexican government to pay back at least part of the money owed to them.[30]

Cecilio Santillana, a former *bracero* who picked beets, cherries, and cotton, and shoveled manure on farms across the United States in the 1940s and 1950s, told the *San Francisco Chronicle* in 2006 why he opposed an effort to expand temporary worker programs. "I'm against it, because they may do to the new workers what they did to us," he said. "We suffered a lot."[31]

How are guest workers treated now?

The H-1 and H-2 guest worker programs include provisions for protecting labor rights, but as the Southern Poverty Law Center notes, these "exist mainly on paper. Government enforcement of guest worker rights is historically very weak."[32]

Workers who come to the United States with H-2 guest worker visas are generally signed up in their home countries by labor recruiters who make travel and visa arrangements. H-2B workers in particular are often charged exorbitant fees for visas, transportation, and other costs, and many begin their employment indebted to recruiters, contractors, or employers. If the workers leave their jobs or get fired, they lose their visa status. Sometimes employers hold on to the workers' passports and other documents to keep them from leaving.[33]

In the H-2A program for agricultural workers, employers must provide workers with free housing, but the living quarters are often lacking in sanitation services, overcrowded, and otherwise inadequate. Employers are required to reimburse travel costs to the job site for H-2A workers who complete at least half the agreed-upon period of employment, and round-trip travel costs for workers who complete the full job period. Employers don't always comply with these rules. (The H-2B program doesn't actually require employers to provide housing or reimburse travel costs, although under Department of Labor regulations they are supposed to do so.)

H-2A workers are supposed to be paid according to a federally mandated state-by-state pay scale, known as the "adverse effect wage rate," which the Department of Labor sets above the local minimum wage to avoid depressing local pay. Payment for H-2B workers is according to a "prevailing wage," which is often just the local minimum wage. But employers routinely violate wage and overtime requirements, and workers are often cheated out of the pay they're promised.[34]

In the film *H-2 Worker*, a timekeeper in the Florida sugarcane fields confessed that the bosses made him illegally alter documents to reflect fewer hours than the H-2 guest workers had actually labored. "It's very painful to know that a man is up there working all day, and only makes 16, or 18, or 21 dollars, and when his day is completed and he goes to his place of rest, he only go with three hours on his ticket. That's cruel." These abuses continue. Employers using the H-2A program "frequently violate the law," Bruce Goldstein, executive director of the Farmworker Justice Fund in Washington, told a reporter in 2006. And "H-2B workers often face an even worse situation with regard to wages than H-2A workers," according to the Southern Poverty Law Center.[35]

If workers want to keep their jobs, and want a chance at getting hired for the program again in the future, they stay quiet and put up with such abuses.[36] "Employers have tremendous bargaining power over workers who are too fearful to challenge unfair or illegal conduct," Goldstein said.[37]

Conditions are no better in the J-1 programs, which mostly lack even the minimal protections that are routinely ignored in the H-2 programs. Adding to the problem, the programs' State Department administrators have little experience in labor issues. College students in other countries pay hefty fees to recruiters—often thousands of dollars—and generally end up working long hours at U.S. hotels, restaurants, ski resorts, fast-food chains, farms, amusement parks, and even in the national park system, employed by private concessionaires.[38] Many receive no more than minimum wage, and have to pay rent to their employers for substandard housing. The students with trainee visas are supposed to receive skilled jobs in their areas of expertise, but some find themselves in the same low-end jobs as those in the Summer Work Travel program.

In February 2012 the State Department's own Office of the Inspector General (OIG) noted critics' charges that the J-1 programs are "little more than expeditious vehicles for importing low- or no-cost labor into the United States." The OIG investigators said they "question[ed] the appropriateness of allowing what are essentially work programs to masquerade as cultural exchange activities."[39]

What happens when "guest workers" defend their rights?

Temporary workers are commonly told that if they speak to legal aid attorneys, union organizers, reporters, or priests about their employment, they'll be fired, deported, and blacklisted.[40] "Usually when [a guest worker] is seen talking to someone like me they're on a plane home the next day," United Farm Workers (UFW) organizer Eric Nicholson said in 2006.[41] In the film *H-2 Worker*, sugar farm supervisor Dale Kelly explained how he dealt with cane cutters from Jamaica who protested or complained about abuses: "If we get some bad people, we just submit their names to the Jamaican government that we don't want them back, and they won't come back."

In November 1986, at least one hundred sugarcane cutters at the Okeelanta Corporation in Florida stopped working to protest that the company was paying too little per row of cane and was falsifying their hours. The workers refused to go back to the fields until the hourly wage promised to them in the contract was honored. The company responded by bringing in Palm Beach County riot police agents with attack dogs and forcibly shipping the entire crew of H-2 workers—not only those who protested—back to Jamaica.[42] "People were running about, and when I look at the door, it was a policeman with a dog and a gun, ordering us to get out," one of the Okeelanta workers explained in the film *H-2 Worker.* "After I get out through the door, I seen another one with a gun holding me, ordering me to get on the bus." Another worker explained, "Now they send 350 men home without time to gather their clothes or possessions. Within a week's time the men were replaced with 350 other workers sent from the islands."[43]

Despite these adverse conditions, sometimes guest workers have been able to fight back, win back pay, and expose the abuses in the programs. Starting in 2006 the Signal International marine oil rig company used the H-2B program to bring some five hundred skilled metal workers from India to repair offshore oil rigs damaged by Hurricane Katrina. The workers each paid from $10,000 to $20,000 to recruiters, who told them the temporary jobs would lead to permanent residency. Instead the workers found themselves living in substandard housing, underpaid, and subjected to racial discrimination; the green cards they were promised turned out to be a fiction. When the workers got together to protest, Signal managers tried to deport several of the leaders. Acting on advice from officials from Immigration and Customs Enforcement (ICE), the managers attempted to bus several of the workers directly to an airport from the company's Pascagoula, Mississippi, shipyard; the attempt was blocked by immigrant rights activists at the gates.

About two hundred of the workers filed at least eleven separate lawsuits against Signal International and the recruiters in U.S. federal courts, and the U.S. Equal Employment Opportunity Commission (EEOC) also sued Signal for discriminating against the workers based on race and national origin, since the Indian workers were subjected to worse conditions than the company's other workers. In July 2015 Signal reached a $20 million settlement covering all the claims, but the company filed for bankruptcy the same day, requiring the settlement amount to be renegotiated in bankruptcy court. In December 2015 the final settlement amount was awarded: $5 million distributed among 476 workers, an average of just over $10,500 per worker.[44]

In August 2011, more than three hundred foreign students in the J-1 Summer Work Travel program went on strike to protest a series of labor abuses at a plant in Pennsylvania where they worked for contractors packing Hershey's chocolate products. The National Guestworkers Alliance, an activist organization that emerged out of the struggle of the Signal workers, supported the strikers. Local union leaders got involved too, charging that Hershey's was using the J-1 program through subcontractors to replace higher-paid union members. The resulting media attention led companies in the Hershey's supply chain to make a settlement with the U.S. Department of Labor that required them to pay $213,000 in unpaid wages and $143,000 for health and safety infractions.[45]

The publicity forced the State Department to announce changes to the J-1 program, but problems have continued. In March 2013 fourteen J-1 workers walked off the job at three locations operated by a McDonald's franchise in the Harrisburg, Pennsylvania, area. After a Labor Department investigation, the franchise agreed in February 2014 to pay $205,977 in back wages and damages to 291 employees, including 178 J-1 workers. "McDonald's is just the latest in a long line of corporations that have hijacked the U.S. guest worker program to get cheap, exploitable labor," National Guestworkers Alliance executive director Saket Soni told *The Nation* magazine.[46]

Do guest worker programs hurt U.S. workers?

Employers often claim they need temporary worker programs because shortages of U.S.-based workers are hurting certain industries, especially farming. H-1 and H-2 employers are supposed to make sure that no U.S. residents will do the work before they can bring in guest workers, but enforcement is lax. Employers have found many ways to get around the H-1 and H-2 requirements, and the J-1 program doesn't even have such safeguards. "There are plenty of people who will do the job if you pay them enough," José Oliva, director of the National Network of Workers Centers for the National Interfaith Committee for Worker Justice, told a reporter in 2007. "The pretension that there aren't enough workers here and you have to go and import them is just a way of expanding this slave labor program rather than paying decent wages."[47]

Some companies actually increased their use of guest worker programs as U.S. unemployment rates soared after the 2008 financial crisis. Walmart, the giant retail firm, applied to bring in seventy-nine H-1B technical workers in 2007; in 2014 the company was applying for 513 workers, more than six times as many. The total number of Walmart's H-1B applications over the eight years was 1,800, according to an April 2014 report by the AFL-CIO, though this is just part of the story. Walmart outsources much of its technical work to consulting firms. From 2007 to 2014 consulting firms filed a total of 14,844 H-1B applications for work in Bentonville, Arkansas, where Walmart has its corporate headquarters. According to the AFL-CIO, "The evidence suggests that Walmart is a key driver of the H-1B visa usage in Bentonville."[48]

The use of temporary workers creates downward pressure on wages for other workers, and probably would even if employers didn't violate wage requirements. The Department of Labor admits that the "prevailing wage rate" it uses for the H-1 and H-2 programs is lower than the actual average rates in the affected industries. One study found that in 2010 H-2B landscape workers and crab pickers in Maryland were making between three and five dollars an hour less than resident workers in the same occupations. Research in 2008 indicated that nationally wages either declined or remained stagnant in six of seven common H-2B occupations from 2000 to 2007.[49]

According to the Economic Policy Institute, H-2 workers earn about the same on average as unauthorized workers. Guest workers, like undocumented workers, face many challenges to defending their rights, and often feel compelled to accept low wages and abusive work conditions. This creates a "race to the bottom," hurting wages and conditions for all U.S. workers.[50]

Tougher border enforcement fuels guest worker programs. Stan Eury, executive director of the North Carolina Growers Association, cited the risks of crossing the border illegally to claim that the workers he recruited from Mexico through the H-2A program were getting a good deal: "As we enforce the borders, the cost to sneak in is more. Some will die in the deserts. But [an H-2A worker] won't. He'll ride over here in an air-conditioned tour bus watching a movie."[51]

Employers can also exploit guest workers to influence labor disputes. H-2 workers aren't supposed to be hired during a strike or a lockout, according to the regulations, but nothing stops employers from using them as a threat. Berry pickers at the Sakuma Brothers Farm in Burlington, Washington, formed a union, Families United for Justice (Familias Unidas por la Justicia), and held several brief strikes during the summer of 2013. In 2014 the farm applied for H-2A visas for 438 people to work in the summer harvest. Management backed off after some 400 U.S.-based workers sent letters applying for the jobs, disproving the claim of a labor shortage. As of July 2016 the union was still trying to win a contract, and supporters had organized a boycott of Sakuma berries.[52]

Can guest worker programs be improved?

An immigration reform bill passed in June 2013 by the U.S. Senate (but not by the House of Representatives) sought to replace existing guest worker programs with new ones for agricultural workers and "lower-skilled workers." Based on employers' need for workers, the Department of Agriculture would set the limit for how many agricultural visas would be issued, and a new Bureau of Immigration and Labor Market Research would decide how many visas should be issued for non-agricultural workers each year, with the number starting at 20,000, but going as high as 200,000 after five years. For the first time, agricultural and lower-skilled guest workers would have a limited option to apply for green cards.[53]

Some immigration reform advocates, including the AFL-CIO, consider such guest worker provisions an improvement, since they include stronger labor safeguards and allow for green cards. Other advocates are skeptical. Congress members might negotiate away the green card option in the process of getting a reform passed, Farmworker Justice Fund director Goldstein pointed out about a similar proposal in 2006. Other advocates noted that employers routinely ignore labor protections in the current programs and would be likely to do the same in a new program.

The idea of basing the number of guest workers on employers' needs is also problematic. Economist and former U.S. Labor Secretary Robert Reich supported the compromises that resulted in the 2013 proposal, but warned: "As soon as any increase in demand might begin to push their wages higher, employers can claim a 'labor shortage'—allowing in more guest workers, who will cause wages to drop back down again." The French newspaper *Le Monde Diplomatique* dismissed the 2013 bill as "mostly intended to supply cheap and docile guest workers for short-term use by employers."[54]

Some labor activists are trying to combat guest worker program abuses with unionization drives. In September 2004, the Ohio-based Farm Labor Organizing Committee (FLOC) signed agreements with the North Carolina Growers Association and the Mount Olive Pickle Company, settling a five-year boycott and extending union representation to more than 8,000 H-2 workers from Mexico.[55] In April 2006, the United Farm Workers signed a nationwide agreement with the international labor-contracting firm Global Horizons, after fighting the company for years over its abusive practices.[56]

However, these agreements remain controversial, and many advocates question whether their protections can be enforced, given the built-in imbalances of temporary worker programs. Fighting abuses in the programs can also be dangerous. In 2007 FLOC sent organizer Santiago Rafael Cruz to the union's office in Monterrey, a major city in northern Mexico. His goal was to organize and educate farm workers heading to H-2A jobs in the United States. Less than two months later he was found beaten to death in the union office. FLOC officials and Mexican human rights advocates feel he was murdered because he was fighting corruption among the groups that recruit temporary workers.[57]

11. Why Do We Jail and Deport Immigrants?

DEPORTATION AND DETENTION ARE PART of the process by which a nation determines which foreign citizens to allow in—and which to keep out. Non-citizens aren't considered to have a legal right to be here; their presence is instead seen as a privilege the government can revoke at will.[1]

Officially, detention and deportation are not considered punishment. In practice, they often violate constitutional and human rights principles, and are plagued by bias at every level. Race impacts who ends up without legal status, who has contact with the criminal justice system, and who is targeted for detention and deportation.

Despite growing public opposition, detention and deportation persist, and have expanded greatly in recent years, partly because private companies profit from these policies and lobby to keep them in place.[2] As immigration scholar Tanya Golash-Boza notes, this "immigration-industrial complex" is fueled by "(a) a rhetoric of fear; (b) the confluence of powerful interests; and (c) a discourse of other-ization."[3]

What is deportation?

When a national government expels a non-citizen from the country, it's known as deportation. Officially, the U.S. government now calls the process "removal." Since 2003, the U.S. agency with the main responsibility for detaining and deporting immigrants is Immigration and Customs Enforcement (ICE), a branch of the Department of Homeland Security (DHS).

A growing number of deportations—83 percent of formal removals in 2013—are summary proceedings, meaning the person being deported is denied the right to a hearing.[4] Mexican citizens apprehended near the southern U.S. border are sometimes "returned" instead of "removed." "Return" means they sign away their rights to a formal removal proceeding and avoid the penalties associated with deportation. Since 2004, arriving immigrants have been increasingly denied this option and have instead been routinely put through a formal removal process, expedited or otherwise, which then subjects them to felony charges if they subsequently re-enter the United States.[5]

Is deportation new?

In the 1800s, deportation was rare. Non-citizens viewed as "undesirable" were occasionally expelled from the United States, and more often excluded as they first arrived or when they returned from trips abroad. People targeted for such treatment included political dissidents, labor activists, and "alien enemies"; sex workers and others accused of "moral turpitude"; people who because of their economic status were deemed "likely to become a public charge"; and Asians, especially Chinese people in the late 1800s.[6]

In 1889, the Supreme Court upheld the discriminatory exclusion of Chinese immigrants as a matter of sovereignty, squarely within the realm of the executive and legislative branches of government, and virtually exempt from judicial review. In 1893, in *Fong Yue Ting v. United States*, the Supreme Court confirmed that immigrants have no due process rights in deportation proceedings. Although the discriminatory laws these rulings upheld were abolished in 1943, the legal doctrines behind them remain largely in effect, serving as the basis for the government's power to deport any non-citizen, for any reason.[7]

From 1918 to 1921, Attorney General A. Mitchell Palmer directed a series of raids targeting foreign-born Communist, Socialist, and anarchist radicals for deportation in what was known as the "Red Scare." Famous anarchists Emma Goldman and Alexander Berkman were among nearly 250 people deported on a ship to Russia, the *Buford*.[8] During the Great Depression of the 1930s, a campaign of mass "repatriation" targeted Mexican workers and families. As many as two million people—Mexicans and U.S.-born citizens of Mexican descent—were deported or forced to leave the United States in what historian Mae Ngai has described as "a racial removal program." Tens of thousands more Mexican workers were driven out of the country in 1954 in Operation Wetback.[9]

The 1986 Immigration Reform and Control Act (IRCA), though providing a path to citizenship for millions of out-of-status immigrants, also expanded deportations by criminalizing the hiring of unauthorized workers, boosting border enforcement, and accelerating the removal of non-citizens with criminal convictions.[10]

A decade later, the 1996 Illegal Immigration Reform and Immigrant Responsibility Act (IIRIRA) and the Antiterrorism and Effective Death Penalty Act (AEDPA) made deportation mandatory for certain classes of immigrants, stripping judges of their authority to determine whether someone should be allowed to stay in the United States. The new laws led to a six-fold increase in the annual number of deportations. From 1997 through 2014, well over five million people were deported, over two and a half times more than were deported during the entire previous century.[11]

Who gets deported, and why?

People end up in the deportation system after they are:

- Caught entering the United States without permission, or deemed "excludable" or "inadmissible" and not allowed to enter.
- Apprehended by the Border Patrol while living or traveling within 100 miles of the border.
- Arrested in raids on workplaces or homes, after having entered without permission, stayed longer than allowed, or violated the terms of their visa (by working without authorization, for example).
- Ordered deported by an immigration judge, including asylum seekers whose petitions or appeals are denied.
- Convicted of crimes. Some non-citizens are deported when they complete their jail sentences. Others end up in removal proceedings despite having served sentences many years ago and having long since complied with all parole, probation, and rehabilitation requirements.[12]

Deportees are disproportionately from Mexico, Guatemala, Honduras, and El Salvador. People from these four countries were nearly 96 percent of those deported in 2013, although they made up only 69 percent of the total unauthorized immigrant population.[13]

People who are deported may also be:

- Deeply rooted in the United States. A majority of immigrants arrested at or near the border are recent arrivals, although an increasing number are returning after having been previously deported. Of those removed from the interior of the United States in 2013, 60 percent had been here at least a year, 47 percent had been here at least three years, and 17 percent had been here a decade or more.[14]
- Parents of U.S. citizen children. In 2013, ICE carried out more than 72,000 removals of immigrants who said they had one or more U.S.-born children.[15]
- Green card holders. From 1997 to 2007, nearly 10 percent of the people deported on criminal grounds had been lawful permanent residents.[16]

- U.S. citizens. Under the law, only non-citizens can be deported. However, thousands of U.S. citizens have likely been wrongfully deported from the United States—for example, when the government refuses to accept the documents that prove their nationality.[17]

Unlike people fighting charges in criminal court, immigrants fighting deportation have no right to a court-appointed lawyer at public expense. In 2010, over 57 percent of immigrants in removal proceedings nationwide were unrepresented in immigration court. A study of immigrants facing removal in New York between 2005 and 2010 found that those with legal representation were about six times more likely to win their cases than those without.[18]

Do most deportees have criminal convictions?

In 2014, 56 percent of the combined 315,943 removals and returns carried out by ICE involved immigrants with criminal convictions. ICE likes to draw attention to its deportation of non-citizens who have been convicted of crimes—"felons, not families," as President Obama put it. Such false dualities between "good" and "bad" immigrants ignore the fact that non-citizens with criminal convictions have families, too, and deserve a fair chance.

When people think of crime, they often think of violence. But only 29 percent of these "criminal removals" from 2003 to 2013 were based on serious or violent offenses, according to a Migration Policy Institute analysis. Another 18 percent were of people convicted of violating immigration laws, and 12 percent were related to a drug possession charge. The definition of an "aggravated felony"—resulting in deportation—was expanded in 1996, and includes offenses like working with a fake ID, filing a false tax return, failure to appear in court, and shoplifting, as long as they result in a sentence of one year or more, even if the sentence is suspended and the person does no jail time. Shoplifting is also considered a "crime involving moral turpitude," as are fraud and forgery. Some of these crimes can trigger deportation even with a six-month sentence, regardless of whether part or all of the sentence is suspended.[19]

From 2003 to 2013, the proportion of "criminal" deportees whose most serious lifetime conviction was a violation of immigration law nearly tripled, going from 11 percent in 2003 to over 30 percent in 2013. Contributing to this increase was "Operation Streamline," a program started in December 2005 and expanded in 2008 under which unauthorized border crossers are virtually compelled to plead guilty to criminal charges of illegal entry and to serve up to 180 days in federal prison before being deported. Violations of immigration law also include reentry into the United States after a previous deportation, punishable with up to three years in prison.[20]

Criminal prosecutions on charges of unauthorized entry and reentry increased nearly 160 percent between 2005 and 2011, even as total apprehensions by DHS dropped about 50 percent over the same period.[21] Immigration-related prosecutions accounted for 57 percent of all federal criminal prosecutions during FY2014.[22]

What happens to people who are deported?

People who are deported lose their jobs, their families, their property, their friends, their homes. Immigrants who have spent most of their lives in the United States have an especially hard time; deportation becomes a form of forced exile from the place they consider home, and requires them to adapt to an environment they may not remember, or in some cases have never known. (At least 673 Cambodians have been deported since 2002; many of them were born in refugee camps in Thailand, came to the United States as children, and had never seen Cambodia before they were deported.) Sometimes people who are deported have no family or friends to help them in their country of origin, and don't even speak the language.

The more time immigrants have spent living outside their country of nationality, and the younger they were when they left, the more likely they are to be viewed as perpetual outsiders when they return. But nearly everyone who is deported will find the country they left behind and their own place within it significantly changed in their absence. Deportees may also experience stigma and social rejection because of their status as deportees, and may suffer violence and persecution at the hands of authorities or others.[23]

Reflecting on her in-depth interviews with longtime U.S. resident men deported to Jamaica and Guatemala, immigration scholar Tanya Golash-Boza notes that although they were never U.S. citizens, "they perceive themselves to be members of U.S. society, and consider their deportation to be one of the worst punishments imaginable."[24]

Under current laws, people who are deported are barred from returning to the United States for five to twenty years, or for life, depending on how and why they were deported.[25] If they return to the United States without permission, they are forced into a vulnerable clandestine existence; if caught, they may face jail sentences for "illegal reentry" or summary deportation under "reinstatement of removal," with no chance to plead their case.[26]

That doesn't stop people from returning. With their lives, families, and friends back in the United States, and limited employment opportunities with low pay in their country of origin, many deportees try to come back illegally. For some, knowing how their families suffer in their absence makes their exile unbearable.[27] In interviews with 300 Salvadoran deportees in 2002, researchers collaborating with the resettlement assistance agency Bienvenido a Casa in El Salvador found that 52 percent of those deported had left a spouse or child in the United States, and that 38 percent of the deportees planned to return to the United States.[28]

"Home is where the heart is," a Dominican deportee wrote in a January 2005 letter to New York sociologist David Brotherton. "Better to live in prison in New York than free in the D.R. We simply don't care about getting caught for reentry, that's the sad truth."[29]

DEPORTED LABOR

Among deportees who don't try to return to the United States, many have trouble finding steady employment, making it even

harder for them to adjust. But in Mexico and Central America, those who speak English with a U.S. accent and understand U.S. cultural cues have been increasingly recruited for jobs handling customer service and technical assistance calls for U.S. and international companies. Because deportees who grew up in the United States "sound American," the outsourced call centers can avoid complaints from U.S.-based customers about foreign accents; indeed, the customers likely have no idea that their call is being answered from abroad. The company saves on labor costs: call-center workers in Mexico earn, on average, a third of what U.S. workers earn for the same job, according to the Mexican Institute of Teleservices.[30]

Call-center outsourcing companies are apparently keeping track of the cities where deportees are settling in order to determine where to open new facilities. One company told a reporter that the Mexican government sometimes gives out information about call center jobs to people who find themselves on the Mexican side of the U.S. border after having been deported.[31]

Since the passage of the DR-CAFTA trade pact between the United States and Central America in 2005, the call center industry has also grown rapidly in Central America. The number of call center jobs in El Salvador grew from 800 in 2004 to 12,000 in 2011, part of a dramatic recent expansion of the country's service sector; services represented 60 percent of the country's Gross Domestic Product (GDP) in 2011.[32] By comparison, remittances from Salvadorans living abroad were only 16 percent of the GDP in 2011.[33] Over the same 2004–2011 period, the U.S. government carried out some 118,000 deportations to El Salvador, with annual removals more than doubling between 2005 and 2007.[34] In 2011, each deportation cost the federal government at least $12,500.[35]

What happens to the families of deportees?

Deportation is devastating for families. The removal of a breadwinner often plunges partners and children into economic crisis, at increased risk of becoming homeless and going hungry. The median income for households headed by at least one unauthorized immigrant is $36,000 per year; that income drops to around $15,400, below the poverty line, when a primary earner is detained or deported.[36]

Over 90 percent of deportees are male, so women are disproportionately left behind caring for children.[37] In the general population, 41 percent of families headed by single women have incomes at or below the official poverty line, compared to 24 percent of families headed by single men.[38] Fathers who are deported often struggle financially to meet their own needs, and are unlikely to be in a position to provide child support. Indeed, family members left behind in the United States may have to send money to support their deported relative.[39]

Children are traumatized by the loss of a parent to deportation. For partners left behind when a family wage earner is deported, employment pressures and financial worries can pile on top of stress, anxiety, and health problems. A 2013 analysis concluded that these combined factors reduced the estimated life spans of the partners of deportees by an average of 2.2 years.[40]

"Letisha, Kristina, and Christopher ask for their dad everyday," wrote Barbara Facey, a member of the group Families for Freedom whose husband, Howard, was deported to Jamaica in 2003. "Their grades are dropping, and the school counselor says they are depressed. Childcare is really hard. When a family friend who was supposed to get Christopher from school was late a few times, the principal threatened to call Children's Services. With all this pressure, I don't have the time to properly treat my heart condition."[41]

Women are also deported, even if they are the sole caregivers for children. One mother described, in tears, how she was transferred from one immigration jail in New Jersey to another while her children were visiting her, just before being deported to the Dominican Republic. "They said my kids were running after the van. Priscilla was running after the van, 'Mommy, Mommy,' but I didn't want to see it. It was awful."[42]

When parents are detained or deported, social service agencies or family courts may terminate their parental rights, deeming them "unfit" simply because they are unavailable. The Applied Research Center (now called Race Forward: The Center for Racial Justice Innovation) estimated in 2011 that at least 5,000 children had landed in foster care because their parents were detained or deported.[43]

The economic impact of deportation makes it hard to maintain close ties. For example, families may not be able to afford passport fees and travel costs to send U.S.-born children to visit or live with the deported parent. Children who do leave the United States to join deported parents may have trouble transitioning to an unfamiliar school system in their new country, and may also face discrimination as children of returnees.[44]

Deported people and their families suffer directly, but just the threat of deportation traumatizes families, and especially children, by creating fear and "a sense of vulnerability that reverberates throughout immigrant communities."[45] A 2007 report by the Urban Institute on the impact of immigration raids documented symptoms including diminished appetite, weight loss, insomnia, nightmares, depression, anxiety, aggression and acting out among children following a parent's arrest and threatened deportation.[46]

What is immigration detention?

Immigration detention is the federal government's practice of jailing people it wants to deport. In some cases, the detainees are going through a legal process to see whether they can remain in the United States. Other detainees are simply being held until their deportation can be arranged.

The conditions of detention make it seem like detainees are being punished for a crime. But being present in the United States without permission is not a crime; it is a civil violation, and jailing people for civil violations was supposed to have ended when debtors' prisons were officially abolished in the nineteenth century.[47] Because the courts have long accepted the argument that the administrative detention of immigrants isn't punishment, no one has yet managed to successfully challenge the practice as unconstitutional.[48]

Is immigration detention new?

Immigration detention has existed in the United States for over a century. The best-known detention center was the one at Ellis Island, where the U.S. government processed arriving immigrants—and detained those deemed excludable—from 1892 to 1954.

In 1954, the U.S. government announced it would only detain immigrants in rare cases when an individual was considered likely to be a security threat or flight risk. Detention grew common again in the 1970s; from 1973 to 1980, the number of people in detention on any given day—the average daily population—almost doubled, from 2,370 to 4,062. In 1981, mass detention was used to contain an exodus of "boat people" who reached the shores of Florida after fleeing turmoil in Haiti.[49]

Immigration detention expanded dramatically following the 1996 laws. The average daily number of people in immigration detention grew by more than 350 percent between 1995 and 2013, from 7,475 to 33,811. Annual "admissions" into detention—the number of people who become detained at some point over the course of a year—went from 85,730 in 1995 to 440,557 in 2013, a more than 400 percent increase.[50] On an average day in 2012, an additional 23,700 noncitizens were in the custody of the federal Bureau of Prisons (BOP), not in immigration detention but serving sentences for immigration crimes like illegal entry and illegal reentry.[51]

Why are so many people detained?

Since at least 2010, Congress has allocated funding to maintain and pay for a minimum annual quota of available immigration detention beds nationwide, whether or not those beds are actually used.

Officials and politicians have at times disagreed about whether the government is in fact mandated to detain the number of immigrants needed to fill the quota, which stood at 34,000 in 2014.[52]

Advocates have been campaigning to abolish the quota. A January 2014 letter signed by 136 civil rights, human rights, legal services, community, and faith-based organizations noted that the number "is arbitrary, and the concept of a legislatively mandated detention quota is an aberration among law enforcement agencies."[53]

In addition to the overall "bed quota" mandated by Congress, many of the government's contracts for specific detention centers require ICE to pay for a guaranteed minimum number of detention beds, whether or not these beds are filled.[54] In a 2014 report, the U.S. Government Accountability Office (GAO) urged ICE to fill each facility's guaranteed minimum in order to avoid paying for unused beds and to hold more immigrants at facilities that offer a "tiered pricing structure," under which lower bed rates kick in after the number of detainees exceeds the minimum. "ICE could conserve resources by better filling the capacity above the guaranteed minimum, as it costs ICE less per detainee to house detainees in these facilities," the GAO wrote.[55]

As detention has grown, the people directly affected by it and other concerned rights advocates have worked to raise awareness of its human and financial costs. These efforts have seemed at times to have an impact: five months into fiscal year 2015, the daily average number of immigrants detained was 26,374, falling short of that year's 34,000 quota by more than 20 percent.[56] On May 15, 2015, the *New York Times* editorial board wrote that it was "time to end mass detention. . . . Shut the system down."[57]

Who are the detainees?

People locked up in immigration detention include:

- Asylum seekers. People who arrive in the United States without proper documentation and request asylum are generally subject to mandatory detention, without bond, while their cases are reviewed.[58] According to government statistics, 15,769 asylum applicants were detained at some point during FY 2010.[59] Asylum seekers represented only 4 percent of admissions into detention that year, but were nearly 10 percent of the daily population, since their average stay was 150 percent longer than the overall average for all detainees.[60]

- People facing deportation because of past criminal convictions, or upon release from prison. The 1996 immigration laws made detention mandatory, with no right to release on bond, for people convicted of any of a wide range of specified types of criminal offenses.[61]

- People who cannot be removed from the United States, either because they are stateless, or because their country of origin does not accept deportees.[62]

ICE is supposed to release vulnerable people instead of detaining them. However, many vulnerable people remain in immigration detention. For example:

- Torture survivors. The Center for Victims of Torture and the Torture Abolition and Survivor Support Coalition International estimated in a 2013 report that between October 2010 and February 2013, the U.S. government likely detained as many as 6,000 torture survivors who were seeking asylum.[63]

- Lesbian, gay, and transgender immigrants. An estimated seventy-five transgender people are in U.S. immigration detention on an average day, about one in every 500 detainees. Ninety percent of them are transgender women, many of whom are seeking asylum from persecution.[64] Between October 2013 and October 2014, out of 104 immigrants who told an ICE officer that they were afraid of being in detention because of their sexual orientation or gender identity, eighty-one were placed in detention anyway, according to records obtained from ICE through a Freedom of Information Act request.[65]

- Pregnant women. In July 2014, the online media outlet *Fusion* revealed that since 2012 at six ICE detention centers, at least 559 women had been detained while pregnant, even though ICE claimed that it no longer detained pregnant women. The average stay in detention for pregnant women was just four days shorter than the average for all detainees, *Fusion* reported.[66]

- Children traveling alone. U.S. Customs and Border Protection took 68,541 unaccompanied children into custody at the southwestern border in fiscal year 2014, up from 38,759 the previous year, and nearly nine times the 7,787 who were apprehended in 2005.[67] Under the Homeland Security Act of 2002, unaccompanied children are not supposed to be detained longer than three days.[68] However, a study by the National Immigrant Justice Center found that from 2008 to 2012, the Department of Homeland Security violated its own rules by detaining at least 1,366 children in thirty adult detention facilities around the country.[69]

- Parents with children. In 2014 CBP apprehended 68,445 "family units" at the southwestern border, compared to 14,855 the previous year. Most were asylum seekers from Central America and Mexico.[70] As of June 2015, about 2,600 women and children remained detained in special "family" detention centers.[71]

- People with intellectual disabilities and mental illness. Immigration officials estimate that about 15 percent of detainees suffer from mental illness. Detention frequently aggravates mental illness and interrupts care and treatment.[72]

Where are people detained?

From fiscal years 2011 through 2013, ICE used 166 facilities to hold detainees for seventy-two hours or more, according to an October 2014 GAO report. Just over half of the detainees were in twenty-two facilities owned and operated by ICE or private companies, or by ICE and private companies jointly. The remaining detainees were in 144 other facilities, primarily local jails holding both immigration detainees and other imprisoned people, either separately or together, under agreements with ICE.[73]

Between 2008 and 2013, the number of facilities ICE uses to detain people declined dramatically, by about 62 percent, even as the number of people entering immigration detention grew more than 16 percent.[74] As the number of facilities dropped, the share of immigration detention beds operated by for-profit prison corporations grew: from 49 percent in 2009 to 62 percent as of March 2015, according to a report by the nonprofit organization Grassroots Leadership. Nine of the ten largest ICE detention centers are privately run.[75]

LOCKING UP KIDS

In July 1985, four girls ages thirteen to sixteen seeking refuge from war-ravaged El Salvador sued the U.S. government and two private for-profit contractors over their detention. One of the plaintiffs was detained at a facility run by the Corrections Corporation of America (CCA) in Laredo, Texas, where authorities subjected her to strip search procedures—including vaginal and anal inspections—every time her attorney visited. The other girls, including lead plaintiff Jenny Lisette Flores, were held at a detention center in Pasadena, California, operated by Behavioral Systems Southwest. The children were not allowed to see visitors, and were not provided with any opportunities for education or recreation.

At the time, U.S. border and immigration authorities were detaining immigrant children—as many as 2,000, according to advocates—together with unrelated adults under prison-like conditions. The numbers had grown after the government changed its policy in September 1984 and began releasing unaccompanied minors only to a parent or guardian; previously children could be released to any responsible adult. Advocates said the new policy scared away unauthorized parents, who feared arrest if they tried to claim their children.[76]

Flores v. Reno was finally resolved in 1997 with the legally binding "Flores Settlement Agreement," mandating specific protections for minors in immigration custody. Some of the settlement's rules were codified into law over a decade later with the passage of the 2008 Trafficking Victims Protection Reauthorization Act.[77] Under the Flores settlement rules, unaccompanied minors from Canada or Mexico are generally returned home "voluntarily" after a few days in custody. Children from other countries must be transferred within seventy-two hours to the Department of Health and Human Services Office of Refugee Resettlement (ORR), which releases them to a sponsor or a shelter and provides support services through its Division for Unaccompanied Children's Services.[78]

In the early years after *Flores*, when children arrived with a parent or guardian, the families were generally either released together, or the adults were placed in detention centers and the children transferred to ORR custody.[79] But ICE changed its practice in 2006 and began detaining women with children at the 500-bed T. Don Hutto facility in Taylor, Texas, operated for profit by CCA. Hutto subjected children and their mothers to harsh prison conditions. After several years of advocacy, litigation, media attention, and growing protests over conditions at the facility, in 2009 ICE stopped detaining children at Hutto; it is still used as a detention center for women.[80]

In June 2014, ICE stepped up family detention again, instituting a "no bond, no release" policy as part of what the government called an "aggressive deterrence strategy" to discourage a wave of families fleeing violence in Central America from making the journey to the United States to seek asylum.

ICE initially used a temporary 672-bed facility in Artesia, New Mexico, to detain the newly arrived women with children. In August 2014, as the flow of asylum seekers continued, ICE contracted with GEO Group to detain children with their mothers in a 532-bed prison in Karnes City, Texas. Advocates immediately raised serious concerns about inadequate conditions, a lack of due process, and the impact of detention on the mental and physical health of children and their mothers, and urged that ICE shut down both facilities and start releasing families. "Our conclusion is simple: there is no way to humanely detain families," wrote the Lutheran Immigration and Refugee Service and the Women's Refugee Commission in an October 2014 report. "Detention traumatizes families, undermines the basic family structure, and has a devastating psycho-social impact."

Instead of ending family detention, in December 2014, ICE shut down the Artesia facility and moved detained women and children into a brand new 2,400-bed facility operated by CCA in Dilley, Texas.[81] The problems continued at Dilley: "CCA and ICE officials have engaged in a pattern and practice of harassing and obstructing legal efforts to defend" the families detained there, according to attorney Laura Lichter, part of a team that volunteered to represent the detainees.[82]

Between July of 2014 and May 31, 2015, a total of 6,381 individuals were booked into "family residential centers," according to ICE. At the end of this period, 29 percent of them remained in detention; 11 percent of those still detained had been held sixty days or longer.[83]

The courts haven't been sympathetic to the government's practice of incarcerating children. On February 20, 2015, the U.S. District Court in the District of Columbia barred the federal government from using deterrence of mass migration as a motivating factor in its decision to detain Central American mothers and children seeking asylum.[84] In July 2015, U.S. District Judge Dolly Gee in California ruled that the conditions of family detention at the Dilley and Karnes facilities constituted a serious violation of the *Flores* settlement, and the children and their parents held there should be released without delay. Gee also found that the Border Patrol had "wholly failed" to guarantee "safe and sanitary" conditions for children in its temporary holding facilities.[85]

How long do people spend in detention?

Whereas most immigration detainees are locked up for less than a month, others remain detained for years, and sometimes have to sue the government to win their freedom. Many detainees say the worst part of detention is that they have no idea how long they will be held, and no way to find out.[86] Asylum seekers generally spend much longer in detention than other migrants. In 2010, their average stay was eighty days. Nearly 11 percent of asylum seekers were held longer than six months.[87]

Detention can drag on as cases wind through the immigration court system and are appealed to backlogged federal courts. As of May 2015, the average immigration court case took 555 days—more than eighteen months—to complete.[88] Even after all appeals are exhausted, and a final deportation order is confirmed, many immigrants find themselves detained for further months or years. Some immigrants who never even challenge their deportation remain jailed for long periods due to bureaucratic delays or problems getting travel documents.

For years, the government contended that it could hold detainees for as long as it took to deport them, and if it couldn't deport them, it could detain them indefinitely. In the June 2001 *Zadvydas v. Davis* decision, the Supreme Court ruled that detention loses its meaning when removal is not foreseeable, such as when detainees are stateless or their country refuses to issue travel documents. The court set six months as a reasonable time frame for the government to remove people who have exhausted all appeals and have been issued final deportation orders. After six months, the burden shifts to the government to remove the detainee promptly, prove that removal is foreseeable in the very near future, or else release the detainee.[89] The Supreme Court's January 2005 decision in *Clark v. Martinez* confirmed that this principle also applies to non-citizens who were paroled into the United States after being deemed "inadmissible," and whose countries would not take them back. That case involved Cubans who had arrived in the 1980 Mariel boatlift and were subsequently convicted of crimes.[90]

In 2013, ICE says it released 3,652 people based on the *Zadvydas* ruling, out of a total of 36,000 people released from detention that year.[91] The agency has not consistently complied with the Supreme Court's mandate, and detainees with a final removal order generally have to stay locked up for six months, then submit a formal request to ICE headquarters asking for release. If ICE still doesn't let them out, detainees must sue the agency in federal court through a habeas petition to win their freedom. Several hundred habeas petitions are filed each year by immigration detainees.[92]

At the end of December 2012, according to ICE records, 4,793 people were still in detention after at least six months. On average, these detainees had spent over a year in detention, and twelve of them had spent between six and eight years in detention.[93] The longest-held immigration detainees are Aurelio Marquez-Coromina and Manuel Reyes-Pena, Cubans detained since 1995 and 1993, respectively, after completing criminal sentences. The U.S. government claims they are too dangerous to release but has declined to transfer them to mental health facilities as might be done with U.S. citizens deemed dangerous and mentally ill.[94]

Even those released under the *Zadvydas* ruling don't have an easy time. They are left without any kind of meaningful status, and many remain under threat of being deported if their country of origin changes its policy and decides to take them back. They don't qualify for any kind of public assistance. They are eligible to apply for work permits, but their applications may be denied. "Most of them are just kind of living day by day, the ones that I see," said Hoang Tu, a California attorney who has represented Vietnamese immigrants released under *Zadvydas*. "They don't have anything, pretty much," Tu said. "They just exist."[95]

How bad is detention really?

"With only a few exceptions, the facilities [for immigration detention] were built, and operate, as jails and prisons to confine pre-trial and sentenced felons," noted corrections policy adviser Dora Schriro in a 2009 report for ICE.[96] Immigrant detainees are handcuffed or shackled during transportation; they wear prison uniforms and have limited freedom of movement within facilities. They may endure invasive strip and body cavity searches, overcrowded conditions or solitary confinement, neglect of basic medical and hygienic needs, denial of outdoor recreation and contact visits, food lacking in quantity and quality, and may be subjected to verbal, physical, and sexual abuse.[97]

In immigration detention, "the use of intimidation as a tool to instill fear and control over people being detained is the norm," explains former detainee Khalil Alvaro Cumberbatch. "Correctional officers treat the control of showers, use of phones, participating in recreational time, and access to the law library to challenge one's immigration proceedings as privileges that can be revoked at a whim in order to control people's behavior."[98]

Detainees who file complaints, speak to the press, or organize protests may be punished with solitary confinement, transfer, or accelerated deportation despite pending claims or appeals.[99]

Detention standards were adopted by the immigration agency in 2000, then updated in 2008 and again in 2011. However, the standards have never been legally binding, numerous exceptions are allowed for unspecified "security" reasons, and the rules are written in a way that makes them impossible to enforce.[100] Many of the facilities ICE uses to hold detainees are not even required to meet the standards.[101] As of January 2014, only about 54 percent of ICE detainees were in facilities covered by the 2011 standards.[102]

Social worker Olivia Lopez, who was employed from October 2014 to April 2015 at the Karnes family detention center run by Geo Group in Texas, said that on the forms she had to fill out for each detainee during weekly mental health monitoring sessions, she was instructed to leave blank the section designated for noting any concerns raised by the detainee, and not to write anything "beyond that the resident had been instructed on the referral process."[103]

Problems in detention facilities include:

- **Lack of access to lawyers.** Immigrants in detention who are represented by an attorney are three to six times more likely to succeed in their cases than detainees who are not represented. Yet roughly two-thirds of detained immigrants have no legal representation at any point in their removal proceedings.[104] Detainees aren't entitled to government-funded legal representation, and most can't afford to pay private lawyers. A 2010 study found that 10 percent of detainees had no access to nonprofit attorneys and 78 percent were in facilities that didn't allow lawyers to schedule private calls with their clients. The immigration agency does give detainees a list of legal service agencies to call, but the list information may be incorrect or out of date, and not all the listed agencies can actually help detainees.[105]

- **Transfers.** The immigration agency moves detainees from jail to jail, sometimes thousands of miles away, without informing their attorneys or relatives, or allowing them to make a phone call. This policy separates detainees from their attorneys, family, and friends, making it harder for them to win their claims. In a 2011 report analyzing twelve years of data, Human Rights Watch found that 46 percent of detainees were transferred more than once, with an average transfer distance of 370 miles. The largest number of out-of-state transfers involved detainees sent to Louisiana, Mississippi, and Texas, adding to the difficulty of fighting their cases in court. These three states combined have a ratio of one immigration attorney for every 510 detainees, and all three are served by the Fifth Circuit Court of Appeals, which is known for decisions that are unfavorable to immigrants.[106]

- **Lack of medical care.** Medical treatment for immigrant detainees is grossly inadequate. Serious conditions are left untreated for weeks, months, or even years, or are "treated" with over-the-counter medications like aspirin, according to information from Human Rights Watch and from investigative reporters.[107] Starting in 2009, under pressure from a lawsuit, ICE began releasing information about people who had died in its custody since October 2003. National Public Radio (NPR) reporter Daniel Zwerdling investigated dozens of these deaths. "In many cases, I found the evidence showed that they begged for medical care for days before they died and they couldn't get it," he noted in a 2009 interview.[108] By the end of November 2016, the list of people who had died in detention had grown to 166 names. Some committed suicide; most appeared to have died from treatable medical conditions.[109]

- **Physical abuse.** In November 2004 NPR's Zwerdling reported that guards at Hudson County Correctional Center in New Jersey had beaten two detainees while they were handcuffed, as other guards and supervising officers watched. After the story aired, a jail spokesperson confirmed the incident and said the county would fire two guards and file administrative charges against nine others.[110] Other journalists have reported on similar incidents at detention facilities, and it's logical to assume that many more go without being reported, since the threat of retaliation is powerful.

- **Sexual abuse.** In October 2011, the American Civil Liberties Union of Texas announced it had obtained government documents through the Freedom of Information Act concerning 185 allegations of sexual abuse in immigration detention facilities around the country. An ACLU attorney described the allegations as "the tip of the iceberg," since sexual abuse is grossly underreported in the outside world, and even more likely to be underreported in detention.[111] The 2003 Prison Rape Elimination Act (PREA) made all sexual contact between guards and prisoners illegal, but as of 2016, DHS had not even set a deadline for implementing PREA at the 143 local jails that held 68 percent of female detainees and 47 percent of all detainees.[112] A 2013 inquiry by the Government Accountability Office (GAO) found that even when detainees manage to lodge complaints of abuse, local facilities don't always report the complaints to the federal government. And when they do, the government doesn't always track the claims or report them properly.[113] In a 2010 report, Human Rights Watch referred to the immigration detention system as "a place where abuses can be hidden until, often, the victims are shipped away."[114]

- **Psychological trauma.** Detention causes lasting trauma and emotional distress, especially for vulnerable populations. Studies conducted by the U.S. Commission on International Religious

Freedom, Physicians for Human Rights, and the Bellevue/New York University Program for Survivors of Torture found disturbingly high levels of depression, anxiety, post-traumatic stress disorder, and worsened psychological health among detained asylum seekers.[115] Many who had suffered torture and abuse in their home countries reported feeling dehumanized by the conditions they faced in detention, as well as confused and isolated by the lack of information about when—or whether—they would be released, and anxious and fearful about the possibility of being returned to the country where they were tortured.[116]

- **Solitary confinement.** Detainees are confined in isolation when they file complaints or try to organize other detainees. After leading a January 2003 hunger strike at Passaic County Jail in New Jersey, New York City–based Palestinian activist Farouk Abdel-Muhti was transferred to York County Jail in Pennsylvania, 177 miles from his attorneys and friends, and kept in solitary confinement there for eight months. According to its own rules, the immigration agency was supposed to conduct a weekly review of its reasons for keeping a detainee in segregation. When an attorney asked the immigration agency for its records of these reviews, the agency promptly moved Abdel-Muhti back to a New Jersey jail, where he was returned to the general detainee population. (Abdel-Muhti, whose high blood pressure and thyroid condition worsened during his two years in detention, died of a massive heart attack on July 21, 2004, just 100 days after he was freed by order of a federal judge. He was fifty-six years old.)[117]

THE STORY OF S.

S., a young woman with no criminal record who had suffered repeated sexual and physical abuse throughout her childhood and was seeking asylum, was detained by the immigration agency for almost nine months in a county jail in upstate New York, alongside people arrested for child abuse, prostitution, and drug crimes. Whenever friends came to visit S., her time

in the visiting room would be interrupted every hour as guards took her out for routine strip searches, and made her spread her buttocks so they could visually inspect her anus.

Her health deteriorated so much in detention that she was eventually taken to a local surgeon for a medical exam. "Because the surgeon works outside of the jail, in order to go see him I must wear leg irons, belly chains, handcuffs, and a handcuff box. It is very humiliating to be taken to a doctor's office and paraded through the front door in shackles in front of eight to twelve other patients, but not as humiliating as being told to 'hurry up,' then falling over when I do (four days later my ankle is still swollen and bruised). Then when I got into the office and the doctor tried to do a physical exam, he couldn't because of the belly chains. The doctor did tell me (the officer wouldn't leave the room) that he wanted me to have a colonoscopy and a biopsy. But I was told that if I agree to have the procedure that officers from the jail would have to be present . . . I refused the procedure."

Thanks to pressure from attorneys, advocates, and elected officials, S. was freed in June 2004. Immigration officials first demanded assurances that a local refugee service agency could provide her with a safe room at its shelter. Then they released her to the street—in an unfamiliar city—without even money for a phone call, and without notifying her attorneys or the refugee agency, which had expected to pick her up. In the end, S. was allowed to live with friends in another state and check in via telephone monthly while she appealed her asylum case. Her medical problems resolved soon after leaving detention.[118]

How are detainees' families affected?

For a family facing the prospect of permanent separation or collective exile, the detention of a loved one adds further stress, anxiety, and financial burden. Families scramble to pay thousands of dollars in legal fees or to find free or low-cost help, and to pull together any documents needed for the case, so their loved one can fight deportation. The prolonged detention of a wage earner hits families hard, economically and emotionally. Children are affected emotionally by separation from a detained (or deported) parent, and the trauma and fear they experience can affect their health and well-being, as well as their performance in school.[119]

For the 47 percent of immigrants who are detained in local jails, family visits, when permitted, often take place through glass barriers, with no contact allowed. In some of these facilities, in-person visits have been replaced altogether with long-distance video conferencing.[120] When in-person visits are possible, they can often be emotionally devastating for detainees and their families. Children may be traumatized by seeing a parent in prison, and detainees may be subjected to humiliating and invasive physical inspections before and after (and sometimes during) each visit.[121]

Family members who don't have legal status may be unable to visit at all, either because they lack the necessary identification to enter the detention center as a visitor, or because they fear being arrested by immigration authorities if they try. When detainees are moved to jails far from their homes, most families can no longer afford to make the trip.[122]

The high cost of phone calls from detention centers adds an additional burden on families. In October 2015, following more than a decade of sustained activist campaigning, the Federal Communications Commission (FCC) moved to cap rates for all phone calls made from detention centers, jails, and prisons nationwide. However, as of November 2016, a federal court had blocked the rate reductions while it considered a challenge brought by companies profiting from prison phone services.[123]

Is detention necessary?

The official purpose of detention is to prevent people from "absconding" by keeping them in jail until they are sent back to their countries of origin. The immigration agency also uses detention as a tool to

pressure detainees to stop fighting their cases and accept deportation, as well as to discourage more people from coming to the United
States. Rather than welcoming people fleeing persecution in other
countries, the U.S. government puts them in the position of having to
decide which is worse: to remain detained in U.S. jails for years or to
return to the persecution they fear at home.

Detention tips the scales of justice toward the government's side by
making it harder for people to win their legal battles against deportation. Without detention, people arrested by immigration could
remain with their families and in their jobs while they seek legal help
to win their cases.

Would people really "abscond" if we got rid of detention? Under
a 1997–2000 alternative pilot program run by the nonprofit Vera
Institute of Justice, which provided immigrants facing deportation
proceedings with legal information, referrals, and court date remind-
ers, and required a community member to act as guarantor, between
88 percent and 94 percent of immigrants showed up for their first five
court hearings. (This high rate of compliance is partly because par-
ticipants who volunteered for the pilot program met certain selection
criteria: they had strong community ties, had complied with reporting requirements in the past, and weren't considered a public safety
threat.) Similar results emerged from two other community-based
programs run by nonprofits at around the same time. The annual cost
of monitoring immigrants in the three programs was a fraction of the
cost of detaining them.[124]

How much does detention cost?

The daily cost of detaining an immigrant varies in different federal
facilities and local jails around the country. In 2013, the National
Immigration Forum estimated that the average cost was $159 per
detainee per day, including payroll and operational expenses.[125] With
more than 32,000 immigrants held in detention on any given day
during 2014, that adds up to more than $1.8 billion a year, paid for by
our federal taxes.[126] That number increases even more if you include

the money the federal government spends jailing unauthorized immigrants on criminal charges of unauthorized entry and reentry—an estimated $5.5 billion between 2005 and 2011.[127]

Shifting to alternatives to detention, including bond and release on recognizance, would reduce detention costs dramatically. The National Immigration Forum found that the cost of alternative programs in 2013 ranged from 0.17 cents to $17 a day for each immigrant. "If ICE limited its use of detention to individuals who have committed violent crimes, the agency could save nearly $4 million a night, or $1.44 billion annually—a 79 percent reduction in costs," the report concluded.[128]

Who profits from detention?

Employers profit indirectly when the threat of deportation and detention makes workers vulnerable, but private prison contractors profit directly from immigration detention: 62 percent of detainees were in privately managed facilities as of 2015. The largest share of the business goes to CCA and GEO Group (formerly Wackenhut Corrections Corporation). These two companies together operate 72 percent of privately contracted immigration detention beds, including eight of the ten largest ICE detention centers.[129]

Private prison companies increase their profits by paying immigration detainees as little as a dollar a day—13 cents an hour—to do jobs that would normally be done by paid staff: cleaning, preparing meals, clerical work, landscaping, laundry and barber services, for example. In some cases detainees even prepare meals for other government institutions.[130] At a GEO Group facility in Aurora, Colorado, detained immigrants "assisted in preparing catered meals for law enforcement events sponsored by GEO," according to a lawsuit brought by the detainees.

In 2013, at least 60,000 immigration detainees worked in detention centers, according to ICE data cited by the New York Times. Their compensation generally comes in the form of credits toward food, toiletry items, and phone calls, all sold at inflated prices. At county jails, some detainees are paid nothing for their labor, or are paid with sodas or candy bars. ICE data shows about 5 percent of detained immigrants who work are not paid at all, the *New York Times* reported. At the Aurora facility, detainees are forced to work in shifts to clean the jail pods for no pay, and are threatened with solitary confinement if they refuse.[131]

In 2012, GEO Group's profits from labor cost savings were estimated to be between $33 million and $72 million; for CCA, the estimate was $30 million to $77 million.[132]

Private companies profit from the management not only of what ICE calls "Contract Detention Facilities," but also of the Service Processing Centers that ICE owns, and of many of the local and county jails that contract with ICE to hold nearly half of all immigration detainees. In general, immigration detention contracts offer higher profit margins for private companies than regular prison contracts, in part because immigration detainees aren't provided with the education, recreation, treatment, and rehabilitation programs granted to other kinds of prisoners.[133] Even in jails managed by government agencies, private profits are made through contracts for services including food, uniform laundering, transportation, telephone calls, video visitation, and money transfer services. Two companies, Global Tel Link and Securus, together controlled about 80 percent of the $1.2 billion market for prison phone service in 2012.[134]

Private companies profit from detention bond services, too, and from "alternatives to detention," including electronic monitoring, in which a GPS tracking device is attached to the ankle of a person under ICE supervision.[135] A Geo Group subsidiary, BI Incorporated, has provided such "supervision services" under contract with ICE since 2004, when it managed an initial pilot program for the tracking devices. Geo Group bought the company in 2011; in September 2014 Geo announced that a new BI Incorporated contract with ICE is "expected to generate approximately $47 million in annualized revenues."[136]

Former top government officials also reap big profits from the detention and security business. The *New York Times* reported in June 2006 that at least ninety former officials at the Department of Homeland Security or the White House Office of Homeland Security, including Homeland Security Secretary Tom Ridge, had become executives, consultants, or lobbyists for companies that collectively do billions of dollars' worth of domestic security business. Among them was Victor X. Cerda, who in July 2005 left his job as acting director of Detention and Removal Operations for ICE, and was immediately hired by a law firm representing government contractors. One of his first lobbying clients was the GEO Group. While Cerda was still running detention operations for the government, a GEO Group subsidiary had won a contract to operate a 1,000-bed detention complex in Texas. In his private sector role, Cerda was able to help GEO prepare new bids, the *Times* reported, and even to directly represent GEO Group in meetings with officials from his old department.[137]

Another example is David Venturella, who ran detention and removal operations at the now-defunct Immigration and Naturalization Service (INS) and subsequently at ICE. He first defected to the private sector in 2004, working for two companies dealing with "homeland security issues," then went back to the government in 2008 to head the "Secure Communities" enforcement program. In 2012, Venturella joined GEO Group as executive vice president; he was promoted in 2014 to senior vice president, and leads the company's "business and proposal development efforts."[138]

In July 2014, GEO Group voted to expand its board of directors from six to seven members, adding former ICE chief Julie Myers Wood. Wood is the CEO of Guidepost Solutions LLC, a company specializing in "monitoring, compliance, international investigations and risk management solutions." She served as Department of Homeland Security assistant secretary in charge of ICE from 2006 to 2008.[139]

12. Can We Open Our Borders?

POLITICIANS, ACTIVISTS, AND EDITORIAL writers on all sides of the immigration debate often refer to our current immigration system as "broken." But the system works very well for the private prison industry and the industries that profit by selling weapons and equipment to the U.S. government to control the southwestern border. The current system also makes it easier for unscrupulous employers to exploit undocumented workers, and provides a large pool of useful scapegoats that politicians can blame for the failures of their policies.

"Open borders" may sound radical, but if you break down what it might mean in practice, and how we could get there, true freedom of movement looks a lot better than what we have now.

What do we mean by open borders?

The term "open borders" can mean different things to different people, but usually it refers to a relatively unrestricted movement of people and goods between nations. This use of the term includes everything from completely uncontrolled borders, like those between U.S. states, to borders where most people can cross, after showing identification and passing through customs, as happens when U.S. citizens enter Mexico. Sometimes when people talk about open borders, they are really talking about "free trade"—that is, the free movement of goods—combined with an expanded use of guest worker programs, but these often come with increased restrictions on border crossing.[1]

Some people believe a country loses its sovereignty or identity if it doesn't restrict its borders. But many nations, including the United States until the twentieth century, have maintained their laws, their form of government, and their national identity while leaving their borders more or less open.[2] The separate national identities, languages, and cultures of European countries remain apparently unaffected by their participation in the largely border-free European Union (EU). No one thinks Spain and Sweden are the same country, or confuses Italy with Germany. In 2007, fifteen years after borders were opened, a public opinion survey run by the European Commission found that 90 percent of people in the EU considered themselves attached or very attached to their own countries, with 52 percent saying they were very attached.[3]

Is freedom of movement a human right?

International law currently recognizes "freedom of movement" as a right, but balances that right with the right of governments to choose who should be let in and who should be kept out. The 1948 Universal Declaration of Human Rights and the 1966 International Covenant on Civil and Political Rights are supposed to guarantee the "right to freedom of movement and residence within the borders of each state," and the "right to leave any country, including [one's] own, and to return to [one's] country."[4] Minor exceptions allow countries to keep people from leaving if they are suspects in a criminal investigation. But the major obstacle to "freedom of movement" is that having the right to leave your own country doesn't mean you have the right to enter another.

Some open borders proponents ask why this right is omitted. A city or town would be committing a human rights violation if it denied entry to people from other cities or towns in the same country; why then is a nation allowed to deny entry to citizens of other nations?[5] Scholars who have studied the issue, such as geography professor Joseph Nevins and historian Aviva Chomsky, argue that it is inherently discriminatory for a country to exclude some people simply because of their nationality. Nevins calls the practice "global apartheid," since most cases of immigration exclusion involve richer nations, often with historically whiter populations, keeping out citizens of poorer nations with predominantly non-white populations.[6]

The official definition of "freedom of movement" also aggravates inequality between richer and poorer countries. By this definition a wealthy nation can restrict the entry of lower-skilled workers from a poor nation, but the poor nation is violating a human right if it tries to keep its own most skilled citizens—doctors and scientists, for example, who may have been educated at public expense—from moving to higher-paying jobs in the wealthy nation. The result is an increased "brain drain" of talented and educated people from poorer nations to richer ones.[7]

Has "open borders" been attempted?

The United States had an open immigration policy for its first ninety-nine years. Goods were subject to restrictions and tariffs, but people were free to immigrate. The first federal immigration law came in 1875, when Congress, under pressure from racists, began limiting the immigration of people from China.

Later laws excluded all Chinese laborers and set up a small entry tax (1882); created a literacy requirement and barred anarchists (1917–18); and put strict limits on immigration from the Eastern Hemisphere (1921 and 1924). For the most part, people were free to cross the border from Mexico until the Border Patrol was established in 1924. Until 1965, people from Western Hemisphere nations could generally enter the United States legally if they could pay a visa fee, prove they were literate, and pass a medical inspection.[8]

Western Europe has generally had free movement of people among its nations since the creation of the European Economic Community in 1958. In 1985, France, Germany, Belgium, Luxembourg, and the Netherlands created a territory without internal borders—the "Schengen area," named for a town in Luxembourg where the first agreements were signed. Within the Schengen area there are no border controls: no one checks your documents as you enter one nation from another, and you don't need a passport to travel.

Since the European Union (EU) was formed in 1993, citizens of a growing number of European countries have been able to travel freely throughout the region and work legally in any country. They can bring their families with them, and close family members who are not European citizens can work legally, too.[9] By the end of 2015, twenty-six European countries had joined the Schengen area, including some that are not part of the EU.[10]

Across the Atlantic, the Union of South American Nations (Unasur) has eliminated travel barriers among its twelve member countries, allowing its citizens to cross regional borders with only their national identification documents. As of late 2015, half of those countries—the six belonging to the regional bloc Mercosur—also allow their citizens to live and work in any of the six. This free mobility is supposed to be extended to the remaining countries, but as of late 2015 no date had been set for implementation.[11]

Does the European Union really have open borders?

Europe doesn't really have true freedom of movement. A number of European countries have restricted job access for migrants from the newer EU member states.[12] And the EU countries have consolidated efforts to keep out immigrants from Africa and Asia under a policy popularly known as "Fortress Europe," which, similar to U.S. border policy, causes the deaths of hundreds of people each year who try to migrate. In 2005, a total of 673 migrants died en route to Europe, most of them Africans who drowned in the Mediterranean Sea while trying to reach Italy or Spain. The toll has increased dramatically since then; some 1,500 migrants drowned in the first four months of 2015, many of them refugees fleeing armed conflicts in Iraq, Syria, and Libya.[13] Like the United States, Europe has faced criticism from international human rights organizations for its harsh policies toward migrants.[14]

In fact, growing European integration appears to be tightly linked with shutting out the outside world, including migrants and refugees from countries that were once European colonies and are still dominated economically by Europe. "The Europeans come to Africa," an African asylum seeker told a 1997 immigrants' rights conference in France. "They take all its riches. . . . We only own 13 percent of our natural resources. It is France that is there, everywhere. . . . It would be better to go home, if we could work there in true cooperation. We'd be better off in the sun, under the coconut palms."[15]

Several EU countries, as well as the United States, remain deeply involved in recent Middle Eastern and African conflicts and in the arms trade generally, so they share responsibility for the violence sending millions of refugees to Europe. No one wants to be forcibly displaced from their homes. Instead of attempting to block people from seeking safety, wouldn't it make more sense for powerful countries to stop fueling these wars, and to try to prevent them instead?[16]

Has freedom of movement caused problems in Europe?

In a 2005 opinion survey, most EU citizens ranked "freedom to travel and work" as the European Union's most meaningful achievement.[17]

When the EU's border-free zone was first extended to Southern Europe in the early 1990s (Italy in 1990; Spain, Portugal, and Greece in 1992), many northern Europeans feared their countries would be flooded by people from the poorer Southern nations who were seeking better-paying jobs. Some people did migrate in that direction, but as it turned out, many went the other way: retirees from Germany and the United Kingdom moved to Spain, France, Greece, or Portugal in search of better weather, cheaper living, and opportunities for leisure. Unemployment rates in most EU nations shrank between 1993 and 2002; unemployment in the region as a whole dropped by more than two percentage points.[18]

The potential problems were greater when eight Eastern European countries, along with the Mediterranean island nations of Cyprus and Malta, joined the European Union on May 1, 2004.

These ten countries had a combined population of more than 100 million people with an average income roughly half that of the other European Union members. The UK government, which put no restrictions on the new arrivals, had predicted that no more than 13,000 people would come each year from the new EU member states, but in the subsequent two years, about 500,000 Eastern Europeans registered as workers in the United Kingdom. The influx sparked public concern, leading Britain to impose restrictions on workers from Bulgaria and Romania, which joined the European Union as member states in 2007.[19]

But the feared economic consequences of mass migration from new EU member states to the more prosperous Western European states largely failed to materialize. "Although there will be continuing migration from east to west . . . geographical mobility within Europe has been, and is likely to remain, relatively low," the Ireland-based European Foundation for the Improvement of Living and Working Conditions concluded in an October 2006 report.[20]

Did Europe's standard of living collapse after borders opened?

In 1975, before the borders were opened, production workers in manufacturing in the original fifteen EU countries were making 80 percent as much as U.S. workers. By the 1990s they were generally making more than workers here—17 percent more in 2004.[21] From 1994 to 2003, the Gross Domestic Product (GDP) as measured in per capita purchasing power standards tended to equalize across the European Union, going slightly down in six of the region's wealthier countries and up in four, while generally rising in the poorer countries. Certainly, no European country saw its standard of living drop dramatically over the decade after the borders were opened.[22]

The EU has suffered serious economic problems since the global financial crisis of 2007 and 2008, but there's no indication that these resulted from Europe's open border policy. Nobel Prize–winning economist Paul Krugman cites a "widespread consensus among economists (though not, alas, among politicians) that Europe's woes were mainly caused by mood swings among private investors," much as unrealistic investment schemes were a major cause of the mortgage crisis in the United States during the same period.[23]

In June 2016, British citizens voted in a referendum to withdraw the United Kingdom from the EU. EU opponents frequently cited increased immigration as one of their objections to the EU, but this was largely because the British media and political establishment had created a distorted view of immigration. According to a 2011 survey, British citizens thought on average that 31.8 percent of the UK population was foreign born, while the actual percentage at the time was 12.7 percent. The largest share of immigrants and refugees came from Southern Asia, East Asia, and Southeast Asia—regions including former British colonies—rather than from the EU.[24]

How can we keep criminals and terrorists out without borders?

Since immigration restriction has not proven effective in preventing crime or terrorism,[25] there's no reason to think that reducing or eliminating repressive immigration policies will make us more vulnerable to criminal or terrorist acts. Certainly, no amount of border control can prevent the kind of decentralized, technologically networked terror attacks that have become increasingly common in recent years.

The European Union has addressed safety concerns by enhancing information sharing among member nations and expanding cooperation with non-member nations. A database has been created among the member nations that includes information about people's identities as well as stolen or lost items. The EU has a European Police Office (Europol) that coordinates intelligence sharing and a European arrest warrant. In addition, even countries in the Schengen area are still free to institute temporary border patrol at times of crisis.[26]

If we really had freedom of movement, some kinds of crime would virtually disappear, such as human trafficking, violent assaults and kidnappings of migrants, and the false document trade. Also, immigrants would be less afraid of cooperating with police to report serious crimes.

Is opening the borders part of "free trade"?

Some efforts at trade liberalization and economic integration have followed the European model, which includes the free internal movement of people as well as goods, services, and money. But the United States created a very different model with the North American Free Trade Agreement (NAFTA), which took effect in 1994 for the United States, Canada, and Mexico. NAFTA allows corporations to move goods, services, and money across borders, but it shuts workers out. This kind of free trade, which the United States has sought to expand into Central and South America, is designed to help wealthy and powerful sectors increase their profits and build their political and economic muscle by keeping workers exploited and lowering labor costs. (In Europe, meanwhile, wealthy and powerful sectors have found ways to profit from the free flow of labor and of goods.)

While the European Union made some efforts to equalize economic conditions among its member nations, NAFTA has done nothing to reduce the wage gap between the United States and Mexico. On the contrary, it has contributed to a "race to the bottom," which only benefits employers looking for cheap labor, and big companies looking for new markets. At the same time, NAFTA has had a devastating impact on small-scale farmers in Mexico, leaving them few options for survival, other than coming to the United States to work as undocumented immigrants.[27]

Could freedom of movement actually work here?

If we take into account the increasingly interconnected global economy, and we expand our ideas about basic human rights, we might come up with a progressive U.S. immigration policy that looks something like this:

- We could allow everyone who is living here and wants to remain a chance to achieve citizenship. Many undocumented immigrants are de facto citizens already, since they have lived here for over a decade and feel that they belong here; we could grant them full rights, with no limiting conditions and no punishment.
- We could grant a full and complete amnesty. No one would be disqualified from entry or from citizenship based on past "illegal" stays, deportations, or criminal records.
- We could put an end to deportation and detention. Yes, even for people who have committed crimes. There are legal mechanisms in place for criminal prosecution and extradition. Our justice system should be fair and impartial in holding offenders accountable, not dependent on citizenship status, race, ethnicity, income level, or any other discriminatory factor.
- We could let visitors come here without an obstructionist visa process. People can fill out an entry form online or at the airport or border—the way people from Western Europe, Australia, Canada, Chile, and a few of the wealthier Asian countries do currently through the U.S. visa waiver program, and the way U.S. citizens do when they visit most other countries.[28]
- If visitors decide they want to stay, we could encourage them to contribute their skills, dreams, values, and political engagement to build a more equitable society—as students, workers, entrepreneurs, community volunteers, or caregivers for friends and relatives. People who want to work should be provided with Social Security numbers and information about their labor rights, and allowed to work without restrictions. We could establish streamlined processes for recognizing their skills and qualifications.

- We could grant freedom of movement in all directions, allowing people to go back and forth as desired between the United States, their country of origin, and any other nation without penalties or time limits.
- We could fully respect dual or multiple nationalities, allowing people to affirm U.S. citizenship without renouncing their citizenship elsewhere. (There's nothing wrong with having close ties or allegiances to more than one place.)

Wouldn't we be flooded with immigrants?

Initially, if we opened our borders, we might see a lot of new immigrants arriving, as happened when the EU admitted Eastern European countries in 2004. But border restrictions are only one of the many factors that shape migration patterns. Even though the U.S. government tightened controls on the southwestern border from 1991 to 2007, the undocumented population from Mexico increased dramatically during the period. When the number of undocumented immigrants stabilized later, in 2007–2008, it was largely because of an economic crisis in the United States.[29]

Puerto Rico is an example of what happens when people are allowed to migrate freely from a poorer country to a wealthier one. The U.S. Congress in effect opened the border with Puerto Rico in 1917 when it made all of the island's residents U.S. citizens, but only about 60,000 Puerto Ricans migrated to the United States in the two decades from 1920 to 1940. However, Puerto Rican migration soared after 1948 when the U.S. government started Operation Bootstrap, a program reorienting the economy from agriculture to manufacturing for export. The program resulted in major job losses and dislocations of the rural population; as many as 694,000 Puerto Ricans moved to the mainland from 1950 to 1970.

The Puerto Rican economy started stabilizing in the 1970s. Net migration to the mainland—the difference between the people who enter and the people who leave—fell to just 11,000 for the ten years from 1990 to 2000. But migration jumped again after long-standing corporate tax breaks were ended in 2006; the tax change helped create a new economic crisis on the island just as the 2007–2009 U.S. recession was about to strike. Net migration to the mainland in the three years from 2010 to 2013 was 48,000.[30]

If the U.S. government renounced the sort of policies that disrupt the economies of its southern neighbors, migration from those countries would likely stabilize just as Puerto Rican migration did in the 1970s and 1980s. Once people realize that they can come and go without problems, we could expect to see many immigrants returning to their home countries for frequent or extended visits. New immigrants who come here to work would be able to save money sooner, rather than laboring for years to pay off debts to smugglers. People could choose to come here for seasonal or temporary jobs, and return home to spend the rest of the year with their families. Such back-and-forth migration used to be common, especially among Mexicans working in the United States, until enforcement grew tougher, increasing the risks of crossing the border. Many immigrants feel torn between an original homeland and an adopted country, not quite belonging in either. Dividing their time between the two homes can help them to feel whole again.

Under a truly international open borders policy, migration could flow in all directions, so that workers dissatisfied with conditions in the United States could move to countries that offer universal healthcare, childcare, and paid vacations. In 2005, when Ireland's economy was booming, a total of 4,300 U.S. citizens moved to Ireland, whereas only 1,700 Irish citizens moved to the United States, according to Ireland's Trade and Employment Ministry.[31] U.S. workers might want to move south of the border for better weather and cheaper housing when they retire; many already do this, just as many retirees from Northern Europe have moved to the Southern European countries. Of course, this should be a personal choice, not something people are forced to do because their pension income isn't enough to support them in their own country.

What would be the costs and benefits of opening the borders?

It's logical to think that opening up the borders would create opportunities to:

- Save billions in tax dollars by reducing bureaucracy and ending immigration enforcement;
- Increase tax revenue by allowing millions more immigrants to work legally;
- Raise wages and improve working conditions by encouraging labor organizing;
- Free up resources to enhance the enforcement of labor, employment, and health and safety protections;
- Boost the travel industry by allowing people to come and go without restrictions;
- Reduce violent crime by eliminating the fear that keeps victims from reporting it;
- Improve social and economic stability by allowing families to stay together;
- Greatly reduce or eliminate deaths on the border, human trafficking, and the illegal trade in false documents.

Research suggests that ending restrictions on labor mobility would raise overall economic output in both poorer and wealthier countries.[32] But what's good for the economy in a general sense is not always good for workers. In many economic sectors, workers are already pitted against one another globally because their jobs can be moved across borders, even if they themselves are not able to migrate. For jobs that can't be easily moved across borders, labor mobility can bring that "race to the bottom" home, pushing down wages and working conditions by expanding the pool of available workers competing for the same jobs.

Given that situation, it's understandable that many U.S. workers want to protect "American jobs" for "American workers." However, the solution to the race to the bottom is for workers to join together across borders, and across ethnic and racial lines, to organize for better wages and working conditions. Restricting immigration actually makes the situation worse for U.S. workers, because instead of stopping immigrants from coming here, it just makes it harder for them to defend their labor rights when they get here.[33]

Do people have a "right not to migrate"?

Most people would rather build a better future in the place they know as home, instead of having to uproot themselves from land, family, and community. That's why, along with the right to migrate, we should work to expand "the right not to migrate." As documented by labor journalist David Bacon, this slogan has become a popular demand of indigenous people from the southern Mexican state of Oaxaca.[34]

Most of the major problems we face now are global and have to be dealt with globally. True freedom of movement would ideally be part of a global economic and social transformation that addresses the root causes of migration by improving the standard of living for the world's poorest people, protecting human rights, and expanding freedom and opportunity for everyone.

Some first steps could be to repeal or renegotiate NAFTA and all other unequal trade agreements; halt the international arms trade; and end the U.S. government's military, political, and economic interventions in world affairs—a major cause of displacement. Instead, the United States could take a stand for justice and freedom through international actions that respect sovereignty and human rights. We could begin a dialogue about ways to redistribute wealth and pay reparations to people affected by the theft and appropriation of resources over past centuries. We could compel U.S.-influenced international financial institutions to reverse policies that cause poverty and suffering around the world—and to forgive the debts of impoverished nations. Instead of paying for wars, military occupations, and bank bailouts, we could devote our tax dollars to building a society in which we could all realize our full human potential. And we'll need to get serious about slowing global warming, which is likely to be a major driver of forced migration in the future.[35]

How can we work toward freedom of movement?

Some would argue that a radical shift in immigration policy requires sweeping changes in the society. It's true that the forces that oppose a real reform are strong. But there's a lot we can do to improve conditions right now, while building toward more fundamental changes in the future.

We could start by pushing for a general amnesty for undocumented immigrants,[36] and for an open border among the three NAFTA nations and the other regional blocs with which the United States has trade pacts.[37]

Arguing for such demands provides opportunities to open up fact-based dialogues at the grassroots level, across and within communities, allowing us to listen and talk to each other. That could lead us to broad, clear, and democratic visions of what we really want, and how to achieve it. We can learn the history of peoples and communities, including those we call our own: what has worked in the past, what hasn't, how we ended up in this current global crisis, and how we might get out of it. We can work to dismantle racism and to address complex issues of belonging and identity. There are thousands of resources—books, films, oral histories—to help us learn. We could share these resources by setting up screenings, discussions, and study groups; by creating our own media, using the internet, and just talking to each other. And above all, we could join together and organize: as workers, students, and neighbors.

Most people everywhere share the same desires: for a good quality of life, access to healthcare, and fairness for all; for opportunities to express ourselves, to be productive, and to fulfill our goals and dreams; and for a sustainable environment for the next generation. By organizing powerful networks of solidarity locally, nationally, and globally, we can build a better future together.[38]

Afterword

DONALD TRUMP ASSUMED THE U.S. presidency in January 2017, shortly after we finished writing the revised edition of this book.

His election campaign relied on myths, stereotypes, and outright hatred of unauthorized immigrants—particularly those from Mexico—and of Muslims. Among his first actions in office were executive orders and other directives targeting these segments of the population.

The new president's anti-immigrant rhetoric relies on many claims that researchers disproved years ago, for example:

- that undocumented immigrants commit a disproportionate share of violent crimes;
- that their numbers are continuing to rise;
- that they cost taxpayers a fortune in social services;
- that Muslim immigrants represent a terrorist threat.

Trump's policy initiatives include stepped-up enforcement measures that are costly, inhumane, and ineffective at best—and likely counterproductive, at least when it comes to the interests of working- and middle-class people.

One of the first policies the administration tried to put in effect was a temporary ban on entry by non-citizens from seven majority-Muslim countries and a four-month ban on entry by any refugee. Evidence from the early 2000s shows that profiling Muslims and refugees does nothing to prevent terrorism; instead, it may divert resources from smart, effective police work.

Trump continues to push for a "wall" along the southwestern border, even though the current massive and expensive display of border enforcement (including more than 600 miles of fencing) has failed to stop unauthorized entry in the past and may even have led to an increase in the size of the undocumented population.

Trump appears to be taking steps to carry out deportations at a more intense pace than was seen under previous administrations. Past experience shows that the main effect of deportation raids is to terrify unauthorized workers and drive them even further into the underground economy, making it harder for all workers to fight for better labor conditions.

A resistance movement is swelling and will continue to grow. We can expect to see more developments like the spontaneous airport protests that took place against the "Muslim ban" in late January, and the rapid response networks that sprang up during a nationwide round of deportations in the middle of February.

But protest is not enough. Trump's victory happened in part because so many of us are uncomfortable talking to people who don't share our views. Even if the most vocal opponents of immigration don't easily change their minds, their arguments can influence others who might be more willing to engage in dialogue. If we can bring ourselves to hear their concerns instead of dismissing or silencing them, we have a chance to shift the political climate.

This is an especially good time for serious dialogue about the realities of immigration. Trump's election has had the paradoxical effect of undercutting common misconceptions on the subject.

Previously many politicians and media commentators tried to make their claims about immigration appear moderate, rational, and fact-based. This effort has vanished with the new administration. We now have a president who describes immigrants from Mexico as rapists bringing drugs and crime, and a senior White House adviser who goes on national television to pass off falsehoods as "alternative facts." Many people are becoming more open to seeing U.S. immigration policies for what they really are: brutal, racist, and harmful, even to most of the native-born population.

Reaching out beyond our immediate circles can be difficult. It's much easier just to talk with people who already agree with us and to dismiss those who don't. But it's necessary—and possible—to get anti-immigrant ideas out in the open and to debate them.

We encourage people to take up the challenge, and we hope you find this book to be a useful tool in your efforts.

—JANE GUSKIN AND DAVID L. WILSON
March 2017

Immigration and the Law: A Chronology

Except where otherwise indicated in these endnotes, information provided in the chronology comes from the text of the relevant laws or court rulings. See http://thepoliticsofimmigration.org for links and updates.

1789 (**ratified**): U.S. Constitution. Article I, section 8 gives Congress the power to "establish an uniform Rule of Naturalization." Article I, section 9, says that prior to 1808 Congress may not prohibit the "Migration or Importation of such Persons as any of the States now existing shall think proper to admit"—implying that starting in 1808 Congress can control immigration policy and the importation of people as slaves. Section 9 also guarantees habeas corpus, the right to challenge a person's imprisonment; nothing in the text limits this right to citizens.

1790: Naturalization Act. Establishes that "any Alien being a free white person, who shall have resided within the limits and under the jurisdiction of the United States for the term of two years, may be admitted to become a citizen" if "he is a person of good character."

1791 (**ratified**): First ten amendments to the Constitution (Bill of Rights). Guarantee basic rights of freedom of religion and of speech, the right to protest, the right to freedom from unreasonable searches, and the right to due process, including the right to remain silent. Nothing in the text limits these rights to citizens;

several rights are specifically guaranteed to "the people" or a "person."

1795: Naturalization Act. Increases the residency requirement to five years, for "free white persons," and requires renunciation of "allegiance and fidelity" to any other country.

1798: Alien and Sedition Acts.

- Naturalization Act increases residency requirement to fourteen years.

- Alien Friends Act allows the government to detain and deport foreigners considered "dangerous" to the peace and safety of the United States.

- Alien Enemies Act allows the detention and deportation of any male over fourteen from an "enemy" nation during times of war.

- Sedition Act restricts free speech.

1807: Act to Prohibit the Importation of Slaves. Congress's first use of its authority to regulate immigration and the importation of persons. Effective January 1, 1808, the Act bans importing "any negro, mulatto, or person of colour, with intent to hold, sell, or dispose of . . . as a slave, or to be held in service or labour."

1848: Treaty of Guadalupe Hidalgo. Gives the United States control over Texas, California, and the southwestern states; Article 9 allows the more than 100,000 people living there who identify as Mexicans the option of choosing U.S. citizenship—but in practice, their citizenship rights and property ownership are not respected. The more than 200,000 Native Americans in the territory are described in Article 11 as members of "savage tribes" and placed "under the exclusive control of the government of the United States."[1]

1857: *Dred Scott v. Sandford.* The Supreme Court rules that only white people can be U.S. citizens, barring all African Americans from citizenship, even free black people who had previously been citizens.

1868 (**ratified**): Fourteenth Amendment. Establishes that "all persons born or naturalized in the United States, and subject to the jurisdiction thereof, are citizens of the United States and of the State wherein they reside." No state is allowed to "deprive any person of life, liberty, or property, without due process of law; nor deny to any person within its jurisdiction the equal protection of the laws."

1870: Naturalization Act. Extends naturalization law to cover "aliens of African nativity and persons of African descent"; Asians and other people of color are not mentioned and so remain excluded from naturalization under the 1790 and 1795 laws.

1875: Immigration Act (Page Act). The first immigration law to bar people from entering the United States because of their nationality or ethnicity. It prohibits "the immigration of any subject of China, Japan, or any Oriental country" without the immigrant's consent, the immigration of people convicted of non-political felonies, and "the importation into the United States of women for the purposes of prostitution." The unstated purpose is to prevent single Chinese women from immigrating and marrying Chinese men already in the United States, since their U.S.-born children would be citizens under the Fourteenth Amendment.[2]

1882: Chinese Exclusion Act. Excludes all Chinese laborers, skilled and unskilled, from entering the United States for ten years, and provides for deportation of "any Chinese person found unlawfully within the United States." Chinese laborers already in the country are mostly permitted to stay; if they leave the United States, they can receive a certificate from a local customs inspector allowing them to reenter later. The Act also bars states from granting citizenship to any Chinese person.

1882: Immigration Act. Imposes a 50-cent tax on foreigners entering at U.S. ports and denies entry at a port for people convicted of non-political crimes and for any "lunatic, idiot, or any person unable to take care of himself or herself without becoming a public charge." Puts the Secretary of the Treasury in charge of immigration; states continue to carry out local immigration functions, but in coordination with the federal government.

1885: Contract Labor Law (Foran Act). Prohibits the contracting of foreign workers to come to the United States in order "to perform service or labor of any kind." The ban does not cover "private secretaries, servants, or domestics"; professionals such as artists and actors are also exempted, as are skilled laborers if resident workers for a specific purpose "cannot otherwise be obtained."

1889: Supreme Court decision in *Chae Chan Ping v. United States* (Chinese Exclusion Case). The unanimous ruling establishes that Congress can restrict immigration or deport immigrants because of a nation's "duty" to "preserve its independence and give security against foreign aggression and encroachment" by a foreign nation, "whether from the foreign nation acting in its national character or from vast hordes of its people crowding in upon us."

1891: Immigration Act. Amends 1882 Immigration Act to create Office of Superintendent of Immigration under the Treasury Department, consolidating the responsibility of the federal government over immigration enforcement. (In 1894 the agency is renamed the Bureau of Immigration.) The Act also increases regulation of the border and expands the list of deportable and excludable foreigners to include "paupers," polygamists, and people with "a loathsome or a dangerous contagious disease." Deportation can only take place within one year after the immigrant enters the United States, in contrast to the Chinese Exclusion Act, which has no time limit for deportations.

1892: Ellis Island. Government opens a new facility on a small New York Harbor island to process immigrants arriving on the East Coast. Almost 12 million immigrants pass through the station before it is closed in 1954.[3]

1892: Geary Act. Extends the Chinese Exclusion Act for an additional ten years. Requires Chinese laborers and other people of Chinese descent to acquire a "certificate of residence" by presenting "at least one credible white witness" who can testify to their legal presence. Orders one year of hard labor and subsequent deportation for those who cannot prove they are legally present. (Chinese Exclusion Act is renewed again in 1902 and made permanent in 1904.)

1893: Supreme Court decision in *Fong Yue Ting v. United States*. Dismisses a legal challenge to the Geary Act, ruling: "The right to exclude or to expel aliens, or any class of aliens, absolutely or upon certain conditions, in war or in peace, is an inherent and inalienable right of every sovereign nation." Upholds the deportation of Fong Yue Ting and two other Chinese immigrants, based on their failure to find "at least one credible white witness" to testify about their resident status.

1898: Supreme Court decision in *United States v. Wong Kim Ark.* Supreme Court upholds birthright citizenship for people born in the United States to non-citizens (other than representatives of foreign governments). Wong Kim Ark was born in California to Chinese immigrant parents; when he tried to return to the United States after a trip abroad, he was denied reentry under the rules of the Chinese Exclusion Act. His successful challenge of his exclusion solidifies the *jus soli* principle ("right of the soil," a legal term for citizenship determined by place of birth).

1903: Immigration Act (Anarchist Exclusion Act). Expands the list of deportable and excludable foreigners to include epileptics, prostitutes, "professional beggars," people with a history of mental illness, and anarchists; this is the first exclusion based on political beliefs since the Alien and Sedition Acts of 1798. Extends the period of time in which excludable immigrants can be deported to three years, and provides for the deportation of "any alien who becomes a public charge by reason of lunacy, idiocy, or epilepsy" within two years of arriving. Levies a head tax of $2. (The Act is renewed in 1907 with some amendments.)

1903: Bureau of Immigration is transferred to the newly created Department of Commerce and Labor.

1906: Naturalization Act. Establishes fixed fees and uniform naturalization forms, and makes knowledge of English a requirement. Changes the Bureau of Immigration to the Bureau of Immigration and Naturalization.

1907: Expatriation Act. For the first time defines the citizenship of women married to foreigners. Women assume the citizenship of their husbands, and a woman with U.S. citizenship forfeits it if she marries a foreigner, unless he becomes naturalized. Repealed by the Married Women's Act of 1922 (Cable Act).

1907: "Gentlemen's Agreement" between the U.S. and Japanese governments. Japanese immigration, especially to California, increased following the Chinese Exclusion Act, as did anti-Japanese backlash. In order to avoid any U.S. legislation barring Japanese immigrants, Japan agrees to stop allowing its citizens to emigrate to the United States, and the United States agrees to continue allowing the entry of spouses and children of Japanese immigrants already present.[4]

1913: California Alien Land Law (Webb-Haney Act). Prohibits "aliens ineligible to citizenship" from owning property in the state. This law is aimed principally at Asian immigrants, who are excluded from citizenship under the Naturalization Act of 1870.

1913: The Organic Act of the Department of Labor. Divides the Department of Commerce and Labor into separate departments; the Bureau of Immigration and Naturalization is moved to the Department of Labor and divided into the Bureau of Immigration and the Bureau of Naturalization.

1917: Immigration Act (Asiatic Barred Zone Act). Denies entry to immigrants from the "Asiatic Barred Zone," an area encompassing most of Asia and the Pacific Islands, excluding Japan and eastern China. (Chinese are already barred under the 1882 law, and the 1907 U.S.-Japan "Gentlemen's Agreement" remains in effect.) Exceptions are made to allow the entry of professional, wealthy, and highly educated Asians. The Act also sets a literacy requirement for immigrants over sixteen and a head tax for entry into the country; it further expands the list of excludable people to cover "feeble-minded persons," alcoholics, and all persons "mentally or physically defective." The only two exceptions are people fleeing religious persecution and immediate family members of admissible foreign nationals.

1917: Jones-Shafroth Act (Jones Act). Extends U.S. citizenship to all citizens of Puerto Rico, although Puerto Ricans have the option to refuse U.S. citizenship for six months after the Act takes effect.

1921: Emergency Quota Act. Limits immigration to a total of about 350,000 a year, with no more from each country than 3 percent of the number of immigrants from that country living in the United States in 1910. This is intended to freeze immigration from Eastern and Southern Europe at the 1910 level.

1922: Supreme Court decision in *Ozawa v. United States*. Upholds the government's power to deny naturalization to an Asian immigrant under the 1790 and 1795 laws.

1923: Supreme Court decision in *United States v. Bhagat Singh Thind*. Denies citizenship rights to migrants from the Indian subcontinent who arrived in the United States before the Immigration Act of 1917 excluded them. The ruling led to the retroactive denaturalization of Indian Americans who had become citizens. In California, where many Punjabi immigrants had become farmers, this denaturalization subjected them to the Alien Land Law of 1913, which banned "aliens ineligible for citizenship" from ownership or long-term leasing of agricultural land.[5]

1924: Immigration Act (National Origins Act, Johnson-Reed Act). Limits immigration to a total of about 165,000 a year through 1928, with no more from each country than 2 percent of the number of immigrants from that country living in the United States in 1890. (After 1927, the quotas are to be based on an estimate of the national origins of the entire U.S. population as of 1920.) Prohibits most immigration of people who are ineligible for citizenship, principally Asians. There is no numerical limit on immigration from independent countries in the Western Hemisphere, although legal immigration is restricted by entry rules including head taxes and literacy requirements. Effectively ends the U.S.-Japan "Gentlemen's Agreement." Specifies that immigrants who enter in violation of the Act can be deported "at any time after entering the United States," and that immigrants have the "burden of proof" to show that they entered lawfully. Sets up the visa process for people seeking to enter the United States.

1924: Labor Appropriation Act. Establishes the Border Patrol under the Department of Labor, in part to prevent the smuggling of alcohol during Prohibition. The government recruits 450 people, mostly chosen from a list of applicants for jobs as federal railway postal clerks, to patrol the 1,950-mile border.[6]

1929: Proclamation 1872. Implements the 1924 National Origins Act as amended by joint committees in 1927 and 1928, reducing the overall annual limit on immigration to 150,000. Quotas are now based on an estimate of the national origins of the entire U.S. population as of 1920 (as mandated in the 1924 Immigration Act), but excluding all people of African or indigenous descent, those with ancestry in Latin America, and Asians: "aliens ineligible to citizenship or their descendants." Each country gets a minimum quota of 100; even the Asian countries, officially, although their citizens cannot use the quotas, since they remain barred. The

United Kingdom now has more than one-third of the quota slots. Western Hemisphere nations remain exempt from the quota.[7]

1929–1936: Mexican Repatriation. Between 500,000 and two million Mexicans and U.S.-born Mexican Americans are deported or forced to leave the United States.[8]

1933: Executive Order 6166. Combines the Bureau of Immigration and the Bureau of Naturalization into the Immigration and Naturalization Service (INS). The new agency remains in the Labor Department until President Roosevelt moves it into the Department of Justice in 1940.

1934: Philippine Independence Act (Tydings-McDuffie Act). Authorizes a ten-year process leading to independence for the Philippines. Ends the extension of U.S. nationality to Filipinos and sets an annual quota of fifty for Filipino immigration to the United States (except for Hawaii, then a U.S. territory). The Philippines become independent on July 4, 1946.

1940: Alien Registration Act (Smith Act). Requires the registration and fingerprinting of all foreigners in the United States over the age of fourteen. Provides for deportation of immigrants who "at the time of entering the United States, or . . . at any time thereafter" belonged to a group advocating the overthrow of the U.S. government.

1940: Nationality Act. Reaffirms restrictions on the naturalization of Asian immigrants and their descendants; only Filipinos who served honorably in the U.S. military are exempted. Restores the citizenship of women who lost their U.S. citizenship by marrying an alien.

1942–1964: "*Bracero*" Program. Created to remedy an apparent shortage of agricultural and other workers during the Second World War, the program expands through the middle 1950s. Although the program is intended as an alternative to the "revolving door" of unauthorized migration, the number of undocumented farmworkers increases dramatically during the period. The workers have 10 percent of their wages withheld for a trust fund, which mysteriously disappears; the Mexican government eventually agrees to reimburse the workers and their survivors early in the twenty-first century.[9]

1943: Chinese Exclusion Repeal Act (Magnuson Act). Repeals several laws, including the Chinese Exclusion Act of 1882. Limits entry to 105 Chinese people a year, based on the quota system established in 1924. Amends the 1940 Nationality Act to allow the naturalization of Chinese people and their descendants, but not other Asians.

1946: Luce Celler Act. Grants naturalization rights to Filipinos and Asian Indians, and allows 100 people a year from each of the two nationalities to immigrate.

1948: Displaced Persons Act. Temporary emergency legislation in response to the refugee crisis in Europe following the Second World War. Eventually brings in 399,698 refugees, who are counted against future national origins system quotas. President Truman objects that the bill effectively excludes "more than 90 percent of the remaining Jewish displaced persons" in Europe. He signs it only because the bill is passed on the last day of the congressional session and a refusal to sign would mean "there would be no legislation on behalf of displaced persons until the next session of the Congress."[10]

1952: Immigration and Nationality Act (McCarran-Walter Act). Consolidates earlier legislation into one act covering both immigration and naturalization. Passed at the height of the Cold War, the law maintains the basic quota system from the 1920s, with about 85 percent of the openings reserved for Northern and Western Europe. Residents of a colonial possession are limited to 100 of the slots in the possessing country's annual quota; residents of the British West Indies colonies are especially affected. The Act continues and expands the exclusion of immigrants on grounds of health, criminal records, and "moral turpitude"; it maintains exclusions for political activities and now adds membership in the U.S. Communist Party and advocacy of "world communism" to the grounds for exclusion. For the first time naturalization is open to all races and ethnic groups. President Truman vetoes the bill, finding it discriminatory; Congress overrides his veto.[11]

1953: Refugee Relief Act. Additional temporary measure in response to the European refugee crisis. Provides for up to 205,000 visas. Most are for European refugees and "escapees" from Communist countries, but there are up to 2,000 visas for Palestinians residing in the Middle East, and 7,000 for Asians. The Act expires at the end of 1956.

1954: Supreme Court decision in *Galvan v. Press*. Upholds the power of Congress to deport immigrants because of past membership, however brief, in the Communist Party. Justices Black and Douglas dissent; Black notes that the petitioner, a longtime U.S. resident, was a Communist Party member for just two years, at a time when the U.S. government recognized the party as "perfectly legal."

1954: "Operation Wetback." U.S. immigration officials, assisted by local authorities, launch a campaign to deport undocumented Mexican agricultural workers. Officials claim as many as 1.3 million Mexicans fled or were deported, but historians say the actual number is much lower. The operation's goal is to force undocumented workers into the *bracero* program; the number of *braceros* in 1954 rises to 300,000, up from 200,000 the previous year.[12]

1957: Refugee-Escapee Act. Among other measures, amends the 1953 Refugee Relief Act to allot a proportion of "special non-quota immigrant visas" to "refugees-escapees," defined as anyone fleeing a "Communist-dominated, or Communist-occupied area," or a country "within the general area of the Middle East," for fear of persecution on the basis of race, religion, or political opinion.

1958: Hungarian Escape Act. Grants permanent status to nearly 40,000 Hungarians who had been allowed to enter the United States temporarily ("paroled," in immigration jargon) as refugees after the Soviet-backed Hungarian government crushed a 1956 uprising.

1960: Fair Share Act. Grants the attorney general authority to parole large groups of refugees. This addresses the continuing problem of Hungarian refugees and of others still living in displaced person camps after the Second World War.

1961: Immigration and Nationality Act. Amends the 1952 law to limit the judicial review of final orders of deportation to specific courts of appeals.

1962: Migration and Refugee Assistance Act. Provides funding for relief of refugees, including resettlement of people who "because of persecution or fear of persecution on account of race, religion, or political beliefs, fled from a nation or area of the Western Hemisphere"—a reference to Cubans opposing the leftist government that took power in Cuba in January 1959.

1965: Immigration and Nationality Act (Hart-Celler Act). Amends the 1952 INA to end the national origin quota system as of 1968; bars discrimination in the granting of visas based on "race, sex, nationality, place of birth, or place of residence." The Act institutes a system of preferences mostly based on family relations to U.S. residents, with some preferences for professionals and people with special skills. It also includes the first formal restrictions on immigration from the Americas; starting in 1968 total immigration is limited to 170,000 a year for the Eastern Hemisphere and 120,000 for the Western Hemisphere. Refugees are defined as people fleeing persecution in "any Communist or Communist-dominated country or area," people fleeing persecution in a Middle Eastern country, or "persons uprooted by a catastrophic natural calamity"; the number of refugees is limited to 6 percent of total immigration. Epilepsy is removed from the list of grounds for exclusion, but "sexual deviation" is added.

1966: Cuban Adjustment Act. Allows Cuban immigrants to apply for permanent resident status if they were admitted or paroled into the United States after January 1, 1959, and have lived here for at least two years.

1968: Protocol Relating to the Status of Refugees (1967) signed by United States. The Protocol updates the 1951 Convention on the Status of Refugees, which originally applied only to European refugees displaced by the Second World War; the United States never signed the 1951 Convention.

1980: Refugee Act. Trades the anti-communist definition of a refugee for the humanitarian definition laid out in the 1967 UN Protocol. Distinguishes refugees (people who apply for refugee status from another country) from asylum seekers (people who apply for asylum after arriving in the United States). Allows acceptance of about 50,000 refugees and 5,000 asylum seekers; the president can expand the numbers in an emergency situation if there are "grave humanitarian concerns" or the expansion "is otherwise in the national interest." Allows the attorney general to parole immigrants into the country but only for "compelling reasons in the public interest." Reduces from two years to one the wait for Cubans to gain residency under the Cuban Adjustment Act.

1980: Mariel Boatlift. Some 130,000 Cubans land in Florida in a "freedom flotilla" from the Cuban port of Mariel; President Carter paroles them into the United States and allows them to apply for asylum. Some 25,000 Haitians arrive in Florida at about the same time and are also paroled into the United States; most are not granted asylum. A clause in the 1986 IRCA eventually allows "Cuban/ Haitian entrants (status pending)" to seek permanent residence.[13]

1982: Supreme Court decision in *Plyler v. Doe*. Strikes down a Texas law denying public funding for the education of undocumented immigrants. The decision is based on the "equal protection of the laws" requirement of the Fourteenth Amendment; it notes that undocumented children are not responsible for their immigration status.

1986: Immigration Reform and Control Act (IRCA). Allows undocumented immigrants who have lived in the United States since before 1982 to apply for legal residence; same provisions for people who worked ninety days in agriculture in the year ending May 1, 1986. Requires employers to obtain proof of work eligibility from all new hires and establishes penalties for employers who hire undocumented immigrants ("employer sanctions"). Mandates a 50 percent increase in the number of Border Patrol personnel. Establishes "diversity visas," also known as the "visa lottery," for 1987 and 1988 for countries with low immigration levels.

1990: Immigration Act. Modifies number of immigrants admitted (worldwide and by country); modifies asylum requirements and family preference requirements. Establishes "Family Unity" to defer deportation for children and spouses of legalized immigrants (mostly those legalized through the 1986 IRCA). Institutes Temporary Protected Status (TPS) for immigrants if the U.S. government has designated their countries as unsafe. Makes the diversity visa permanent; creates a new visa category for up to 10,000 immigrants a year who invest at least $1 million in "a new commercial enterprise." "Sexual deviation" is removed from the list of grounds for exclusion.

1994: FY1995 Commerce, Justice, State (CJS) Appropriations Act. Adds section 245(i) to INA; this provides a temporary process allowing some out-of-status immigrants to pay a fine and apply for adjustment of status without leaving the United States. Affects applicants with residency petitions sponsored by an employer or by immediate family members who are citizens or permanent residents.

1994: Cuba-U.S. Joint Communiqué ("Wet Foot Dry Foot"). Cubans who reach land in the United States are admitted to the country, but Cubans who are intercepted by the U.S. Coast Guard while at sea will be returned to Cuba.[14]

1994: California Proposition 187. California voters approve a state referendum mandating laws against the use of false immigration documents and cutting off state funding for all "public social services," "publicly funded healthcare" (including prenatal care), and public education (including elementary and secondary education) for undocumented immigrants. Teachers and health workers are required to turn in their students and patients suspected of being undocumented. Federal courts strike down parts, notably those affecting education (which violate the 1982 *Plyler v. Doe* decision) and healthcare.[15]

1996: Antiterrorism and Effective Death Penalty Act (AEDPA). Allows exclusion or deportation of foreigners supporting organizations that the president designates as terrorist; the government can use secret evidence in the deportation process. Expands the list of "crimes of moral turpitude" that can result in deportation.

1996: Personal Responsibility and Work Opportunity Reconciliation Act (PRWORA). Drastically reduces public assistance for lawful permanent residents who entered the United States after August 1996, including food stamps, Supplemental Security Income (SSI), Temporary Assistance for Needy Families (TANF), and Medicaid; bars federal welfare funding for undocumented immigrants.

1996: Illegal Immigration Reform and Immigrant Responsibility Act (IIRIRA). Cuts filing deadline for asylum cases to one year; allows immigration officers to deny entry to asylum applicants. Introduces "expedited removal," which authorizes immigration officers in many situations to order a foreigner deported without a hearing before an immigration judge. Drastically increases the number of crimes for which a legal resident can be deported. Makes detention mandatory for immigrants convicted of certain crimes. Expands the Border Patrol. Makes it harder to qualify for suspension of deportation, now renamed "cancellation of removal."

1997: Nicaraguan Adjustment and Central American Relief Act (NACARA). Allows Nicaraguans and Cubans to apply for permanent residence; gives some out-of-status Guatemalans, Salvadorans, and former Soviet bloc nationals a chance to seek suspension of deportation under pre-1996 rules.

1997: *Flores v. Reno* settlement. Mandates specific protections for unaccompanied minors in immigration custody; when possible, the minors are to be released to a sponsor or a shelter and provided with support services. Some of the binding settlement's rules are codified into law with the passage of the 2008 Trafficking Victims Protections Reauthorization Act.

1998: Haitian Refugee Immigration Fairness Act (HRIFA). Allows nearly 50,000 Haitians to seek permanent residence under a process similar to that granted to Cubans and Nicaraguans under NACARA.

1999: Supreme Court decision in *ADC v. Reno* (Los Angeles Eight). Rules that immigrants can be deported based on their political affiliations and do not have the right to challenge such selective targeting in federal court, or to find out the government's reasons for targeting them.

2000: Legal Immigration and Family Equity Act (LIFE Act). Extends deadline for filing section 245(i) applications from January 14, 1998, to April 30, 2001; 245(i) is no longer available after that date. Grants "late amnesty" to plaintiffs in class action suits whose legalization applications under IRCA were unfairly denied. Creates a temporary "V" visa allowing spouses and minor children of lawful permanent residents to enter the country if they've been waiting more than three years for a green card. Permanently expands visa options for family members and fiancés and fiancées of U.S. citizens.

2000: Battered Immigrant Women Protection Act (Title V of the Victims of Trafficking and Violence Protection Act). Expands access to relief for battered immigrant women, and creates the "U" non-immigrant visa for victims of domestic violence, trafficking, slavery, and certain other crimes who cooperate with law enforcement, allowing them to gain permanent residency in some cases.

2001: Supreme Court decision in *Zadvydas v. Davis*. Holds that immigrants cannot be detained indefinitely if they are ordered deported but have no country to return to; detention in these cases generally should not exceed six months.

2001: Uniting and Strengthening America by Providing Appropriate Tools Required to Intercept and Obstruct Terrorism (USA PATRIOT) Act. Amends the 1952 INA to expand the definition of non-citizens who are inadmissible or deportable for terrorism-related reasons. These reasons now include espousal of terrorism, association with foreign or domestic terrorist organizations, or family relationship (being the child or spouse of a terrorism suspect). Whether an organization is terrorist is determined by the secretary of state without any procedural safeguards. The attorney general can now order the detention and deportation of any alien suspected of terrorism; the suspect is able to challenge the detention only through a habeas corpus suit, with limited opportunities to appeal.[16]

2002: National Security Entry-Exit Registration System (NSEERS). A program initiated by the Department of Justice in 2002 and taken over by the Department of Homeland Security in 2003. All males sixteen years old or older who are on temporary non-immigrant visas and come from a list of twenty-five countries are required to register at immigration offices, where they are fingerprinted, photographed, and interrogated. All but one of the listed countries have predominantly Muslim populations. More than 80,000 non-citizens are registered, thousands are deported, and no terrorists are identified. The program is not used after April 2011 and is terminated on December 23, 2016, following a grassroots campaign to dismantle it.[17]

2002: Homeland Security Act. Creates the Department of Homeland Security (DHS). In March 2003, the INS is dismantled and its functions are moved into separate DHS agencies, the names of which are later clarified as Customs and Border Protection (CBP), Immigration and Customs Enforcement (ICE), and Citizenship and Immigration Services (USCIS). The Act transfers responsibility for unaccompanied minors to the Office of Refugee Resettlement (ORR), and confirms that the *Flores* Settlement Agreement terms apply to the new agencies.

2005: Supreme Court decision in consolidated cases of *Clark v. Martinez* and *Benitez v. Rozos*. Extends the logic of the *Zadvydas* ruling to "inadmissible" detainees, limiting their detention. The plaintiffs are Cubans who were paroled into the United States at the time of the 1980 Mariel boatlift.

2005: REAL ID Act. Approved as part of an Emergency Supplemental Appropriations Act. Imposes federal standards on states for issuing driver's licenses and other identification documents. Expands terrorism-related grounds for deeming aliens inadmissible. Makes it more difficult to win political asylum. Impedes the use of habeas corpus and limits judicial review in challenges to removal orders (although not to detention). Expands technological and communications infrastructure in border enforcement, and increases the Department of Homeland Security's waiver authority to construct barriers along the border. Includes the "Save Our Small and Seasonal Businesses Act of 2005," which makes available more H-2B temporary worker visas.

2005: HR 4437 (Sensenbrenner Bill). The House of Representatives tries to criminalize out-of-status immigrants by lumping together unlawful presence with "illegal entry," increasing the maximum sentence to a year and a day, and turning the crime into a felony. The bill, which also would have criminalized humanitarian support for undocumented immigrants, sparks mass protests by millions of immigrants in the spring of 2006. In May 2006, the Senate passes the Comprehensive Immigration Reform Act (S. 2611), which includes limited amnesty provisions providing certain categories of unauthorized immigrants with a path to citizenship. The two incompatible bills die in conference.[18]

2006: Secure Fence Act. Authorizes the construction of nearly 700 miles of fencing along the U.S.-Mexico border, along with an "interlocking surveillance camera system" in one sector.

2008: William Wilberforce Trafficking Victims Protection Reauthorization Act. Strengthens provisions of the Battered Immigrant Women Protection Act of 2000. Codifies into law some of the *Flores v. Reno* settlement rules for the protection of unaccompanied minors.

2009: DHS Appropriations Act for FY 2010. Requires immigration authorities to "maintain a level of not less than 33,400 detention beds." This is the first time Congress has set a quota for the number of detention beds; the number rises to 34,000 by 2015.[19]

2010: Supreme Court ruling in *Padilla v. Kentucky*. Allows some immigrants who plead guilty to a criminal offense to challenge the resulting removal order if their attorney failed to properly inform them that their plea would result in deportation.

2012: Deferred Action for Childhood Arrivals (DACA). President Obama issues an executive order allowing undocumented people under age thirty-one who came here before their sixteenth birthdays to apply for a two-year renewable work permit and a reprieve from deportation. To qualify, applicants must be in or have completed school or military service, and must have no significant criminal record. Some 1.2 million young people are estimated to be eligible for the program.[20]

2014: Deferred Action for Parental Accountability (DAPA). President Obama proposes a three-year deferment and work permit for many undocumented parents with children who are U.S. citizens or lawful permanent residents. DAPA and a proposed DACA expansion are blocked by a deadlocked Supreme Court in 2016.[21]

Notes

1. Who Are the Immigrants?

1. Eric Foner and John A. Garraty, eds., "Black Migration," *The Reader's Companion to American History* (Boston: Houghton Mifflin, 1991), accessed at Answers.com on February 22, 2007, http://www.answers.com/topic/black-migration.

2. Synopsis of "Underground Railroad," Historica Minutes, Historica Foundation of Canada website, accessed April 6, 2015, https://www.historicacanada.ca/content/heritage-minutes/underground-railroad; "Underground Railroad in Canada," Parks Canada website, http://www.pc.gc.ca/APPS/CP-NR/release_e.asp?bgid=479&andor1=bg, accessed April 6, 2015.

3. Felix Salmon, "The 'Illegal' Index: Which News Organizations Still Use the Term 'Illegal Immigrant'?" *Fusion*, November 20, 2014; Lawrence Downes, "What Part of 'Illegal' Don't You Understand?" *New York Times*, October 28, 2007.

4. Pilar Melero, "The Impact of Immigration Raids on Families," *Milwaukee Journal Sentinel*, August 10, 2006.

5. Jie Zong and Jeanne Batalova, "Frequently Requested Statistics on Immigrants and Immigration in the United States," Migration Policy Institute, February 26, 2015. The total of 44 million was calculated based on the number of naturalized citizens, LPRs, and undocumented immigrants in 2013; temporary legal residents were excluded. The 2013 figure of 13.5 million LPRs was obtained by taking the 2012 number (13.3 million), subtracting the 779,929 LPRs who naturalized in 2013 (both of these from the above-cited source), and adding the 990,553 people who became lawful permanent residents in 2013. See *DHS 2013 Yearbook of Immigration Statistics*, Table 6, "Persons Obtaining Lawful Permanent Resident Status

by Type and Major Class of Admission: Fiscal Years 2004 to 2013," http://www.dhs.gov/publication/yearbook-immigration-statistics-2013-lawful-permanent-residents, accessed November 8, 2015, Refugee/asylee numbers based on total number of individuals granted refugee or asylum status in 2013: 108,134. Refugees must adjust to LPR status one year after arriving; asylees are entitled but not required to do so, therefore the number of people with asylum status but not LPR status may be higher, but no figures seem to be available on this. See also (for 2012 numbers): Pew Hispanic Center, *Statistical Portrait of the Foreign-Born Population in the United States, 2012*, April 29, 2014, Table 1; Jeffrey S. Passel, D'Vera Cohn, and Ana Gonzalez-Barrera, *Population Decline of Unauthorized Immigrants Stalls, May Have Reversed*, Pew Hispanic Center, September 23, 2013, 9–10; Jeffrey S. Passel and D'Vera Cohn, *Unauthorized Immigrant Population: National and State Trends, 2010*, Pew Hispanic Center, February 1, 2010, 9–10. The Pew Hispanic Center became a part of the Pew Research Center in 2004 and in 2013 was renamed "Pew Research Center's Hispanic Trends Project." See http://www.pewresearch.org/2013/08/14/pew-hispanic-center-renamed-pew-research-centers-hispanic-trends-project/.

6. Jeffrey S. Passel and D'Vera Cohn, "Unauthorized Immigrant Population table for Half a Decade," Pew Research Center, July 22, 2015.

7. Jeffrey S. Passel and D'Vera Cohn, "Unauthorized Immigrant Totals Rise in 7 States, Fall in 14: Decline in Those From Mexico Fuels Most State Decreases," Pew Research Center, November 18, 2014. As of 2014, Pew estimated that the number of undocumented workers had decreased slightly to 8 million, about 5 percent of the U.S. labor force. Jeffrey S. Passel and D'Vera Cohn, "Size of U.S. Unauthorized Immigrant Workforce Stable After the Great Recession," Pew Research Center, November 3, 2016.

8. Pew Hispanic Center, *Statistical Portrait of the Foreign-Born Population in the United States, 2009*, February 17, 2011, Tables 9 and 9a.

9. Pew Research Center Hispanic Trends, "Median Household Income, by Nativity and Region of Birth: 2013," Table 33, in *Statistical Portrait of the Foreign-Born Population in the United States, 1960 –2013*, June 22, 2015.

10. Sandra L. Colby and Jennifer M. Ortman, "Population by Race and Hispanic Origin: 2014 and 2060," Table 2, in U.S. Census Bureau, *Projections of the Size and Composition of the U.S. Population: 2014 to 2060*, March 2015; Zong and Batalova, "Frequently Requested Statistics on Immigrants and Immigration in the United States."

11. Passel, Cohn, and Gonzalez-Barrera, *Population Decline of Unauthorized Immigrants Stalls, May Have Reversed*, 15; Passel and Cohn, *Unauthorized Immigrant Population: National and State Trends, 2010*, 11.

12. Pew Hispanic Center, *Modes of Entry for the Unauthorized Migrant Population*, May 22, 2006, 3–4.

13. Jeffrey S. Passel and D'Vera Cohn, *Share of Unauthorized Immigrant Workers in Production, Construction Jobs Falls Since 2007*, Pew Hispanic Center, March 26, 2015. "Agricultural" or "farm" labor as used here also

includes jobs in fishing, forestry, and hunting. In 2012, unauthorized workers made up 26 percent of the labor force in these industries, but these industries accounted for less than 1 percent of all wage and salary workers in the United States. The U.S. Department of Agriculture (USDA) cites the National Agricultural Workers Survey (NAWS) in estimating that about half of hired crop farm workers lacked legal status in 2009; the NAWS excludes livestock, poultry, and fishery employees. USDA Economic Research Service, "Farm Labor: Overview," http://www.ers.usda.gov/topics/farm-economy/farm-labor/background.aspx#Numbers, accessed August 12, 2015.

14. Passel and Cohn, *Share of Unauthorized Immigrant Workers in Production, Construction Jobs Falls Since 2007*, March 26, 2015, Table 2.1.

15. Eduardo Porter, "Illegal Immigrants Bolstering Social Security with Billions," *New York Times,* April 5, 2005. Stephen Goss, Alice Wade, J. Patrick Skirvin, Michael Morris, K. Mark Bye, and Danielle Huston, *Effects of Unauthorized Immigration on the Actuarial Status of the Social Security Trust Funds*, Social Security Administration, April 2013, 4; and see "Do Immigrants Pay Taxes?" (chapter 6).

16. Jeffrey S. Passel and D'Vera Cohn, *A Portrait of Unauthorized Immigrants in the United States*, Pew Hispanic Center, April 14, 2009, 16–17. The lower pay is partly explained by undocumented workers tending to be younger and less well educated, but an important factor is the "wage penalty" for being undocumented. See also "Why Do They Work For Less?" (chapter 6).

17. Authors' calculation based on data in Hoefer, Rytina, and Baker, *Estimates of the Unauthorized Immigrant Population Residing in the United States: January 2011*; and Jeffrey S. Passel and D'Vera Cohn, *US Unauthorized Immigration Flows Are Down Sharply Since Mid-Decade*, Pew Hispanic Center, September 1, 2010, 5.

18. Percentages based on Zong and Batalova, "Frequently Requested Statistics on Immigrants and Immigration in the United States"; Passel and Cohn, "Unauthorized Immigrant Population Stable for Half a Decade"; and authors' calculation of a foreign-born population of 44 million.

19. Vernon M. Briggs, Jr., *Mass Immigration and the National Interest: Policy Directions for the New Century*, 3rd ed. (Armonk, NY: M. E. Sharpe, 2003), 135.

20. Rick Lyman and Brenda Goodman, "New Data Shows Immigrants' Growth and Reach," *New York Times*, August 15, 2006.

21. Jennifer Van Hook, Frank D. Bean, and Jeffrey Passel, "Unauthorized Migrants Living in the United States: A Mid-Decade Portrait," Migration Information Source (MIS), Migration Policy Institute (MPI), September 1, 2005.

22. Passel and Cohn, *Unauthorized Immigrant Population: National and State Trends, 2010*, 9; Immigration Policy Center, *Mexican Migration Patterns Signal a New Immigration Reality: Fewer Mexicans are Entering the U.S., Fewer Are Leaving, and Mexican American Births Now Outpace Immigration*

from Mexico, August 2011; Passel and Cohn, "Unauthorized Immigrant Population Stable for Half a Decade."

23. Briggs, *Mass Immigration and the National Interest*, 48, 71. In 2015, the Pew Research Center projected that the proportion of foreign born in the United States could soon reach and pass its 1910 peak of 14.7 percent. Pew Research Center, *Modern Immigration Wave Brings 59 Million to U.S., Driving Population Growth and Change through 2065*, September 28, 2015.

24. Briggs, *Mass Immigration and the National Interest*, 88–89; Irving Bernstein, *The Lean Years: A History of the American Worker, 1920–1933* (Chicago and New York: Haymarket Books, 2010), 322–23; Dennis Wepman, *Immigration* (New York: Facts on File, 2007), 231; "World War II and Immigration," North American Immigration, http://northamericanimmigration.org/319-world-war-ii-and-immigration.html, accessed April 6, 2015.

25. Fred Dews, "What Percentage of U.S. Population Is Foreign Born?" *Brookings Now*, Brookings Institution, October 3, 2013.

26. In 2013, 80 percent of the just under one million people who obtained legal resident status came from Asia and the Americas, and only 9 percent came from Europe. Their top ten countries of origin were Mexico, China, India, the Philippines, the Dominican Republic, Cuba, Vietnam, South Korea, Colombia, and Canada. Department of Homeland Security (DHS) Office of Immigration Statistics, "Persons Obtaining Lawful Permanent Resident Status by Region and Selected Country of Last Residence: Fiscal Years 1820 to 2013," *Yearbook of Immigration Statistics: 2013*, Table 2, http://www.dhs.gov/publication/yearbook-immigration-statistics-2013-lawful-permanent-residents, accessed November 8, 2015.

27. Jill H. Wilson and Audrey Singer, "Immigrants in 2010 Metropolitan America: A Decade of Change," Brookings Institution, October 13, 2011.

28. David M. Reimers, *Still the Golden Door: The Third World Comes to America,* 2nd ed. (New York: Columbia University Press, 1992), 220–23.

29. Rachel L. Swarns, "Failed Amnesty Legislation of 1986 Haunts the Current Immigration Bills in Congress," *New York Times*, May 23, 2006. The Census Bureau later appears to have revised its 1980 estimate downward, to just over two million. Jeffrey S. Passel, "Estimating the Number of Undocumented Aliens," U.S. Department of Labor, Bureau of Labor Statistics, *Monthly Labor Review*, September 1, 1986.

30. Transatlantic Trends, *Immigration Survey 2011*, question 28a; Katy Long, *Huddled Masses: Immigration and Inequality* (London: Thistle Publishing, 2014), 9–10.

2. Why Do People Immigrate?

1. Vernon M. Briggs, Jr., *Mass Immigration and the National Interest: Policy Directions for the New Century*, 3rd ed. (Armonk, NY: M. E. Sharpe, 2003), 51–53; David A. Gerber, *American Immigration: A Very Short Introduction* (Oxford: Oxford University Press, 2011), 79–80; Bill Ong Hing, *Defining America Through Immigration Policy* (Philadelphia: Temple University Press,

2004), 28; Corinne K. Hoexter, *From Canton to California: The Epic of Chinese Immigration* (New York: Four Winds Press, 1976), 32, 125; Campbell Gibson and Kay Jung, "Historical Census Statistics on Population Totals By Race, 1790 to 1990," in U.S. Census Bureau, http://www.census.gov/population/www/documentation/twps0056/twps0056.html, accessed July 22, 2014; Shmuel Ettinger, "Jewish Emigration in the 19th Century," MyJewishLearning.com, http://www.myjewishlearning.com/history/Modern_History/1700-1914/Emigration.shtml, accessed July 15, 2014.

2. Carlos Sandoval and Catherine Tambini, directors, *Farmingville*, 2003, Camino Bluff Productions, Inc.

3. UN Department of Economic and Social Affairs, Population Division, "Trends in International Migrant Stock: The 2013 Revision," September 2013 database, http://www.un.org/en/development/desa/population/migration/data/estimates2/estimatestotal.shtml, accessed January 5, 2016. This UN report estimates the numbers of migrants, defined as people living at least one year outside their country of birth. However, for about 20 percent of the total countries this data was unavailable and the country of citizenship was used instead, which results in some over- and undercounting; the inclusion of refugees among the foreign-born population is also inconsistent among countries.

4. Gerber, *American Immigration*, 68–69.

5. See "Are immigrants different from other people?" (chapter 1).

6. United States Institute of Peace, "Truth Commission: Guatemala," http://www.usip.org/publications/truth-commission-guatemala, accessed July 18, 2014; BBC News, "Timeline: El Salvador," August 16, 2012; Roger Peace, "The Anti-Contra War Campaign: Organizational Dynamics of a Decentralized Movement," *International Journal of Peace Studies* 13/1 (Spring/Summer 2008), 63–83.

7. Danielle Renwick and Stephanie Hanson, "FARC, ELN: Colombia's Left-Wing Guerrillas," CFR Backgrounder, Council on Foreign Relations, December 1, 2014. As of 2013, 10 percent of Colombia's population was displaced, including more than 5.3 million internally displaced people and over 400,000 refugees, according to UNHCR data. *UNHCR 2013 Global Report: Colombia*, http://www.unhcr.org/53980a010.html, accessed January 1, 2015; "Hay 400,000 colombianos refugiados en el extranjero: Acnur," *El Colombiano* (Medellín), August 11, 2014.

8. SOA Watch, "Most Notorious SOA Graduates," http://www.soaw.org/about-the-soawhinsec/soawhinsec-grads/notorious-grads, accessed July 18, 2014.

9. Saskia Sassen, "Why Migration?," *Race, Poverty & the Environment* 4/2 (1993): 15–20; Eric Toussaint, "Domination of the United States on the World Bank," Committee for the Abolition of Illegitimate Debt (CADTM), September 1, 2014.

10. Ben Alpers, "The Strange, Transatlantic Career of 'Neoliberalism,'" Society for U.S. Intellectual History, January 4, 2011.

11. Valeria Mosini, *Reassessing the Paradigm of Economics: Bringing Positive*

Economics Back Into the Normative Framework (London: Routledge, 2012), 125–27.

12.   Justin Akers Chacón and Mike Davis, *No One Is Illegal* (Chicago: Haymarket Books, 2006), 109; James D. Cockcroft, *Mexico's Hope: An Encounter with Politics and History* (New York: Monthly Review Press, 1998), 154; Tim L. Merrill and Ramón Miró, eds., *Mexico: A Country Study* (Washington, D.C.: GPO for the Library of Congress, 1996); World Bank, World Development Indicators database, http://data.worldbank.org/indicator/NY.GDP.MKTP. CD, accessed July 4, 2013.

13.   John Ross, *The Annexation of Mexico* (Monroe, ME: Common Courage Press, 1998), 174; Cockcroft, *Mexico's Hope*, 290–91, 210.

14.   U.S. Government Accountability Office (GAO), *Mexico's Financial Crisis: Origins, Awareness, Assistance, and Initial Efforts to Recover*, February 23, 1996, 2.

15.   Deborah James, "Food Security, Farming, CAFTA and the WTO," n.d., http://www.globalexchange.org/campaigns/cafta/Agriculture.html; Reuters, "Mexico: Corn Shortage Forces Farm Shakeup," October 23, 1995; Eduardo Zepeda, Timothy Wise, and Kevin Gallagher, *Rethinking Trade Policy for Development: Lessons From Mexico under NAFTA*, Carnegie Endowment for International Peace, December 2009, 12.

16.   Zepeda et al., *Rethinking Trade Policy for Development*, 10–11.

17.   Ibid., 14.

18.   Cockcroft, *Mexico's Hope*, Table 5, 155.

19.   "Cost of Living Comparison between Mexico and United States," Numbeo.com, https://www.numbeo.com/cost-of-living/compare_countries.jsp, accessed July 4, 2014; Jim Pickell, "What Is the Cost Of Living in Mexico Compared to the US, Canada And Europe?" *SanDiegoRed.com*, May 13, 2012; U.S. Department of Labor, Bureau of Labor Statistics (BLS), "Indexes of Hourly Compensation Costs in U.S. Dollars for Production Workers in Manufacturing, 32 Countries or Areas and Selected Economic Groups 1975–2004," November 2005; BLS, "International Comparisons of Hourly Compensation Costs for Production Workers in Manufacturing, 2004," November 18, 2005; David Bacon, *The Children of NAFTA: Labor Wars on the U.S./Mexico Border* (Berkeley and Los Angeles: University of California Press, 2004), 53.

20.   Zepeda et al., *Rethinking Trade Policy for Development*, 13.

21.   As of 2015 the country's debt was over $77 billion. "Philippines Total Gross External Debt" (2001 and 2015), Trading Economics, http://tradingeconomics.com/philippines/external-debt, accessed February 26, 2017.

22.   National Network for Immigrant and Refugee Rights, with Sasha Khokha, Ulla Nilsen, Jon Fromer, and Francisco Herrera, *Uprooted: Refugees of the Global Economy*, 28 min. (2001).

23.   Akers Chacón and Davis, *No One Is Illegal*, 105; Paul Friedrich, *Agrarian Revolt in a Mexican Village* (Chicago: University of Chicago Press, 1977), passim; Dan La Botz, *Democracy in Mexico: Peasant Rebellion and Political Reform* (Boston: South End Press, 1995), 54–55.

24. Holly Sklar, *Washington's War on Nicaragua* (Boston: South End Press, 1988), 9–12.

25. Ibid., 45.

26. Ibid., 62–64.

27. Tim Merrill, *Nicaragua: A Country Study*, "The Chamorro Era, 1990-," Library of Congress Federal Research Division, December 1993, http://www.loc.gov/item/94021664; Sarah J. Mahler and Dusan Ugrina, "Central America: Crossroads of the Americas," Florida International University, published April 1, 2006, in Migration Information Source, a project of the Migration Policy Institute.

28. Alexis Henríquez, "Los 20,000 Km Más Letales," *La Prensa Gráfica,* January 17, 2006.

29. U.S. Agency for International Development (USAID), *Fiscal Year 2005 Budget Justification to the Congress,* February 20, 2004, 604.

30. U.S. Census Bureau, "Region and Country or Area of Birth of the Foreign Born Population, 1960 to 1990," http://www.census.gov/population/www/documentation/twps0029/tab03.html, accessed May 22, 2015; Megan Davy, "The Central American Foreign Born in the United States," Migration Policy Institute, April 1, 2006.

31. National Democratic Institute for International Affairs, *The 1990 General Elections in Haiti: International Delegation Report, 1991,* http://aceproject.org/regions-en/countries-and-territories/HT/reports/Final%20Report%20Haiti%201990.pdf/view, accessed May 14, 2015; Human Rights Watch (HRW), *World Report 1995—Haiti,* http://www.hrw.org/reports/1995/wr95/americas-07.htm, accessed May 14, 2015.

32. Kathleen Newland and Elizabeth Grieco, "Spotlight on Haitians in the United States," Migration Policy Institute, April 1, 2004; Ruth Ellen Wasem, *U.S. Immigration Policy on Haitian Migrants,* Congressional Research Service, May 17, 2011; Chiamaka Nwosu and Jeanne Batalova, "Haitian Immigrants in the United States," Migration Policy Institute, May 29, 2014.

33. Allan Nairn, "Aristide Banks on Austerity," *Multinational Monitor,* July/August 1994; Marc Cohen, *Planting Now: Agricultural Challenges and Opportunities for Haiti's Reconstruction,* Oxfam, October 2010, 8.

34. Wasem, *U.S. Immigration Policy on Haitian Migrants*; U.S. Census Bureau, "The Population With Haitian Ancestry in the United States: 2009," October 2010; Nwosu and Batalova, "Haitian Immigrants in the United States."

35. Jens Manuel Krogstad and Ana Gonzalez-Barrera, "Number of Latino Children Caught Trying to Enter U.S. Nearly Doubles in Less Than a Year," Pew Research Center, June 10, 2014; Jens Manuel Krogstad, Ana Gonzalez-Barrera, and Mark Hugo Lopez, "Children 12 and Under Are Fastest Growing Group of Unaccompanied Minors at U.S. Border," Pew Research Center, July 22, 2014.

36. United Nations High Commissioner for Refugees, *Children on the Run: Unaccompanied Children Leaving Central America and Mexico and the Need for International Protection,* March 12, 2014, 6; Elizabeth Kennedy, *No*

Childhood Here: Why Central American Children are Fleeing Their Homes, Immigration Policy Center, July 1, 2014.

37. Roque Planas and Ryan Grim, "Here's How the U.S. Sparked a Refugee Crisis on the Border, in 8 Simple Steps," *Huffington Post,* July 18, 2014.

38. Human Rights Watch (HRW), "World Report 2015—Honduras," http://www.hrw.org/world-report/2015/country-chapters/honduras, accessed May 15, 2015; HRW, "World Report 2015: Mexico," http://www.hrw.org/world-report/2015/country-chapters/mexico, accessed May 15, 2015; David Huey, "The US War on Drugs and Its Legacy in Latin America," *The Guardian,* February 3, 2014; Ted Galen Carpenter, "The Child Migrant Crisis Is Just the Latest Disastrous Consequence of America's Drug War," *Washington Post,* July 21, 2014; Laura Carlsen, "Blowback on the Border: America's Child Refugee Crisis," *Foreign Policy in Focus,* July 18, 2014; Clare Ribando Seelke and Kristin Finklea, *U.S.-Mexican Security Cooperation: The Mérida Initiative and Beyond,* Congressional Research Service, May 7, 2015.

39. Dan Beeton, "The Legacy Children of the Honduran Coup," Al Jazeera America, June 28, 2014; Human Rights Watch, "World Report 2015: Honduras."

40. Sklar, *Washington's War on Nicaragua,* 192.

41. John Ross, *Rebellion From the Roots: Indian Uprising in Chiapas* (Monroe, ME: Common Courage Press, 1995), 21.

42. David Gonzalez, "Latin Sweatshops Pressed by U.S. Campus Power," *New York Times,* April 4, 2003; Kim Bhasin, "Can You Make Clothes Without Sweatshop Labor? This Dominican Factory Is Trying," *Huffington Post,* October 9, 2014; John M. Kline and Edward Soule, *Alta Gracia: Four Years and Counting,* Georgetown University Reflective Engagement Initiative, August 2014; Alta Gracia website: http://altagraciaapparel.com/, accessed January 31, 2015.

43. United Students Against Sweatshops (USAS), "Simultaneous Labor Protests In Four Countries Target Hemisphere's Largest Supplier of Adidas and Nike," August 21, 2012; USAS, "Victory: Gildan Union Leaders in Haiti Rehired!" January 24, 2012; Rick Westhead, "Gildan Vows Minimum Wage for Haitian Garment Workers," *Toronto Star,* November 18, 2013.

44. Sarah Newell, Robert Ascherman, and Garrett Strain, "After Rana Plaza: Setting the Record Straight on the Bangladesh Safety Accord," United Students Against Sweatshops, June 18, 2014.

45. BangladeshAccord.org, "Accord on Fire and Building Safety in Bangladesh."

46. Joe Bardwell, "A Victory for Labour Rights: The International Solidarity Movement Shows What It Can Do," Business and Human Rights Resource Centre, London and New York, October 13, 2014, https://business-human-rights.org/; Metal Workers Union of the Philippines (MWAP), "MWAP Statement on the Conclusion of NXP Cabuyao Struggle," September 27, 2014.

47. International Transport Workers Federation (ITF), "Panama Port Workers' Victory Leads to Start of Collective Negotiations," October 3, 2014;

David Bacon, "Panamanian Longshore Workers Join the ILWU," *ILWU Dispatcher*, March 3, 2015.

3. Does the United States Welcome Refugees?

1. United Nations High Commissioner for Refugees (UNHCR), *The 1951 Convention Relating to the Status of Refugees and Its 1967 Protocol*, September 2011, http://www.unhcr.org/4ec262df9.html.

2. The 1969 Organization of African Unity (OAU) Convention defined "refugees" to include those who "owing to external aggression, occupation, foreign domination or events seriously disturbing public order" are compelled to seek refuge outside their country of origin. In the 1984 Cartagena Declaration on Refugees, Latin American nations recognized as refugees those people who cross an international border "because their lives, security or freedom have been threatened by generalized violence, foreign aggression, internal conflicts, massive violations of human rights or other circumstances which have seriously disturbed public order." International Organization for Migration (IOM), "Key Migration Terms," http://www.iom.int/key-migration-terms.

3. For the U.S. government, refugees are people who have been granted that status before they arrive here. If you come to the United States (with or without a visa) and then seek refugee status, the government classifies you as an asylum seeker; if officials approve your claim, you become an "asylee," with the same rights as a refugee. UNHCR, "Asylum-Seekers," http://www.unhcr.org/pages/49c3646c137.html; Jeanne Batalova, "Refugees and Asylees in the United States," Migration Policy Institute, July 13, 2009, http://www.migrationpolicy.org/article/refugees-and-asylees-united-states-1.

4. In 2015 the UNHCR also dealt with some 201,400 former refugees who had returned to their countries of origin (returnees); 2.3 million returned internally displaced people (IDPs); 3.7 million stateless people; and 870,700 other "persons of concern." UNHCR, *UNHCR Global Trends 2015*, http://www.unhcr.org/en-us/global-trends-2015.html, accessed November 5, 2016. The Palestinian refugees under UNRWA's protection are 750,000 people who between 1946 and 1948 fled or were expelled from lands seized for the creation of Israel, and four generations of their descendants. UNRWA was founded in May 1950, seven months before the UNHCR. UNCHR, "History of UNHCR," http://www.unhcr.org/pages/49c3646cbc.html, accessed October 23, 2014; United Nations Relief and Works Agency for Palestine Refugees in the Near East (UNRWA), "Who We Are," http://www.unrwa.org/who-we-are.

5. Alexander Betts, *Survival Migration: Failed Governance and the Crisis of Displacement* (Ithaca, NY: Cornell University Press, 2013); Tamer Afifi and Jill Jäger, editors, *Environment, Forced Migration and Social Vulnerability* (Heidelberg and New York: Springer, 2010), xv.

6. Afifi and Jäger, *Environment, Forced Migration and Social Vulnerability*, xv, 239–40. The same violence that pushes people to flee can also prevent

them from doing so—as in Colombia, where the military and other armed groups have at times impeded people from migrating by imposing bans on leaving the community, maintaining strict control over who can enter or exit, restricting the entry of supplies, or surrounding localities with anti-personnel mines. Martha Inés Villa, "Desplazamiento forzado en Colombia. El miedo: un eje transversal del éxodo y de la lucha por la ciudadanía," *Controversia* 187, December 2006, Bogotá, Colombia, published by Centro de Investigación y Educación Popular (CINEP), Corporación Región, Escuela Nacional Sindical (ENS), Foro Nacional por Colombia, Instituto Popular de Capacitación (IPC).

7. Refugee Act of 1980, http://www.gpo.gov/fdsys/pkg/STATUTE-94/pdf/STATUTE-94-Pg102.pdf; Displaced Persons Act of 1948, http://library.uwb.edu/guides/usimmigration/62%20stat%201009.pdf; Refugee Relief Act of 1953, http://www-rohan.sdsu.edu/dept/polsciwb/brianl/docs/1953RefugeeReliefAct.pdf; 1952 INA, http://library.uwb.edu/guides/usimmigration/66%20stat%20163.pdf.

8. Bockley, "A Historical Overview of Refugee Legislation"; Marc R. Rosenblum and Idean Salehyan, "Norms and Interests in US Asylum Enforcement," *Journal of Peace Research* 41/6 (November 2004): 679, 683–84. The United States signed the 1967 Protocol in November 1968; it never signed the original 1951 Convention. UNHCR, "States Parties to the 1951 Convention relating to the Status of Refugees and the 1967 Protocol," http://www.unhcr.org/3b73b0d63.html, accessed October 23, 2014; Refugee Act of 1980. See also Chronology for language referring to communism in Refugee Relief Act of 1953, Refugee-Escapee Act of 1957, and Immigration Act of 1965.

9. Julián Aguilar, "Analysis Reveals Asylum Records of Judges," *Texas Tribune*, July 31, 2011. For more on the relationship between foreign policy concerns and asylum decisions, see Rosenblum and Salehyan, "Norms and Interests in US Asylum Enforcement."

10. In July 1938, *Fortune Magazine* polled Americans about their "attitude toward allowing German, Austrian and other political refugees" (primarily Jewish refugees from those countries) into the United States. Two-thirds of respondents opposed letting in any of the refugees; another 18 percent wanted to keep existing restrictions in place. In a January 1943 poll by the National Opinion Research Center, 78 percent of respondents said it would be a "bad idea" to let more immigrants come into the United States after the war. In September 1944, the same firm asked whether respondents felt "a certain number" of people from specific groups should be allowed in after the war, or whether they should be stopped from coming at all: 46 percent responded that Jews should be kept out; the only groups that were less popular were Germans (59 percent) and Japanese (75 percent). Hadley Cantril and Mildred Strunk, *Public Opinion, 1935–1946* (Princeton: Princeton University Press, 1951), 306–7, 1150. See also Leonard Dinnerstein, *Antisemitism in America* (New York and Oxford: Oxford University Press, 1994).

11. United States Holocaust Memorial Museum (USHMM), "The Voyage of the *St. Louis*," http://www.ushmm.org/wlc/en/article. php?ModuleId=10005267, accessed November 1, 2014; Associated Press, "'Against All Odds' Exhibit Shows How American Jews Rescued Europe's Refugees During the Nazi Era," *HuffingtonPost.com*, May 20, 2013.

12. In 1938, more than 300,000 Germans—mostly German Jews fleeing the Nazis—applied for U.S. visas; just over 20,000 applications were approved. By the end of June 1939, some 309,000 German, Austrian, and Czech Jews had applied for the 27,000 places granted under that year's combined quota for Germany and Austria. Constitutional Rights Foundation, "Educating About Immigration," http://crfimmigrationed.org/index.php/lessons-for-teachers/144-hl5, accessed October 10, 2014. Between 1933, when Hitler took power, and 1941, when the United States entered the war, the U.S. government admitted only about 250,000 refugees from Europe, many of them academics and professionals. Vernon M. Briggs, Jr., *Mass Immigration and the National Interest: Policy Directions for the New Century*, 3rd ed. (Armonk, NY: M. E. Sharpe, 2003), 95–96.

13. USHMM, "The Voyage of the *St. Louis*."

14. An admirer of the Nazis, Trujillo also hoped the offer would improve his regime's international image, recently tarnished by its own attempt at "ethnic cleansing": the Dominican military's October 1937 massacre of 15,000 unarmed Haitians and Dominicans of Haitian descent near the border between the two countries. As Trujillo soaked up international praise for his offer to accept up to 100,000 European refugees, his government then took steps to restrict immigrants of the "Semitic race," requiring them to show farming experience and valid citizenship (the Nazis had stripped Austrian and German Jews of their nationality), and to pay a $500 residency fee. In the end, the Dominican Republic took in only 757 European Jews, most of whom later left for the United States when visa restrictions were loosened after the Second World War. Allen Wells, *Tropical Zion: General Trujillo, FDR, and the Jews of Sosúa* (Durham, NC, and London: Duke University Press, 2009); USHMM, "The Evian Conference," http://www.ushmm.org/outreach/en/article.php?ModuleId=10007698, accessed November 4, 2014.

15. The return voyage carried 907 passengers, of which 288 went to Britain and 619 to the Netherlands, Belgium, or France. (One refugee died during the outgoing voyage, while one who attempted suicide remained hospitalized in Havana, and later joined his family in Britain.) Of those who went to the Continent, only eighty-seven managed to flee to safety before the Nazis invaded Western Europe in May 1940. The others were trapped: 254 of them died, and 278 survived the war. USHMM, "The Voyage of the *St. Louis*"; Sarah A. Ogilvie and Scott Miller, *Refuge Denied: The St. Louis Passengers and the Holocaust* (Madison: University of Wisconsin Press, 2006). The Dominican government reportedly offered to accept the refugees in exchange for a $500 per person landing fee, but the American

Jewish Joint Distribution Committee (JDC) rejected the offer because the fee applied only to Jews, and because of what JDC director Joseph Hyman described as "some unfavorable information" about "the suitability of settling in Santo Domingo." C. Paul Vincent, "The Voyage of the *St. Louis* Revisited," *Holocaust Genocide Studies* 25/2 (Fall 2011): 252–89.

16. USHMM, "Seeking Refuge in Cuba, 1939," http://www.ushmm.org/wlc/en/article.php?ModuleId=10007330, accessed November 1, 2014.

17. USHMM, "United States Policy Toward Jewish Refugees, 1941–1952," http://www.ushmm.org/wlc/en/article.php?ModuleId=10007094, accessed October 4, 2015.

18. The Nazis also persecuted and killed hundreds of thousands of non-Jewish people on the basis of their religion, perceived race, political opinion, or "social group," including Roma (Gypsies), people with disabilities, Jehovah's Witnesses, Communists, and homosexuals. USHMM, "Mosaic of Victims: In Depth," http://www.ushmm.org/wlc/en/article.php?ModuleId=10007329, accessed January 11, 2015.

19. For example, Swedish diplomat Raoul Wallenberg saved as many as 90,000 Hungarian Jews by distributing Swedish documents and setting up safe houses under diplomatic protection in Budapest. USHMM, "Raoul Wallenberg," http://www.ushmm.org/research/research-in-collections/search-the-collections/bibliography/raoul-wallenberg, accessed January 11, 2015. Aristides de Sousa Mendes, the Portuguese consul in Bordeaux, France, defied direct orders from Lisbon and issued 30,000 visas to refugees, a third of them Jews, over twelve days in June 1939, with help from several colleagues and an activist local rabbi (Sousa Mendes Foundation website, http://sousamendesfoundation.org)/, accessed January 9, 2015. The closest equivalent among U.S. diplomats was Hiram "Harry" Bingham IV, a U.S. vice consul in Marseille, who assisted efforts by journalist Varian Fry and others to get documents to some 2,500 refugees—most of them prominent artists or intellectuals—seeking to escape occupied France in 1940 and 1941. USHMM, "Varian Fry," http://www.ushmm.org/wlc/en/article.php?ModuleId=10005740, accessed January 9, 2015; Holocaust Survivors and Remembrance Project, "The Hiram 'Harry' Bingham IV Case," http://isurvived.org/2Bingham-IV_Case/07-BIV_FinalOutcome.html, accessed January 9, 2015. Fry reportedly said of Bingham: "He does everything he can to help us, within American law." The U.S. government recalled Bingham and replaced him with a vice consul who, according to Fry, "seemed to delight in making autocratic decisions and refusing as many visas as he possibly could." Hiram "Harry" Bingham IV Quotes, http://www.hirambinghamrescuer.com/quotes.html, accessed January 10, 2015, citing Varian Fry, *Surrender on Demand, 1945* (Boulder, CO: Johnson Books, 1997), 10, 215–16.

20. USHMM, "Preventing Future Genocide and Protecting Refugees," transcript of Ogata speech, April 30, 1997, http://www.ushmm.org/confront-genocide/speakers-and-events/all-speakers-and-events/

preventing-future-genocide-and-protecting-refugees, accessed January 10, 2015.

21. Authors' analysis of data from Department of Homeland Security (DHS) Office of Immigration Statistics, *Yearbook of Immigration Statistics: 2013*, Table 13, "Refugee Arrivals: 1980 to 2013," http://www.dhs.gov/sites/default/files/publications/immigration-statistics/yearbook/2013/RFA/table13.xls, accessed January 1, 2015; Donald M. Kerwin, *The Faltering U.S. Refugee Protection System: Legal and Policy Responses to Refugees, Asylum Seekers, and Others in Need of Protection*, Migration Policy Institute Report, May 2011; David M. Reimers, *Still the Golden Door: The Third World Comes to America*, 2nd ed. (New York: Columbia University Press, 1992), 164.

22. Migration Policy Institute, "U.S. Annual Refugee Resettlement Ceilings and Number of Refugees Admitted, 1980–Present," http://www.migrationpolicy.org/programs/data-hub/charts/us-annual-refugee-resettlement-ceilings-and-number-refugees-admitted-united, accessed November 5, 2016.

23. Average calculated from totals of combined defensive and affirmative asylum grants for people from all countries from 2000 to 2013; data extracted from the UNHCR Population Statistics Database, http://popstats.unhcr.org/en/overview, accessed November 12, 2014.

24. In 2015, the top six countries hosting refugees were Turkey (2.5 million), Pakistan (1.6 million), Lebanon (1.1 million), Iran (979,400), Ethiopia (736,100), and Jordan (664,100). UNHCR, *UNHCR Global Trends 2015*.

25. UNHCR, "Annual Report Shows a Record 33.3 Million Were Internally Displaced in 2013," May 14, 2014.

26. UNHCR, *UNHCR Global Trends 2013*; UNHCR, "Resettlement," http://www.unhcr.org/pages/4a16b1676.html, accessed January 2, 2015.

27. UNHCR, *The State of the World's Refugees 1993;* see "Going Home: Voluntary Repatriation," (chapter 6); http://www.unhcr.org/3eeedf3d5.html, accessed January 2, 2015.

28. Katy Long, *The Point of No Return: Refugees, Rights, and Repatriation*, Oxford Scholarship Online, September 2013.

29. UNHCR, *The 1951 Convention Relating to the Status of Refugees and Its 1967 Protocol*.

30. Long points out in *The Point of No Return*, "Too often, repatriation has been presented as a 'natural' best solution to refugees' exile, when in fact the assumptions that underpin this claim—that people belong in a particular, fixed place—reflect the interests of the politically powerful in retaining the status quo international order, rather than the capacity of return to realize the rights of the displaced."

31. Jeff Crisp, "When You Can't—or Don't Want to—Go Home Again," RefugeesInternational.org, http://refugeesinternational.org/blog/when-you-cant-go-home-again; UNHCR, "Global Consultations on International Protection/Third Track: Voluntary Repatriation" (EC/GC/02/5), April 25, 2002.

32. UNHCR, *UNHCR Global Trends 2013*; UNHCR, "Resettlement."

33. UNHCR, *UNHCR Global Trends 2015*.

34. USCIS, "Iraqi Refugee Processing Fact Sheet," June 6, 2013, http://www.uscis.gov/humanitarian/refugees-asylum/refugees/iraqi-refugee-processing-fact-sheet.

35. Christina Alexander, "Who Pays the Airfare to Transport Refugees to the U.S., and How Does It Work?" Immigrant Connect Chicago, November 30, 2010.

36. The one-year rule was imposed as part of the 1996 Illegal Immigration Reform and Immigrant Responsibility Act (IIRIRA). IIRIRA text, http://www.uscis.gov/iframe/ilink/docView/PUBLAW/HTML/PUBLAW/0-0-0-10948.html, accessed October 1, 2014.

37. U.S. Department of Justice, Executive Office for Immigration Review, *Asylum and Withholding of Removal Relief: Convention Against Torture Protections*, January 15, 2009.

38. USCIS, "Green Card Through Refugee or Asylee Status," http://www.uscis.gov/green-card/green-card-through-refugee-or-asylee-status, accessed October 7, 2015.

39. Kathryn M. Bockley, "A Historical Overview of Refugee Legislation: The Deception of Foreign Policy in the Land of Promise," *North Carolina Journal of International Law & Commercial Regulation* 21 (Fall 1995): 253.

40. U.S. Citizenship and Immigration Services (USCIS), "Green Card for a Cuban Native or Citizen," http://www.uscis.gov/green-card/other-ways-get-green-card/green-card-cuban-native-or-citizen, accessed October 6, 2015; Ruth Ellen Wasem, *Cuban Migration to the United States: Policy and Trends*, Congressional Research Service (CRS), June 2, 2009.

41. Reimers, *Still the Golden Door*, 160; Briggs, *Mass Immigration and the National Interest*, 136–37, 143–45.

42. Silvia Pedraza, "Cuba's Revolution and Exodus," *The Journal of the International Institute* 5/2 (Winter 1998), http://hdl.handle.net/2027/spo.4750978.0005.204.

43. Wasem, *Cuban Migration to the United States: Policy and Trends*.

44. Reimers, *Still the Golden Door*, 165–75.

45. Wasem, *Cuban Migration to the United States: Policy and Trends*. These U.S. policies may be affected in the future by the normalization of U.S.-Cuban relations that began in December 2014. On January 12, 2017, a week before leaving office, President Barack Obama ended the "wet foot/dry foot" policy, saying that Cubans arriving in the United States without permission would be treated like other migrants. Julie Hirschfeld Davis and Frances Robles, "Obama Ends Exemption for Cubans Who Arrive Without Visas," *The New York Times*, January 12, 2017.

46. Greg Philo, Emma Briant, and Pauline McDonald, *Bad News for Refugees* (London: Pluto Press 2013), 18.

47. Richard Perkins and Eric Neumayer, "The Organized Hypocrisy of Ethical Foreign Policy: Human Rights, Democracy and Western Arms Sales,"

Geoforum 41/2 (2010): 247–56. The United States consistently transfers twice as much in weapons as do France, Germany, and the United Kingdom combined, according to Stockholm International Peace Research Institute (SIPRI) data at http://armstrade.sipri.org/armstrade/page/toplist.php, accessed March 3, 2017.

48. Expedited removal doesn't apply to Canadians trying to enter the United States as visitors, or Cubans entering the country by air. In theory, Cubans arriving by land or sea have faced expedited removal. However, the Department of Homeland Security has claimed the right to process Cubans under regular removal proceedings, which has allowed them to seek administrative relief through the Cuban Adjustment Act. Board of Immigration Appeals, *Matter of E-R-M- & L-R-M-, Respondents*, decided June 3, 2011; Nolo Network, "When Expedited Removal Allows Deportation Without a Hearing," http://www.nolo.com/legal-encyclopedia/when-expedited-removal-allows-deportation-without-hearing.html, accessed April 5. 2015; Research Directorate, Immigration and Refugee Board of Canada, Ottawa, Responses to Information Requests (RIRs) ZZZ102626.E, January 31, 2008.

49. In February 2014, U.S. Citizenship and Immigration Services (USCIS) raised the bar on credible fear, instructing asylum officers that applicants must "demonstrate a substantial and realistic possibility of succeeding" in their cases in order to qualify for an asylum hearing. Sara Campos, Esq., and Joan Friedland, Esq., *Mexican and Central American Asylum and Credible Fear Claims: Background and Context*, American Immigration Council special report, May 21, 2014.

50. Human Rights First, *How to Repair the U.S. Asylum and Refugee Resettlement Systems*, December 2012, citing USCRIF Report on Expedited Removal, 54.

51. In October 2013 immigration legal aid and advocacy organizations reported that some asylum seekers were waiting up to two months for a credible fear interview. National Immigrant Justice Center, "Immigration Legal Service Groups Demand Data on Asylum Seekers Waiting for Credible and Reasonable Fear Interviews," October 14, 2013, https://www.immigrantjustice.org/press_releases/FOIA-asylum-seekers-credible-fear.

52. See "How bad is detention really?" (chapter 11).

53. The Leadership Conference on Civil and Human Rights, "Immigration Reform Update: The 1996 Immigration Laws and Their Impact on Civil Rights," *Civil Rights Monitor* 11/3, http://www.civilrights.org/monitor/vol11_no3/art7p1.html, accessed October 1, 2014; IIRIRA text.

54. Until 2010, Immigration and Customs Enforcement (ICE) rules mandated detention as the default for asylum seekers who had passed their credible fear interviews. Agents had discretion to release certain asylum seekers "in limited circumstances" for compelling humanitarian or public interest reasons—for example, if they were pregnant, juvenile, had serious medical conditions, or would be serving as witnesses, as long as they could show

they were not a "flight risk" or a danger to society. Effective January 4, 2010, ICE Directive No. 11002.1 reversed the mandatory detention policy, taking the position that detention of asylum seekers is generally assumed not to be in the public interest, as long they are not a flight risk or a danger to society. This directive remained in effect as of 2015, but ICE has often ignored it. In December 2013, an organizer from the National Immigrant Youth Alliance (NIYA) detained at the El Paso Processing Center identified nearly 100 people who were eligible for parole, yet were still being held there. ICE, *Parole of Arriving Aliens Found to Have a "Credible Fear" of Persecution or Torture*, November 6, 2007; ICE, *Parole of Arriving Aliens Found to Have a Credible Fear of Persecution or Torture*, December 8, 2009; Campos and Friedland, *Mexican and Central American Asylum and Credible Fear Claims*; National Immigrant Youth Alliance Press Release, "NIYA Infiltrates El Paso Immigration Detention Center: Finds Hundreds of Cases of Wrongly Detained," December 9, 2013.

55.   A November 2013 report by the Center for Victims of Torture and the Torture Abolition and Survivor Support Coalition International estimated that between October 2010 and February 2013, the U.S. government likely detained as many as 6,000 asylum seekers who were survivors of torture. Detained asylum seekers interviewed for the report described feeling dehumanized by the conditions they faced in detention, as well as confused and isolated by the lack of information about when, or whether, they would be released, and anxious and fearful about the possibility of being returned to the country where they were tortured and persecuted. Center for Victims of Torture (CVT) amd Torture Abolition and Survivor Support Coalition, International (TASSC), *Tortured & Detained: Survivor Stories of U.S. Immigration Detention*, November 2013.

56.   Americans for Immigrant Justice, *The "Hieleras": A Report on Human & Civil Rights Abuses Committed by U.S. Customs & Border Protection*, August 7, 2013.

57.   Physicians for Human Rights, *Broken Laws, Broken Lives: Medical Evidence of Torture by US Personnel and its Impact*, June 2008; Physicians for Human Rights and Human Rights First, *Leave No Marks: Enhanced Interrogation Techniques and the Risk of Criminality*, August 2007.

58.   Human Rights Watch and Seton Hall Law, *"At Least Let Them Work": The Denial of Work Authorization and Assistance for Asylum Seekers in the United States*, November 2013.

59.   Andrew I. Schoenholtz, Philip G. Schrag, Jaya Ramji-Nogales, *Lives in the Balance: Asylum Adjudication by the Department of Homeland Security* (New York: NYU Press, 2014), 127–37. The researchers looked at asylum grant rates in 329,361 affirmative cases evaluated on their merits by DHS adjudicators between 1996 and 2009. Latin American and Caribbean applicants who entered without inspection were also more likely to be from Haiti or Central America, while those who entered with visas were more likely to be from Colombia and Venezuela. One asylum officer suggested that men

without dependents who entered without inspection were likely to be seen as economic migrants, persecutors, or terrorists; for them, legal representation would "somewhat mediate the threat." However, representation hurt applicants if their lawyers were seen as incompetent or accustomed to filing fraudulent applications.

60. TRAC Immigration, "Asylum Denial Rate Reaches All Time Low: FY 2010 Results, a Twenty-Five-Year Perspective," http://trac.syr.edu/immigration/reports/240/ .

61. Human Rights First, *U.S. Detention of Asylum Seekers: Seeking Protection, Finding Prison*, June 2009.

62. Individual officers within each regional office were assigned cases at random. Yet between asylum officers in San Francisco who adjudicated at least one hundred cases of Indian nationals, grant rates by officer ranged from 6 percent to over 90 percent. Among Miami officers who interviewed at least one hundred Haitians, grant rates ranged from 5 percent to 85 percent. Los Angeles officers who handled at least one hundred Chinese cases granted asylum at rates ranging from 1 percent to 99 percent. *Lives in the Balance*, 163; see also Schoenholtz, Schrag, and Ramji-Nogales, links to *Lives in the Balance* and "Rejecting Refugees" supplemental materials.

63. GAO, *U.S. Asylum System*.

64. Human Rights First, *How to Repair the U.S. Asylum and Refugee Resettlement Systems*, December 2012, citing Human Rights First, *The Asylum Filing Deadline: Denying Protection to the Persecuted and Undermining Governmental Efficiency*, September 2010; and Philip G. Schrag, Andrew I. Schoenholtz, Jaya Ramji-Nogales, and James P. Dombach, "Rejecting Refugees: Homeland Security's Administration of the One-Year Bar to Asylum," *William and Mary Law Review* (December 2010).

65. U.S. Government Accounting Office (GAO), *U.S. Asylum System: Significant Variation Existed in Asylum Outcomes Across Immigration Courts and Judges*, September 2008.

66. TRAC Immigration, "Asylum Disparities Persist, Regardless of Court Location and Nationality," September 24, 2007. In 2009, TRAC reviewed updated data and found that the gap between judges' asylum approval rates had diminished in ten of the fifteen busiest courts, but that significant disparities still existed. TRAC Immigration, "Latest Data from Immigration Courts Show Decline in Asylum Disparity," June 22, 2009.

67. Banks Miller, Linda Camp Keith, and Jennifer S. Holmes, *Immigration Judges and U.S. Asylum Policy* (Philadelphia: University of Pennsylvania Press, 2014).

68. Chris Dolan, Liza Schuster, Matt Merefield, *The Impact of Deportation: Some Reflections on Current Practice*, Refugee Law Project, 2014, http://www.refugeelawproject.org/files/briefing_papers/The_Impact_of_Deportation.pdf; *Amnesty International, Eritrea: Sent Home to Detention and Torture*, May 2009, Index: AFR 64/002/2009; Caroline Moorhead, "The End of All Hope," *The Guardian*, August 23, 2006; Bernadette Lyodu, "Uganda: The

Silent Practice of Deportations," *Pambazuka News*, May 6, 2010; Human Rights Watch document detailing thirteen cases of alleged torture of failed Tamil asylum seekers, available at http://www.hrw.org/sites/default/files/related_material/UK%20Sri%20Lanka%20deportees%20tortured%20final_0.pdf, accessed December 24, 2014; Edmund Rice Centre interim research update, "Failed Asylum Seekers: Sri Lanka," August 21, 2014; Catherine Ramos, *Unsafe Return II*, Justice First, October 3, 2013, http://justicefirst.org/.

69. Human Rights Watch, "Haiti: Prosecute Duvalier," January 17, 2011.
70. Bockley, "A Historical Overview of Refugee Legislation"; Ruth Ellen Wasem, *U.S. Immigration Policy on Haitian Migrants*, Congressional Research Service, May 17, 2011; U.S. District Court, Southern District of. Florida, *Haitian Refugee Center v. Civiletti*, 503 F. Supp. 442 (S.D. Fla. 1980), decided July 2, 1980.
71. Wasem, *U.S. Immigration Policy on Haitian Migrants*, Congressional Research Service, January 15, 2010; see also Wasem, *U.S. Immigration Policy on Haitian Migrants*, 2011.
72. U.S. Embassy, Port-au-Prince, "Haiti—United States: Agreement to Stop Clandestine Migration of Residents of Haiti to the United States," September 23, 1981, International Legal Materials 20/5 (September 1981): 1198–1202; Wasem, *U.S. Immigration Policy on Haitian Migrants*, 2010.
73. See "What happens when people do try to fix their countries?" (chapter 2).
74. Wasem, *U.S. Immigration Policy on Haitian Migrants*, 2010; Clifford Krauss, "U.S., in New Policy, Will Not Pick Up All Haiti Refugees," *New York Times*, May 22, 1992.
75. David G. Savage, "Haitian Intercept Policy Backed by High Court," *Los Angeles Times*, June 22, 1993; Douglas Farah, "Coast Guard Patrols, Clinton's Switch on Repatriation Delay Haitian Exodus," *Washington Post*, January 21, 1993.
76. Michael Ratner, "How We Closed the Guantánamo HIV Camp: The Intersection of Politics and Litigation," *Harvard Human Rights Journal* 11 (Spring 1998): 187–220.
77. Anne T. Gallagher and Fiona David, *The International Law of Migrant Smuggling* (New York: Cambridge University Press, 2014), 100; Wasem, *U.S. Immigration Policy on Haitian Migrants*, 2010.
78. Melanie Nezer, *Resettlement at Risk: Meeting Emerging Challenges to Refugee Resettlement in Local Communities*, Hebrew Immigrant Aid Society (HIAS), February 2013; Ryan J. Foley, "Burmese Refugees Flock to Iowa Meatpacking Town," Associated Press, May 5, 2013; Rehka Basu, "New Challenges Are Now Facing Burma's Refugees Living in Iowa," *Des Moines Register*, April 6, 2014.
79. USCIS, "Refugees," http://www.uscis.gov/humanitarian/refugees-asylum/refugees, accessed October 8, 2015; USCIS, "Asylum," http://www.uscis.gov/humanitarian/refugees-asylum/asylum, accessed October 8, 2015.
80. Justine Drennan, "The U.S. Is Deporting Cambodian Refugees and

Orphaning Their Children," *Foreign Policy in Focus*, August 19, 2014. See "What happens to people who are deported?" (chapter 11).

81.   USCIS, "Temporary Protected Status," https://www.uscis.gov/humanitarian/ temporary-protected-status, accessed November 6, 2016; East Bay Sanctuary Covenant, "Temporary Protected Status (TPS)," https://eastbaysanctuary. org/temporary-protected-status-tps/, accessed November 6, 2016; Madeline Messick, Claire Bergeron, "Temporary Protected Status in the United States: A Grant of Humanitarian Relief that Is Less than Permanent," Migration Policy Institute, Migration Information Source, July 2, 2014.

82.   Susan Gzesh, "Central Americans and Asylum Policy in the Reagan Era," Migration Information Source, Migration Policy Institute, April 1, 2006; Megan Davy, "The Central American Foreign Born in the United States," Migration Policy Institute, April 1, 2006. For the Central American wars, see "What happens when people do try to fix their countries?" (chapter 2).

83.   Gzesh, "Central Americans and Asylum Policy in the Reagan Era"; Text of United States District Court N. California decision, *American Baptist Churches et al., v. Richard Thornburgh et al.*, 760 F. Supp. 796 (1991).

84.   ILW Immigration Daily, "The 208 Final Rule," December 6, 2000.

85.   American Immigration Law Center (AILC), "Immigration Through the Nicaraguan Adjustment and Central American Relief Act (NACARA), Section 203," http://www.ailc.com/services/residency/nacara203_main. htm, accessed May 14, 2015; American Immigration Lawyers Association, "INS Announces HRIFA Procedures," May 11, 1999. For more on these laws, see Chronology.

4. Why Can't They Just "Get Legal"?

1.   For a general discussion of this subject, see Cecilia Menjivar and Daniel Kanstroom, eds., *Constructing Immigrant "Illegality": Critiques, Experiences, and Responses* (New York: Cambridge University Press, 2014).

2.   Aarti Shahani, "Legalization and De-Legalization," *Gotham Gazette*, April 4, 2006.

3.   Sharokina Shams, "Immigrants Disagree on Obama's Reform Plan," *KCRA Sacramento*, November 20, 2014.

4.   The respondents were 55 percent Latino, 30 percent Asian, and 15 percent European or African. More than half of them were naturalized U.S. citizens. "Legal Immigrants: A Voice of Reason in the Immigration Debate, First Multilingual Poll of Legal Immigrants," *New American Media*, March 28, 2006, prepared by Bendixen and Associates for New American Media in partnership with LCCR (Leadership Conference on Civil Rights) Education Fund and Center for American Progress.

5.   Josh Marshall, "Are Legal Immigrants the Biggest Victims?" *TalkingPointsMemo.com*, November 24, 2014.

6.   Schomburg Center for Research in Black Culture, New York Public Library, "The Abolition of the Slave Trade," http://abolition.nypl.org/essays/us_ slave_trade/ accessed September 17, 2015. Most of the enslaved Africans

were brought to the United States between 1651 and 1810. The slave trade was banned in 1808; the more than 6,000 Africans who arrived between 1811 and 1860 would have been smuggled in illegally.

7. Christopher Tomlins, "Reconsidering Indentured Servitude: European Migration and the Early American Labor Force, 1600-1775," *Labor History* 42/1 (February 2001): 5–43; Richard Hofstadter, *America at 1750: A Social Portrait* (New York: Vintage, 1973), 36.

8. U.S. Congress, "An Act to Prohibit the Importation of Slaves into any Port or Place Within the Jurisdiction of the United States," enacted March 2, 1807, http://avalon.law.yale.edu/19th_century/sl004.asp.

9. American Women, Law Library of Congress, "Memory," http://memory. loc.gov/ammem/awhhtml/awlaw3/immigration.html, accessed September 17, 2015.

10. Office of the Historian, U.S. Department of State, "Milestones: 1866–1898," https://history.state.gov/milestones/1866-1898/chinese-immigration; U.S. Congress, Immigration Act of 1924, approved May 26, 1924, http://tucnak. fsv.cuni.cz/~calda/Documents/1920s/ImmigAct1924.html, accessed September 15, 2015; History Matters, "Who Was Shut Out?: Immigration Quotas, 1925–1927," American Social History Project/Center for Media and Learning (Graduate Center, CUNY) and the Roy Rosenzweig Center for History and New Media (George Mason University), http:// historymatters.gmu.edu/d/5078, accessed September 17, 2015.

11. The 1924 law had no quotas for citizens of independent countries in the Americas, but people from colonial possessions were subject to the quotas for the possessing countries. The intention was apparently to reduce immigration by English-speaking black people, notably from Jamaica, which was still a British colony. The U.S. consulate in Kingston, Jamaica, was issuing about thirty immigrant visas a day before the law took effect; under the new law U.S. officials slashed the number of visas to ten a month. Lara Putnam, *Radical Moves: Caribbean Migrants and the Politics of Race in the Jazz Age* (Chapel Hill: University of North Carolina Press, 2013), 88–95.

12. Mae M. Ngai, *Impossible Subjects: Illegal Aliens and the Making of Modern America* (Princeton: Princeton University Press, 2004), 60, 68, 131. See "What happened to the Mexican '*braceros*'?" (chapter 10).

13. Ibid., 61–62.

14. Roger Daniels, "The Immigration Act of 1965: Intended and Unintended Consequences," IIP Digital, U.S. Department of State, April 3, 2008.

15. Aviva Chomsky, *Undocumented: How Immigration Became Illegal* (Boston: Beacon Press, 2014), 59. See also "Are politicians stirring up a panic about immigration?" (chapter 1).

16. Under the 1952 Immigration and Nationality Act (INA), the U.S. government can impose both criminal and civil penalties for violations of immigration law. Criminal charges are presented in federal court, and civil violations generally involve removal proceedings in immigration court, a separate administrative system under the Department of Justice that

provides defendants with fewer due process guarantees. (In immigration proceedings, you have no right to a court-appointed lawyer.) Under INA Section 275 (8 U.S.C. 1325), "illegal entry" is a federal criminal misdemeanor with a maximum sentence of six months in jail and a fine. "Illegal reentry"—returning to the United States without permission after being deported—is a more serious felony crime. Unlawful presence is a violation of a civil statute. Brett Snider, "Is Illegal Immigration a Crime? Improper Entry v. Unlawful Presence," FindLaw, July 9, 2014,; Alison Siskin, Andorra Bruno, Blas Nunez-Neto, Lisa M. Seghetti, and Ruth Ellen Wasem, *Immigration Enforcement within the United States,* Congressional Research Service, April 6, 2006; 8 U.S. Code sec.1325, Improper entry by alien, at Cornell Law School Legal Information Institute, https://www.law.cornell.edu/uscode/text/18/1546, accessed September 18, 2015.

17. 18 U.S. Code sec. 1546, Fraud and misuse of visas, permits, and other documents, at Cornell Law School Legal Information Institute, https://www.law.cornell.edu/uscode/text/18/1546, accessed September 18, 2015.

18. American Immigration Council (AIC), "Supreme Court Rejects Government's Argument in Aggravated Identity Theft Case," http://www.immigrationpolicy.org/supreme-court/supreme-court-rejects-governments-argument-aggravated-identity-theft-case, accessed September 18, 2015. The *knowing* use of another person's information to circumvent immigration laws is included in the federal crime known as "aggravated identity theft." This is different from the common definition of identity theft—the use of other people's identities to defraud them or steal from them. 18 U.S. Code sec. 1028A, Aggravated identity theft, at Cornell Law School Legal Information Institute, https://www.law.cornell.edu/uscode/text/18/1028A.

19. Mexperience.com, "Mexican Visas and Immigration," http://www.mexperience.com/lifestyle/living-in-mexico/visas-and-immigration/#2, accessed September 20, 2015.

20. AIC, "Why Don't They Just Get In Line? The Real Story of Getting a 'Green Card' and Coming to the United States Legally," http://www.immigrationpolicy.org/just-facts/why-don%E2%80%99t-they-just-get-line, accessed September 18, 2015.

21. Jie Zong and Jeanne Batalova, "Frequently Requested Statistics on Immigrants and Immigration in the United States," AIC, February 26, 2015. For more on refugees and asylees, see chapter 3.

22. AIC, "Why Don't They Just Get In Line?"; AIC, "How the United States Immigration System Works: A Fact Sheet," http://www.immigrationpolicy.org/just-facts/how-united-states-immigration-system-works-fact-sheet, accessed September 18, 2015; Randall Monger and James Yankay, *U.S. Lawful Permanent Residents: 2013,* Department of Homeland Security Office of Immigration Statistics, May 2014.

In 2014 the State Department issued 467,370 visas for people to settle here (not all were used that year), with 259,393 going to immigrants other than

U.S. citizens' immediate family members. U.S. State Department, "Report of the Visa Office 2014," Table 1, http://travel.state.gov/content/dam/visas/Statistics/AnnualReports/FY2014AnnualReport/FY14AnnualReport-TableI.pdf, accessed September 20, 2015.

23. AIC, "How the United States Immigration System Works"; Zong and Batalova, "Frequently Requested Statistics on Immigrants and Immigration in the United States"; UniteFamilies.org, "Frequently Asked Questions (FAQ)," http://www.unitefamilies.org/eng/faq/#impacted2, accessed September 20, 2015.

24. Celler himself was opposed to race-based limits on immigration; he'd originally intended to base preferences on skills and training that would be "especially advantageous" to the United States. Rep. Michael Feighan, a conservative Democrat from Ohio, was responsible for the family preference clause, which the American Legion lauded as "a naturally operating national-origin system." Tom Gjelten, "In 1965, A Conservative Tried To Keep America White. His Plan Backfired," *NPR*, October 3, 2015; Vernon M. Briggs, Jr., *Mass Immigration and the National Interest: Policy Directions for the New Century*, 3rd ed. (Armonk, NY: M. E. Sharpe, 2003), 129.

25. AIC, "How the United States Immigration System Works."

26 Thomas Alexander Aleinikoff, David A. Martin, and Hiroshi Motomura, *Immigration and Citizenship: Process and Policy*, 4th ed. (St. Paul, MN: West Publishing Company, 1998), 295, as cited in Charles J. Ogletree, Jr., "America's Schizophrenic Immigration Policy: Race, Class, and Reason," *Boston College Law Review* 41/4 (July 2000), 755–770.

27. The Diversity Immigrant Visa Program allows for 55,000 visas, but 5,000 of these are set aside for the Nicaraguan Adjustment and Central American Relief Act (NACARA). AIC, "How the United States Immigration System Works." For NACARA, see "Refugee Case Study: Central America." (chapter 3). The 2017 Diversity Visa was not open to natives of Bangladesh, Brazil, Canada, China (mainland-born), Colombia, Dominican Republic, Ecuador, El Salvador, Haiti, India, Jamaica, Mexico, Nigeria, Pakistan, Peru, Philippines, South Korea, United Kingdom (except Northern Ireland) and its dependent territories, and Vietnam. U.S. Department of State website, "Instructions for the 2017 Diversity Immigrant Visa Program (DV-2017)," https://travel.state.gov/content/dam/visas/Diversity-Visa/DV-Instructions-Translations/DV-2017-Instructions-Translations/DV-2017%20Instructions%20and%20FAQs.pdf. In 2015, the diversity visa program received nearly 9.4 million qualified entries. U.S. Department of State website, "DV 2015 - Selected Entrants," http://travel.state.gov/content/visas/en/immigrate/diversity-visa/dv-2015-selected-entrants.html, accessed January 17, 2016. "Visas are apportioned among six geographic regions based on immigration rates to the United States over the last five years, with a greater number of visas going to regions with lower rates of immigration to the United States." Embassy of the United States, Tashkent,

Uzbekistan, "Diversity Visas," http://uzbekistan.usembassy.gov/dv.html, accessed January 16, 2016.

28. U.S. Citizenship and Immigration Services (USCIS), "About the EB-5 Visa," https://www.uscis.gov/working-united-states/permanent-workers/employment-based-immigration-fifth-preference-eb-5/about-eb-5-visa, accessed January 19, 2016.

29. Jim Gardner, "Bring Me Your Rich, Yearning to Invest; Ex-Scourge of Illegal Aliens Now Bringing 'Yacht People' Ashore," *Orange County Business Journal*, July 20, 1992.

30. Walter F. Roche Jr. and Gary Cohn, "INS insiders profit on immigrant dreams," *Baltimore Sun*, February 20, 2000.

31. Rebecca Daugherty, "Appeals Court Rules that Government Cannot Withhold Information on Official in the Name of Privacy," *The News Media & The Law* (Reporters Committee for Freedom of the Press) 27/1 (Winter 2003): 26; Walter F. Roche Jr., "Judges Rule for Release of Report in Visa Case, Ex-INS lawyer Virtue Accused of Favoritism in Investment Program," *Baltimore Sun*, November 26, 2002.

32. Alana Semuels, "Should Congress Let Wealthy Foreigners Buy Green Cards?" *The Atlantic*, September 21, 2015; U.S. Citizenship and Immigration Services, Immigrant Petition by Alien Entrepreneur (I-526) and Petition by Entrepreneur to Remove Conditions (I-829), Service-wide Receipts, Approvals, Denials, Fiscal Year(s): 2005–2012 (Third Quarter), July 19, 2012.

33. For countries to be considered for the visa waiver program, they must comply with certain security standards and their citizens must have a low rate of denial when applying for U.S. visitor visas; still, these criteria don't guarantee a country's acceptance into the program, which is granted "at the discretion of the U.S. government." U.S. Department of State, "Visa Waiver Program," http://travel.state.gov/content/visas/en/visit/visa-waiver-program.html, accessed September 23, 2015; U.S. Department of State, "Citizens of Canada and Bermuda," accessed October 26, 2015, http://travel.state.gov/content/visas/en/visit/canada-bermuda.html;   Alison Siskin, Congressional Research Service, "Visa Waiver Program," December 11, 2015.

34. U.S. Department of State, "Non-Immigrant Visa Statistics," http://travel.state.gov/content/visas/en/law-and-policy/statistics/non-immigrant-visas.html, accessed September 23, 2015. For example, Mexicans applying for U.S. visas in 2015 had to pay a $160 fee, at a time when about 13 percent of Mexico's workforce was being paid a minimum wage of less than $5 a day. U.S. Embassy, Mexico City, website, "Visas to the U.S.: How to Apply," http://mexico.usembassy.gov/visas/non-immigrant-visas/how-to-apply.html, accessed September 23, 2015; Anthony Harrup, "Mexico Raises Minimum Wage for 2015 by 4.2%, In Line With Inflation," *Wall Street Journal*, December 19, 2014. Denial rates for U.S. visitor visas range widely for different countries; for Mexico in 2014 it was 15.6 percent, compared

to 1.8 percent for Uruguay, 36.8 percent for Honduras and 58.2 percent for Haiti. U.S. Department of State website, "Adjusted Refusal Rate - B-Visas Only by Nationality Fiscal Year 2014," http://travel.state.gov/content/dam/visas/Statistics/Non-Immigrant-Statistics/RefusalRates/FY14.pdf, accessed January 17, 2016.

35. Consular officers are supposed to provide reasons for the denial, but these reasons may include that the applicant did not "overcome the presumption of being an intending immigrant," and officers are not required to explain how they reached this conclusion. U.S. Department of State website, "Visa Denials," https://travel.state.gov/content/visas/en/general/denials.html, accessed January 17, 2016.

36. Philip Shenon, "Judge Denounces U.S. Visa Policies Based on Race or Looks," *New York Times*, January 23, 1998.

37. U.S. Department of State, "Entering the United States," http://www.travel.state.gov/content/visas/en/general/entering.html, accessed September 23, 2015. At some airports, U.S. immigration officials inspect travelers prior to their departure on U.S.-bound flights and may prevent them from boarding. For example, in December 2015, U.S. authorities at London's Gatwick airport stopped an entire British family from boarding a flight to Los Angeles, even though the family had obtained prior authorization for the trip through the visa waiver program. Esther Addley and Amanda Holpuch, "US stops British Muslim Family From Boarding Flight to Visit Disneyland," *The Guardian*, December 22, 2015.

38. U.S. Department of State, "Student Visa," http://www.travel.state.gov/content/visas/en/study-exchange/student.html, accessed September 23, 2015.

39. USCIS, "Temporary (Nonimmigrant) Workers," http://www.uscis.gov/working-united-states/temporary-workers/temporary-nonimmigrant-workers, accessed June 1, 2015. For more on exchange programs, see "What are the current guest worker programs?" (chapter 10).

40. Bendixen & Associates, *Report of Findings from October 2005 Poll of Undocumented Immigrants*, Manhattan Institute for Policy Research and National Immigration Forum, March 30, 2006. See "Who are the undocumented immigrants?" (chapter 1).

41. Department of Homeland Security Yearbook of Immigration Statistics: "2013 Lawful Permanent Residents," Table 6, "Persons Obtaining Lawful Permanent Resident Status by Type and Major Class of Admission: FYs 2004 to 2013," http://www.dhs.gov/sites/default/files/publications/table6_4.xls, accessed January 17, 2016. This number is down from 2005, when a total of 738,302 people adjusted to LPR status, and 900,000 applications remained pending a decision. Kelly Jefferys and Nancy Rytina, *U.S. Legal Permanent Residents: 2005*, Department of Homeland Security, Office of Immigration Statistics, Policy Directorate, Annual Flow Report, April 2006. More recent DHS reports haven't given the number of pending applications, but according to attorney William Stock, as of 2014 over a

million cases, including naturalization and residency petitions, remained pending for over six months.

42. Immigration Equality, "The Provisional Unlawful Presence Waiver," http://www.immigrationequality.org/get-legal-help/our-legal-resources/path-to-status-in-the-u-s/the-provisional-unlawful-presence-waiver/, accessed September 23, 2015. For a few years there was a clause called Section 245(i), which was first added to the Immigration and Nationality Act in 1994, and which has sometimes been referred to, incorrectly, as an "amnesty." It allowed people in the EWI category to pay a $1,000 fine and adjust their status, without having to return to their country and apply for a visa. Section 245(i) expired on January 14, 1998, but the Legal Immigration Family Equity Act (LIFE), signed by President Bill Clinton on December 21, 2000, brought it back temporarily, creating a brief window of opportunity for immigrants who could get their petitions filed by April 30, 2001. Thousands applied during that four-month period, creating a major backlog. The new law also temporarily broadened the opportunities for "labor certification," the process by which employers can sponsor their employees for green cards. Rómulo E. Guevara, "Cutting Off Loose Ends: DOL Proposes to End Substitutions, Permanent Validity, and Improper Commerce of Labor Certifications," ILW.com, March 14, 2006.

43. Allan Wernick, "Marriage Allows Those on Visitor's Visas to Change Status," *NY Daily News*, November 24, 2015.

44. Immihelp.com, "Bona Fide Marriage Documentation," http://www.immihelp.com/greencard/bona-fide-marriage-documentation.html, accessed October 27, 2015.

45. Andy J. Semotiuk, "Spousal Immigration Processing Times Cause Frustration," *Forbes*, March 11, 2015. Processing for petitions by permanent resident spouses in the northeastern United States was taking more than a year as of September 2015. U.S. Citizenship and Immigration Services (USCIS), "USCIS Processing Time Information for the Vermont Service Center," https://egov.uscis.gov/cris/processingTimesDisplay.dom, accessed September 25, 2015.

46. U.S. Citizenship and Immigration Services (USCIS), "Same-Sex Marriages: Statement from Secretary of Homeland Security Janet Napolitano on July 1, 2013," http://www.uscis.gov/family/same-sex-marriages, accessed September 25, 2015.

47. U.S. Department of Labor, Office of Foreign Labor Certification, "Foreign Labor Certification," http://www.foreignlaborcert.doleta.gov/about.cfm, accessed September 25, 2015.

48. Ben A. Rissing and Emilio J. Castilla, "House of Green Cards: Statistical or Preference-Based Inequality in the Employment of Foreign Nationals," *American Sociological Review* 79/6 (2014):1226–55.

49. Julia Nissen, "New Attacks on Birthright Citizenship: 'Anchor Babies' and the 14th Amendment," Council on Hemispheric Affairs, August 24, 2010.

50. Jeffrey S. Passel and D'Vera Cohn, *Unauthorized Immigrant Population:*

National and State Trends, 2010, Pew Hispanic Center, February 1, 2010, 12; Bendixen & Associates, *Report of Findings from October 2005 Poll of Undocumented Immigrants.*

51.   Joanna Dreby, *How Today's Immigration Enforcement Policies Impact Children, Families, and Communities: A View from the Ground,* Center for American Progress, August 2012; New York University School of Law Immigrant Rights Clinic, *Insecure Communities, Devastated Families: New Data on Immigrant Detention and Deportation Practices in New York City,* July 23, 2012, 18.

52.   8 U.S. Code sec. 1229b. Cancellation of removal; adjustment of status, https://www.law.cornell.edu/uscode/text/8/1229b, accessed May 22, 2015; Richard Hanus, "Exceptional and Extremely Unusual Hardship: BIA Reverses Immigration Judge Ruling on an Undocumented Family of Six," *Immigration Law Facts and Issues,* September 26, 2002.

53.   U.S. Department of Justice, Executive Office for Immigration Review (EOIR) Office of Planning, Analysis, & Technology, *FY 2005 Statistical Year Book,* Table 15, February 2006; EOIR, *FY 2010 Statistical Year Book,* Table 15, January 2011; EOIR, *FY 2014Statistics Yearbook,* Table 16, March 2015. EOIR, "Procedures Further Implementing the Annual Limitation on Suspension of Deportation and Cancellation of Removal," November 30, 2016.

54.   Van Gosse, "Birthright Citizenship Is Bedrock Americanism," *Huffington Post,* September 27, 2010; James Oliver Horton, "Weevils in the Wheat: Free Blacks and the Constitution, 1787–1860," in *This Constitution: A Bicentennial Chronicle,* Fall 1985, http://www.apsanet.org/imgtest/freeblacksconstitution.pdf; U.S. Supreme Court, *Alexander Murray v. The Schooner Charming Betsy,* 1804, https://supreme.justia.com/cases/federal/us/6/64/; U.S. Supreme Court, *Scott v. Sandford,* dissent by Justice John McLean, March 6, 1857, http://www.law.cornell.edu/supremecourt/text/60/393#writing-USSC_CR_0060_0393_ZD, dissent by Justice Benjamin R. Curtis, http://www.law.cornell.edu/supremecourt/text/60/393#writing-USSC_CR_0060_0393_ZD1.

55.   U.S. Supreme Court, *United States v. Wong Kim Ark,* March 28, 1898, http://www.law.cornell.edu/supct/html/historics/USSC_CR_0169_0649_ZO.html.

56.   Rhonda Brownstein, "Anti-Immigrant Republican Brian Bilbray's Bizarre Crusade on the 14th Amendment," *AlterNet,* September 1, 2008; Julianne Hing, "Lawmakers in 14 States Coordinate Birthright Citizenship Attack," *ColorLines,* January 5, 2011; Eric Foner, "Born in the U.S.A. Is What Makes Someone American," *Bloomberg Opinion,* August 17, 2010.

57.   United Nations High Commissioner for Refugees (UNHCR) press release, "UNHCR Urges Dominican Republic to Restore Nationality," December 5, 2013; Inter-American Commission on Human Rights (IACHR) press release, "IACHR Wraps Up Visit to the Dominican Republic," December 6, 2013.

58. Jennifer Van Hook with Michael Fix, *The Demographic Impacts of Repealing Birthright Citizenship*, Migration Policy Institute, September 2010.

59. USCIS, "Naturalization Fact Sheet," http://www.uscis.gov/archive/archive-news/naturalization-fact-sheet, accessed September 25, 2015.

60. Most applicants must also pay an $85 biometric fee. U.S. Citizenship and Immigration Services, "N-400, Application for Naturalization," https://www.uscis.gov/n-400, accessed March 5, 2017. Fee waivers are available for those earning less than 150 percent of the poverty level. Allan Wernick, "Permanent Residents Who Want to Vote in 2016 Should Apply for U.S. Citizenship," New York *Daily News*, September 29, 2015.

61. Information from the co-authors' conversations with the applicant and his legal representative.

62. H. G. Reza, "For Citizenship Delayed, 10 Taking U.S. to Court," *Los Angeles Times*, August 1, 2006; American Civil Liberties Union of Southern California, "Ten Area Residents, ACLU, CAIR File Class Action Lawsuit, Seek to Fix Broken Citizenship Process," August 1, 2006; American Civil Liberties Union of Southern California, "ACLU/SC Wins Citizenship for Seven," October 5, 2006.

63. ACLU of Southern California, *Muslims Need Not Apply: How USCIS Secretly Mandates the Discriminatory Delay and Denial of Citizenship and Immigration Benefits to Aspiring Americans*, August 2013; Sonali Kolhatkar, "How the FBI Secretly Denies Muslim Immigrants Their Citizenship," *Common Dreams*, August 29, 2013; Karen McVeigh, "FBI Granted Power to Delay Citizenship for Muslims, ACLU Report Says," *The Guardian*, August 21, 2013. In 2015, attorney William Stock wrote on his firm's website that the previous year over a million naturalization or residency cases remained pending with USCIS for over six months, and that many of these were likely delayed over FBI name checks: "While most applicants for citizenship can expect an interview within six months of filing the application, a significant number (by the FBI's estimates, about 10 percent of all applicants) will not be scheduled for interview on their application for years." William A. Stock, "Immigrants Challenge Lengthy Processing Delays in Court with Mixed Results," Klasko Immigration Law Partners, LLP, May 4, 2015.

5.Is it Easy to Be "Illegal"?

1. National Academies Press, *The Integration of Immigrants into American Society*, September 21, 2015, 9-3.

2. See "Who gets deported, and why?" (chapter 11).

3. Nicholas Riccardi, "Why Illegal Immigrants Fear Leaving: As Border Control Has Tightened, Many Have Sent for Their Families Instead of Risking a Visit," *Los Angeles Times*, April 12, 2006. See "Has border enforcement cut the flow of migrants?" (chapter 9).

4. Heather Courtney, *Los Trabajadores/The Workers*, New Day Films, 2001.

5. U.S. Constitution, Fourteenth Amendment.

6.   U.S. Supreme Court, *United States v. Christopher Lee Armstrong et al., No. 95-157*, May 13, 1996.

7.   Daniel González, "'Wilson 4' Avoid Deportation: Judge Tosses Case over Profiling; Feds Plan Appeal," *Arizona Republic*, July 22, 2005; Scott Simon, "Arizona's 'Wilson 4' Remain in Legal Limbo," NPR, October 22, 2005.

8.   In October 2016, a federal court charged Arpaio with criminal contempt for failing to comply with the court order. Two weeks later he was voted out of office. Associated Press, "Joe Arpaio Racially Profiled Latinos in Arizona, Judge Rules," *The Guardian*, May 25, 2013; David Schwartz, "Arizona Sheriff Ordered to Undergo Training to Stop Racial Profiling," Reuters, October 29, 2014; Megan Cassidy, "Maricopa County Sheriff Joe Arpaio Officially Charged with Criminal Contempt," *The Arizona Republic*, October 25, 2016; Fernanda Santos, "Sheriff Joe Arpaio Loses Bid for 7th Term in Arizona," *The New York Times*, November 9, 2016.

9.   In the absence of any evidence of alienage, such as documents or the testimony of another person, the courts have ruled that a person's silence to questions about alienage cannot be construed as an admission that they are an alien. "If the 'burden' of proof were satisfied by a respondent's silence alone, it would be practically no burden at all," the Board of Immigration Appeals (BIA) noted in a 1990 decision overturning a deportation order. *BIA Interim Decision #3143, Matter of Guevara, In Deportation Proceedings A-29017722*, decided by BIA September 14, 1990, and January 31, 1991.

10.   Reuters, "1,200 Caught in Immigration Raids at IFCO Systems Plants," *USA Today*, April 20, 2006; Alfonso Chardy, "Fears of Mass Arrests Keep Undocumented Immigrants Off South Florida Streets," *Miami Herald*, April 27, 2006.

11.   Nancy Hiemstra, "This Is Fear: ICE Raids on Parents and Children," *Huffington Post*, January 8, 2016.

12.   See "Do immigrants commit more crimes than non-immigrants?" (chapter 8).

13.   Southern Poverty Law Center (SPLC), *Under Siege: Life for Low-Income Latinos in the South*, March 31, 2009. See also Crime Victims' Institute, Sam Houston State University, *Victimization of Immigrants*, October 2008.

14.   Leslye E. Orloff and Nomi Dave, "Identifying Barriers: Survey of Immigrant Women and Domestic Violence in the D.C. Metropolitan Area," *Poverty and Race* 6/4 (August 31, 1997); Leslye E. Orloff and Rachel Little, "Somewhere to Turn: Making Domestic Violence Services Accessible to Battered Immigrant Women: A How-To Manual for Battered Women's Advocates and Service Providers," Ayuda, Inc. (May 1999, updated July 2011).

15.   Family Violence Prevention Fund, *Intimate Partner Violence in Immigrant and Refugee Communities: Challenges, Promising Practices and Recommendations*, March 2009.

16.   SPLC, *Under Siege*; Alfonso A. Castillo, "Judge: Day Laborers' Rights Violated," *Newsday*, February 12, 2005; Naimah Jabali-Nash, "Four New York Teens Sentenced in 2008 Hate Crime," CBS News, August 26, 2010.

17. Brad Knickerbocker, "National Acrimony and a Rise in Hate Crimes," *Christian Science Monitor*, June 3, 2005; Riad Z. Abdelkarim, "Surge in Hate Crimes Followed by Official U.S. Targeting of Muslim, Arab Men," *Washington Report on Middle East Affairs*, April 1, 2003; U.S. Department of Justice, Bureau of Justice Statistics, "U.S. Residents Experienced About 293,800 Hate Crime Victimizations in 2012: Unchanged From 2004," press release, February 20, 2014; Meagan Meuchel Wilson, "Hate Crime Victimization, 2004–2012 Statistical Tables" from BJS National Crime Victimization Survey, 2003–2012; FBI Hate Crime Statistics Reporting Program, (2003–2012), February 20, 2014; Abby Haglage, "Hate Crime Victimization Statistics Show Rise in Anti-Hispanic Crime," *The Daily Beast*, February 20, 2014.

18. Cindy Y. Rodriguez, "New York City Next In Line to Issue ID Cards to Undocumented Residents," CNN, February 24, 2014: Janice Kephart, "Driver's License Insecurity: A Terrorist's Back Door," Center for Immigration Studies, September 2012. See also "How did the September 11 hijackers get here?" (chapter 8).

19. National Immigration Law Center (NILC), "Why Denying Driver's Licenses to Undocumented Immigrants Harms Public Safety and Makes Our Communities Less Secure," January 2008.

20. NILC, "Inclusive Policies Advance Dramatically in the States: Immigrants' Access to Driver's Licenses, Higher Education, Workers' Rights, and Community Policing," August 2013, updated October 2013, 1–4; Rodriguez, "New York City next in line to issue ID cards to undocumented residents"; Aaron Morrison, "Immigrant Identification Card: New York's ID Program Watched by Immigration Reform Advocates Across Nation," *International Business Times*, January 15, 2015.

21. U.S. Supreme Court, *Plyler v. Doe, No. 80-1538*, June 15, 1982.

22. NILC, *Basic Facts about In-State Tuition for Undocumented Immigrant Students*, April 2006.

23. Samuel G. Freedman, "Behind Top Student's Heartbreak, Illegal Immigrants' Nightmare," *New York Times*, September 1, 2004.

24. David Epstein, "Dream Deferred," *Inside Higher Ed*, July 28, 2006.

25. NILC, *Basic Facts about In-State Tuition for Undocumented Immigrant Students*, June 2014; NILC, "State Laws & Policies," http://www.nilc.org/eduaccesstoolkit2a.html#tables, accessed April 18, 2015.

26. The Pew Research Center estimates that 1.1 million young immigrants were eligible for DACA. NILC and United We Dream, "Frequently Asked Questions: The Obama Administration's Deferred Action for Childhood Arrivals (DACA)," http://www.nilc.org/FAQdeferredactionyouth.html, accessed April 20, 2015; Jens Manuel Krogstad and Ana Gonzalez-Barrera, "If original DACA program is a guide, many eligible immigrants will apply for deportation relief," Pew Research Center, December 5, 2014; U.S. Citizenship and Immigration Services, "Number of I-821D, Consideration of Deferred Action for Childhood Arrivals by Fiscal Year, Quarter, Intake, Biometrics and

Case Status: 2012–2015 (September 30)," http://www.uscis.gov/sites/default/files/USCIS/Resources/Reports%20and%20Studies/Immigration%20Forms%20Data/All%20Form%20Types/DACA/I821_daca_performance-data_fy2015_qtr4.pdf, accessed December 28, 20/15. For more on DACA, see "Are DAPA and DACA amnesty programs?" (chapter 10).

27. Immanuel Ness, *Immigrants, Unions, and the New U.S. Labor Market* (Philadelphia: Temple University Press, 2005), 1–5; Rebecca Smith and Eunice Hyunhye Cho, "Workers' Rights on ICE: How Immigration Reform Can Stop Retaliation and Advance Labor Rights," National Employment Law Project (NELP), February 2013.

28. See "Why do they work for less?" (chapter 6). Few studies actually compare the pay and working conditions for undocumented and documented workers; most analyses of this issue instead rely on comparisons of conditions for immigrants and the native born, or for Latino or Hispanic workers (who make up a majority of the undocumented labor force) versus those of other ethnicities.

29. Richard D. Vogel, "Harder Times: Undocumented Workers and the U.S. Informal Economy," *Monthly Review* 58/3 (July-August 2006); Roger Lowenstein, "The Immigration Equation," *New York Times Magazine*, July 9, 2006. Median annual earnings for high school dropouts are calculated from weekly earnings in U.S. Bureau of Labor Statistics, *Highlights of Women's Earnings in 2004*, Table 1, September 2005.

30. Flippen Chenoa A., "Laboring Underground: The Employment Patterns of Hispanic Immigrant Men in Durham, NC," *Social problems* (February 2012), 21–42.

31. Steven Greenhouse, "Low-Wage Workers Are Often Cheated, Study Says," *New York Times*, September 1, 2009; Annette Bernhardt, Ruth Milkman, Nik Theodore, Douglas Heckathorn, Mirabai Auer, James DeFilippis, Ana Luz González, Victor Narro, Jason Perelshteyn, Diana Polson, and Michael Spiller, *Broken Laws, Unprotected Workers: Violations of Employment and Labor Laws in America's Cities*, Center for Urban Economic Development, National Employment Law Project, and UCLA Institute for Research on Labor and Employment, September 2009, 42–43; Bernhardt, Spiller, and Polson, "All Work and No Pay: Violations of Employment and Labor Laws in Chicago, Los Angeles and New York City," *Social Forces* 91/3 (2013): 725–46.

32. Stephen Franklin and Darnell Little, "Fear of Retaliation Trumps Pain: Deaths, Injuries on the Job Soar for Illegal Immigrants," *Chicago Tribune*, September 3, 2006; Pia M. Orrenius and Madeline Zavodny, "Do Immigrants Work in Riskier Jobs?" *Demography* 46/3 (August 2009): 535–51; Katherine Loh and Scott Richardson, "Foreign-born Workers: Trends in Fatal Occupational Injuries, 1996–2001," *Monthly Labor Review*, U.S. Bureau of Labor Statistics, June 2004.

33. Chip Mitchell, "Immigrant job deaths up 14% in two years," Chicago Public Radio, May 8, 2013; AFL-CIO, "Death on the Job: Latino and Immigrant Workers Increasingly at Risk," May 6, 2014.

34. Thomas Maier, "Death on the Job: Immigrants at Risk" (five-part series), *Newsday* (Long Island), July 22–26, 2001; Occupational Safety and Health Administration, Office of the Inspector General, *Evaluation of OSHA's Handling of Immigrant Fatalities in the Workplace*, September 30, 2003; Center for Popular Democracy, *Fatal Inequality: Workplace Safety Eludes Construction Workers of Color in New York State*, October 25, 2013; for more on OSHA, see "How much does enforcement cost us?" (chapter 9).

35. Franklin and Little, "Fear of Retaliation Trumps Pain."

36. Liz Chandler, "He Came for the American Dream and Found an American Nightmare," *Charlotte Observer*, September 17, 2006.

37. See, for example, the small grassroots Laundry Workers Center in New York City, the subject of a 2014 documentary, *The Hand That Feeds*, http://thehandthatfeedsfilm.com/; Sadhbh Walshe, "¡Sí se puede! How Immigrant Workers Won Fair-Wage Battle on Their Terms," *The Guardian*, April 21, 2015.

38. U.S. Equal Employment Opportunity Commission (EEOC), "Employment Rights of Immigrants Under Federal Anti-Discrimination Laws," http://www.eeoc.gov/eeoc/publications/immigrants-facts.cfm, accessed April 21, 2015.

39. U.S. Labor Department, Wage and Hour Division (WHD), "Questions and Answers About the Minimum Wage," http://www.dol.gov/whd/minwage/q-a.htm, accessed April 21, 2015.

40. The study did not indicate whether the workers were undocumented, but out-of-status immigrants make up a large part of the city's low-wage work force. Shannon Firth, "Special Report: Employers Turn Their Backs on Undocumented Workers Injured on the Job," *Voices of New York*, April 1, 2013; Annette Bernhardt, Diana Polson, and James DeFilippis, *A Survey of Employment and Labor Law Violations in New York City*, National Employment Law Project (NELP), 2010.

41. Rebecca Smith and Amy Sugimori (National Employment Law Project), and Ana Avendaño and Marielena Hincapié (National Immigration Law Center), *Undocumented Workers: Preserving Rights and Remedies after Hoffman Plastic Compounds v. NLRB*, April 2003.

42. Mark Hamblett, "Court Rejects Bid to Obtain Workers' Files," *New York Law Journal*, June 17, 2002; *Zeng Liu et al. v. Donna Karan International, Inc. et al., 00 Civ. 4221 (WK), 2002 U.S. Dist. LEXIS 10542*, U.S. District Court for the Southern District of New York, June 11, 2002.

43. NILC, *Immigrants' Rights Update*, 16/6 (October 21, 2002).

44. U.S. Supreme Court, *Hoffman Plastic Compounds, Inc. v. NLRB*, March 27, 2002; Smith, Sugimori, Ana Avendaño, and Marielena Hincapié, *Undocumented Workers*.

45. Equal Employment Opportunity Commission, "EEOC Reaffirms Commitment to Protecting Undocumented Workers from Discrimination," press release, June 28, 2002, http://www.eeoc.gov/press/6-28-02.html; EEOC, "Rescission of Enforcement Guidance on Remedies Available to

Undocumented Workers Under Federal Employment Discrimination Laws," Directives Transmittal #915.002, June 27, 2002.

46.   WHD, "Fact Sheet #48: Application of U.S. Labor Laws to Immigrant Workers: Effect of Hoffman Plastics decision on laws enforced by the Wage and Hour Division," revised July 2008.

47.   The full text of the U.S. Constitution is available, with explanations, at https://www.law.cornell.edu/constitution/.

48.   U.S. Supreme Court, *Scott v. Sanford*, March 6, 1857.

49.   "Illegals have no right to protest U.S. laws," *News-Times* (Danbury, CT), April 11, 2006.

50.   Martin Luther King, Jr., "Letter from a Birmingham Jail," April 16, 1963, http://www.africa.upenn.edu/Articles_Gen/Letter_Birmingham.html.

51.   Justia.com, "The Power of Congress to Exclude Aliens," http://law.justia.com/constitution/us/article-1/36-aliens.html, accessed April 21, 2015; Jennifer Chacón, "Who Is Responsible for U.S. Immigration Policy?," *Insights on Law and Society* 14/3 (Spring 2014).

52.   GNN (Guerrilla News Network) interview with Riva Enteen, Program Director at the San Francisco chapter of the National Lawyer's Guild, ca. November 2002, posted at http://www.oocities.org/hal9000report/hal91.html, accessed November 25, 2016.

53.   Frederick Douglass, "If There Is No Struggle, There Is No Progress," from BlackPast.org, http://www.blackpast.org/1857-frederick-douglass-if-there-no-struggle-there-no-progress, accessed November 28, 2016.

6. Are Immigrants Hurting Our Economy?

1.   Miriam Valverde, "Donald Trump says illegal immigration costs $113 billion a year," PolitiFact, September 1, 2016; Congressional Budget Office, *The Impact of Unauthorized Immigrants on the Budgets of State and Local Governments,* December 2007.

2.   Fiscal Policy Institute, *Immigrants and the Economy: Contribution of Immigrant Workers to the Country's 25 Largest Metropolitan Areas,* December 2009, 5; Steven A. Camarota, *The High Cost of Cheap Labor: Illegal Immigration and the Federal Budget,* Center for Immigration Studies, August 2004; Commission on Behavioral and Social Sciences and Education (CBASSE), *The New Americans: Economic, Demographic, and Fiscal Effects of Immigration* (Washington, D.C.: National Academies Press, 1997), 9–12.

3.   World Bank, "GDP (current US$)," accessed August 1, 2014; Congressional Budget Office, *Report on the Troubled Asset Relief Program—October 2012,* October 11, 2012; Daniel Trotta, "Iraq War Costs U.S. More than $2 Trillion: Study," Reuters, March 14, 2013.

4.   See "How much does enforcement cost us?" (chapter 9).

5.   See, "How many immigrants are here?" (chapter 1).

6.   Jeffrey S. Passel and D'Vera Cohn, *Unauthorized Immigrant Population: National and State Trends, 2010,* Pew Hispanic Center, February 1, 2010,

9; Institute on Taxation and Economic Policy (ITEP), *Undocumented Immigrants' State and Local Tax Contributions,* July 2013.

7.   See "Who are the undocumented immigrants?" (chapter 1). The SSA figure likely comes from a calculation of returns filed using an ITIN. Tax data for 2013 shows more than 3.5 million returns filed with an ITIN—2.65 percent of all tax filers. The number and proportion of ITIN filers rose from 2012, when just over 3.4 million filers represented 2.60 percent of all filers. Returns are counted as being filed with an ITIN if anyone listed on the form uses an ITIN. Authors' analysis of data downloaded from Brookings Institution website, http://www.brookings.edu/research/interactives/eitc.

8.   ITEP, *Undocumented Immigrants' State and Local Tax Contributions.* No information appears to be available about the numbers or proportion of ITIN filers who are paid off the books, or as "independent contractors."

9.   Center for Poverty Research, University of California Davis, "What are the annual earnings for a full-time minimum wage worker?," http://poverty.ucdavis.edu/faq/what-are-annual-earnings-full-time-minimum-wage-worker, accessed August 2, 2014; Internal Revenue Service 1040 form for 2013, http://www.irs.gov/pub/irs-prior/f1040--2013.pdf, accessed August 2, 2014.

10.   D. A. Barber, "The 'New' Economy?" *Tucson Weekly,* January 8, 2003; Rick Newman, "The New Underground Economy: More people than ever may be working off-the-books—and spending freely," *U.S. News & World Report,* March 18, 2013; Joshua Zumbrun, "More Americans Work in the Underground Economy," *Bloomberg Businessweek,* March 28, 2013.

11.   Albor Ruiz, "Study estimates that illegal immigrants paid $11.2B in taxes last year, unlike GE, which paid zero," New York *Daily News,* April 20, 2011; Robert S. McIntyre, Matthew Gardner, Richard Phillips, *The Sorry State of Corporate Taxes: What Fortune 500 Firms Pay (or Don't Pay) in the USA, and What They Pay Abroad—2008 to 2012,* Citizens for Tax Justice and Institute on Taxation and Economic Policy, February 2014; Jane G. Gravelle, *Tax Havens: International Tax Avoidance and Evasion* (Washington, D.C.: Congressional Research Service, January 15, 2015).

12.   Testimony of Robert J. Rector before Senate Judiciary Subcommittee on Immigration, February 2, 1996, excerpted in *Melting Pot or Boiling Point? The Issues of Immigration* (Hudson, WI: Gary E. McCuen Publications, 1997), 78.

13.   Stephen Ohlemacher, "Social Security Cheap Compared with Europe's," Associated Press, August 12, 2012; Tanya Broder and Jonathan Blazer, *Overview of Immigrant Eligibility for Federal Programs,* National Immigration Law Center, October 2011.

14.   Shawn Fremstad, *Immigrants and Welfare Reauthorization,* Center on Budget and Policy Priorities, February 4, 2002; Amanda Levinson, "Immigrants and Welfare Use," Migration Policy Institute, August 1, 2002; Broder and Blazer, *Overview of Immigrant Eligibility for Federal Programs;* U.S. Department of Health and Human Services, *Barriers to Immigrants'*

Access to Health and Human Services Programs, May 2012, Office of the Assistant Secretary for Planning and Evaluation (ASPE) research brief prepared by the Urban Institute; Mark H. Greenberg, Jodie Levin-Epstein, Rutledge Q. Hutson, Theodora J. Ooms, Rachel Schumacher, Vicki Turetsky, and David M. Engstrom, "The 1996 Welfare Law: Key Elements and Reauthorization Issues Affecting Children," *Children and Welfare Reform* 12/1 (Winter–Spring 2002).

15. Leighton Ku and Brian Bruen, *The Use of Public Assistance: Benefits by Citizens and Non-Citizen Immigrants in the United States*, Cato Institute Working Paper, February 19, 2013.

16. Broder and Blazer, *Overview of Immigrant Eligibility for Federal Programs.*

17. Pew Hispanic, "Unauthorized Immigrants Today: A Demographic Profile," http://www.immigrationpolicy.org/just-facts/unauthorized-immigrants-today-demographic-profile, accessed April 11, 2015; U.S. Department of Education, National Center for Education Statistics, "Fast Facts," https://nces.ed.gov/fastfacts/display.asp?id=66, accessed April 11, 2015; U.S. Department of Education, "10 Facts About K-12 Education Funding," http://www2.ed.gov/about/overview/fed/10facts/index.html, accessed August 2, 2014; National Conference of State Legislatures, "Immunizations Policy Issues Overview," April 4, 2011.

18. The Child Tax Credit can only reduce taxes owed; the Additional Child Tax Credit is refundable. "Your Federal Income Tax," Internal Revenue Service (IRS) Publication 17 (2015); IRS, "Ten Facts About the Child Tax Credit," February 10, 2011.

19. Timothy Casey and Laurie Maldonado, "Worst Off: Single-Parent Families in the United States: A Cross-National Comparison of Single Parenthood in the U.S. and Sixteen Other High-Income Countries," LegalMomentum. org, December 2010.

20. Kelly Phillips Erb, "Viral 'Tax Loophole' Video Is Misleading: Taxpayer Fraud Is a Much Bigger Problem," *Forbes*, May 15, 2012; Marshall Fitz and Sarah Jane Glynn, "Attacks Against the Child Tax Credit Suggest Compassionate Conservatism Is Dead," Center for American Progress, May 30, 2012, https://americanprogress.org.

21. The 1996 welfare reform law barred federal funding for prenatal care for undocumented pregnant women. In 2002 the U.S. Department of Health and Human Services issued regulations allowing states to provide such care by extending Children's Health Insurance Program (CHIP) coverage to unborn children. As of November 2013, eighteen states provided prenatal care to undocumented women through either the CHIP program or state funding. Catholic Legal Immigration Network, Inc. website, "Eighteen States Offer Prenatal Care to Undocumented Immigrant Women (Nov. 2013)," https://cliniclegal.org/resources/articles-clinic/eighteen-states-offer-prenatal-care-undocumented-immigrant-women-nov-2013, accessed January 19, 2016; Nebraska Appleseed, "LB599: Restoring Prenatal Care in Nebraska," Mar. 29, 2012; Robin D. Gorsky and John P. Colby, Jr.,

"The Cost Effectiveness of Prenatal Care in Reducing Low Birth Weight in New Hampshire," *Health Services Research* 24/5 (December 1989): 583–98; C. Annette DuBard and Mark W. Massing, "Trends in Emergency Medicaid Expenditures for Recent and Undocumented Immigrants," *Journal of the American Medical Association*, March 14, 2007; Phil Galewitz, "Medicaid Helps Hospitals Pay for Illegal Immigrants' Care," *Kaiser Health News*, February 12, 2013; Sy Mukherjee, "Why Undocumented Immigrants Should Have Access to Taxpayer-Funded Health Care," ThinkProgress, May 24, 2013. A 2006 study by the Rand Institute gave a lower figure for government health care spending for undocumented immigrants. Evelyn Larrubia, "Illegal Immigrants' Healthcare Bill Is Tallied," *Los Angeles Times*, November 15, 2006. For claims that undocumented mothers have children to get legal status, see "What about the 'anchor babies'?" (chapter 4).

22. Eduardo Porter, "Illegal Immigrants Are Bolstering Social Security with Billions," *New York Times*, April 5, 2005; John Lantigua, "Illegal Immigrants Pay Social Security Tax, Won't Benefit," Cox Newspapers, *Seattle Times*, December 28, 2011; Stephen Goss, Alice Wade, J. Patrick Skirvin, Michael Morris, K. Mark Bye, and Danielle Huston, "Effects of Unauthorized Immigration on the Actuarial Status of the Social Security Trust Funds," Social Security Administration, April 2013, 3.

23. Larrubia, "Illegal Immigrants' Healthcare Bill Is Tallied"; National Immigration Law Center, "Immigrants and the Affordable Care Act (ACA)," January 2014.

24. See "Are undocumented workers more exploited?" (chapter 5).

25. Tamyra Carroll Garcia, Amy B. Bernstein, and Mary Ann Bush, "Emergency Department Visitors and Visits: Who Used the Emergency Room in 2007?," National Center for Health Statistics (NCHS), May 2010; Mary Engel, "Study Finds Immigrants' Use of Healthcare System Lower Than Expected," *Los Angeles Times*, November 27, 2007; Alexander N. Ortega, Hai Fang, Victor H. Perez, John A. Rizzo, Olivia Carter-Pokras, Steven P. Wallace, Lillian Gelberg, "Health Care Access, Use of Services, and Experiences Among Undocumented Mexicans and Other Latinos," *Archives of Internal Medicine*167/21 (November 26, 2007).

26. John Dorscher, "ER Use in Dade Less Than Expected," *Miami Herald*, July 18, 2006; Julia Preston, "Texas Hospitals Reflect the Debate on Immigration," *New York Times*, July 18, 2006.

27. Ruth E. Hernández Beltrán, "Still Unknown How Many Undocumented Immigrants Died in 9/11," *La Oferta* (San Jose, CA) from Spanish news agency EFE, September 15, 2006.

28. Cara Buckley, "With Millions in 9/11 Payments, Bereaved Can't Buy Green Cards," *New York Times*, September 3, 2006.

29. Migration Policy Institute, "The Global Remittances Guide," http://www.migrationpolicy.org/programs/data-hub/global-remittances-guide, accessed March 3, 2015; Lindsay Koshgarian, "Penny on the Dollar: US Foreign Aid Is About One Percent of Spending," National Priorities Project, August 12, 2014;

Congressional Budget Office, *Migrants' Remittances and Related Economic Flows*, February 2011; Inter American Development Bank press release, "Remittances to Latin America stabilizing after 15% drop last year—MIF," March 4, 2010; World Bank annual remittances data, http://siteresources. worldbank.org/EXTDECPROSPECTS/Resources/476882-1157133580628/ RemittancesData_Inflows_May10(Public).xls, accessed September 5, 2011.

30.   Jeff Cox, "US companies now stashing $2 trillion overseas," CNBC, November 12, 2014.

31.   *Merco Press*, "Walmart is Latin America's single largest employer, says Latin Business," August 5, 2010; Galina Hale and Bart Hobijn, "The U.S. Content of 'Made in China,'" *Federal Reserve Bank of San Francisco Economic Letter*, August 8, 2011.

32.   Kevin O'Neil, "Remittances from the United States in Context," Migration Policy Institute, June 1, 2003; Justin Akers Chacón and Mike Davis, *No One Is Illegal* (Chicago: Haymarket Books, 2006), 164.

33.   Aaron Terrazas, "Salvadoran Immigrants in the United States," Migration Policy Institute, January 5, 2010; Alfonso Gonzales, "The FMLN Victory and Transnational Salvadoran Activism: Lessons for the Future," *NACLA Report on the Americas*, July 2009. For the number of Salvadorans living here with TPS, see "Are refugees sent home when their countries become safer?" (chapter 3).

34.   Stephen Moore, Lowell Gallawy, and Richard Vedder, "Immigration and Unemployment: New Evidence," March 1994, quoted in *Melting Pot*, 103.

35.   Rakesh Kochhar, "Growth in the Foreign-Born Workforce and Employment of the Native Born," Pew Hispanic Center, August 10, 2006.

36.   John Irons and Andrew Fieldhouse, "Let the tax cuts for the rich expire," *Milwaukee Journal Sentinel*, August 17, 2010; Seth D. Michaels, "Luxury Goods Are the Only Growth Industries—and That's Bad," *TalkingPointsMemo.com*, February 6, 2014; Robert Reich, "The Four Biggest Right-Wing Lies About Inequality," Robert Reich blog, May 5, 2014, http:// robertreich.org/.

37.   Testimony of James S. Holt before Subcommittee on Immigration and Claims of the House Judiciary Committee, December 7, 1995, excerpted in *Melting Pot*, 137–38.

38.   Department of Agriculture (USDA) Economic Research Service, "Farm Labor: Overview," http://www.ers.usda.gov/topics/farm-economy/farm-labor/background.aspx, accessed August 12, 2015. The data comes from the Labor Department's National Agricultural Workers Survey (NAWS). See also "Who are the undocumented immigrants?" and its endnotes (chapter 1).

39.   Jeffrey S. Passel and D'Vera Cohn, *A Portrait of Unauthorized Immigrants in the United States*, Pew Hispanic Center, April 14, 2009, 16; Jeffrey S. Passel, *The Size and Characteristics of the Unauthorized Migrant Population in the U.S.: Estimates Based on the March 2005 Current Population Survey*, Pew Hispanic Center, March 7, 2006.

40. George J. Borjas, *Heaven's Door: Immigration Policy and the American Economy* (Princeton: Princeton University Press, 1999), 79, italics in original.

41. Moshe Adler, *The Effect of Immigration on Wages: A Review of the Literature and Some New Data*, Empire State College, SUNY, May 1, 2008; Moshe Adler, "Pitting Worker Against Worker," *TruthDig.org*, April 30, 2010.

42. *The New Americans*, 6–7, 219–28.

43. Roger Lowenstein, "The Immigration Equation," *New York Times Magazine*, July 9, 2006. Annual earnings for dropouts are calculated from Department of Labor Bureau of Labor Statistics (BLS), "Median Weekly Earnings By Educational Attainment in 2014," January 23, 2015.

44. Pia Orrenius and Madeline Zavodny, *The Minimum Wage and Latino Workers*, Institute for the Study of Labor discussion paper, November 2010; Janelle Jones and John Schmitt, "Low-Wage Latino Workers," Center for Economic and Policy Research, April 4, 2012.

45. Dean Calbreath, "Experts Say Exodus of Illegal Immigrants Could Stagger Economy," *San Diego Union-Tribune*, September 5, 2006.

46. Matthew Hall, Emily Greenman, and George Farkas, "Legal Status and Wage Disparities for Mexican Immigrants," *Social Forces* 89/2 (2010): 491–513.

47. Pedro P. Orraca-Romano and Erika García Meneses, "Why Are the Wages of the Mexican Immigrants and Their Descendants So Low in the United States?" *Estudios Económicos* 31/2 (July-December 2016): 305–37.

48. Jeffrey S. Passel and D'Vera Cohn, *Share of Unauthorized Immigrant Workers in Production, Construction Jobs Falls, Since 2007*, Pew Hispanic Center, March 26, 2015, Table 1, http://www.pewhispanic.org.

49. See "Are undocumented workers more exploited?" (chapter 5).

50. Francisco L. Rivera-Batiz, "Undocumented workers in the labor market: An analysis of the earnings of legal and illegal Mexican immigrants in the United States," *Journal of Population Economics* 12/1 (1999): 100, 106; Julie A. Phillips and Douglas A. Massey, "The New Labor Market: Immigrants and Wages After IRCA," *Demography* 36/2 (May 1999): 244; Hall, Greenman, and Farkas, "Legal Status and Wage Disparities for Mexican Immigrants"; Patrick Oakford, *Administrative Action on Immigration Reform: The Fiscal Benefits of Temporary Work Permits*, Center for American Progress, September 2014, 14–17.

51. Paul Krugman, "Wages, Wealth and Politics," *New York Times*, August 18, 2006; Steven Greenhouse and David Leonhardt, "Real Wages Fail to Match a Rise in Productivity," *New York Times*, August 28, 2006.

52. Heidi Shierholz, *Fix It and Forget It: Index the Minimum Wage to Growth in Average Wages*, Economic Policy Institute briefing paper, December 17, 2009.

53. Rebecca M. Blank, "Was Welfare Reform Successful?" *The Economists' Voice* 3/4 (2006); June E. O'Neill and M. Anne Hill, *Gaining Ground? Measuring the Impact of Welfare Reform on Welfare and Work*, Manhattan Institute, Civic Report No. 17, July 2001. For an example of the effects of outsourcing,

see Will Kimball and Robert E. Scott, "China Trade, Outsourcing and Jobs," Economic Policy Institute, December 11, 2014.

54. Julia Preston and Steven Greenhouse, "Immigration Accord by Labor Boosts Obama Effort," *New York Times*, April 13, 2009.

55. Bryan C. Baker, *Naturalization Rates among IRCA Immigrants: A 2009 Update*, Department of Homeland Security Office of Immigration Statistics, October 2010.

56. Calbreath, "Experts Say Exodus of Illegal Immigrants Could Stagger Economy"; Raul Hinojosa Ojeda, Robert McCleery, Enrico Marcelli, Fernando de Paolis, David Runsten, and Marysol Sanchez, *Comprehensive Migration Policy Reform in North America: The Key to Sustainable and Equitable Economic Integration*, North American Integration and Development Center, School of Public Policy and Social Research, University of California, Los Angeles, August 29, 2001, 28, 30; Raúl Hinojosa-Ojeda, *Economic Stimulus through Legalization*, William C. Velázquez Institute white paper, January 23, 2009.

57. Teófilo Reyes, "AFL-CIO, in Dramatic Turnaround, Endorses Amnesty for Undocumented Immigrants," *Labor Notes*, April 1, 2000.

58. David Bacon, *The Children of NAFTA: Labor Wars on the U.S./Mexico Border* (Berkeley and Los Angeles: University of California Press, 2004), 284, 301.

59. Chip Mitchell, "Before Sit-In, Workers Beat Racial Tensions," *Chicago Public Radio*, December 17, 2008; Esther J. Cepeda, "The Immigrant Story That Wasn't: Laid Off Republic Windows Employees Just Regular Working Stiffs," *Huffington Post*, December 9, 2008; David Brooks, "Hora de que los pequeños nos pongamos de pie," *La Jornada* (Mexico), December 11, 2008.

7. Is Immigration Hurting Our Health, Environment, or Culture?

1.   National Academies of Sciences, Engineering, and Medicine, *The Integration of Immigrants into American Society* (Washington, DC: National Academies Press, 2016), 399.

2.   Eddy Ng and Isabel Metz, "Multiculturalism as a Strategy for National Competitiveness: The Case for Canada and Australia," *Journal of Business Ethics* 128/2 (May 2015): 253–66.

3.   Maggie Fox, "Vectors or Victims? Docs Slam Rumors That Migrants Carry Disease," NBC News, July 9, 2014.

4.   Immigration Act of 1891, http://library.uwb.edu/static/USimmigration/26%20stat%201084.pdf; Ruth Ellen Wasem, Congressional Research Service, *Immigration Policies and Issues on Health-Related Grounds for Exclusion*, August 13, 2014.

5.   At ports of entry on the Texas-Mexico border, the U.S. Public Health Service "disinfected" groups of incoming migrants and forced them to undergo physical exams. Lower-class Asians arriving in San Francisco were subjected to similar treatment and often detained at Angel Island to await laboratory testing for parasites. Even among Europeans, ethnicity

was medicalized; Eastern European Jews, for example, were seen as prone to "poor physique." During the great wave of immigration between 1891 and 1924, fewer than 1 percent of all arriving immigrants—and 4 percent of Chinese immigrants—were turned back for medical reasons. Mexican "*bracero*" guest workers were sprayed with DDT into the late 1950s. Howard Markel and Alexandra Minna Stern, "The Foreignness of Germs: The Persistent Association of Immigrants and Disease in American Society," *Milbank Quarterly* 80/4 (2002); David Dorado Romo, "Crossing the Line," *Los Angeles Times*, February 27, 2006. On the history of U.S. government attempts to regulate health and morality through immigration policy, see Deirdre M. Moloney, *National Insecurities: Immigrants and U.S. Deportation Policy Since 1882* (Chapel Hill: University of North Carolina Press, 2012).

6.   Dr. Jean William Pape, who treated Haiti's first AIDS cases, concluded that the disease was likely brought to Haiti by U.S. tourists. In 1987, Philippine Health Department statistics showed that the heaviest concentration of AIDS cases in the Philippines was among prostitutes working near two U.S. military bases, Clark Air Base and Subic Bay Naval Base, suggesting that HIV had been introduced there by U.S. soldiers. The issue spurred local opposition to the bases, which were closed in 1992. Laura Beil, "The Infancy of AIDS: Epidemic's Early Years Could Hold Clues to Disease's Future," *Dallas Morning News*, February 22, 1999, available at http://sks. sirs.swb.orc.scoolaid.net/cgi-bin/hst-article-display?id=SNY5419-0-108&type=ART&artno=0000097485; Mark Fineman, "U.S. Bases, Politics Involved; Philippines Face Difficult Obstacles in AIDS Fight," *Los Angeles Times*, March 30, 1987.

7.   Michael Ratner, "How We Closed the Guantánamo HIV Camp: The Intersection of Politics and Litigation," *Harvard Human Rights Journal* 11 (Spring 1998).

8.   U.S. Citizenship and Immigration Services (USCIS), "Human Immunodeficiency Virus (HIV) Infection Removed from CDC List of Communicable Diseases of Public Health Significance," last reviewed/ updated May 18, 2010, http://www.uscis.gov/archive/archive-news/human-immunodeficiency-virus-hiv-infection-removed-cdc-list-communicable-diseases-public-health-significance; Gay Men's Health Crisis (GMHC), *Undermining Public Health and Human Rights: The United States HIV Travel and Immigration Ban*, January 2010. Health and Human Services (HHS) manages the list of barred diseases. To the question, "Why are HHS and CDC removing only HIV infection when other sexually transmitted diseases (STDs) are still on the list of diseases that prevent entry?" CDC responded that this was because specific legislation in 2008 mandated the removal of HIV/AIDS from the list, and "because . . . HIV is not spread through casual contact." CDC, Immigrant and Refugee Health, "General Questions and Answers: Final Rule Removing HIV Infection from U.S. Immigration Screening," http://www.cdc.gov/immigrantrefugeehealth/

laws-regs/hiv-ban-removal/final-rule-general-qa.html, accessed January 27, 2016. However, none of the STDs on the list are spread by casual contact, and the CDC could simply remove them without legislation—only HIV/AIDS was added to the list by Congress, and thus had to be removed by Congress as well as by HHS. The likely answer is that other STDs, once cured, cannot be detected or serve as a basis for excluding whole categories of people; it was the broad exclusion of people living with HIV/AIDS that motivated activists to win the legislative change through a political battle. No similar social movement exists to push for reform of the remaining medical criteria. For a discussion of ongoing issues relating to the HIV/AIDS ban, see Heidemarie F. Kremer, "USA: Banning People with HIV from Attending the AIDS 2012 Conference," *openDemocracy*, July 18, 2012.

9. CDC, "Immigrant and Refugee Health: Communicable Diseases of Public Health Significance," http://www.cdc.gov/immigrantrefugeehealth/exams/diseases-vaccines-included.html, accessed April 25, 2015; USCIS Policy Manual, vol. 8, Part B, "Health-Related Grounds of Inadmissibility," chap. 6, "Communicable Diseases of Public Health Significance," http://www.uscis.gov/policymanual/HTML/PolicyManual-Volume8-PartB.html. There were only seventy-seven new cases of leprosy in the United States in 2014, nearly all of them among immigrants. The disease is fully curable with antibiotics, and is spread only through prolonged and close physical contact with an infected person who has not yet received treatment. Leprosy has been on the decline for decades; its worldwide prevalence fell by 90 percent from 1980 to 2000. Donald G. McNeil Jr., "Where the Doctors Recognize Leprosy," *New York Times*, October 24, 2006; World Health Organization (WHO), "Leprosy: Fact sheet No.101," updated January 2014, http://www.who.int/mediacentre/factsheets/fs101/en/; CDC, "Summary of Notifiable Diseases, United States, 2005," *Morbidity and Mortality Weekly Report* 64/16 (May 1, 2015).

10. CDC, "Immigrant and Refugee Health: Communicable Diseases of Public Health Significance"; USCIS, "Communicable Diseases of Public Health Significance." The inclusion of venereal diseases on the list of grounds for medical inadmissibility appears to have less to do with public health and more to do with morality; until 1990, immigration law also barred the entry of those deemed "sexually deviant," a category that formerly included homosexuals.

11. CDC, "Trends in Tuberculosis: United States, 2005," *Morbidity and Mortality Weekly Report* 55/11 (March 24, 2006); CDC, "Fact Sheet: Trends in Tuberculosis, 2014," http://www.cdc.gov/tb/publications/factsheets/statistics/TBTrends.htm, accessed January 24, 2016. Spread of the tuberculosis bacteria can largely be prevented by guaranteeing adequate ventilation (six air changes per hour, negative air pressure, and air exhausted to the outside of the building). However, prisons, detention centers, and even health centers rarely reach those standards. A 1992 survey of 729 U.S. medical facilities showed that 26 percent of isolation rooms and 89 percent of emergency rooms failed to meet minimum ventilation

recommendations. Public Health Agency of Canada, "Guidelines for Preventing the Transmission of Tuberculosis in Canadian Health Care Facilities and Other Institutional Settings," *Canada Communicable Diseases Report* 22S1 (April 1996).

12. Christine K. Olson, Mary P. Naughton, and Luis S. Ortega, "Health Considerations for Newly Arrived Immigrants & Refugees," CDC Health Information for International Travel (2014), chap. 9; USCIS, "Communicable Diseases of Public Health Significance."

13. Unless visitors show signs of obvious medical distress, border agents rarely pull them aside for health questioning; in any case, officers at ports of entry are not trained to diagnose illness. Ruth Ellen Wasem, Congressional Research Service, *Immigration Policies and Issues on Health-Related Grounds for Exclusion*, August 13, 2014.

14. CDC, "Immigrant and Refugee Health: Refugee Health Guidelines," http://www.cdc.gov/immigrantrefugeehealth/guidelines/refugee-guidelines.html, accessed January 27, 2016.

15. This concern could be easily addressed by ending the detention of asylum seekers. See "Why Do We Jail and Deport Immigrants?" (chapter 11).

16. The top seven causes of U.S. deaths in 2013 were heart disease, cancer, chronic lower respiratory diseases, accidents, strokes, Alzheimer's disease, and diabetes. U.S. Department of Health and Human Services, Centers for Disease Control and Prevention (CDC), "Leading Causes of Death," http://www.cdc.gov/nchs/fastats/leading-causes-of-death.htm, accessed April 25, 2015.

17. National Academies of Sciences, Engineering, and Medicine, "Americans Have Worse Health Than People in Other High-Income Countries; Health Disadvantage Is Pervasive Across Age and Socio-Economic Groups," press release, January 9, 2013.

18. National Academies of Sciences, Engineering, and Medicine, *The Integration of Immigrants into American Society*, 401.

19. Some 12.9 percent of U.S. adults were uninsured in the fourth quarter of 2014; the number had been 17.1 percent a year earlier but fell as the 2010 Affordable Care Act (Obamacare) started taking effect. Jenna Levy, "In U.S., Uninsured Rate Sinks to 12.9%," Gallup, January 7, 2015.

20. See "Are Unauthorized Immigrants a Burden on Our Health Care System?" (chapter 6).

21. S. P. Wallace, J. M. Torres, T. Z. Nobari et al., *Undocumented and Uninsured: Barriers to Affordable Care for Immigrant Populations*, Commonwealth Fund and the UCLA Center for Health Policy Research, August 2013; Frank Seo, "We Can't Afford Immigrants Not Being Insured," *Truthout*, April 28, 2015.

22. "World Bank health work flawed, still pushing privatisation of services," Bretton Woods Project website, July 10, 2009, http://www.brettonwoodsproject.org/; Ann-Louise Colgan, Africa Action Position Paper: "Hazardous to Health: The World Bank and IMF in Africa," April

2002. A study of post-Communist Eastern European countries found IMF lending programs were "associated with significantly worsened tuberculosis incidence, prevalence, and mortality rates," even after controlling for other factors. David Stuckler, Lawrence P. King, Sanjay Basu, "International Monetary Fund Programs and Tuberculosis Outcomes in Post-Communist Countries," *PLOS Medicine*, July 22, 2008. For the impact of structural adjustment policies on migration, see "How do U.S. economic policies affect migration?" (chapter 2).

23.   Amy Lieberman, "Where will the climate refugees go?" Al Jazeera, December 22, 2015.

24.   Stephanie Innes, "Border crossers can be threat to environment," *Arizona Daily Star*, September 28. See also "Can't we seal off the border?" (chapter 9).

25.   Amanda Peterson Beadle, "Anti-Immigrant Group Runs False TV Ad Blaming Global Warming on Immigrants Entering the U.S.," *ThinkProgress*, April 19, 2012; Worldwatch Institute website, "The State of Consumption Today," http://www.worldwatch.org/node/810, accessed May 23, 2015; Nigel Purvis, "Greening U.S. Foreign Aid through the Millennium Challenge Account," Brookings Institution Policy Brief 119, June 2003.

26.   Steven A. Camarota and Leon Kolankiewicz, *Immigration to the United States and World-Wide Greenhouse Gas Emissions*, Center for Immigration Studies (CIS), August 2008.

27.   Gregory J. Lengyel (Colonel, USAF), *Department of Defense Energy Strategy: Teaching an Old Dog New Tricks*, Brookings Institution, August 2007, 10–11; Sohbet Karbuz, "How Much Energy Does the U.S. Military Consume?: An Update," *Daily Energy Report*, August 5, 2013. The U.S. military is also the world's largest single polluter, generating an estimated 750,000 tons of toxic waste annually—more than the five largest chemical companies in the United States combined. Project Censored, "U.S. Military's War on the Earth," April 29, 2010; Alexander Nazaryan, "The US Department of Defense Is One of the World's Biggest Polluters," *Newsweek*, July 17, 2014.

28.   Todd Litman, *Evaluating Public Transit as an Energy Conservation and Emission Reduction Strategy*, Victoria Transport Policy Institute; Rocky Mountain Institute, "Fuel savings potential trucks vs rail intermodal," http://www.rmi.org/RFGraph-Fuel_savings_potential_trucks_rail_intermodal, accessed May 4, 2015; Steve Hargreaves, "China Trounces U.S. in Green Energy Investments," CNN, April 17, 2013.

29.   Immigrants who come from warmer climates may consume more energy in northern U.S. winters than they would at home, but this would be a relatively minor problem: a majority of immigrants settle either in major urban areas like New York that have low carbon footprints, or in places with warmer climates like California and Florida. Beadle, "Anti-Immigrant Group Runs False TV Ad."

30.   Committee on Women, Population and the Environment (CWPE), "Women,

Population & the Environment: Call for a New Approach," presented at the United Nations Summit on Environment and Development in Rio de Janeiro, 1992, http://cwpe.org/resources/environment/newapproach; Nicholas Eberstadt, "Drunken Nation: Russia's Depopulation Bomb," *WorldAffairsJournal.org*, Spring 2009; Lindsay Abrams, "Russia's Environmental Crisis: Exiled Activist Sounds Off to Salon," *Salon*, May 26, 2014.

31.   Cathi Tactaquin, "The Greening of the Anti-Immigrant Agenda," National Network for Immigrant and Refugee Rights, *Network News*, Spring 1998.

32.   Steven A. Camarota, *Birth Rates Among Immigrants in America: Comparing Fertility in the U.S. and Home Countries*, CIS, October 2005.

33.   Jeffrey S. Passel and Paul Taylor, *Unauthorized Immigrants and Their U.S.- Born Children*, Pew Research Center, August 11, 2010; Gretchen Livingston and D'Vera Cohn, *U.S. Birth Rate Falls to a Record Low: Decline Is Greatest Among Immigrants*, Pew Research Center, November 29, 2012.

34.   CWPE, "Women, Population & the Environment: Call for a New Approach."

35.   David M. Reimers, *Still the Golden Door: The Third World Comes to America*, 2nd ed. (New York: Columbia University Press, 1992), 127; Secretaría de Gobernación (Mexico), "La Población de México Alcanzó los 105.3 Millones a Mediados de Año," July 20, 2004; INEGI—Instituto Nacional de Estadística Geografía e Informática (Mexico), chart, July 19, 2006; Tim L. Merrill and Ramón Miró, eds., *Mexico: A Country Study* (Washington, D.C.: Government Publishing Office for the Library of Congress, 1996).

36.   Brian Dixon, "Guest Opinion: Overpopulation the Cause of Common Problems," *Tucson Citizen*, November 16, 2006; Population Connection, "Empowering Women Empowers Us All," http://www. populationconnection.org/article/empowering-women-empowers-us/, accessed December 13, 2016. Population Connection (then called Zero Ppulation Growth) had anti-immigration activist John Tanton as its president briefly in the 1970s, but the group then rejected his far-right agenda. Christopher Hayes, "Keeping America Empty: How one small-town conservationist launched today's anti-immigration movement," *In These Times*, April 24, 2006. For a thorough discussion of the way in which "environmental degradation is blamed on poor populations of color on the basis of highly xenophobic, classist, racist, and sexist assumptions about uncontrolled fertility, immorality, criminality, selfishness, and danger," see Jessica LeAnn Urban, *Nation, Immigration, and Environmental Security* (New York: Palgrave Macmillan, 2008).

37.   Political Research Associates, "Immigrants and the Environment," May 5, 2002; Zhou Yu, "Does immigration induce urban sprawl? A dynamic demographic analysis for the United States," University of Texas at Austin, School of Architecture, 2002.

38.   Lori M. Hunter, "The Spatial Association Between U.S. Immigrant Residential Concentration and Environmental Hazards," *International Migration Review* 34/2 (Summer 2000): 460–88; Rachel Wilf and Jorge

Madrid, "New EPA Rules Help Communities of Color Breathe Easier: New Standards Will Reduce Health and Economic Costs," Center for American Progress, April 20, 2012; Douglas Fischer, "Climate Change Hits Poor Hardest in U.S.," *Scientific American*, May 29, 2009.

39.   In 2012, 49.8 percent of Hispanic adults and 35.5 percent of all Hispanics were born outside the United States; 52 percent of the foreign-born population came from Latin America. Jens Manuel Krogstad and Mark Hugo Lopez, "Hispanic Nativity Shift: U.S. births drive population growth as immigration stalls," Pew Research Center Hispanic Trends, April 29, 2014; Pew Research Center, Hispanic Trends, "U.S. Foreign-Born Population Trends," *Modern Immigration Wave Brings 59 Million to U.S., Driving Population Growth and Change Through 2065*, September 28, 2015; Roberto Ontiveros, "Huge Majority of Latinos Concerned About the Air Pollution, Environmental Issues—Poll," *Latino Post*, August 30, 2015; Earthjustice, "Latinos and the Environment," http://earthjustice.org/features/poll-latino-opinion, accessed October 29, 2015; Gary M. Segura and Adrian Pantoja, "Polling Memo and Summary for National Release: 2015 Environmental Attitudes Survey," *Latino Decisions*, July 22, 2015. A 2002 study concluded that "foreign-born respondents are very similar to Hispanics in their opinions about the human-environment relationship"— although it found that those opinions leaned more toward the belief that "humans have a right to modify the environment and control nature, the environmental crisis is exaggerated, and the balance of nature is not all that delicate." H. Ken Cordell, Carter J. Betz, Gary T. Green, "Recreation and the Environment as Cultural Dimensions in Contemporary American Society," *Leisure Sciences* 24/1 (2002): 3–41.

40.   Lori M. Hunter, "A Comparison of the Environmental Attitudes, Concern, and Behaviors of Native-Born and Foreign-Born U.S. Residents," *Population and Environment* 21/6 (July 2000): 565–80; Max J. Pfeffer and J. Mayone Stycos, "Immigrant Environmental Behaviors in New York City," *Social Science Quarterly* 83/1 (March 2002).

41.   Philip Radford, "The Environmental Case for a Path to Citizenship," *Huffington Post*, March 14, 2013.

42.   Southwest Network for Environmental and Economic Justice, http://weact.org/Coalitions/EJLeadershipForumonClimateChange/EJLeadershipForumMembers/SNEEJ/tabid/553/Default.aspx, accessed May 6, 2015; "Invisible 5" website, http://www.invisible5.org/index.php?page=kettlemancity, accessed May 6, 2015.

43.   David Bacon, "Watsonville Teachers and Students Take on Methyl Iodide Pesticide," *Truthout*, July 14, 2012. See also Steve Early, *Refinery Town: Big Oil, Big Money, and the Remaking of an American City* (Boston: Beacon Press, 2017).

44.   Bill Ong Hing, *Defining America through Immigration Policy* (Philadelphia: Temple University Press, 2004), 3.

45.   Cato Institute, *Immigration Reform Bulletin*, October 2010.

46. Pew Research Center, Hispanic Trends, *Modern Immigration Wave Brings 59 Million to U.S.*

47. Monica Whatley and Jeanne Batalova, "Limited English Proficient Population of the United States," Migration Policy Institute, July 25, 2013; Chhandasi Pandya, Margie McHugh, and Jeanne Batalova, *Limited English Proficient Individuals in the United States: Number, Share, Growth, and Linguistic Diversity*, Migration Policy Institute, December 2011. See also "Is the new wave really new?" (chapter 1).

48. James Thomas Tucker, *The ESL Logjam: Waiting Times for Adult ESL Classes and the Impact on English Learners*, National Association of Latino Elected and Appointed Officials (NALEO) Educational Fund, September 2006.

49. Winnie Hu, "New York City Libraries Struggle to Meet Demand for English-Language Classes," *New York Times*, August 6, 2014.

50. Claude S. Fischer and Michael Hout, *Century of Difference: How America Changed in the Last One Hundred Years* (New York: Russell Sage Foundation, 2006), 42–43.

51. Cato Institute, *Immigration Reform Bulletin,* from Miranda E. Wilkerson and Joseph Salmons, "'Good Old Immigrants of Yesteryear,' Who Didn't Learn English: Germans in Wisconsin," *American Speech* 83/3 (2008): 259.

52. Pandya, McHugh, and Batalova, *Limited English Proficient Individuals in the United States.*

53. Stephen Krashen, "Bilingual Education, the Acquisition of English, and the Retention and Loss of Spanish," in *Research on Spanish in the U.S.: Linguistic Issues and Challenges,* ed. Ana Roca (Somerville, MA: Cascadilla Press, 2000); Viorica Marian and Anthony Shook, "The Cognitive Benefits of Being Bilingual," *Cerebrum: The Dana Forum on Brain Science*, September–October 2012; Ng and Metz, "Multiculturalism as a Strategy for National Competitiveness: The Case for Canada and Australia"; Joy Kreeft Peyton, Donald A. Ranard, Scott McGinnis, eds., *Heritage Languages in America: Preserving a National Resource: Language in Education: Theory and Practice* (McHenry, IL: Center for Applied Linguistics and Delta Systems, 2001).

54. Louis Menand, "Patriot Games: The New Nativism of Samuel P. Huntington," *The New Yorker*, May 17, 2004.

55. James P. Smith, "Assimilation Across the Latino Generations," *American Economic Review* (May 2003): 315–19, cited in Miriam Jordan, "Once here illegally, Mexican family savors children's success," *Wall Street Journal*, July 20, 2005; Jacob L. Vigdor, *Measuring Immigrant Assimilation in the United States*, Manhattan Institute for Policy Research Civic Report No. 53, May 2008.

56. Harvard University Open Collections Program, "Dillingham Commission (1907–1910)," http://ocp.hul.harvard.edu/immigration/dillingham.html; Commission on Behavioral and Social Sciences and Education (CBASSE), *The New Americans: Economic, Demographic, and Fiscal Effects of Immigration* (Washington, D.C.: National Academies Press, 1997), 12–13.

57. David R. Roediger, *Working Toward Whiteness: How America's Immigrants*

Became White: The Strange Journey from Ellis Island to the Suburbs (New York: Basic Books, 2006).

58. Evelio Grillo, *Black Cuban, Black American* (Houston: Arte Público Press, 2000).

59. Que-lam Huynh, Thierry Devos, and Laura Smalarz. "Perpetual Foreigner in One's Own Land: Potential Implications for Identity and Psychological Adjustment," *Journal of Social and Clinical Psychology* 30/2 (2011): 133–62.

60. National Academies of Sciences, Engineering, and Medicine, *The Integration of Immigrants into American Society*, 346–355.

61. Hing, *Defining America through Immigration Policy*, 28–50, 259–63.

62. Vigdor, "Measuring Immigrant Assimilation in the United States"; N. C. Aizenman, "Study Says Foreigners in U.S. Adapt Quickly," *Washington Post*, May 13, 2008.

63. John Ross, *The Annexation of Mexico* (Monroe, ME: Common Courage Press, 1998), 27–38.

64. Natural Resources Conservation Council, U.S. Department of Agriculture, *Native American Contributions*, http://www.nrcs.usda.gov/Internet/FSE_DOCUMENTS/nrcs141p2_024206.pdf, accessed December 13, 2014.

65. Kimberly Sambol-Tosco, "The Slave Experience: Education, Arts, & Culture," PBS, http://www.pbs.org/wnet/slavery/experience/education/history2.html.

66. Deborah J. Schildkraut, "Defining American Identity in the Twenty-First Century: How Much 'There' Is There?" *The Journal of Politics* 69/3 (2008): 597–615, cited in Tomás R. Jiménez, *Immigrants in the United States: How Well Are They Integrating into Society?* (Washington, D.C.: Migration Policy Institute, May 2011), 16–17.

8. Are Immigrants a Threat?

1. See "Do most deportees have criminal convictions?" (chapter 11).

2. Research Perspectives on Migration, a joint project of the International Migration Policy Program of the Carnegie Endowment for International Peace and the Urban Institute, *Immigration and the Justice System* 1/5 (July–August 1997).

3. Kristin F. Butcher and Anne Morrison Piehl, "Cross-City Evidence on the Relationship between Immigration and Crime," *Journal of Policy Analysis and Management* 17/3 (1998): 457–93.

4. Rubén G. Rumbaut and Walter A. Ewing, *The Myth of Immigrant Criminality and the Paradox of Assimilation*, Immigration Policy Center, February 21, 2007; Walter A. Ewing, Daniel E. Martínez, and Rubén G. Rumbaut, *The Criminalization of Immigration in the United States*, American Immigration Council, July 9, 2015. It is reasonable to believe that the comparative rate of immigrant incarceration would be even lower if we were to exclude incarceration for immigration crimes.

5. Ted Chiricos and Sarah Eschholz, "The Racial and Ethnic Typification of Crime and the Criminal Typification of Race and Ethnicity in Local

Television News," *Journal of Research in Crime and Delinquency* 39/4 (2002): 400–420.

6.   "Racial bias and news media reporting: New research trends," *Journalist's Resource*, May 20, 2015; Travis L. Dixon, "Good Guys Are Still Always in White? Positive Change and Continued Misrepresentation of Race and Crime on Local Television News," *Communication Research*, April 2, 2015.

7.   National Hispanic Media Coalition, *The Impact of Media Stereotypes on Opinions and Attitudes Towards Latinos*, September 2012.

8.   Eileen Poe-Yamagata and Michael A. Jones, *And Justice for Some*, April 2000, updated January 2007 by Christopher Hartney and Fabiana Silva, National Council on Crime and Delinquency; Mark Soler, "Public Opinion on Youth, Crime and Race: A Guide for Advocates," *Building Blocks for Youths*, Center for Children's Law and Policy, http://www.cclp.org/, October 2001.

9.   Francisco A. Villarruel and Nancy E. Walker, "Donde Está la Justicia? A Call to Action on Behalf of Latino and Latina Youth in the U.S. Justice System," *Building Blocks for Youth*, July 2002.

10. Lynn Langton, and Matthew Durose, *Police Behavior during Traffic and Street Stops, 2011*, U.S. Department of Justice, Bureau of Justice Statistics, September 2013, 9.

11. See "Are most deportees criminals?" (chapter 11). Examples of plea bargains leading to deportation appear in Human Rights Watch, *Forced Apart: Families Separated and Immigrants Harmed by United States Deportation Policy*, July 16, 2007.

12. Sean Gardiner, "U.S. Deportation Policy," *Newsday*, April 4, 2004.

13. See "What happens to people who are deported?" and "What happens to the families of deportees?" (chapter 11).

14. Kirk Semple, "Study: Deportations Don't Lead to Lower Crime Rates," *New York Times*, September 3, 2014; Thomas J. Miles and Adam Cox, "Does Immigration Enforcement Reduce Crime? Evidence from 'Secure Communities,'" *Journal of Law and Economics* (November 2014).

15. Mahwish Khan , "Public Safety on ICE: How Do You Police a Community That Won't Talk to You?" *America's Voice*, August 24, 2011.

16. Gabrielle Banks, "Other Nations Don't Trail Offenders: Megan's Law Can't Follow Deportees," *Pittsburgh Post-Gazette*, September 23, 2006. This is not to suggest that parole policies or monitoring programs like those instituted under Megan's Law necessarily make people safer, but if the tracking of U.S. citizen sex offenders is seen as an important form of protection, shouldn't the same be true of foreign-born offenders?

17. Brianna Lee, "U.S. Deportation Policies Have Close Ties to Central American Violence," *International Business Times*, July 14, 2014; Douglas Farah and Pamela Phillips Lum, *Central American Gangs and Transnational Criminal Organizations: The Changing Relationships in a Time of Turmoil*, International Assessment and Strategy Center, February 2013. Some researchers say assessments like the one from the Treasury Department

overstate MS-13's unity and strength. Carlos Garcia, "6 Common Misconceptions About the MS13 Street Gang," Insight Crime, February 25, 2016, http://www.insightcrime.org/.

18. General Accounting Office (GAO), *September 11: More Effective Collaboration Could Enhance Charitable Organizations' Contributions in Disasters,* Report to the Ranking Minority Member, Committee on Finance, U.S. Senate, December 2002; Rick Hampson, "For families of Muslim 9/11 victims, a new pain," *USA Today,* September 9, 2010; Kamal Kobeisi, "Remembering the Muslims who were killed in the 9/11 attacks," *Al Arabiya,* September 11, 2011; About.com, "List of Muslim Victims of September 11th Attack," compiled from the Islamic Circle of North America, *Newsday* victims database, and news reports, http://islam.about.com/blvictims.htm, accessed August 4, 2015.

19. Andrew Gumbel, "Oklahoma City Bombing: 20 years later, key questions remain unanswered," *The Guardian,* April 13, 2015.

20. Scott Shane, "Homegrown Extremists Tied to Deadlier Toll Than Jihadists in U.S. Since 9/11," *New York Times,* June 24, 2015; New America, "Deadly Attacks Since 9/11," http://www.newamerica.org/in-depth/terrorism-in-america/, accessed December 23, 2016; Charles Kurzman and David Schanzer, *Law Enforcement Assessment of the Violent Extremism Threat,* Triangle Center on Terrorism and Homeland Security, June 25, 2015. The survey authors note that their "data was collected in early 2014, before the self-proclaimed Islamic State (also known as ISIS) began actively recruiting Americans. However, in follow-up telephone interviews . . . after ISIS stepped up recruitment, the officers we spoke with did not modify their initial responses in light of the new threat."

21. Muzaffar A. Chishti, Doris Meissner, Demetrios G. Papademetriou, Jay Peterzell, Michael J. Wishnie, Stephen W. Yale-Loehr, *America's Challenge: Domestic Security, Civil Liberties, and National Unity After September 11,* Migration Policy Institute, June 26, 2003.

22. Mary Beth Sheridan, "15 Hijackers Obtained Visas in Saudi Arabia," *Washington Post,* October 31, 2001.

23. GAO, *Border Security: Visa Process Should Be Strengthened as an Antiterrorism Tool,* Report to the Chairman, Subcommittee on National Security, Veterans Affairs, and International Relations, Committee on Government Reform, House of Representatives, October 2002.

24. Sean Gallagher, "Goodbye to Lifeandliberty.gov—and hundreds of other dead .gov domains," *Ars Technica,* April 8, 2015.

25. Dan Eggen and Julie Tate, "U.S. Campaign Produces Few Convictions on Terrorism Charges," *Washington Post,* June 12, 2005; David Cole, "Are We Safer?," February 8, 2006, reprinted in *New York Review of Books,* March 9, 2006.

26. Center on Law and Security, New York University School of Law, February 2005, *Terrorist Trials: A Report Card.*

27. Cole, "Are We Safer?"

28. Coleen Rowley's letter, dated February 26, 2003, quoted in Mark Dow, *American Gulag: Inside U.S. Immigration Prisons* (Oakland: University of California Press, 2005), 26.

29. Cole, "Are We Safer?"

30. Greg Palast report (transcript), BBC News, *Newsnight*, November 6, 2001.

31. Michael Springman interview, July 3, 2002, on *Dispatches*, hosted by Rick MacInnes-Rae on CBC Radio News (Canadian Broadcasting Corporation), unofficial transcript posted at http://911review.org/Wiki/ SpringmanInterview.shtml.

32. Palast, *Newsnight*.

33. *Harpal Singh Cheema, Rajwinder Kaur v. Immigration and Naturalization Service*, No. 02-71311, June 24, 2004. The saying "one man's terrorist is another man's freedom fighter" was popularized in the 1980s by President Ronald Reagan. Israeli activist Uri Avnery claims to have invented the expression. Uri Avnery, "The Reign of Absurdiocy," Gush Shalom website, November 28, 2015.

34. Camille T. Taiara, "After Years in Limbo—More Immigrant Detainees Choose 'Voluntary' Deportation," *New American Media* (Disappeared in America series), August 7, 2006.

35. "Dal Khalsa: BJP Conspiring with Prison Department to Stop Prof. Bhullar's Parole," *Sikh24.com*, June 19, 2015.

36. Pat McDonnell Twair, "Iranian Brothers' American Dream Turned Into a Nightmare" (Special Report), *Washington Report on Middle East Affairs* (July 2005): 44–45, 66; Kelly Thornton, "Iranian Brothers Scarred by Accusations, Detention; 4 Held 3 1/2 Years in Los Angeles Jail," *San Diego Union-Tribune*, June 18, 2006.

37. Michael Isikoff, "Ashcroft's Baghdad Connection," *Newsweek Online*, September 25, 2002; Michael Isikoff, "Terror Watch: Shades of Gray," *Newsweek Online*, October 12, 2004.

38. McDonnell Twair, "Iranian Brothers' American Dream Turned Into a Nightmare." The Mirmehdi brothers later sought compensation and an apology from the U.S. government. U.S. courts rejected their claims. In 2014 they asked the UN Working Group on Arbitrary Detention and the Washington, D.C.-based Inter-American Commission for Human Rights to take up their case. Brenda Gazzar, "San Fernando Valley-based Iranian brothers turn to international tribunals over U.S. detentions," *Los Angeles Daily News*, April 22, 2014. The U.S. State Department removed the MEK from its list of terrorist organizations in 2012 under intense pressure from prominent U.S. supporters. Scott Shane, "Iranian Dissidents Convince U.S. to Drop Terror Label," *New York Times*, September 21, 2012; Conor Friedersdorf, "Is One Man's Terrorist Another Man's Freedom Fighter?" *The Atlantic*, May 16, 2012.

39. Jim Lobe, "When Is a Terrorist 'Mastermind' Not a Terrorist?" *InterPress Service/Global Information Network*, October 25, 2006; Michael Fox, "Venezuela Demands Posada Carriles Extradition on 30th Anniversary of

Bombing," *Venezuelanalysis.com*, October 9, 2006; Alfonso Chardy, "Judge: Posada Carriles' Time in Detention 'Well Beyond' Limit," *Miami Herald*, November 4, 2006; Tim Weiner, "Cuban Exile Could Test U.S. Definition of Terrorist," *New York Times*, May 9, 2005.

40. David Brooks, "Luis Posada Carriles, absuelto en Texas," *La Jornada* (Mexico), April 8; David Brooks, "Liberan en EU al segundo del grupo de los cinco de Cuba," *La Jornada*, February 27, 2014.

41. Chishti et al., *America's Challenge.*

42. Tom Winter, "Russia Warned U.S. About Tsarnaev, But Spelling Issue Let Him Escape," *NBC News*, March 25, 2014.

43. Chishti et al., *America's Challenge.*

44. Nina Bernstein, "Questions, Bitterness and Exile for Queens Girl in Terror Case," *New York Times*, June 17, 2005. Adama Bah's case is the subject of a 2011 documentary, *Adama,* http://itvs.org/films/adama.

45. Chishti et al., *America's Challenge.*

46. Scott Long, Jessica Stern, and Adam Francoeur, *Family, Unvalued: Discrimination, Denial, and the Fate of Binational Same-Sex Couples under U.S. Law*, Human Rights Watch/Immigration Equality report, May 2006; Alicia J. Campi, "The McCarran-Walter Act: A Contradictory Legacy on Race, Quotas, and Ideology," American Immigration Law Foundation (AILF) Immigration Policy Brief, 2004.

47. Michel Shehadeh, "A Never-Ending Saga: 'The Case of the Los Angeles Eight,'" *Washington Report on Middle East Affairs*, April/May 1997; American Civil Liberties Union, "California Judge Ends 20-Year-Old Deportation Case Against Palestinians," January 30, 2007.

48. U.S. Supreme Court, Janet Reno, *Attorney General et al. v. American-Arab Antidiscrimination Committee et al.*, No. 97–1252, February 24; Anthony Lewis, "Abroad at Home," *New York Times*, March 13, 1999.

49. William Branigin, "Secret U.S. Evidence Entangles Immigrants, Rarely Used Law Now Falls Most Heavily on Arabs," *Washington Post*, October 19, 1997.

50. Martin Merzer, "Muslim Cleric to Be Deported; Case Watched by Civil Libertarians," *Miami Herald*, August 19, 2002; "U.S. Deports Palestinian Detainee After Seven-Year Legal Fight," Associated Press, August 23, 2002.

51. David Cole, "National Security State," *The Nation*, November 29, 2001 (December 17, 2001 issue).

52. ICE, news release, "Owner of Tarrasco Steel arrested in ICE probe for hiring illegal alien workers at critical infrastructure construction sites," August 3, 2007; Karin Brulliard and Paul Duggan, "55 Illegal Immigrants Arrested at Dulles Site," *Washington Post*, June 15, 2006. The same reasoning was used for decades to argue against allowing gay people to work in sensitive jobs—although not to disqualify other potential blackmail risks, such as employees who are cheating on their spouses. Gregory B. Lewis, "Barriers to Security Clearances for Gay Men and Lesbians: Fear of Blackmail or Fear of Homosexuals?," *Journal of Public Administration Research and Theory* 11/ (October 1, 2001): 539–58.

53. Jacqueline Charles, "Diplomats Puzzled by Claim Migrants Use Haiti to Enter U.S.," *Miami Herald*, April 25, 2003; National Immigration Law Center (NILC), "AG's Precedent Decision Denies Haitian's Release on Bond Based on Generalized National Security Concerns," *NILC Immigrants' Rights Update* 17/3 (June 3, 2003); Lawyers' Committee for Human Rights (now Human Rights First), "Attorney General Ashcroft Calls for Blanket Detentions of Haitian Asylum Seekers: New Precedent Decision Portrays Haitians as Risks to National Security," *Asylum News* 13 (April 28, 2003).

9. Enforcement: Is It a Solution?

1. Matt Apuzzo and Michael S. Schmidt, "U.S. to Continue Racial, Ethnic Profiling in Border Policy," *The New York Times*, December 5, 2014.

2. Nancy Hiemstra, "Performing Homeland Security within the US Immigrant Detention System," *Environment and Planning D: Society and Space* 32/4 (August 1, 2014): 571–88.

3. Steve Benen, "The House GOP's immigration plan: 'Deport 'em all,'" MSNBC, August 1, 2014.

4. Pew Research Center for the People and the Press, "Public Divided Over Increased Deportation of Unauthorized Immigrants," February 27, 2014.

5. As of March 2008, Pew Research Center estimated that just over 36 percent of unauthorized immigrants (including children) lived in families with at least one U.S.-born citizen child. Jeffrey S. Passel and D'Vera Cohn, "A Portrait of Unauthorized Immigrants in the United States (III. Demographic and Family Characteristics)," Pew Research Center's Hispanic Trends Project, April 14, 2009. No updated data appears to be available, but the figure is presumably higher now. Not included in that definition of mixed-status families are unauthorized immigrants who have U.S. citizen partners (or partners with some other form of status) but no U.S.-born children. Since 2001, people who entered the United States without a valid entry permit are not generally eligible to adjust their status within the United States—even with a U.S. citizen as a spouse, child, or other immediate relative—leaving such mixed-status families in limbo for years. Marisa Cianciarulo, "Seventeen Years Since the Sunset: The Expiration of 245(i) and Its Effect on U.S. Citizens Married to Undocumented Immigrants," *Chapman Law Review* 18/2 (January 1, 2015): 451–79.

6. Russ Bynum, "Messy Aftermath of Immigration Raids Outrages Small Georgia Town," Associated Press, September 15, 2006.

7. Bill Ong Hing, *Defining America Through Immigration Policy* (Philadelphia: Temple University Press, 2004), 161, 165. See "Are politicians stirring up a panic about immigration?" (chapter 1) for an estimate of the undocumented population in 1980.

8. Marshall Fitz, Gebe Martinez, and Madura Wijewardena, "The Costs of Mass Deportation," Center for American Progress, March 19, 2010. A breakdown of the $23,482 cost per deportation is found in the "Fast Facts on Deportation" section.

9. Blas Nuñez-Neto, Stephen R. Viña, *Border Security: Fences along the U.S. International Border*, Congressional Research Service (CRS), Library of Congress, updated December 12, 2006.

10. Hing, *Defining America through Immigration Policy*, 185–87.

11. Doris Meissner, Donald M. Kerwin, Muzaffar Chishti, and Claire Bergeron, *Immigration Enforcement in the United States: The Rise of a Formidable Machinery*, Migration Policy Institute, January 2013, 18; Customs and Border Protection, "Enacted Border Patrol Program Budget by Fiscal Year (Dollars in Thousands)," http://www.cbp.gov/sites/default/files/documents/BP%20Budget%20History%201990-2014_0.pdf, accessed April 16, 2014.

12. Department of Homeland Security, *Budget-in-Brief Fiscal Year 2015*, 50.

13. As with using arrest statistics to measure crime, this method is problematic in that it only counts those who get caught. Also, because it counts apprehensions, not people, migrants are presumably overcounted, since they may be stopped and returned several times before they successfully enter the United States. It would be logical to think that the apprehensions correlate more strongly to the number of Border Patrol agents who are tasked with apprehending people than to the number of migrants crossing the border. However, no clear correlations of this nature emerge from the authors' regression analysis of the available data.

14. Authors' analysis of data from United States Border Patrol, "Nationwide Illegal Alien Apprehensions Fiscal Years 1925–2015," https://www.cbp.gov/sites/default/files/documents/BP%20Total%20Apps%20FY1925-FY2015.pdf, accessed April 28, 2016.

15. See "Is there a 'new wave' of immigration?" (chapter 1).

16. Olga R. Rodriguez, "New Wall Not Expected to Stop Migrants," Associated Press, October 6, 2006; Douglas S. Massey, "Beyond the Border Buildup: Towards a New Approach to Mexico-U.S. Migration," *Immigration Policy in Focus* 4/7 (September 2005).

17. Massey, "Beyond the Border Buildup"; Hing, *Defining America through Immigration Policy*, 201.

18. Massey, "Beyond the Border Buildup"; Meissner, Kerwin, Chishti, and Bergeron, *Immigration Enforcement in the United States*, 33–34; Spencer S. Hsu, "Border Deaths Are Increasing," *Washington Post*, September 30, 2009; Maria Jimenez, "Humanitarian Crisis: Migrant Deaths at the U.S.-Mexico Border," ACLU of San Diego & Imperial Counties, Mexico's National Commission of Human Rights, October 1, 2009, 13–16. The U.S. government did not start tracking border deaths until 1998, so no official statistics are available for earlier years. Deaths at the southwestern border were at their highest in fiscal years 2005 and 2012, with nearly 500 deaths in each of those years. The death tally varied across the period from 2005 to 2015; on average, 365 people died each year crossing the southwestern border during this time. When we look at deaths per 1,000 apprehensions, we see a fairly consistent increase from 1998 to 2012, followed by a steep drop. Authors' analysis

of data from U.S. Border Patrol, "Nationwide Illegal Alien Apprehensions Fiscal Years 1925–2015" and United States Border Patrol, Southwest Border Sectors, Southwest Border Deaths By Fiscal Year, https://www.cbp.gov/sites/default/files/documents/BP%20Southwest%20Border%20Sector%20Deaths%20FY1998%20-%20FY2015.pdf, accessed April 28, 2016.

19. Hing, *Defining America through Immigration Policy*, 199.

20 Massey, "Beyond the Border Buildup"; Wayne Cornelius, "Evaluating Enhanced US Border Enforcement," Migration Information Source, Migration Policy Institute, May 1, 2004.

21. U.S. Government Accountability Office (GAO), *Secure Border Initiative, Technology Deployment Delays Persist and the Impact of Border Fencing Has Not Been Assessed*, 2009, 21–23; Chad C. Haddal, Yule Kim, and Michael John Garcia, *Border Security: Barriers Along the U.S. International Border*, CRS, March 16, 2009, 27; Massey, "Beyond the Border Buildup"; Meissner, Kerwin, Chishti, and Bergeron, *Immigration Enforcement in the United States*, 30–31.

22. Haider Rizvi, "Border Fence Could Spell Environmental Disaster," published on *Common Dreams*, October 3, 2006, available at https://groups.yahoo.com/neo/groups/helptheanimals/conversations/topics/12128; Chris Clarke, "Immigration's Impact," *Earth Island Journal* 21/4 (Autumn 2006); Melissa Gaskill, "United States Border Fence Threatens Wildlife," *Nature News*, August 2, 2011; Jesse R. Lasky, Walter Jetz, and Timothy H. Keitt, "Conservation Biogeography of the US-Mexico Border: A Transcontinental Risk Assessment of Barriers to Animal Dispersal," *Diversity and Distributions* 17/4 (2011): 673; Brady McCombs, "Rain washes away 40 feet of US-Mexico border fence," *Arizona Daily Star*, August 10, 2011; Bryan Gerhart, "Arizona Border Fence Causes Flood and Self-Destructs—as Predicted," *ColorLines*, August 12, 2011.

23. Jordan Fabian, "U.S.-Mexico border 'more secure than ever,' official says," *Univision News*, August 4, 2011.

24. GAO, *Military Personnel: DOD Needs to Improve the Transparency and Reassess the Reasonableness, Appropriateness, Affordability, and Sustainability of Its Military Compensation System*, July 19, 2005, summary.

25. Bob Ortega, "Secrecy Continues to Shroud Killings by Border Agents," *Arizona Republic*, September 14, 2014; Garrett M. Graff, "The Green Monster: How the Border Patrol became America's most out-of-control law enforcement agency," *Politico*, November–December 2014.

26. Brian Bennett, "Border Patrol's Use of Deadly Force Criticized in Report," *Los Angeles Times*, February 27, 2014.

27. Daniel E. Martinez, Guillermo Cantor, and Walter A. Ewing, "No Action Taken: Lack of CBP Accountability in Responding to Complaints of Abuse," American Immigration Council, May 6, 2014.

28. American Friends Service Committee press release, "Border Communities and Migrant Families Used as Political Pawn by Administration Considering Troops on Border," May 12, 2006.

29. "D.A. Doubts Military Version of Border Shooting," Associated Press, June 4, 1997; "Grand Jury Doesn't Indict Marine in Border Shooting; Jurors Say Marines Followed Rules of Engagement," CNN, August 14, 1997.

30. "Can We Put an End to Human Smuggling?," Migration Policy Debates, Organization for Economic Cooperation and Development (OECD), December 2015; Hein de Haas, "Smuggling Is a Reaction to Border Controls, Not the Cause of Migration," *Hein de Haas.com* (blog), October 5, 2013; Hein de Haas, "Don't Blame the Smugglers: The Real Migration Industry," *Hein de Haas.com*, September 23, 2015.

31. Catherine Rampell, "Why Are Mexican Smugglers' Fees Still Rising?," *New York Times Economix Blog*, May 18, 2009; Bryan Roberts, Gordon Hanson, Derekh Cornwell, and Scott Borger, DHS Office of Immigration Statistics, Working Paper, "An Analysis of Migrant Smuggling Costs along the Southwest Border," November 2010, 5, Fig. 2.

32. Jorge Morales Almada, "Los 'polleros' han cambiado de tácticas," *La Opinión*, December 21, 2014; Rodriguez, "New Wall Not Expected to Stop Migrants"; Bryan Roberts, Gordon Hanson, Derekh Cornwell, and Scott Borger, *An Analysis of Migrant Smuggling Costs along the Southwest Border*, Department of Homeland Security Office of Immigration Statistics, November 2010, 3–5; Massey, "Beyond the Border Buildup." These prices are presumably for Mexicans; crossing has always been considerably more expensive for Central Americans or other non-Mexicans crossing into the United States from Mexico. Even as Mexican migration slowed during the recession, migrants from Honduras, El Salvador, and Guatemala continued to attempt to enter the United States at relatively steady rates, and were even more likely to use smugglers than Mexicans.

33. Roberts, Hanson, Cornwell, and Borger, *An Analysis of Migrant Smuggling Costs along the Southwest Border*, 6–7.

34. Morales Almada, "Los 'polleros' han cambiado de tácticas."

35. "Can We Put an End to Human Smuggling?," OECD Migration Policy Debates.

36. Onell R. Soto, "At Border, Rise Seen in Corrupt Workers," *San Diego Union-Tribune*, October 22, 2006.

37. GAO, *Border Security: Additional Actions Needed to Strengthen CBP Efforts to Mitigate Risk of Employee Corruption and Misconduct*, December 2012; Graff, "The Green Monster."

38. Ralph Vartabedian, Richard A. Serrano, and Richard Marosi, "Rise in Bribery Tests Integrity of Border," *Los Angeles Times*, October 24, 2006.

39. See "How illegal is immigration, anyway?" (chapter 4).

40. Meissner, Kerwin, Chishti, and Bergeron, *Immigration Enforcement in the United States*, 96–98; Alistair Graham Robertson, Rachel Beaty, Jane Atkinson, and Bob Libal, *Operation Streamline: Costs and Consequences*, Grassroots Leadership, September 19, 2012, 23; Carla N. Argueta, *Border Security: Immigration Enforcement Between Ports of Entry*, CRS, April 19, 2016, 8.

41. Lisa Seghetti, *Border Security: Immigration Enforcement Between Ports of Entry*, CRS, December 18, 2014, 11.This report was originally available at http://www.fas.org/sgp/crs/homesec/R42138.pdf but has been replaced at that URL, apparently without explanation, by the above-cited report by Argueta with the same title, dated April 16, 2016. Both reports contain the same background on Operation Streamline (8), but Argueta's 2016 version does not include the recidivism rates for migrants subjected to specific enforcement consequences. Seghetti's version includes that data for 2011 and 2012, noting that "changes in recidivism rates may not be wholly attributable to differences among the consequences because the Border Patrol takes account of migrants' migration histories and other factors when assigning people to different enforcement outcomes" (11). A February 2016 report by Argueta discusses in more detail the recidivism rate's "weaknesses as a performance measurement," noting, among other concerns: "A decreasing recidivism rate that may be interpreted as a successful increase in deterrence could also be the result of a falling apprehension rate." Carla Argueta, *Border Security Metrics Between Ports of Entry*, CRS, February 16, 2016. The discrepancies between the different reports suggest that CRS may have had the 2014 report rewritten after determining that it overstated the significance of the recidivism rates.

42. Ted Robbins, "Claims of Border Program Success Are Unproven," National Public Radio, September 13, 2010; Robertson, Beaty, Atkinson, and Libal, "Operation Streamline," 16.

43. Robbins, "Claims of Border Program Success Are Unproven"; Connor Radnovich, "Legal, civil rights groups urge a halt to Operation Streamline," *Cronkite News* (PBS, AZ), February 21, 2013; Robertson, Beaty, Atkinson, and Libal, *Operation Streamline*, 16.

44. Marc R. Rosenblum and Doris Meissner, "The Deportation Dilemma: Reconciling Tough and Humane Enforcement," Migration Policy Institute, April 2014, 43.

45. United States Sentencing Commission, *Illegal Reentry Offenses*, April 2015, 25–26.

46. Robertson, Beaty, Atkinson, and Libal, *Operation Streamline*, 7–9, 23. In a 2015 report, the Department of Homeland Security's Office of the Inspector General (OIG) confirmed that the Border Patrol "does not track or estimate" the costs of Operation Streamline, or differentiate them from the costs of other enforcement programs. DHS OIG, "Streamline: Measuring Its Effect on Illegal Border Crossing," May 15, 2015.

47. Robertson, Beaty, Atkinson, and Libal, *Operation Streamline*, 12–14; Joanna Lydgate, *Assembly-Line Justice: A Review of Operation Streamline*, Chief Justice Earl Warren Institute on Race, Ethnicity & Diversity, UC Berkeley Law School, 7–9; Robbins, "Claims of Border Program Success Are Unproven."

48. Amanda Sakuma, "Operation Streamline: An immigration nightmare for Arizona courts," MSNBC, June 22, 2014; Meissner, Kerwin, Chishti, and Bergeron, *Immigration Enforcement in the United States*, 96–98; Lydgate,

Assembly-Line Justice, 12–16; Robertson, Beaty, Atkinson, and Libal, *Operation Streamline*, 1.

49.   U.S. Citizenship and Immigration Services, http://www.uscis.gov/i-9-central/penalties, accessed January 1, 2015.

50.   Andorra Bruno, *Immigration-Related Worksite Enforcement: Performance Measures*, CRS, August 7, 2013, 5.

51.   Meissner, Kerwin, Chishti, and Bergeron, *Immigration Enforcement in the United States*, 77; *Immigration Enforcement: Weaknesses Hinder Employment Verification and Worksite Enforcement Efforts*, statement of GAO director for Homeland Security and Justice Richard M. Stana to the Senate Committee on the Judiciary, June 19, 2006, 7–8.

52.   Bruno, *Immigration-Related Worksite Enforcement*, 6.

53.   David Bacon, "No Justice with No-Match Rule," *The American Prospect*, September 10, 2007.

54.   Julia Preston, "Illegal Workers Swept From Jobs in 'Silent Raids,'" *New York Times*, July 9, 2010.

55.   Meissner, Kerwin, Chishti, and Bergeron, *Immigration Enforcement in the United States*, 78; Michelle Chen, "Troubled 'E-Verify' Program Highlights Dysfunctional Immigration System," *In These Times*, September 14, 2009; Marc Rosenblum and Lang Hoyt, "The Basics of E-Verify, the US Employer Verification System," Migration Policy Institute, July 2011.

56.   National Network for Immigrant and Refugee Rights (NNIRR), "NNIRR's first 25 years: A chronology of activities, issues and struggle in the human rights of all migrants," 2011; NNIRR, *Portrait of Injustice: The Impact of Immigration Raids on Families*, October 1998; "INS: Raids, Do Not Hire," *Rural Migration News* (University of California at Davis) 5/2 (April 1999).

57.   "Operation Tarmac terrorizes families," *People's World*, January 9, 2003; Lucio Guerrero, "Immigration groups protest airport raids; Illegal workers bear brunt of U.S. terror probe, activists say," *Chicago Sun-Times*, December 13, 2002. See "Are immigrant workers a national security risk?" (chapter 8).

58.   "Massive Raid Reflects New ICE Strategy?," *Immigration News Briefs*, April 22, 2006; Nina Bernstein, "Immigrants Panicked by Rumors of Raids," *New York Times*, April 29, 2006; Alfonso Chardy, "Fears of Mass Arrests Keep Undocumented Immigrants off South Florida Streets," *Miami Herald*, April 27, 2006; Miriam Jordan and Paulo Trevisani Jr., "Illegal Immigrants Skip Work Amid Unfounded Rumors of Government Roundup," *Wall Street Journal*, April 28, 2006; Miguel Perez and Elizabeth Llorente, "False Raid Rumors Spread, Panicking Local Immigrants," *Bergen Record*, April 27, 2006. For more on the April 2006 raids, see "How can you tell who's undocumented?" (chapter 5).

59.   *Immigration News Briefs*, December 15, 2006. For background on raids and protests generally from 2006 to 2008, see *Immigration News Briefs* for those years at http://immigrationnewsbriefs.blogspot.com/; see also National Network for Immigrant and Refugee Rights, Human Rights Immigrant

Community Action Network, *Over-Raided, Under Siege: U.S. Immigration Laws and Enforcement Destroy the Rights of Immigrants*, January 2008.

60. "Massive Raid at Kosher Meat Plant in Iowa," *Immigration News Briefs*, June 2, 2008; Erik Camayd-Freixas, "Interpreting the Largest ICE Raid in U.S. History: A Personal Account," *New York Times*, June 13, 2008.

61. *Immigration News Briefs*, August 10, 2008.

62. Julia Preston, "27-Year Sentence for Plant Manager," *New York Times*, June 21, 2010.

63. "Mississippi Factory Raided, 595 Arrested," *Immigration News Briefs*, August 30, 2008.

64. For example, Federico Peña, a former Denver mayor and co-chair of Obama's presidential campaign, participated in a pro-immigrant march in Denver on August 28, 2008, during the Democratic Convention, carrying a banner stating: "Immigrant Rights Are Human Rights." *Immigration News Briefs*, September 7, 2008.

65. ICE Worksite Enforcement Fact Sheet, April 1, 2013, https://www.ice.gov/factsheets/worksite. Accessed June 8, 2016.

66. Preston, "Illegal Workers Swept From Jobs in 'Silent Raids'"; Bruno, *Immigration-Related Worksite Enforcement*, 6.

67. Jeffrey S. Passel and D'Vera Cohn, "Share of Unauthorized Immigrant Workers in Production, Construction Jobs Falls since 2007," Pew Research Center Hispanic Trends Project, March 26, 2015; Passel and Cohn, *Unauthorized Immigrant Population: National and State Trends, 2010*, Pew Hispanic Center, February 1, 2011, 17.

68. Letter from Congressional Budget Office Director Peter R. Orszag to Rep. John Conyers Jr., April 4, 2008.

69. See "Who are the undocumented immigrants?" (chapter 1).

70. "Lack of Worksite Enforcement and Employer Sanctions," Hearing before Subcommittee on Immigration, Border Security, and Claims of the Committee on the Judiciary, House of Representatives, June 21, 2005. For a more recent discussion of the impact of subcontracting and similar arrangements on immigrant workers, see Chenoa A. Flippen, "Laboring Underground: The Employment Patterns of Hispanic Immigrant Men in Durham, NC," *Social Problems* 59/1 (February 1, 2012): 21–42.

71. Steven Greenhouse, "Illegally in U.S., and Never a Day Off at Wal-Mart," *New York Times*, November 05, 2003; Steven Greenhouse, "Wal-Mart to Pay U.S. $11 Million in Lawsuit on Illegal Workers," *New York Times*, March 19, 2005; Associated Press, "Workers of Wal-Mart Subcontractors Arrested," November 18, 2005; Dave Jamieson, "Warehouse Workers at Walmart-Contracted Facility Allege Abusive Conditions, Wage Theft," *Huff Post Latino Voices*, October 18, 2011.

72. "Lack of Worksite Enforcement and Employer Sanctions." See also "Why do they work for less?" (chapter 6).

73. William Stockton, "Mexicans Expecting No Good of Immigration Law," *New York Times*, November 6, 1986.

74. David Bacon, "The Law that Keeps Workers Chained," October 2, 1999, http://dbacon.igc.org/Imgrants/29ChainLaw.htm; see also Bacon, "After 9/11, Immigrant Workers In the Crosshairs," December 15, 2002, http:// dbacon.igc.org/Imgrants/15WrkrsInCrosshairs.htm; Marielena Hincapié, Tyler Moran, and Michele Waslin, "The Social Security Administration No-Match Program: Inefficient, Ineffective, and Costly," *Immigration Policy in Focus* (published by Immigration Policy Center) 6/2 (May 2008).

75. Glen Warchol, "Unions Denounce the Firing of Miners," *Salt Lake Tribune*, December 11, 2004.

76. William Petroski, "Immigration Raid: Union Fears Action Hurts Probe," *Des Moines Register*, May 12, 2008.

77. David Bacon, "Hundreds of Union Janitors Fired Under Pressure From Feds," *Truthout*, May 7, 2010; David Bacon and Bill Ong Hing, "The Rise and Fall of Employer Sanctions," *Fordham Urban Law Journal* (2010); David Bacon, *The Right to Stay Home: How US Policy Drives Mexican Immigration* (Boston: Beacon Press, 2013), 196.

78. Jessica M. Vaughan, "Attrition through Enforcement: A Cost-Effective Strategy to Shrink the Illegal Population," Center for Immigration Studies (CIS), April 2006.

79. Meissner, Kerwin, Chishti, and Bergeron, *Immigration Enforcement in the United States*, 103–6; Michele Waslin, *The Secure Communities Program: Unanswered Questions and Continuing Concerns*, Immigration Policy Center Special Report, November 29, 2011; Immigration Policy Center, "The 287(g) Program: A Flawed and Obsolete Method of Immigration Enforcement," November 29, 2012.

80. Secure Communities was implemented in all jurisdictions nationwide in 2013; it then ended in 2014 and was replaced in July 2015 with the "Priority Enforcement Program." Department of Homeland Security, Immigration and Customs Enforcement (ICE), "Secure Communities," 2016, https://www. ice.gov/secure-communities, accessed June 12, 2016; Thomas J. Miles and Adam Cox, "Does Immigration Enforcement Reduce Crime? Evidence from 'Secure Communities,'" *Journal of Law and Economics* (November 2014).

81. Michele Waslin, *Discrediting "Self Deportation" as Immigration Policy: Why an Attrition Through Enforcement Strategy Makes Life Difficult for Everyone*, Immigration Policy Center special report, February 2012, 2, 5–9; Immigration Policy Center, *Q&A Guide to State Immigration Laws: What You Need to Know If Your State Is Considering Anti-immigrant Legislation*, special report, February 16, 2012.

82. Justin Peter Steil and Ion Bogdan Vasi, "The New Immigration Contestation: Social Movements and Local Immigration Policy Making in the United States, 2000–2011," *American Journal of Sociology* 119/4 (2014): 1110. Steil and Vasi show a marked jump in local anti-immigrant ordinances starting after the 2006 pro-immigrant mobilizations.

83. Debra A. Hoffmaster, Gerard Murphy, Shannon McFadden, and Molly Griswold, *Police and Immigration: How Chiefs Are Leading their*

Communities through the Challenges, Police Executive Research Forum, March 2011, iv–vi; Julia Preston, "Police Chiefs Wary of Immigration Role," *New York Times*, March 3, 2011.

84. Jennifer Chacon, "Who is Responsible for U.S. Immigration Policy?" *Insights on Law and Society* (Spring 2014); Anti-Defamation League (ADL), "The Anti-Immigrant Movement's Focus on Pro-Immigrant Legislation," November 27, 2013.

85. Maribel Hastings, "Some African-Americans in Alabama see HB 56 as 'a giant step backwards,'" *Huffington Post*, October 27, 2011.

86. Leslie Berestein Rojas, "LA County Supes renew controversial partnership between Sheriff's Dept. and ICE," KPCC, Southern California Public Radio, October 7, 2014; Cindy Carcamo, "States back off from enacting immigration laws," *Los Angeles Times*, October 12, 2013; Amanda Peterson Beadle, "Alabama Settles Last Legal Challenge to State's Self-Deportation Law," *Immigration Impact*, October 15, 2014; ADL, "The Anti-Immigrant Movement's Focus on Pro-Immigrant Legislation"; Catalina Restrepo, "Annual Review of State-Level Immigration Policy Still Trending Pro-Immigrant," *Immigration Impact*, August 11, 2015. See "Can immigrants get driver's licenses?" (chapter 5). The shifting climate in 2012 coincided with a wave of highly visible organizing by the undocumented youth commonly referred to as "dreamers," as evidenced by *Time* magazine's June cover story featuring "undocumented Americans" as the "person of the year" and the Obama administration's introduction that same month of the Deferred Action for Childhood Arrivals (DACA) policy granting work authorization eligibility to undocumented college students and graduates who arrived as children.

87. Katie Strang, "Immigration Hurdles Mark (Re)Turning Point for Irish," *Queens Chronicle*, November 2, 2006.

88. Jeffrey S. Passel and D'Vera Cohn, "US Unauthorized Immigration Flows Are Down Sharply Since Mid-Decade," Pew Hispanic Center, September 1, 2010, 5.

89. See "Is there a 'new wave' of immigration?" (chapter 1).

90. Steven A. Camarota and Karen Jensenius, *Homeward Bound: Recent Immigration Enforcement and the Decline in the Illegal Alien Population*, Center for Immigration Studies (CIS), July 2008.

91. Immigration Policy Center, "Throwing Good Money After Bad: Immigration Enforcement," May 26, 2010; Passel and Cohn, "US Unauthorized Immigration Flows Are Down."

92. Adam Hadi, "Construction employment peaks before the recession and falls sharply throughout it," Bureau of Labor Statistics, *Monthly Labor Review*, (April 2011): 24–27; Robertson, Beaty, Atkinson, and Libal, *Operation Streamline*, 26. This pattern may reflect enforcement patterns as much as it does migration patterns, since it relies on apprehensions as a measure of unauthorized entry.

93. Wayne A. Cornelius, Scott Borger, Adam Sawyer, David Keyes, Clare Appleby, Kristen Parks, Gabriel Lozada, and Jonathan Hicken, *Controlling*

Unauthorized Immigration From Mexico: The Failure of "Prevention Through Deterrence" and the Need for Comprehensive Reform, Center for Comparative Immigration Studies (CCIS), June 10, 2008; Editorial, "Immigration Decline," *San Diego Union-Tribune*, June 6, 2009.

94. Jeffrey S. Passel and D'Vera Cohn, *Mexican Immigrants: How Many Come? How Many Leave?*, Pew Hispanic Center, July 22, 2009; Michael S. Rendall, Peter Brownell, and Sarah Kups, *Declining Return Migration From the United States to Mexico in the Late-2000s Recession: A Research Note*, RAND Corporation working paper, July 9, 2011; Immigration Policy Center, *Mexican Migration Patterns Signal A New Immigration Reality: Fewer Mexicans Are Entering the U.S., Fewer Are Leaving, and Mexican American Births Now Outpace Immigration from Mexico*, August 2011.

95. Meissner et al., *Immigration Enforcement in the United States*, 2–3, 9.

96. Department of Homeland Security, *Budget-in-Brief: Fiscal Year 2015*, 50, 64.

97. Department of Labor, *FY 2015 Department of Labor Budget in Brief*, http://www.dol.gov/dol/budget/2015/PDF/FY2015BIB.pdf, 4, 14, 37, 49.

98. Bureau of Labor Statistics, "Census of Fatal Occupational Injuries Summary, 2013," September 11, 2014; Bureau of Labor Statistics, "Employer-Reported Workplace Injury and Illness Summary," December 4, 2014.

99. U.S. House of Representatives Committee on Oversight and Government Reform, *Dollars Not Sense: Government Contracting Under the Bush Administration*, June 2006, 77, available at http://www.halliburtonwatch.org/reports/waxman0606.pdf; GAO, *Homeland Security: Some Progress Made, but Many Challenges Remain on U.S. Visitor and Immigrant Status Indicator Technology Program*, report to congressional committees, February 2005.

100. Alice Lipowicz, "Signed, Sealed, Delivered: Boeing Gets SBI-Net," *Washington Technology*, September 21, 2006; Joseph Richey, "Border for Sale: Privatizing Immigration Control," *Corpwatch*, July 5, 2006.

101. Julia Preston, "Homeland Security Cancels 'Virtual Fence' After $1 Billion Is Spent," *New York Times*, January 14, 2011.

102. See "Who profits from detention?" (chapter 11).

10. What About Amnesty and Guest Worker Programs?

1.   Southern Poverty Law Center, *Close to Slavery: Guestworker Programs in the United States*, February 2013.

2.   American Friends Service Committee, "'Legalization' or 'Amnesty'? Understanding the Debate—What's the Difference Between Comprehensive Immigration Reform, Legalization, and Amnesty?," available at http://immigration.procon.org/view.answers.php?questionID=000770, accessed May 26, 2015.

3.   Andorra Bruno, *Immigration: Registry as Means of Obtaining Lawful Permanent Residence*, Congressional Research Service, August 22, 2001.

4.   Immigration Reform and Control Act (IRCA), Bill Summary & Status, 99th Congress (1985–1986), Library of Congress, http://thomas.loc.gov/cgi-bin/bdquery/z?d099:SN01200:@@@L&summ2=m&%7CTOM:/bss/d099query.html, accessed May 26, 2015.

5.   Vernon M. Briggs, *Mass Immigration and the National Interest: Policy Di-*

rections for the New Century (Armonk, NY: M. E. Sharpe, 2003), 180, 183; Rachel L. Swarns, "Failed Amnesty Legislation of 1986 Haunts the Current Immigration Bills in Congress," *New York Times,* May 23, 2006.

6. U.S. Citizenship and Immigration Services, "Hemispheric Ceilings," http://www.uscis.gov/tools/glossary/hemispheric-ceilings, accessed May 27, 2015.

7. Ronald Reagan, "Statement on Signing the Immigration Reform and Control Act of 1986," November 6, 1986, Ronald Reagan Presidential Library and Museum. For "employer sanctions," see "Can't we cut off the 'job magnet'?" (Chapter 9).

8. "España: Inmigrantes Ilegales Se Apuran a Pedir Residencia," *VOA News,* February 7, 2005; A. Agulló, "800.000 Inmigrantes Podrán Regularizarse a Partir de Hoy," *20minutos.es,* February 7, 2005.

9. "Más de 2,5 Millones de Inmigrantes Regularizados Hasta Septiembre," *Europa Press,* January 1, 2006.

10. "La Inmigración en Cifras," *El País* (Madrid), January 13, 2004.

11. Christian Fraser, "Italy Considers Immigrant Amnesty," BBC News, May 22, 2006.

12. Kate Brick, "Regularizations in the European Union: The Contentious Policy Tool," Migration Policy Institute, *Insights,* December 1, 2011.

13. "Brazil: Amnesty for Illegal Immigrants Sparks Hope and Controversy," *Global Voices,* July 18, 2009; Samuel Novacich, "From Amnesty to Permanent Residency," *Rio Times,* June 7, 2011.

14. See "Is It Easy to Be 'Illegal'"? (chapter 4).

15. Paul Taylor, Mark Hugo Lopez, Jeffrey S. Passel, and Seth Motel, *Unauthorized Immigrants: Length of Residency, Patterns of Parenthood,* Pew Hispanic Center, December 1, 2011.

16. See "What can we do about the 'race to the bottom'?" (chapter 6) and "How much does enforcement cost us?" (chapter 9).

17. "Hasty Call for Amnesty," editorial, *New York Times,* February 22, 2000; Pia M. Orrenius and Madeline Zavodny, "Do Amnesty Programs Reduce Undocumented Immigration? Evidence from IRCA," *Demography* 40/3 (August 2003): 438, 446; Joshua Linder, "The Amnesty Effect: Evidence from the 1986 Immigration Reform and Control Act," *The Public Purpose* (Spring 2011): 13–31; Pia M. Orrenius and Madeline Zavodny, "The Economic Consequences of Amnesty for Unauthorized Immigrants," *Cato Journal* 32/1 (2012): 85–106; "Illegal Immigration, Population Estimates in the United States, 1969–2011," ProCon.org, http://immigration.procon.org/view.resource.php?resourceID=000844, accessed January 10, 2015.

18. National Immigration Law Center and United We Dream, "Frequently Asked Questions: The Obama Administration's Deferred Action for Childhood Arrivals (DACA)," http://www.nilc.org/FAQdeferredactionyouth.html, accessed April 20, 2015.

19. Migration Policy Center, *A Guide to the Immigration Accountability Executive Action,* http://www.immigrationpolicy.org/special-reports/guide-immigration-accountability-executive-action, accessed May 29, 2015; "Who and Where Are the Actual and Potential Beneficiaries of DACA?," *Immigration Impact,* August 12, 2015; Muzaffar Chishti and Faye Hipsman,

"Supreme Court DAPA Ruling a Blow to Obama Administration, Moves Immigration Back to Political Realm," *Migration Policy Institute, Migration Information Source,* June 29, 2016. Presidents Ronald Reagan and George H. W. Bush authorized similar but smaller executive actions to prevent families from being separated while the 1986 amnesty was being implemented. Mark Noferi, "When Reagan and GHW Bush Took Bold Executive Action on Immigration," *The Hill,* October 2, 2014. As of early 2017, there were concerns that DACA might be revoked, or at least not renewed, under the anti-immigrant Trump administration.

20.   U.S. Citizenship and Immigration Services, "Temporary (Non-Immigrant) Workers," http://www.uscis.gov/working-united-states/temporary-workers/temporary-nonimmigrant-workers, accessed June 1, 2015; Jill H. Wilson, *Immigration Facts: Temporary Foreign Workers,* Brookings Institution, June 18, 2013; Southern Poverty Law Center (SPLC), "What is the J-1 Visa Exchange Visitor Program?," in *Culture Shock: The Exploitation of J-1 Cultural Exchange Workers,* February 1, 2014; U.S. State Department, "Exchange Visitor Program: Cap on Current Participant Levels and Moratorium on New Sponsor Applications for Summer Work Travel Program," http://j1visa.state.gov/sponsors/current/regulations-compliance/rulemaking-documents/, accessed June 5, 2015. Hired farmworkers are only about one-third of the total agricultural work force. See "Who are the undocumented immigrants?" (chpater 1) and notes.

21.   U.S. Commission on Immigration Reform, *Binational Study: Migration Between Mexico and the United States,* 1997, vol. 1; Agustín Escobar Latapí, Philip Martin, Gustavo López Castro, and Katharine Donato, *Factors that Influence Migration;* vol. 3; Martin, *Guest Workers: Past and Present.*

22.   Daniel J. Tichenor, *Dividing Lines: The Politics of Immigration Control in America* (Princeton and Oxford: Princeton University Press, 2002), 210; J. Craig Jenkins, "Push/Pull in Recent Mexican Migration to the U.S.," *International Migration Review* 11/2 (Summer 1997): 183, Table 2, data from U.S. Department of Justice Immigration and Naturalization Service.

23.   Vernon M. Briggs, "Guestworker Programs for Low-Skilled Workers: Lessons from the Past and Warnings for the Future," testimony before the Subcommittee on Immigration and Border Security of the Judiciary Committee of the U.S. Senate, February 5, 2004, available at Center for Immigration Studies (CIS), http://www.cis.org/node/536.

24.   Ibid.; Timothy J. Bartik and Susan N. Houseman, eds., *A Future of Good Jobs? America's Challenge in the Global Economy* (Kalamazoo, MI: W. E. Upjohn Institute 2008), 134; SPLC, "A Brief History of Guestworkers in America," *Close to Slavery,* February 2013; U.S. Code Title 22 (1961), chap. 33, Mutual Educational And Cultural Exchange Program, http://www2.ed.gov/about/offices/list/ope/iegps/fulbrighthaysact.pdf.

25.   Stephanie Black, *H-2 Worker,* 1990, http://www.lifeanddebt.org/h2worker/.

26.   Valerie Orleans, "Educator Brings Attention to Historic Period and Its Affect [*sic*] on Her Family," interview with Christine Valenciana, *News and Information,* March 17, 2005, website of California State University,

Fullerton, http://calstate.fullerton.edu/news/2005/valenciana.html, accessed June 3, 2015; Eric Roy, "Righting an Old Wrong," *VOANews.com*, September 29, 2003, http://www.alternet.org/rights/16859/; Wendy Koch, "U.S. urged to apologize for 1930s deportations," *USA Today*, April 5, 2006; California Senate Rules Committee, Senate Floor Analysis of SB 645, May 27, 2005, ftp://www.legislature.ca.gov/pub/05-06/bill/sen/sb_0601-0650/sb_645_cfa_20050527_150338_sen_floor.html; Terry Gross interview with Francisco Balderrama, "America's Forgotten History of Mexican-American 'Repatriation,'" NPR, *Fresh Air*, September 10, 2015.

27. Roy, "Righting an Old Wrong"; Vanessa Martinez, "California apologizes for unconstitutional deportation of 2 million people," *Daily Titan* (California State University, Fullerton), February 27, 2012; MALDEF, "Permanent Monument Honoring Victims and Survivors to Be Housed at LA Plaza," press release, February 26, 2012; Terry Gross interview with Francisco Balderrama, "America's Forgotten History Of Mexican-American 'Repatriation,'"; Adrian Florido, "Mass Deportation May Sound Unlikely, But It's Happened Before," NPR, *Morning Edition*, September 8, 2015.

28. Fred L. Koestler, "Operation Wetback," Handbook of Texas Online, http://www.tshaonline.org/handbook/online/articles/pqo01, accessed June 3, 2015.

29. David M. Reimers, *Still the Golden Door: The Third World Comes to America*, 2nd ed. (New York: Columbia University Press, 1992), 38–40, 44, 54–55; John Ross, *The Annexation of Mexico* (Monroe, ME: Common Courage Press, 1998), 296–300; Jenkins, "Push/Pull in Recent Mexican Migration to the U.S."; David Bacon, "The Political Economy of Immigration Reform: The Corporate Campaign for a U.S. Guest Worker Program," *Multinational Monitor* 25/11 (November 2004); David Bacon, "Is a New Bracero Program in Our Future?" *Z Magazine* 16/10 (October 2003), available at http://dbacon.igc.org/Imgrants/17FastPast.htm.

30. In October 2008 then-Mexican president Felipe Calderón announced that Mexico would pay 38,000 pesos (about $3,455 at the time) to each of the former *braceros* living in the United States or their survivors. This was the result of a class action suit the *braceros* brought in California in 2001. Former workers living in Mexico were promised the same amount several years earlier, but as of March 2016, many of the ex-*braceros* or their survivors were still fighting in court for the payments owed to them. Jesse Greenspan, "Braceros Win $14.6M Settlement After 60-Year Wait," *Law 360*, October 15, 2008, on website for attorneys Lieff, Cabraser, Heimann, & Bernstein, LLP, http://www.lieffcabraser.com/braceros.htm, accessed June 3, 2015; Belén Zapata, "Miles de ex trabajadores inmigrantes en defensa de sus ahorros," CNN Mexico, May 2, 2010; Centro Nacional de Comunicación Social (Cencos), press release, "Ex Braceros Ganan Demanda de Amparo En Contra Del Presidente Enrique Peña Nieto, Esperan Su Respuesta En Demanda Al Pago de Su Fondo de Ahorro," February 28, 2014; Alberto Núñez Hernández, "Ex Braceros Ganamos Juicio y el Gobierno Tendrá Que Hacernos el Pago en Dólares," *Página 24*, March 4, 2016.

31. Tyche Hendricks, "Ex-Braceros Leery of Guest Worker Plan," *San Francisco Chronicle*, May 30, 2006.

32. SPLC, *Close to Slavery*, "Executive Summary."
33. Farmworker Justice website, "H-2B Program," http://farmworkerjustice. org/content/h-2b-guestworker-program, accessed June 8, 2015;Tom Knudson, "Forest Guest Workers Tell of Abuses," *Sacramento Bee*, May 19, 2006; Danna Harman, "Guest Workers Vulnerable," *Christian Science Monitor*, April 25, 2006; SPLC, *Close to Slavery*, "Holding the Deportation Card," February 2013.
34. Farmworker Justice website, "H-2A Guestworker Program," http://farmworkerjustice.org/content/h-2a-guestworker-program, accessed June 8, 2015, and "H-2B Program"; William G. Whittaker, *Farm Labor: The Adverse Effect Wage Rate (AEWR)*, Congressional Research Service (CRS) report for Congress, April 14, 2005; SPLC, *Close to Slavery*, "How Guestworker Programs Operate"; U.S. Department of Labor Wage and Hour Division (WHD), "Fact Sheet #78C: Wage Requirements under the H-2B Program," http://www.dol.gov/whd/regs/compliance/whdfs78c.htm, accessed November 2, 2015; Melinda Pilling, "Employers Must Reimburse Guest Workers' Travel and Immigration Expenses," Rukin Hyland Doria Tindall LLP and Attorneys, April 14, 2014. Department of Labor (DoL) guidelines issued in 2015 strengthen protections for H-2B workers, requiring employers to cover their visa costs and inbound and outbound travel expenses. However, these guidelines are said to "not supersede" the weaker H-2B regulations under immigration law, and a 2016 appropriations bill bars the DoL from using any funds to enforce some of the added protections. Several federal appeals court rulings have held that under the Fair Labor Standards Act (FLSA), H-2A workers are entitled to be promptly reimbursed when the deduction of such costs pushes their wages below the federal minimum; these rulings leave open the possibility that H-2B workers may have the same rights. U.S. Department of Labor, Wage and Hour Division (WHD), "WHD H-2B Side-by-Side Comparison of the 2009 and 2015 Rules," https://www.dol.gov/whd/immigration/h2bfinalrule/h2bsidebyside.htm, accessed June 22, 2016.
35. Black, *H-2 Worker*; Barry Yeoman, "Silence in the Fields," *Mother Jones*, January–February 2001; Eduardo Porter, "Who Will Work the Farms?" *New York Times*, March 23, 2006; SPLC, *Close to Slavery*, "Wage and Hour Abuses," February 2013.
36. Yeoman, "Silence in the Fields."
37. Porter, "Who Will Work the Farms?"
38. Nancy Lofholm, "Visa Program Encourages Seasonal Hiring of Foreign Students While U.S. Youths Go Jobless," *Denver Post*, June 18, 2011.
39. SPLC, "Foreign Students Deceived, Exploited With Little Recourse," *Culture Shock*, February 1, 2014; U.S. State Department Office of Inspections, *Inspection of the Bureau of Educational and Cultural Affairs*, Report Number ISP-I-12-15, February 2012, 24–25, 27–28.
40. David Bacon, "Talking Points on Guest Workers," *Truthout*, July 13, 2005.
41. Kari Lydersen, "Guest Workers Seek Global Horizons: U.S. Company Exploits Migrant Labor," *CorpWatch*, November 3, 2006, updated and corrected April 12, 2007.

42. Marie Brenner, "In the Kingdom of Big Sugar," *Vanity Fair*, February 2001; Black, *H-2 Worker*.

43. Black, *H-2 Worker*.

44. Sunita Sohrabji, "$20 Million Signal Settlement to Indian Guest Workers Reduced to $5 Million," *India West*, January 5, 2016; U.S. Equal Employment Opportunity Commission (EEOC) press release, "Signal International, LLC to Pay $5 Million to Settle EEOC Race, National Origin Lawsuit," December 18, 2015.

45. Julia Preston, "Foreign Students in Work Visa Program Stage Walkout at Plant," *New York Times*, August 17, 2011; Jennifer Gordon, "America's Sweatshop Diplomacy," *New York Times,* August 24, 2011; Josh Eidelson, "McDonald's Guest Workers Stage a Surprise Strike," *The Nation*, March 6, 2013.

46. Eidelson, "McDonald's Guest Workers Stage a Surprise Strike"; David Wenner, "Critics claim program that brought foreign students to local McDonald's is a pipeline for cheap, vulnerable labor," *Patriot-News* (Harrisburg, PA), March 13, 2013; U.S. Department of Labor, "Former McDonald's franchisee agrees to pay nearly $211,000 in unpaid wages, damages and penalties following U.S. Labor Department investigation," press release, February 18, 2014.

47. SPLC, *Close to Slavery*, "Executive Summary"; Lydersen, "Guest Workers Seek Global Horizons."

48. Center for Strategic Research, AFL-CIO, *After Decimating U.S, Manufacturing, Wal-Mart Takes Aim at the Information Technology Sector*, April 1, 2015.

49. Daniel Costa, "H-2B employers and their congressional allies are fighting hard to keep wages low for immigrant and American workers," Economic Policy Institute, October 6, 2011.

50. Daniel Costa, "Frequently Asked Questions about the H-2B Temporary Foreign Worker Program," Economic Policy Institute, June 2, 2016. See also "Who benefits from low wages for immigrants?" (chapter 6).

51. Victoria Bouloubasis, "Be Our Guest Worker," *The American Prospect*, November 7, 2013.

52. David Bacon, "Why Is This Farm Using Guest Workers as Strike Breakers?," *The Nation*, May 2, 2014; Karen Taylor, "Berry pickers hope to block Sakuma Brothers Farm's use of foreign guest workers," KGMI News (Bellingham, WA), March 31, 2015; Boycott Sakuma Berries, "Hundreds of Consumers and Boycott Supporters March with Farm Workers to Sakuma Farms," *Indybay*, July 23, 2016.

53. Migration Policy Center, *A Guide to S.744: Understanding the 2013 Senate Immigration Bill*, http://www.immigrationpolicy.org/special-reports/guide-s744-understanding-2013-senate-immigration-bill, accessed May 29, 2015.

54. Hendricks, "Ex-Braceros Leery of Guest Worker Plan"; Robert Reich, "What Immigration Reform Could Mean for American Workers, and Why the AFL-CIO Is Embracing It," RobertReich.org, April 2, 2013; Benoît Bréville, "Getting in and getting on," *Le Monde Diplomatique* (English), July 2013.

55. Steven Greenhouse, "North Carolina Growers' Group Signs Union Contract for Mexican Workers," *New York Times*, September 17, 2004; Paul Crowley, "Mt. Olive Boycott Officially Ends," *Duke University Chronicle*, September 17, 2004; Farm Labor Organizing Committee (FLOC), "Precedent Setting Agreement Reached, Mt. Olive Pickle Boycott Over," press release, September 16, 2004.
56. Lydersen, "Guest Workers Seek Global Horizons."
57. Claudia Boyd-Barrett, "FLOC, family seek justice in 2007 death," *Toledo* (Ohio) *Blade*, September 8, 2011.

11. Why Do We Jail and Deport Immigrants?

1. Peter L. Markowitz, "Deportation Is Different," *University of Pennsylvania Journal of Constitutional Law* 13/5 (2011): 1299–1361. Markowitz argues that this long-standing legal framing of deportation appears to be shifting; the 2010 Supreme Court ruling in *Padilla v. Kentucky* "marks the beginning of a significant reconceptualization of the nature of deportation toward the realization that it is . . . a unique legal animal that lives in the crease between the civil and criminal labels."
2. Bethany Carson and Eleana Diaz, *Payoff: How Congress Ensures Private Prison Profit with an Immigrant Detention Quota*, Grassroots Leadership, April 2015.
3. Tanya Golash-Boza, "The Immigration Industrial Complex: Why We Enforce Immigration Policies Destined to Fail," *Sociology Compass* 3/2 (2009): 295–309.
4. The percentage of removals that are summary proceedings has grown sharply since 2009, when it was 56.2 percent. Center for Migration Studies, "Immigration Detention: Behind the Record Numbers," February 13, 2014. See also ACLU, *American Exile: Rapid Deportations that Bypass the Courtroom*, December 2014. Summary deportations in 2013 included 193,000 "expedited removals" of people arriving in the United States (mostly at land borders, but also by sea or air), and 171,000 "reinstatements of removal," applied to people who are caught inside the United States after having been previously deported. John F. Simanski, *Immigration Enforcement Actions: 2013*, Department of Homeland Security (DHS) Office of Immigration Statistics Annual Report, September 2014. Expedited removal was introduced in 1996 as part of the Illegal Immigration Reform and Immigrant Responsibility Act (IIRIRA). Initially, it was used only for people entering the United States, but in 2004, DHS began applying it to non-citizens apprehended within 100 miles of the southwestern U.S. border, unless they could demonstrate they had been present in the country over the past fourteen days. In 2006, DHS extended the policy to all U.S. borders. American Immigration Council Immigration Policy Center, "Removal Without Recourse: The Growth of Summary Deportations from the United States," April 28, 2014.
5. Returns include "voluntary departures" and "withdrawals of applications for admission." The growing number of formal removals since 2004 has been outpaced by a steep drop in returns—from more than 1.1 million in

2004 to less than 165,000 in 2014. The combined total of removals and returns declined from 1.4 million in 2004 to less than half that number— 577,000—in 2014. DHS, *Yearbook of Immigration Statistics: 2013*, Enforcement Actions Data Table 39, "Aliens Removed or Returned: Fiscal Years 1892 to 2013," October 1, 2014; DHS Press Office, "DHS Releases End of Year Statistics," December 19, 2014; Walter A. Ewing, "The Growth of the U.S. Deportation Machine: More Immigrants Are Being 'Removed' from the United States than Ever Before," American Immigration Council Immigration Policy Center, March 2014, 6.

6. Deirdre M. Moloney, *National Insecurities: Immigrants and U.S. Deportation Policy Since 1882* (Chapel Hill: University of North Carolina Press, 2012), passim.

7. Markowitz, "Deportation Is Different"; *Chae Chan Ping v. United States*, 130 U.S. 581, May 13, 1889, http://caselaw.lp.findlaw.com/scripts/getcase.pl?court=US&vol=130&invol=581; *Fong Yue Ting vs. United States*, http://caselaw.lp.findlaw.com/scripts/getcase.pl?court=US&vol=149&invol=698.

8. Emma Goldman, "War Resistance, Anti-Militarism, and Deportation, 1917–1919," Emma Goldman Papers, Berkeley Library, University of California, www.lib.berkeley.edu/goldman/MeetEmmaGoldman/warresistance-anti-militarism-deportation1917-1919.html, accessed October 11, 2015.

9. Deportation by federal agents was only one component in these two campaigns. State and local police—and during the Depression, relief agencies—played important roles, and many Mexicans and Mexican-Americans were coerced to leave "voluntarily," or fled to escape the raids. See "What happened to the Mexican '*braceros*'?" (chapter 10).

10. Jonathan Xavier Inda, "Subject to deportation: IRCA, 'criminal aliens', and the policing of immigration," *Oxford University Migration Studies* 1/3 (2013): 292–310, February 13, 2013.

11. Total deportations went from 69,680 in fiscal year 1996 to a high of 438,421 in fiscal year 2013, then dipped slightly to 414,481 in 2014. DHS, *Yearbook of Immigration Statistics: 2013*, Enforcement Actions Data Table 39; see also Ana Gonzalez-Barrera and Jens Manuel Krogstad, "U.S. Deportations of Immigrants Reach Record High in 2013," Pew Research Center, October 2, 2014; DHS Press Office, "DHS Releases End of Year Statistics," December 19, 2014.

12. Title 8 U.S. Code § 1227, "Deportable Aliens," https://www.law.cornell.edu/uscode/text/8/1227, accessed October 12, 2015; Brenda Goodman, "Legislator's Wife Is Allowed to Stay in U.S.," *New York Times,* December 6, 2006. See also "How do we treat asylum seekers?" (chapter 3).

13. The disparity is most striking for Hondurans, who make up 3 percent of the unauthorized and over 8 percent of those deported. Data on removals is from DHS, *Yearbook of Immigration Statistics: 2013*, Enforcement Actions Data, Table 41, "Aliens Removed by Criminal Status and Region and Country of Nationality: Fiscal Years 2004 to 2013," October 1, 2014; data on unauthorized population is from Migration Policy Institute,

"Profile of the Unauthorized Population: US," http://www.migrationpolicy.org/data/unauthorized-immigrant-population/state/US,   accessed June 30, 2016.

14. It is not clear whether these removals include people who had been previously deported and are arrested upon reentry—some "recent arrivals" could be longtime residents attempting to return. Marc R. Rosenblum and Kristen McCabe, *Deportation and Discretion: Reviewing the Record and Options for Change*, Migration Policy Institute, October 2014, 24.

15. Elise Foley, "Deportation Separated Thousands Of U.S.-Born Children From Parents In 2013," *Huffington Post*, June 25, 2014.

16. Human Rights Watch, "Forced Apart (By the Numbers): Non-Citizens Deported Mostly for Nonviolent Offenses," April 2009.

17. Jacqueline Stevens, "U.S. Government Unlawfully Detaining and Deporting U.S. Citizens as Aliens," *Virginia Journal of Social Policy and the Law* 18/3 (July 2011): 606, available at SSRN, http://ssrn.com/abstract=1931703. Attorney Gabriela Rivera notes that the unlawful deportation of U.S. citizens is a "predictable consequence of a system that relies on racial and ethnic stereotypes, empowers officers to act as judge, jury and executioner, and all but prohibits affected individuals from seeking judicial review." ACLU, *American Exile*; Ted Robbins, "In the Rush to Deport, Expelling U.S. Citizens," National Public Radio, October 24, 2011.

18. Data includes both detained and non-detained immigrants; those who were not detained were 5.7 times more likely to prevail if they had representation, while detained immigrants were six times more likely to prevail with representation. New York Immigrant Representation Study, *Accessing Justice: The Availability and Adequacy of Counsel in Immigration Proceedings*, December 2011, 19–20; and *Accessing Justice II: A Model for Providing Counsel to New York Immigrants in Removal Proceedings*, December 2012, 4–5.

19. Rosenblum and McCabe, *Deportation and Discretion*, 15; Grace Meng, "Don't Deport All Criminal Immigrants," *USA Today*, June 6, 2013; Adrian Florido, "Immigration Advocates Challenge Obama's 'Felons Not Families' Policy," NPR, November 1, 2016; Transactional Records Access Clearinghouse (TRAC) immigration report, "Aggravated Felonies and Deportation," June 9, 2006; Washington Courts, *Immigration Resource Guide for Judges*, chap. 7, Washington State Supreme Court Gender and Justice Commission and Minority and Justice Commission, July 2013.

20. Rosenblum and McCabe, *Deportation and Discretion*, 15. See "Can't we increase the penalties for border crossers?" (chapter 9).

21. Authors' analysis of data from Alistair Graham Robertson, Rachel Beaty, Jane Atkinson, and Bob Libal, *Operation Streamline: Costs and Consequences*, Grassroots Leadership, September 2012, from calculations based on TRAC data on convictions and sentence days and U.S. marshals per diem per person paid rates available at http://www.justice.gov/ofdt/perdiem-paid.htm; DHS apprehension data from *DHS Yearbook*

of Immigration Statistics: 2013, Enforcement Actions Table 33, "Aliens Apprehended: Fiscal Years 1925 to 2013," October 1, 2014.

22. Calculation based on numbers for all new federal criminal prosecutions and new immigration prosecutions from TRAC report (summary), "Prosecutions for September 2014 (Fiscal Year 2014)," November 6, 2014.

23. M. Kathleen Dingeman-Cerda and Susan Bibler Coutin, "The Ruptures of Return: Deportation's Confounding Effects," in *Punishing Immigrants: Policy, Politics, and Injustice,* ed. Charis E. Kubrin, Marjorie S. Zatz, and Ramiro Martinez, Jr. (New York: New York University Press, 2012); David Brotherton and Luis Barrios, *Banished to the Homeland: Dominican Deportees and Their Stories of Exile* (New York: Columbia University Press, 2011); Walter Leitner, *Removing Refugees: U.S. Deportation Policy and the Cambodian-American Community,* Leitner Center for International Law and Justice, Spring 2010; total number of Cambodians deported as of FY2015 from Immigration and Customs Enforcement (ICE) removal data for FY2015, Table 41, "Aliens Removed by Criminal Status and Region and Country of Nationality: Fiscal Years 2006 to 2015"; and FY2011, Table 41, "Aliens Removed by Criminal Status and Region and Country of Nationality: Fiscal Years 2002 to 2011"; Deepa Fernandes, *Targeted: Homeland Security and the Business of Immigration* (New York: Seven Stories Press, 2007), 27–28, 102–5, 109.

24. Tanya Golash-Boza, "From Legal to 'Illegal,'" *Constructing Immigrant "Illegality": Critiques, Experiences and Responses,* ed. Cecilia Menjivar and Daniel Kanstroom (New York: Cambridge University Press, 2014), 220.

25. Most non-citizens without criminal convictions, being deported for the first time, are subject to a ten-year bar. Some who are stopped entering the country or near the border may be barred for only five years; those who have been deported more than once may be barred for twenty years. Those who have been convicted of an "aggravated felony," or who have reentered the country after being deported, are subject to a lifetime bar. Certain deportees may be eligible for a "waiver of inadmissibility" that allows them to reapply to enter the United States to reunite with family. Not everyone is eligible: no waivers are available if you were convicted of or have admitted committing a drug offense, other than a single conviction for possession of 30 grams or less of marijuana. Others not eligible for waivers include former lawful permanent residents convicted of an aggravated felony, and anyone convicted of or admitting to acts of murder or torture. Even if you're eligible for a waiver, that doesn't mean you'll get one. The immigration agency has full discretion to grant or reject waivers on a case-by-case basis after weighing all factors, and grant rates vary dramatically within and between the various grounds for inadmissibility. Center for Human Rights and International Justice, Post-Deportation Human Rights Project, Boston College, *Returning to the United States After Deportation: A Guide to Assess Your Eligibility,* August 2011. Authors' analysis on April 24, 2015, of data from Table 20, Immigrant

and Nonimmigrant Visa Ineligibilities (by Grounds for Refusal Under the Immigration and Nationality Act) for 2004–2013, accessible through the page for the annual Report of the Visa Office on the U.S. Department of State website, http://travel.state.gov/content/visas/english/law-and-policy/statistics/annual-reports.html.

26.   Dingeman-Cerda and Coutin, "The Ruptures of Return"; Brotherton and Barrios, *Banished to the Homeland.*

27.   Dingeman-Cerda and Coutin, "The Ruptures of Return"; Damien Cave, "Crossing Over, and Over," *New York Times,* October 2, 2011.

28.   Scott Phillips, Jacqueline Maria Hagan, and Nestor Rodriguez, "Brutal Borders? Examining the Treatment of Deportees During Arrest and Detention," *Social Forces* 85/1 (2006): 93–109.

29.   Brotherton and Barrios, *Banished to the Homeland,* 4. It would be difficult to estimate how many former deportees are living in the United States. About 171,000 of the 438,000 people removed in 2013—39 percent—were subjected to "reinstatement of removal," which is only applicable to people who have reentered the country unlawfully following deportation. If we assume that the ratio of the total number of people apprehended in a given year to the total unauthorized population (26 percent) is the same as the ratio of apprehended reentering deportees in a given year to the total population of reentered deportees, we can estimate that 2.85 million people—about a quarter of the unauthorized population—has been previously deported at some point. (Authors' analysis of data based on Pew Hispanic's estimate of 11.2 million unauthorized population and 2013 removal statistics from John F. Simanski, *Immigration Enforcement Actions: 2013.*)

30.   Seth Freed Wessler, "Call Centers: Returning to Mexico but sounding 'American,'" Al Jazeera America, March 16, 2014.

31.   WBEZ, "No Place Like Home," NPR, *This American Life,* originally aired March 14, 2014.

32.   Guadalupe Hernández, "El sector de servicios ha crecido 29% en seis años," *El Diario de Hoy,* November 20, 2011, available at http://www.revistasumma.com/19886/.

33.   Associated Press, "Remesas a El Salvador crecieron 6.4% en 2011," *La Prensa Gráfica* (San Salvador), January 17, 2012.

34.   DHS, *Yearbook of Immigration Statistics: 2013,* Enforcement Actions Data Table 41, "Aliens Removed by Criminal Status and Region and Country of Nationality: Fiscal Years 2004 to 2013," October 1, 2014. These figures are for removals, not people; they do not necessarily reflect a total number of deportees living in El Salvador, as some people may have been removed more than once over the period in question, and an unknown number of deportees are assumed to have left the country.

35.   See "What if we deport all the 'illegal' immigrants?" (chapter 9). By other estimates, the cost for the whole deportation process is $23,482.

36.   Sara Satinsky, Alice Hu, Jonathan Heller, and Lili Farhang, *Family Unity,*

Family Health: How Family-Focused Immigration Reform Will Mean Better Health for Children and Families, Human Impact Partners, June 2013.

37. Between 2003 and 2013, 91 percent of all DHS deportations were of men, even though only 53 percent of the unauthorized population was male. Rosenblum and McCabe, *Deportation and Discretion*, 11; Hoefer, Rytina, and Baker, *Estimates of the Unauthorized Immigrant Population Residing in the United States: January 2011*, 5.

38. Joanna Dreby, *How Today's Immigration Enforcement Policies Impact Children, Families, and Communities: A View from the Ground*, Center for American Progress, August 2012.

39. Dingeman-Cerda and Coutin, "The Ruptures of Return."

40. Satinsky et al., *Family Unity, Family Health*.

41. Barbara Facey and Carol McDonald, "Bring Back Our Husbands," *ColorLines* RaceWire, June 8, 2004, Alternet.org, http://www.alternet.org/story/18904/.

42. Brotherton and Barrios, *Banished to the Homeland*, 159.

43. *Shattered Families: The Perilous Intersection of Immigration Enforcement and the Child Welfare System*, Applied Research Center (ARC) (now Race Forward: The Center for Racial Justice Innovation), November 2011.

44. Dreby, *How Today's Immigration Enforcement Policies Impact Children, Families, and Communities*.

45. Dingeman-Cerda and Coutin, "The Ruptures of Return."

46. Randolph Capps, Rosa Maria Castaneda, Ajay Chaudry, Robert Santos, *Paying the Price: The Impact of Immigration Raids on America's Children*, Urban Institute/National Council of La Raza, October 31, 2007.

47. Rights advocates note that the current practice in some localities of jailing people for failure to pay traffic tickets and other debts they cannot afford constitutes a modern-day form of debtor's prison. American Civil Liberties Union (ACLU), "Ending Modern-Day Debtors' Prisons," at https://www.aclu.org/feature/ending-modern-day-debtors-prisons, accessed May 2, 2015.

48. César Cuauhtémoc García Hernández, "Immigration Detention as Punishment," University of Denver Sturm College of Law, Legal Research Paper Series, Working Paper No. 13-41, August 22, 2013 (also in *UCLA Law Review* 1346 (2014): 61); see also César Cuauhtémoc García Hernández, "Is DHS Admitting Immigration Detention Is Punishment?," *Immigration*, September 25, 2014.

49. Mark Dow, *American Gulag, Inside U.S. Immigration Prisons* (Berkeley: University of California Press, 2004), 6–7. In the early 1990s, Haitian refugees were detained at the U.S. government's Guantánamo Naval Base in Cuba. See "Haitians face 'floating Berlin wall'" (chapter 3).

50. The 1995 numbers are from Doris Meissner, Donald M. Kerwin, Muzaffar Chishti, and Claire Bergeron, *Immigration Enforcement in the United States: The Rise of a Formidable Machinery*, Migration Policy Institute, January 2013; 2013 data from Simanski, Immigration Enforcement Actions: 2013, Table 5, "Initial Admissions to ICE Detention Facilities by Country of Nationality:

Fiscal Years 2011 to 2013." The fact that detention admissions showed a larger increase than average daily population over the 1995–2013 period suggests a declining average length of stay. Admission totals may also include multiple stints in detention by the same people over the course of a year.

51. American Civil Liberties Union of Texas, *Warehoused and Forgotten: Immigrants Trapped in Our Shadow Private Prison System*, June 2014.

52. National Immigrant Justice Center, "Immigration Detention Bed Quota Timeline," March 2014, http://www.immigrantjustice.org/immigration-detention-bed-quota-timeline, accessed May 5, 2015.

53. Letter from 136 NGOs to Congress, "Re: Immigration detention bed mandate in FY 2015 DHS Appropriations," January 24, 2014.

54. Detention Watch Network and Center for Constitutional Rights, *Banking on Detention: Local Lockup Quotas and the Immigrant Dragnet*, June 2015.

55. GAO, *Immigration Detention*.

56. Joanne Faryon, "U.S. Government Holding Fewer Immigrants in Detention," *inewsource*, April 6, 2015.

57. Editorial, "End Immigration Detention," *New York Times*, May 15, 2015.

58. Detention Watch Network, "Facts about Mandatory Detention."

59. ICE, *Detained Asylum Seekers, Fiscal Year 2009 and 2010, Report to Congress*, August 20, 2012.

60. Percentages calculated by authors using data from ICE, *Detained Asylum Seekers, Fiscal Year 2009 and 2010* and from ICE, *ERO Facts and Statistics 2*, December 12, 2011, http://www.ice.gov/doclib/foia/reports/ero-facts-and-statistics.pdf, accessed May 15, 2015.

61. Mandatory detention applies to people detained upon release from custody after October 8, 1998, following a conviction on one of the designated offenses. César Cuauhtémoc García Hernández, "BIA: mandatory detention applies only if released from custody for allegedly removable offense after October 8, 1998," *crImmigration*, June 28, 2010.

62. Leslie Berestein Rojas, "Why some immigrants with criminal convictions aren't deported," Southern California Public Radio (SCPR), KPCC-FM, March 6, 2015.

63. Center for Victims of Torture (CVT) and Torture Abolition and Survivor Support Coalition, International (TASSC), *Tortured & Detained: Survivor Stories of U.S. Immigration Detention*, November 2013.

64. Cristina Costantini, Jorge Rivas, and Kristofer Ríos, "Why Did the U.S. Lock Up These Women With Men? A Fusion Investigation," *Fusion*, November 19, 2014, based on data from ICE estimates and demographic analysis from the Williams Institute at UCLA.

65. Dara Lind, "The government knows LGBTQ immigrants are often raped in detention. It puts them there anyway," *Vox*, May 14, 2015.

66. Cristina Costantini, "U.S. is locking up pregnant moms despite policy against it," *Fusion*, July 25, 2014. In a November 2014 memo, the Department of Homeland Security clarified that pregnant women should not be detained unless there are "extraordinary circumstances" or

mandatory detention is required. Yet as of June 2015, ICE was continuing to detain pregnant women—at least twelve of them at one facility alone. Perla Trevizo, "Pregnant border crossers being detained more, longer," *Arizona Daily Star*, June 28, 2015; ACLU of Southern California, "Violations of Policy Regarding Detention, Shackling, and Care of Pregnant Women at Mesa Verde Detention Facility," June 18, 2015.

67. U.S. Customs and Border Protection (CBP), "Southwest Border, Unaccompanied Alien Children (FY 2014)," n.d., https://www.cbp.gov/ newsroom/stats/southwest-border-unaccompanied-children/fy-2014, accessed Decembe 27, 2016; American Immigration Council, *Children in Danger: A Guide to the Humanitarian Challenge at the Border*, July 10, 2014.

68. If they're from Canada or Mexico, unaccompanied children are generally returned home "voluntarily"; otherwise they must be transferred within seventy-two hours to the Department of Health and Human Services Office of Refugee Resettlement (ORR), which releases them to a sponsor or a shelter and provides support services. American Immigration Council, *A Guide to Children Arriving at the Border: Laws, Policies and Responses*, June 26, 2015.

69. Department of Homeland Security data obtained by the National Immigrant Justice Center through a Freedom of Information Act (FOIA) lawsuit. Because data was only provided for thirty of the approximately 250 adult detention facilities with which DHS held contracts at the time, the number of children detained with adults is likely much higher. More than 800 of the children spent at least one week in adult custody; some were detained for over a year, and four of them were held longer than 1,000 days. The detention of children with adults violates the terms set by the 1997 *Flores v. Reno* settlement. National Immigrant Justice Center: "Fact Sheet: Children Detained by the Department of Homeland Security in Adult Detention Facilities," May 2013.

70. CBP, "Southwest Border Unaccompanied Alien Children (FY 2014)."

71. Julia Preston, "Judge Orders Release of Immigrant Children Detained by U.S.," *New York Times*, July 25, 2015. Although "family units" are defined as adults with children, nearly all the detention beds in these centers are for mothers with children under age eighteen; adult men who arrive with their families are generally detained separately, sometimes in another state. If a father is apprehended with his minor children, in the absence of the children's mother, the family might be released or held at the Berks County facility, which provides a small amount of bed space for fathers. Lutheran Immigration and Refugee Service (LIRS) and Women's Refugee Commission (WRC) Family Detention, *Locking Up Family Values, Again: The Continued Failure of Immigration Family Detention*, October 2014; Preston, "Judge Orders Stop to Detention of Families at Borders"; Nuri Vallbona, "Judge tentatively rules against restrictive detention facilities for immigrant families," *National Catholic Reporter Online*, May 4, 2015; National Immigrant Justice Center, *Background on Family Detention*, January 2015.

72. Texas Appleseed, *Justice for Immigration's Hidden Population: Protecting the Rights of Persons with Mental Disabilities in the Immigration Court and Detention System*, March 2010; Dana Priest and Amy Goldstein, "Suicides Point to Gaps in Treatment: Errors in Psychiatric Diagnoses and Drugs Plague Strained Immigration System," *Washington Post*, May 13, 2008.

73. GAO, *Immigration Detention: Additional Actions Needed to Strengthen Management and Oversight of Facility Costs and Standards*; Cody Mason, "Dollars and Detainees: The Growth of For-Profit Detention," The Sentencing Project, July 2012; Berks County (PA) website, http://www.co.berks.pa.us/Dept/BCRC/Pages/AboutDepartment.aspx, accessed May 24, 2015.

74. Authors' analysis of admissions data: 2009 data from ICE, *ERO Facts and Statistics 2*, "ICE Detainee Population Statistics by Fiscal Year"; 2013 data from. Simanski, *Immigration Enforcement Actions: 2013*, Table 5. Authors' analysis of facilities data: 2013 data combines numbers of facilities holding detainees over and under seventy-two hours, from GAO report cited above. For 2008, data is from Transactional Records Access Clearinghouse (TRAC), which states that ICE used 654 facilities nationwide to detain immigrants over the twelve-month period from April 2007 through March 2008. (Not all facilities were necessarily in use as of March 2008 or at the end of FY2008. TRAC does not clarify if this number includes facilities holding detainees for less than seventy-two hours.) TRAC Immigration, "Huge Increase in Transfers of ICE Detainees," December 2, 2009. The number of facilities may have continued to drop between 2013 and 2015. As of May 2015, ICE listed on its website only eighty-one facilities across the United States where it detains immigrants. However, some of the facilities still in use—Berks, for example—appeared to be excluded from the list. See ICE, https://www.ice.gov/detention-facilities, accessed May 24, 2015.

75. Carson and Diaz, *Payoff: How Congress Ensures Private Prison Profit with an Immigrant Detention Quota*.

76. At the time the suit was filed, advocates said 2,000 children were being detained nationwide, whereas Immigration and Naturalization Service (INS) Western Regional Commissioner Harold Ezell said the number was 200, and that many of the children were detained together with at least one parent. According to Ezell, the average stay was twenty-eight days. David Holley, Elizabeth Lu, "Judge Orders INS to Free 2 Children: Advocates Say Ruling Could Aid Hundreds of Illegals," *Los Angeles Times*, July 20, 1985.

77. Suzanne Gamboa, "When Migrant Children Were Detained Among Adults, Strip Searched," NBC News, July 24, 2014; David G. Savage, "INS Detention of Children Upheld," *Los Angeles Times*, March 24, 1993.

78. American Immigration Council, *A Guide to Children Arriving at the Border: Laws, Policies and Responses*, accessed August 11, 2015.

79. Alexandra Starr, "Standards for Child Migrants Could Force Detention Centers to Close," NPR, May 13, 2015.

80. Lutheran Immigration and Refugee Service (LIRS) backgrounder: "From Persecution to Prison: Child and Family Detention," August 2014.

81. National Immigrant Justice Center, *Background on Family Detention*; LIRS and WRC Family Detention, *Locking Up Family Values, Again.*.

82. Lichter cited "roadblocks" including preventing attorneys from using computers, phones and wi-fi hotspots, restricting the attire of female attorneys, delaying attorney visits and meetings with clients, conducting invasive searches, and not allowing volunteers even to inform detainees of the availability of free legal help. Laura Lichter, "Life or Death Consequences: Part 2," Association of Immigration Law Attorneys (AILA) Leadership Blog, June 3, 2015.

83. "ICE Statement," KSAT News (San Antonio, TX), June 23, 2015.

84. ACLU press release, "Federal Court Blocks Government From Detaining Asylum Seekers as Tactic to Deter Others From Coming to U.S.," February 20, 2015; *Jenny L. Flores et al. v. Jeh Johnson et al.*, United States District Court, Central District of California, Civil Minutes, July 24, 2015, http://graphics8.nytimes.com/packages/pdf/us/FloresRuling.pdf.

85. Julia Preston, "Judge Orders Release of Immigrant Children Detained by U.S.," *New York Times*, July 25, 2015; *Jenny L. Flores et al. v. Jeh Johnson et al.*

86. According to a Transactional Records Access Clearinghouse (TRAC) analysis, 70 percent of detainees were held thirty days or less in 2013, and half were held eleven days or less. The average time spent in detention was thirty-one days. The data set analyzed was of people leaving detention during November and December of 2012. The TRAC data suggests that most detainees—72 percent—left detention only when they were deported or "voluntarily" returned to their country of origin. Only 21 percent were actually released from detention—and of these, just over 2 percent either won their fight against deportation, or the government decided not to pursue their removal; the rest were freed conditionally to await an outcome. Conditions include bond, electronic monitoring, or orders of supervision or recognizance. People apprehended in the four states that share a border with Mexico made up 70 percent of those leaving detention, and 73 percent of those removed. TRAC Immigration, "Legal Noncitizens Receive Longest ICE Detention," June 3, 2013.

87. A total of 72 percent of asylum seekers were held ninety days or less. In 2009, their average stay was ninety-nine days, with more than 16 percent of detained asylum seekers held longer than six months. ICE, *Detained Asylum Seekers, Fiscal Year 2009 and 2010 Report to Congress.*

88. This average was skewed significantly downward by nationals of Honduras, Guatemala, and El Salvador, who made up 45 percent of the cases and had a combined average processing time of 371 days. (Honduras had the largest number of cases of the three countries, and the lowest average processing time: 294 days.) If these three nationalities are excluded, the average processing time was nearly 706 days—nearly two years. Authors' analysis of data for immigration court proceedings on immigration charges as of May 2015 from TRAC Immigration, "Immigration Court Processing Time by Charge," http://trac.syr.edu/phptools/immigration/court_backlog/court_proctime_charge.php, accessed May 13, 2015.

89. Lutheran Immigration and Refugee Service (LIRS), *Unlocking Liberty: A Way Forward for U.S. Immigration Detention Policy*, October 27, 2011, 40.
90. *Clark v. Martinez* decision, January 12, 2005 (03-878, 03-7434), https://www.law.cornell.edu/supct/html/03-878.ZO.html.
91. Senator Chuck Grassley website, "Senators Introduce Bill to Close Catch-and-Release Loophole," June 11, 2014.
92. According to data from TRAC, thirty-two habeas petitions were filed by "alien detainees" in January 2015; if this number is representative of an average month, the annual number would be 384. TRAC also notes that the January 2015 habeas filings were down nearly 32 percent compared to six-month moving average one year and five years earlier. Not all habeas cases are based on *Zadvydas*; these numbers are for all habeas cases filed by immigration detainees. TRAC Immigration, "Civil Immigration Filings Trending Downward," February 24, 2015.
93. It was not clear how many of these detainees already had final orders of removal, and how many were still appealing their cases through the courts. "TRAC report: Legal Noncitizens Receive Longest ICE Detention," May 22, 2013. The courts have generally not set a time limit on detention for people who are continuing to fight their cases through the appeals process, although some courts have ruled that anyone detained for more than six months should be entitled to a bond hearing before an immigration judge. ACLU Immigrants' Rights Project, *Recommendations for Preventing Prolonged and Arbitrary Immigration Detention*, revised January 2014.
94. Maria Sacchetti, "Cuba deal brings deportation questions: Renewing ties with Cuba raises questions about deportees," *Boston Globe*, December 26, 2014.
95. Leslie Berestein Rojas, "Controversy over foreign-born offenders who aren't deported," Southern California Public Radio (SCPR), KPCC-FM, April 10 2015.
96. Dora Schriro, *Immigration Detention Overview and Recommendations*, ICE, October 6, 2009.
97. Dow, *American Gulag*, 137; Human Rights Watch, *Locked Away: Immigration Detainees in Jails in the United States*, September 1998, available at http://www.refworld.org/docid/3ae6a8400.html; ACLU, Written Statement of the American Civil Liberties Union for a Hearing on "*Holiday on ICE: The U.S. Department of Homeland Security's New Immigration Detention Standards*," submitted to the House Judiciary Subcommittee on Immigration Policy and Enforcement, March 28, 2012, 23.
98. Andrew Lyubarsky and Juan Caballero, *23 Hours in the Box: Solitary Confinement in New Jersey Immigration Detention*, NJ Advocates for Immigrant Detainees and NYU School of Law Immigrant Rights Clinic, June 2015.
99. Daniel González, "ICE accused of punishing Eloy immigration detainee who spoke to media," *Arizona Republic* (Phoenix), August 28, 2015; Suzanne Gamboa, "ICE Can Deport Those Who Complain of Abuse by the Agency," NBC News, August 5, 2014; Heartland Alliance National

Immigrant Justice Center (NIJC) and Physicians for Human Rights (PHR), *Invisible in Isolation: The Use of Segregation and Solitary Confinement in Immigration Detention*, September 2012; ACLU of Massachusetts, *Detention and Deportation in the Age of ICE*, December 2008.

100. The March 2011 *Federal Plain Language Guidelines* instructed U.S. government agencies to use the word "must" to convey obligation, instead of the less precise "shall." Yet "shall" appears 3,833 times in the 2011 *Performance-Based National Detention Standards* (PBNDS), compared to 445 times for "must." ICE, *ICE Performance-Based National Detention Standards 2011* (as modified by February 2013 errata), http://www.ice.gov/doclib/detention-standards/2011/pbnds2011.pdf, accessed June 30, 2015; *Federal Plain Language Guidelines*, March 2011, http://www.plainlanguage.gov/howto/guidelines/bigdoc/fullbigdoc.pdf, accessed June 30, 2015.

101. University of Miami School of Law Human Rights Clinic, American Friends Service Committee (AFSC), and others, *Written Statement on Immigration Detention and Deportation in the United States of America*, report submitted for the 53rd Session of the United Nations Committee Against Torture, November 2014, 8; ICE, "ICE Detention Standards Fact Sheet," February 24, 2012, http://www.ice.gov/factsheets/facilities-pbnds, accessed June 19, 2015.

102. GAO, *Immigration Detention*.

103. "This Is Child Abuse: Social Worker Breaks Silence over Conditions Inside Immigrant Detention Center," *Democracy Now!*, July 29, 2015.

104. Based on data from California and New York: Northern California Collaborative for Immigrant Justice, "Access to Justice for Immigrant Families and Communities. Study of Legal Representation of Detained Immigrants in Northern California," October 2014, 19–20; New York Immigrant Representation Study, *Accessing Justice: The Availability and Adequacy of Counsel in Immigration Proceedings*.

105. New York Immigrant Representation Study, *Accessing Justice*; Donald M. Kerwin, *The Faltering U.S. Refugee Protection System: Legal and Policy Responses to Refugees, Asylum Seekers, and Others in Need of Protection*, Migration Policy Institute, May 2011, 19–21; Amnesty International Report, *USA: Amnesty International's Concerns Regarding Post September 11 Detentions in the USA*, March 14, 2002, 19–20.

106. Human Rights Watch, "Statement of Human Rights Watch to the United States Commission on Civil Rights," March 2, 2015.

107. Human Rights Watch, *Locked Away*; Nina Bernstein, "New Scrutiny as Immigrants Die in Custody," *New York Times*, June 26, 2007.

108. Interview with Daniel Zwerdling by Madeleine Brand, "U.S. to Overhaul Immigrant Detention Policy," *All Things Considered*, NPR, August 6, 2009.

109. American Civil Liberties Union (ACLU) Press Release, "Announcement Prompted by ACLU Lawsuit," August 17, 2009; ICE, "List of Deaths in ICE Custody, Data from October 2003 to November 28, 2016," https://www.ice.gov/sites/default/files/documents/FOIA/2016/detaineeDeaths11_28_2016.pdf, accessed December 23, 2016.

110. Daniel Zwerdling, "Jailed Immigrants Allege Abuse," NPR, multiple reports, November 17–December 9, 2004.

111. ACLU press release, "ACLU of Texas Today Files Federal Lawsuit on Behalf of Women Assaulted at T. Don Hutto Detention Center," October 19, 2011; Written Statement of the American Civil Liberties Union for a hearing on "Holiday on ICE: The U.S. Department of Homeland Security's New Immigration Detention Standards," submitted to the House Judiciary Subcommittee on Immigration Policy and Enforcement, March 28, 2012, 23.

112. Human Rights Watch, *Detained and Dismissed: Women's Struggles to Obtain Health Care in United States Immigration Detention*, Report 1-56432-455-9, March 2009; Carl Takei, ACLU National Prison Project, "Detention Is No Place for Infants, Children, and Families," February 4, 2015. The ACLU notes that ICE's 2011 detention standards regarding sexual abuse and assault, shackling and use of force "have regressed from their 2008 counterparts," and that the sex abuse standards are not compliant with PREA. Statement of the American Civil Liberties Union for a hearing on "Holiday on ICE."

113. GAO, *Immigration Detention: Additional Actions Could Strengthen DHS Efforts to Address Sexual Abuse*, Report to Congressional Requesters, November 2013, updated December 6, 2013; Sarah Childress, "Why Immigrant Detainees Still Aren't Safe from Abuse," *PBS Frontline*, November 20, 2013.

114. Human Rights Watch, *Detained and at Risk: Sexual Abuse and Harassment in United States Immigration Detention*, August 2010.

115. Physicians for Human Rights and the Bellevue/NYU Program for Survivors of Torture, *From Persecution to Prison: The Health Consequences of Detention for Asylum Seekers*, June 2003; Craig Haney, "Conditions of Confinement for Detained Asylum Seekers Subject to Expedited Removal," *Study on Asylum Seekers in Expedited Removal*, United States Commission on International Religious Freedom, Vol. 2: Expert Reports, February 2005.

116. CVT/TASSC, *Tortured & Detained*.

117. Daniel Zwerdling, "The Death of Richard Rust," *All Things Considered*, NPR, December 5, 2005; Human Rights Watch, *Locked Away*. Information on Abdel-Muhti is from firsthand knowledge; the authors were in his support team.

118. Based on co-author Guskin's letters and other communication with asylum-seeker "S.," her attorneys, elected officials, advocates, and immigration officials, January through June 2004.

119. Ajay Chaudry, Randolph Capps, Juan Pedroza, Rosa Maria Castaneda, Robert Santos, and Molly M. Scott, *Facing Our Future: Children in the Aftermath of Immigration Enforcement*, Urban Institute, February 2, 2010; Heather Koball, Randy Capps, Krista Perreira, Andrea Campetella, Sarah Hooker, Juan Manuel Pedroza, William Monson, and Sandra Huerta, *Health and Social Service Needs of US-Citizen Children with Detained or Deported Immigrant Parents*, Urban Institute and Migration Policy Institute, September 2015.

120. In May 2015, Securus Technologies, the industry leader in correctional video visitation services, announced it would stop using contract language that requires facilities to restrict or deny in-person visits; instead, it would leave the choice up to the facility. The company's controversial practice of mandating prison visitation policy was exposed in a January 2015 Prison Policy Institute report that found local jails especially likely to eliminate in-person visits, even when not required by contract language. Bernadette Rabuy, "Securus ends its ban on in-person visits, shifts responsibility to sheriffs," Prison Policy Institute, May 6, 2015; "Securus Technologies Revises Video Visitation Policy—Defers to Prison/Jail Officials on Rules For Onsite Visits," *PRNewswire*, May 4, 2015; Bernadette Rabuy and Peter Wagner, *Screening Out Family Time: The For-Profit Video Visitation Industry in Prisons and Jails*, Prison Policy Institute, January 2015.

121. Even under the improved 2011 detention standards, facilities are allowed to strip-search detainees routinely without cause after contact visits, as long as the facility offers detainees an alternative option of a non-contact visit. ICE, *ICE Performance-Based National Detention Standards 2011*.

122. Koball et al., *Health and Social Service Needs of US-Citizen Children with Detained or Deported Immigrant Parents*.

123. Deirdre Fulton, "In 'Extraordinary Victory,' FCC Votes to Cap Exorbitant Prison Phone Fees," *Common Dreams*, October 22, 2015; Jon Brodkin, "Court Blocks FCC Attempt to Cap Prison Phone Rates," *Ars Technica*, November 4, 2016.

124. Lutheran Immigration and Refugee Service (LIRS), *Alternatives to Detention (ATD): History and Recommendations*, December 6, 2013; LIRS, *Unlocking Liberty*; Oren Root, *The Appearance Assistance Program: An Alternative to Detention for Noncitizens in U.S. Immigration Removal Proceedings*, Vera Institute of Justice, New York, n.d., http://www.vera.org/sites/default/files/resources/downloads/aap_speech.pdf, accessed October 24, 2015. Congress began funding alternative programs in 2003, but these are contracted with private companies instead of community-based nonprofits and often rely on electronic monitoring devices such as ankle bracelets. Studies indicate that instead of providing an alternative to detention, these programs often include immigrants who wouldn't have been detained if the programs hadn't existed. Rutgers School of Law-Newark Immigrant Rights Clinic, in conjunction with the American Friends Service Committee, *Freed But Not Free: A report examining the current use of alternatives to immigration detention*, July 2012.

125. National Immigration Forum, *The Math of Immigration Detention: Runaway Costs for Immigration Detention Do Not Add Up to Sensible Policies*, August 2013.

126. Grassroots Leadership estimates that ICE detained a daily average of 32,163 immigrants during fiscal year 2014. Carson and Diaz, *Payoff*.

127. Robertson, Beaty, Atkinson, and Libal, *Operation Streamline: Costs and Consequences*.

128. National Immigration Forum, *The Math of Immigration Detention*.

129. Three of the ten largest ICE detention facilities are operated by CCA and five are run by GEO; a firm called Management and Training Corporation (MTC) operates another; and the federal government runs one of the ten facilities directly. Carson and Diaz, *Payoff*. CCA and GEO directly benefit from the congressional mandate for filling 34,000 beds and from the "tiered pricing structure"; not surprisingly, they spend millions of dollars lobbying legislators and funding candidates. Michael Cohen, "How for-profit prisons have become the biggest lobby no one is talking about," *Washington Post*, April 28, 2015.

130. Carson and Diaz, *Payoff*; *Alejandro Menocal v. The Geo Group, Inc.*, Class Action Complaint for Unpaid Wages and Forced Labor, October 22, 2014, http://www.clearinghouse.net/chDocs/public/IM-CO-0009-0001.pdf; Ian Urbina, "Using Jailed Migrants as a Pool of Cheap Labor," *New York Times*, May 24, 2014.

131. *Menocal v. The Geo Group, Inc.*; Urbina, "Using Jailed Migrants as a Pool of Cheap Labor."

132. Carson and Diaz, *Payoff*.

133. Meredith Kolodner, "Immigration Enforcement to Benefit Detention Companies," *New York Times*, July 19, 2006.

134. Tom Kutsch, "Study: Private Contracts Encourage Federal Immigrant Detentions," Al Jazeera America, June 12, 2015; Sukey Lewis, "The High Cost of Phone Calls for Inmates," KALW, October 16, 2014; Todd Shields, "Prison Phones Prove Captive Market for Private Equity," *Bloomberg Business*, October 4, 2012.

135. Gabe Ortiz, "Profiting From Immigrants: Bail Bond Company Charges $420 a Month for a GPS Ankle Bracelet," *America's Voice*, October 5, 2015; Patricia Borns, "Verona Immigration Ministry Becomes Nationwide Business," *The News Leader*, June 26, 2015.

136. "The GEO Group Awarded Contract By U.S. Immigration and Customs Enforcement for the Continued Provision of Services Under Intensive Supervision and Appearance Program," *Business Wire*, September 10; Geo Group "History" website, http://www.geogroup.com/history, accessed May 17, 2015; BI Incorporated website, "U.S. Immigration and Customs Enforcement renews contract with BI Incorporated," September 16, 2014.

137. Eric Lipton, "Former Antiterror Officials Find Industry Pays Better," *New York Times*, June 18, 2006.

138. ICE Foundation website, "David Venturella," http://www.icefoundation. org/david-venturella.html, accessed August 2, 2015; GEO Group website, "Management Team: David J. Venturella," http://www.geogroup.com/ David_J__Venturella, accessed August 2, 2015.

139. Darwin Bond-Graham, "Private Prison Corporation Geo Group Expands Its Stable of Former Top Federal Officials," *Counterpunch*, July 25, 2014; Guidepost Solutions website, "Executive Officers: Julie Myers Wood," http:// www.guidepostsolutions.com/about_leadership_julie_myers_wood.php,

accessed August 2, 2015; GEO Group website, "Board of Directors: Julie M. Wood," http://www.geogroup.com/Julie_M__Wood, accessed August 2, 2015.

12. Can We Open Our Borders?

1. Robert L. Bartley, "Open Nafta Borders? Why Not?" *Wall Street Journal*, July 2, 2001. "Comprehensive immigration reform" proposals generally link guest worker programs with tighter border controls. See "Won't amnesty cause more problems later on?" and "Do guest worker programs hurt U.S. workers?" (chapter 10).

2. Alex Nowrasteh, "National Sovereignty and Free Immigration Are Compatible," Cato Institute, April 28, 2014.

3. Denis Sindic, "National Identities: Are they Declining?" Beyond Current Horizons, a partnership headed by the United Kingdom's Department for Children, Schools and Families (DCSF) and Futurelab, December 2008.

4. Universal Declaration of Human Rights, 1948, Article 13, http://www.un.org/Overview/rights.html#a13; International Covenant on Civil and Political Rights, 1966, Article 12, http://www.ohchr.org/EN/ProfessionalInterest/Pages/CCPR.aspx. The U.S. government ratified the Covenant in 1992, and it has energetically denounced violations in certain countries, such as the former East Germany, which used the Berlin Wall from 1961 to 1989 to keep its citizens from leaving, and Cuba, which until 2013 restricted Cubans' freedom to leave by requiring an exit visa. However, the U.S. government also limits the freedom of its citizens to travel: U.S. citizens are free to leave but not to go to certain countries. For example, as of 2015 they were still denied the right to visit Cuba as tourists. U.S. State Department, "U.S. Passports & International Travel: Cuba," http://travel.state.gov/content/passports/en/country/cuba.html, accessed November 28, 2015. In 2016 the Obama administration eased but did not eliminate the restrictions on tourism to Cuba.

5. Teresa Hayter, *Open Borders: The Case Against Immigration Controls*, 2nd ed. (London: Pluto Press, 2004), 151.

6. Joseph Nevins, "Policing Mobility, Maintaining Global Apartheid—From South Africa to the United States," in *Beyond Walls and Cages: Bridging Immigrant Justice and Anti-Prison Organizing in the United States*, ed. Jenna M. Loyd, Matt Mitchelson, and Andrew Burridge (Athens: University of Georgia Press, 2012), 19–26; Aviva Chomsky, *Undocumented: How Immigration Became Illegal* (Boston: Beacon Press, 2014), 32–37. The 1965 immigration law officially barred discrimination in the granting of visas based on "race, sex, nationality, place of birth, or place of residence." In practice, however, these factors can influence who is granted a visitor visa, and the diversity visa and visa waiver programs are based almost entirely on nationality.

7. Hayter, *Open Borders*, 167. One U.S. author openly calls for the United States "to take advantage of the human capital pushing at our doors" by

making it easier for educated foreigners to move here. Michele Wucker, *Lockout* (New York: Public Affairs, 2007), 123. Another advocates this sort of immigration as a "brain gain" for the United States. Darrell M. West, *Brain Gain: Rethinking U.S. Immigration Policy* (Washington, D.C.: Brookings Institution Press, 2010), 13-17.

8.   U.S. Customs and Border Protection, "Border Patrol History," https://www. cbp.gov/border-security/along-us-borders/history, accessed July 10, 2016. See also "How did immigration become 'illegal'?" and "Has Mexican immigration always been 'illegal'?" (chapter 4).

9.   John Pinder and Simon Usherwood, *The European Union: A Very Short Introduction*, second edition (Oxford and New York: Oxford University Press, 2007), 104–3; European Union website, http://europa.eu/, accessed December 3, 2015.

10.   "Schengen Visa Countries List," Schengen Visa Info, www.schengenvisainfo. com/schengen-visa-countries-list/, accessed November 15, 2015; "Free Movement of People within the Schengen Area," Citizens Information Board, www.citizensinformation.ie/en/moving_country/moving_abroad/ freedom_of_movement_within_the_eu/free_movement_of_people_ within_the_schengen_area.html, accessed November 15, 2015. The United Kingdom and the Republic of Ireland, both EU members at the time, had not signed the Schengen agreement but had adopted some of its rules.

11.   "Unasur aprueba plan para libre movilidad de sudamericanos," Globovisión, December 4, 2014; Comunidad Andina website, "Derechos de los Viajeros" and "Derechos de los Trabajadores Andinos," http://www. comunidadandina.org/derechos_ciudadanos/viajeros.html, and http:// www.comunidadandina.org/derechos_ciudadanos/trabajo.html, accessed October 17, 2015.

12.   Human Rights Watch, "EU: Protect the Rights of Migrants and Asylum Seekers in Seville Policy Proposals," letter to EU Heads of State, June 13, 2002.

13.   Barry Lando, "Mediterranean Horrors: Fortress Europe's Vast Moat," *Huffington Post*, April 21, 2015; data for 2005 posted February 2006 by Gabriele del Grande on his Fortress Europe blog, http://fortresseurope. blogspot.com/.

14.   As of 2015 some EU countries restricted employment of Croatian nationals. European Union, "Work Permits," http://europa.eu/youreurope/citizens/ work/work-abroad/work-permits/index_en.htm, accessed December 3, 2015.

15.   Hayter, *Open Borders*, 170.

16.   Lando, "Mediterranean Horrors." See also "Why should we accept refugees?" (chapter 3).

17.   European Foundation for the Improvement of Living and Working Conditions, *Mobility in Europe: Analysis of the 2005 Eurobarometer Survey on Geographical and Labour Market Mobility*, October 23, 2006, v.

18.   Michael Braun and Camelia Arsene, "The Demographics of Movers and Stayers in the European Union," in Adrian Favell and Ettore

Recchi, eds., *Pioneers of European Integration: Citizenship and Mobility in the EU* (Cheltenham, UK, and Northampton, MA: Edward Elgar Publishing, 2009), 26–51; Ettore Recchi, Damian Tambini, Emiliana Baldoni, David Williams, Kristin Surak, and Adrian Favell, "Intra-EU Migration: A Socio-Demographic Overview," PIONEUR Working Paper No. 3, July 2003, available at https://www.academia.edu/4327087/Intra-EU_Migration_A_Socio-demographic_Overview.

19. Sarah Lyall, "Britain to Restrict Workers from Bulgaria and Romania," *New York Times*, October 25, 2006; Pavel Prikryl, "Bienvenidos, Still Not Willkommen: Europe Split over Labor Mobility Restrictions," Center for European Policy Analysis, June 6, 2006.

20. European Foundation for the Improvement of Living and Working Conditions, *Mobility in Europe*, 71–72.

21. U.S. Department of Labor, Bureau of Labor Statistics (BLS), *International Comparisons of Hourly Compensation Costs for Production Workers in Manufacturing, 2004*, November 18, 2005.

22. Recchi, Tambini, Baldoni, Williams, Surak, and Favell, "Intra-EU Migration."

23. Paul Krugman, "Europe the Unready," *New York Times*, November 27, 2015. By "mood swings" Krugman is referring to the actions of investors "who recklessly poured money into southern Europe after the creation of the euro, then abruptly reversed course a decade later." In 2012 British immigration opponents tried to link unemployment to migration, but this was based on research by the United Kingdom Migration Advisory Committee tentatively suggesting a limited connection between unemployment and migration from outside the EU—it showed no connection to freedom of movement within the EU. Katy Long, *Huddled Masses: Immigration and Inequality* (London: Thistle Publishing, 2014), 56.

24. Rocio Cifuentes, "The Think Project, Brexit and the urgent need for better citizenship education," *openDemocracy*, July 8, 2016; Transatlantic Trends, *Immigration Survey, 2011*, question 28a; Long, *Huddled Masses*, 9–10; Migration Observatory at Oxford University, "Top 15 countries of birth of non-UK born residents in 2011 & change on 2001: Great Britain," http://www.migrationobservatory.ox.ac.uk/migration-great-britain-census-fact-sheet, accessed July 10, 2016. See also "Are politicians stirring up a panic about immigration?" (chapter 1).

25. See "Does deportation make us safer?" and "Does the crackdown on immigrants make us safer?" (chapter 8).

26. Pinder and Usherwood, *The European Union*, 105–10.

27. Erica Dahl-Bredine, "U.S. Helped Create Migrant Flow," *National Catholic Reporter*, September 22, 2006. See also "Why do so many Mexicans come here?" (chapter 2).

28. See "Why don't immigrants 'follow the rules'?" and "Is it easy for people to come here as tourists?" (chapter 4).

29. See "What caused the drop in unauthorized immigration?" (chapter 9).

30. "Puerto Rican Emigration: Why the 1950s?" Lehmann College Department

of Latin American and Puerto Rican Studies, http://lcw.lehman.edu/lehman/depts/latinampuertorican/latinoweb/PuertoRico/1950s.htm, accessed December 5, 2015; D'Vera Cohn, Eileen Patten, and Mark Hugo Lopez, *Puerto Rican Population Declines on Island, Grows on U.S. Mainland*, Pew Hispanic Center, August 11, 2014.

31. "Ireland Considering Immigration Deal with U.S.," Reuters, October 25, 2006.

32. Paul Klein and Gustavo Ventura, "Productivity Differences and the Dynamic Effects of Labor Movements," *Journal of Monetary Economics* 56 (2009): 1059–73.

33. See "Do immigrants bring down wages?" and "Why do they work for less?" (chapter 6).

34. David Bacon, *The Right to Stay Home: How US Policy Drives Mexican Migration* (Boston: Beacon Press, 2013).

35. Ellie Mae O'Hagan, "Mass migration is no 'crisis': It's the new normal as the climate changes," *The Guardian*, August 18, 2015.

36. See "Haven't we already had an amnesty?" (chapter 11).

37. Tim Cavanaugh, "No border, no problem: Let's live up to the promise of NAFTA and allow a free flow of people in North America," *Los Angeles Times*, May 23, 2006.

38. For more suggestions, see "How can we address the root causes of immigration?" (chapter 2), and "What can we do about the 'race to the bottom'?" (chapter 6). Resources for action and study—organizations, books, videos, and other materials on immigration issues—are available at the Politics of Immigration's website, http://thepoliticsofimmigration.org/. Links to news articles and other current information can be found on our blog, http://thepoliticsofimmigration.blogspot.com/.

Immigration and the Law: A Chronology

1. Richard Griswold del Castillo, *The Treaty of Guadalupe Hidalgo: A Legacy of Conflict* (Norman: University of Oklahoma Press, 1990), passim.

2. National Women's History Museum, "Chinese American Women: A History of Resilience and Resistance," https://www.nwhm.org/online-exhibits/chinese/6.html, accessed January 25, 2016.

3. The Statue of Liberty-Ellis Island Foundation, "Ellis Island History," http://www.libertyellisfoundation.org/ellis-island-history#Policy, accessed January 25, 2016.

4. Franklin Odo, ed., *The Columbia Documentary History of the Asian American Experience* (New York: Columbia University Press, 2002), 141.

5. Race: Are We So Different?, a project of the American Anthropological Association, "European Immigration and Defining Whiteness," http://www.understandingrace.net/history/gov/eastern_southern_immigration.html, accessed January 26, 2016.

6. U.S. Customs and Border Protection (CBP), "Border Patrol History," http://www.cbp.gov/border-security/along-us-borders/history, accessed January 26, 2016.

7. Michael C. LeMay, *Guarding the Gates: Immigration and National Security* (Westport, CT: Praeger Publishers, 2006), 132–34.

8. Terry Gross interview with Francisco Balderrama, "America's Forgotten History of Mexican-American 'Repatriation,'" NPR, *Fresh Air*, September 10, 2015. See also chapter 10, "What happened to the Mexican '*braceros*'?"

9. David M. Reimers, *Still the Golden Door: The Third World Comes to America*, 2nd ed. (New York: Columbia University Press, 1992), 38–40, 44, 54–55. See also chapter 10, "What happened to the Mexican '*braceros*'?"

10. Roger J. LeMaster and Barnaby Zall, "Compassion Fatigue: The Expansion of Refugee Admissions to the United States," *Boston College International and Comparative Law Review* 6/2 (May 1, 1983): Article 4; Kathryn M. Bockley, "A Historical Overview of Refugee Legislation: The Deception of Foreign Policy in the Land of Promise," *North Carolina Journal of International Law & Commercial Regulation* (Fall 1995); Truman, "Statement by the President Upon Signing the Displaced Persons Act," June 25, 1948, American Presidency Project website, http://www.presidency.ucsb.edu/ws/?pid=12942, accessed January 3, 2017.

11. Bockley, "A Historical Overview of Refugee Legislation"; U.S. Immigration Legislation Online, "1952 Immigration and Nationality Act, a.k.a. the McCarran-Walter Act," summary, http://library.uwb.edu/static/USimmigration/1952_immigration_and_nationality_act.html, accessed January 27, 2016.

12. Fred L. Koestler, "Operation Wetback," Handbook of Texas Online, http://www.tshaonline.org/handbook/online/articles/pqo01, accessed June 3, 2015.

13. Silvia Pedraza, "Cuba's Revolution and Exodus," *Journal of the International Institute* 5/2 (Winter 1998); Ruth Ellen Wasem, *U.S. Immigration Policy on Haitian Migrants*, Congressional Research Service (CRS), January 15, 2010.

14. Ruth Ellen Wasem, *Cuban Migration to the United States: Policy and Trends*, Congressional Research Service, June 2, 2009; Heather Reynolds, "Irreconcilable Regulations: Why the Sun Has Set on the Cuban Adjustment Act in Florida," *Florida Law Review* 63/4 (February 8, 2013): Article 6. See also chapter 3, "Special treatment for Cubans."

15. "Prop. 187 Approved in California," *Migration News* 1/11 (December 1994); Evelyn Nieves, "California Calls Off Effort to Carry Out Immigrant Measure," *New York Times*, July 30, 1999.

16. Charles Doyle, *Terrorism: Section by Section Analysis of the USA PATRIOT Act*, Congressional Research Service, December 10, 2001, 33–36; American Civil Liberties Union (ACLU), "How the Anti-Terrorism Bill Allows for Detention of People Engaging in Innocent Associational Activity," October 23, 2001.

17. "INSEERS Overview," Immigrationlaw.com, updated December 2003; Michele Waslin, "DHS's NSEERS Program, While Inactive, Continues to Discriminate," Immigration Impact, June 28, 2012; Jessie Hellmann, "Obama gets rid of visitor registry before Trump takes over," *The Hill*, December 22, 2016; Center for Constitutional Rights, press release,

"National Security Entry-Exit Registration System (NSEERS) Freedom of Information Act (FOIA) Request," January 3, 2017. See also chapter 8, "Did the government's post-9/11 crackdown help stop terrorism?"

18. Ruth Ellen Wasem, *Brief History of Comprehensive Immigration Reform Efforts in the 109th and 110th Congresses to Inform Policy Discussions in the 113th Congress*, Congressional Research Service, February 27, 2013; "Thousands march for immigrant rights: Schools, businesses feel impact as students, workers walk out," CNN, May 1, 2006.

19. Jennifer Chan, "Immigration Detention Bed Quota Timeline," National Immigrant Justice Center, March 1, 2016.

20. National Immigration Law Center and United We Dream, "Frequently Asked Questions: The Obama Administration's Deferred Action for Childhood Arrivals (DACA)," http://www.nilc.org/FAQdeferredactionyouth.html, accessed April 20, 2015. See also chapter 10, "Is 'Deferred Action' an amnesty program?"

21. Migration Policy Center, "A Guide to the Immigration Accountability Executive Action," November 30, 2014.

Index

to, 111; securing border between U.S. and, 157–58; Texas and California as parts of, 135; Treaty of Guadalupe Hilalgo with, 79, 254; U.S. tourists entering, 70; *see also* borders of U.S.

migrants, 18; entering Europe, 238–39; as refugees or immigrants, 45; smugglers of, 162–64

Migration and Refugee Assistance Act (1962), 262–63

Migration Policy Institute, 148–50, 166, 180

migrations: from Puerto Rico, 244–45; reasons for, 27–28; "right not to migrate," 247–48; *see also* immigration

Miller, Marc, 165–67

minimum wages, 92-93, 95, 97, 104, 116, 197

Miranda, Olga, 176

Mirmehdi brothers, 146–47

Mitchell, Chip, 118

Morgan, Mark Alan, 161

Mount Olive Pickle Company, 202

MS-13 (Mara Salvatrucha; street gang), 142

Mueller, Robert, 145

Mujahedin-e Khalq (MEK), 146–47

municipal ID cards, 89–90

Muñoz, Carlos, 118

Muslims, 142–43; ban on immigration of, 250; immigration raids against, 171; Trump on, 249

Al-Najjar, Mazen, 152

National Academy of Sciences, 102, 114, 132–33

National Council of Resistance of Iran (NCR), 146–47

National Council on Crime and Delinquency, 139

National Guestworkers Alliance, 199

Nationality Act (1940), 260

National Origins Act (1924; Immigration Act; Johnson-Reed Act), 259

National Security Entry-Exit Registration System (NSEERS), 267

Native Americans, 79, 135

naturalization (see citizenship)

Naturalization Act (1790), 253

Naturalization Act (1795), 254

Naturalization Act (1870), 134, 255

Naturalization Act (1906), 257

Nazis, refugees from, 46–49

neoliberalism, 30–31

Neumayer, Eric, 54

Nevins, Joseph, 237

New Haven (Connecticut), 89–90

New York (New York): construction deaths in, 94; English classes in, 131; environmental views in, 129; occupational injuries in, 95

Ngai, Mae, 68, 207

Nicaragua, 30, 35–36, 63-64, 146

Nicaraguan Adjustment and Central American Relief Act (1997; NACARA), 64, 266

Nicholson, Eric, 197

Nixon, Richard, 24

non-immigrants, 18

Noonan, John, 146

North American Free Trade Agreement (NAFTA; 1994), 32–33, 39, 157, 242, 247

North Carolina Growers Association, 202

Norway, 50

NXP Semiconductors (firm), 41

Oaxaca (Mexico), 247

Obama, Barack, 209; DACA executive order issued by, 188, 269; DAPA executive order issued by, 189; elected president, 173

Obama administration: 287(g) program under, 177; Deferred Action